D0209042

*The Cavalry
at Gettysburg*

M

973.7349
c.1

The Cavalry at Gettysburg

A Tactical Study of Mounted Operations
during the Civil War's Pivotal Campaign
9 June–14 July 1863

Edward G. Longacre

RICHMOND
PUBLIC
LIBRARY
CALIFORNIA

University of Nebraska Press
Lincoln and London

MAIN
973.7349 Longacre, Edward
G., 1946-
    The Cavalry at
    Gettysburg :

31143005766739   c. 1

Copyright © 1986 by Associated University Presses, Inc.
All rights reserved
Manufactured in the United States of America

First Bison Book printing: 1993
Most recent printing indicated by the last digit below:
10   9   8   7   6   5   4   3   2   1

Library of Congress Cataloging-in-Publication Data
Longacre, Edward G., 1946–
The Cavalry at Gettysburg: a tactical study of mounted operations during the Civil
War's pivotal campaign, 9 June–14 July 1863 / Edward G. Longacre.
p.   cm.
Originally published: Rutherford, N.J.: Fairleigh Dickinson University Press, c1986.
Includes bibliographical references and index.
ISBN 0-8032-7941-8 (pbk.)
1. Gettysburg Campaign, 1863.   2. United States—History—Civil War, 1861–
1865—Cavalry operations.   3. Pennsylvania—History—Civil War, 1861–1865—
Cavalry operations.   4. Pennsylvania—History—Civil War, 1861–1865—Campaigns.   I. Title.
E475.51.L85   1993
973.7'349—dc20
92-37790   CIP

Reprinted by arrangement with Associated University Presses

∞

for My Parents

Contents

The illustrations appear in two groups, on pages 114–118, and 214–219.

Preface

THE Civil War is the most written-about event in American history, and the Gettysburg campaign is the most written-about episode of that war. It would appear that few gaps in the literature of Gettysburg remain to be filled. This book attempts to plug one of the last.

Many hundreds of books, pamphlets, articles, and essays have dealt with the infantry fighting at Gettysburg. A much smaller number have chronicled the role artillery played in the campaign. But no full-length study has ever considered the contributions made by the mounted forces of the Army of Northern Virginia and the Army of the Potomac between 9 June and 14 July 1863.

One might suppose that cavalry played a minor part in the proceedings, hence a lack of interest in telling its story. Not so. The Gettysburg campaign witnessed the largest and most influential mounted battles ever waged in the Western Hemisphere; in truth, cavalry may have been the deciding factor in the campaign. Even those who reject the last assertion must be intrigued by the might-have-beens born of cavalry's participation in the campaign. For choice, had Robert E. Lee lacked implicit confidence in J. E. B. Stuart and Stuart's cavalry division, he might never had pursued his invasion of Pennsylvania. Then, too, had Stuart not taken the route north he chose to follow during that invasion, Lee might never have stumbled into battle against the army of George Gordon Meade in that crossroads village in Adams County. Furthermore, had it not been for the strategic instincts of the Federal cavalry's John Buford, who chose Gettysburg as a point of defense, the field of battle might have been in southeastern Maryland (Meade's choice), where geographical features might have exercised markedly different influences on the fighting. And had mounted troops not been employed precisely as they were on numerous critical occasions between 1 and 3 July, 1863 (especially during General George E. Pickett's 3 July attack against Meade's center), the Confederates might have prevailed. Admittedly, these remain flights of imagination. Yet, a dispassionate look at the record lends persuasiveness to arguments based on such speculation.

No one exposed to the story of the cavalry at Gettysburg can deny that the horse soldiers of North and South shouldered the major burden of the campaigning. The infantry on both sides served in the climactic combat of 1–3 July as well as in the skirmishing that took place during the three weeks immediately preceding and the fortnight following that period. The cavalry, however, was kept busy on a daily basis, fighting almost constantly on either side of Mason's and Dixon's Line. For example, during the ten days that separated Lee's withdrawal from Gettysburg and his recrossing of the Potomac River, the horsemen North and South fought more than a dozen close-quarters engagements, suffering heavily. During that time, foot troops and artillerymen engaged primarily in long-range skirmishing—most frequently, in marching and countermarching.

The troopers did more than wage combat. They also saw service as scouts, pickets, skirmishers for the infantry, wagon-train and supply-line guards, provost troops, couriers, and escorts for field commanders. In each army, whole brigades of horsemen protected the flanks and rear of the main body, while other mounted units traveled in the forefront to clear a path through unknown territory or to forage for rations and materiel. Such a heavy workload devolved upon soldiers who composed only one-seventh of Lee's and Meade's forces.

Ever afterward, cavalry veterans on both sides took considerable pride in the scope of their Gettysburg service. Thus they were chagrined by the dearth of postwar recognition accorded them. Though producing a heavy flow of prose about Gettysburg, historians tended to overlook the contributions of the cavalry. When the government plotted maps of the Pennsylvania battlefield in the 1870s, its cartographers took little notice of the area three and a half miles east of Gettysburg where the campaign's most decisive mounted combat took place. Only the vigorous protests of cavalrymen succeeded in redressing governmental neglect. Yet, despite the many memoirs and monographs they themselves contributed during the last third of the nineteenth century and early in the twentieth, cavalry veterans proved unable to correct, in proper measure, the wrong that the scribes had dealt them. Gettysburg became fixed in the national consciousness as an infantry and artillery battle: dramatic episodes such as Pickett's Charge and the fighting for Little Round Top and amid the Wheatfield and the Peach Orchard came to be regarded as the salient episodes of the campaign. The horsemen were relegated to limbo—not entirely forgotten, they nevertheless failed to receive recognition commensurate with the significance of their efforts.

Writing in 1905, Brevet Lieutenant Colonel William Brooke Rawle noted the disinclination of historians "to give us . . . credit for having done anything [at Gettysburg]. So fierce was the main engagement, of which the infantry bore the brunt, that the fighting on the part of the cavalry passed almost unnoticed; yet this was one of the few battles of the war in which the three arms of the service fought in combination and at the same time, each within supporting distance and within sight of the other[s], and each in its proper sphere. The turmoil incident to an active campaign allowed us no opportunity to write up our achievements, and no news correspondents were allowed to sojourn with us to do it for us. Full justice has yet to be done."

Over eighty years later, Brooke Rawle's commentary remains valid. A debt is still owed. Here, at least, is an attempt to provide recompense.

***

A note about research:

The Philadelphia area contains indispensable sources on cavalry's participation in the Gettysburg campaign. This is not merely because Philadelphia is the metropolis closest to the battlefield. Many of those who fought in the mounted ranks at Gettysburg (in fact, nearly forty per cent of the Union troopers engaged) were natives or residents of the city, or members of units recruited in the Philadelphia region. A surprisingly large number left published or manuscript memoirs that are readily available today.

The most valuable research tool is a multivolume compilation of postwar correspondence from dozens of participants in the Union and Confederate cavalry. The volumes repose in the William Brooke Rawle collection at the Historical Society of Philadelphia. Only a minute portion of this material has been published, despite its great historical value. It embraces over one thousand pages of eyewitness testimony about the fighting from Brandy Station to Falling Waters, most of it recorded within ten to twenty years after the close of the campaign—so much the better for accuracy.

William Rawle Brooke (he reversed the order of his surname after the war) was the scion of a distinguished Philadelphia family and a nineteen-year-old senior at the University of Pennsylvania when he obtained a commission as a second lieutenant in Company C, 3rd Pennsylvania Cavalry, midway through the Civil War. Diminuative and babyfaced, he went south in May 1863 to take command of a platoon of bearded veterans, some of whom were more than twice his age. Despite a dearth of military experience, he established himself as a popular officer, primarily because he was not afraid to lead in battle. Late that spring and early in the summer he found himself immersed in a whirlpool of conflict, but he escaped without serious injury. He returned home in 1865 as a battle-tempered veteran of twenty-one, with the brevet of lieutenant colonel and an opportunity for a Regular Army commission. He "threw up" the appointment, entered law school, and became a respected member of the Philadelphia bar. Late in life he served as an officer on the board of the Historical Society of Pennsylvania (which his ancestors had helped establish), and in his spare hours he wrote memoirs and historical monographs.

In 1877 Brooke Rawle penned one of the first in-depth studies of cavalry service in the Pennsylvania campaign, "The Right Flank at Gettysburg," one of a series of war reminiscences published in the *Philadelphia Weekly Times*. Later reprinted in pamphlet form and as part of a book-length compilation, the account brought him into contact with many troopers on both sides and influenced him to write other works on the topic, some of which appeared in the prestigious *Journal of the United States Cavalry Association*. He also became a prime mover behind the 1880 Congressional appropriation for the resurveying of the Gettysburg battlefield to include cavalry battle terrain on government maps. And soon after the turn of the twentieth century he edited the chronicle of his regiment's war career, destined to be recognized as one of the finest Civil War unit histories ever published.

In addition to producing a wealth of material on the cavalry at Gettysburg, Brooke Rawle bequeathed to later generations a vast body of literature on the war in general. He and other comrades of the 3rd Pennsylvania Cavalry were charter members of the Military Order of the Loyal Legion of the United States, a Union officers' patriotic and fraternal organization established in Philadelphia in 1865. Over the next several years the legionnaires stocked the local commandery's War Library with twelve thousand volumes, as well as with letters, diaries, memoirs, photographs, and artifacts covering all phases of the conflict—many dealing with cavalry operations. Through such efforts the War Library became one of the largest repositories of Civil War literature in the country. Today, housed at 1805 Pine Street, Philadelphia, it remains an invaluable source of information for Civil War researchers.

Acknowledgments

MANY people helped make researching this book an enjoyable experience—no mean feat under the circumstances (see below). Those who rendered the most extensive assistance include:

Don Alberts, Sandia Park, New Mexico; Ethan Bishop, Shenandoah, Virginia; Barbara Adams Blundell, Essex Institute, Salem, Massachusetts; Robert L. Brake, Waynesboro, Pennsylvania; William G. Burnett, Rocky River, Ohio; Marie T. Capps, United States Military Academy Library, West Point, New York; Gary Christopher, Atwater Kent Museum, Philadelphia, Pennsylvania; Howson W. Cole, Virginia Historical Society, Richmond; John C. Dann, William L. Clements Library, University of Michigan, Ann Arbor; Kathy Georg and Tom Harrison, Gettysburg National Military Park; Bob Hoffert, Bellevue, Nebraska; Elliott Wheelock Hoffman, Newmarket, New Hampshire; Marshall D. Krolick, Chicago, Illinois; Archie Motley, Chicago Historical Society; Anna Jane Moyer, Gettysburg College Library; Mary Jo Pugh, Bently Historical Library, University of Michigan; Doug Rauschenberger, Haddonfield, New Jersey; Nathaniel N. Shipton, Rhode Island Historical Society, Providence; Donald A. Sinclair, Rutgers University Library, New Brunswick, New Jersey; James Pulm Swann, Sr., Atlanta, Georgia; Susan B. Tate, University of Georgia Library, Athens; and the late Dr. Frederick Tilberg, formerly chief historian, Gettysburg National Military Park.

Special acknowledgments go to Professor Russell F. Weigley, Temple University; to my father, Edgar T. Longacre; and to my brother, Lawrence T. Longacre. A word of thanks must also go to John H. Hayes, D.O., who shares my interest in the Civil War and in whose office part of this book was written. This seems only fitting; my two-year, twice-weekly visits to him were necessitated by an allergy I contracted from exposure to the dusty, moldy archives and books I consulted in my research.

13

. . .afterward all anyone would say was, "Oh yes, the cavalry fought at Gettysburg too, didn't it?"

—Bruce Catton, *This Hallowed Ground*

Errata

Page 11, line 14:   *For* Historical Society of Philadelphia
                      read Historical Society of Pennsylvania

Page 60, line 21:   *For* breechloaders with barrels
                      read breechloaders

line 37:   *For* only a handful of mounted units
                      read no mounted units

lines 37–40:   *Delete* All told, fewer than six hundred members of the Cavalry Corps possessed a Spencer rifle; they were scattered through the 8th and 12th Illinois, 3rd Indiana, 8th New York, and 1st West Virginia regiments.

The Antagonists

CAVALRY DIVISION, ARMY OF NORTHERN VIRGINIA (Maj. Gen. James E. B. Stuart)

Hampton's Brigade (Brig. Gen. Wade Hampton, Col. Laurence S. Baker)
1st North Carolina (Col. Laurence S. Baker, Lt. Col. James B. Gordon)
1st South Carolina (Col. John Logan Black, Lt. Col. John D. Twiggs)
2nd South Carolina (Col. M. Calbraith Butler, Maj. Thomas J. Lipscomb)
Cobb's (Georgia) Legion (Col. Pierce M. B. Young)
Jeff Davis (Alabama, Georgia, and Mississippi) Legion (Lt. Col. J. Frederick Waring)
Phillips (Georgia) Legion (Lt. Col. William W. Rich)

Fitz Lee's Brigade (Brig. Gen. Fitzhugh Lee, Col. Thomas T. Munford)
1st Maryland Battalion (Maj. Harry Gilmor, Maj. Ridgely Brown)
1st Virginia (Col. James H. Drake)
2nd Virginia (Col. Thomas T. Munford, Lt. Col. James W. Watts, Maj. Cary Breckinridge)
3rd Virginia (Col. Thomas H. Owen)
4th Virginia (Col. Williams C. Wickham, Capt. William B. Newton)
5th Virginia (Col. Thomas L. Rosser)

Rooney Lee's Brigade (Brig. Gen. W. H. F. Lee, Col. John R. Chambliss, Jr.)
2nd North Carolina (Col. Solomon Williams, Lt. Col. William H. F. Payne, Lt. Col. William G. Robinson)
9th Virginia (Col. Richard L. T. Beale)
10th Virginia [nine companies] (Col. J. Lucius Davis, Maj. Robert A. Caskie)
13th Virginia (Col. John R. Chambliss, Jr., Lt. Col. Jefferson C. Phillips, Maj. Joseph Gillett)

Robertson's Brigade (Brig. Gen. Beverly H. Robertson)
4th North Carolina (Col. Dennis D. Ferebee)
5th North Carolina (Col. Peter G. Evans, Lt. Col. Stephen B. Evans)

17

Jones's Brigade (Brig. Gen. William E. Jones)
6th Virginia (Maj. Cabell E. Flournoy)
7th Virginia (Lt. Col. Thomas Marshall)
11th Virginia (Col. Lunsford L. Lomax, Lt. Col. Oliver R. Funsten)
12th Virginia (Col. Asher W. Harman, Lt. Col. Thomas B. Massie)
35th Virginia Battalion (Lt. Col. Elijah V. White)
Ashby Horse Artillery (Capt. Robert Preston Chew)

Jenkins's Brigade (Brig. Gen. Albert G. Jenkins, Col. Milton J. Ferguson)
14th Virginia (Col. James Cochran, Maj. Benjamin F. Eakle, Capt.
    Edwin E. Bouldin)
16th Virginia (Col. Milton J. Ferguson, Maj. James H. Nounnan)
17th Virginia (Col. William H. French)
34th Virginia Battalion (Lt. Col. Vincent A. Witcher)
36th Virginia Battalion (Maj. James W. Sweeney)
Charlottesville (Virginia) Battery (Capt. Thomas E. Jackson)

Horse Artillery Battalion (Maj. Robert F. Beckham)*
1st Stuart Horse Artillery (Capt. James Breathed)
2nd Stuart Horse Artillery (Capt. William M. McGregor)
2nd Baltimore Battery (Capt. William H. Griffin)
Washington (South Carolina) Artillery (Capt. James F. Hart)
Lynchburg (Virginia) Battery (Capt. Marcellus N. Moorman)

INDEPENDENT COMMAND

Imboden's Brigade (Brig. Gen. John D. Imboden)
18th Virginia (Col. George W. Imboden)
62nd Virginia Mounted Infantry (Col. George H. Smith)
Virginia Partisan Rangers [one company] (Capt. John H. McNeill)
Staunton (Virginia) Artillery [six guns] (Capt. J. H. McClanahan)

***

CAVALRY CORPS, ARMY OF THE POTOMAC (Maj. Gen. Alfred Pleasonton) [After 28
June 1863]

First Division (Brig. Gen. John Buford)
First Brigade (Col. William Gamble)
    8th Illinois (Maj. John L. Beveridge)
    12th Illinois [four companies] ⎫
    3rd Indiana [six companies]   ⎬ (Col. George H. Chapman)
    8th New York (Lt. Col. William L. Markell)
Second Brigade (Col. Thomas C. Devin)

---

*Each battery mounted four cannon.

6th New York [eight companies] (Lt. Col. William H. Crocker, Maj. William E. Beardsley)

9th New York (Col. William Sackett)

17th Pennsylvania (Col. Josiah H. Kellogg)

3rd West Virginia [two companies] (Capt. Seymour B. Conger)

Reserve Brigade (Brig. Gen. Wesley Merritt)

6th Pennsylvania (Maj. James H. Haseltine)

1st United States (Capt. Richard S. C. Lord, Capt. Eugene M. Baker)

2nd United States (Capt. Theophilus F. Rodenbough, Capt. George A. Gordon)

5th United States (Capt. Julius W. Mason)

6th United States (Maj. Samuel H. Starr, Capt. George C. Cram, Capt. Ira W. Claflin, Lt. Nicholas Nolan)

Second Division (Brig. Gen. David McMurtrie Gregg, Col. John B. McIntosh, Col. Pennock Huey)

First Brigade (Col. John B. McIntosh, Col. John P. Taylor)

1st Maryland (Lt. Col. James M. Deems)

1st Massachusetts (Lt. Col. Greely S. Curtis, Capt. Benjamin W. Crowninshield)

1st New Jersey (Maj. Myron H. Beaumont, Maj. Hugh H. Janeway)

1st Pennsylvania (Col. John P. Taylor, Lt. Col. David Gardner)

3rd Pennsylvania (Lt. Col. Edward S. Jones)

Purnell (Maryland) Legion [one company] (Capt. Robert E. Duvall)

Battery H, 3rd Pennsylvania Artillery [two guns] (Capt. William D. Rank)

Second Brigade (Col. Pennock Huey)

2nd New York (Lt. Col. Otto Harhaus)

4th New York (Lt. Col. Augustus Pruyn)

6th Ohio [ten companies] (Lt. Col. William Stedman)

8th Pennsylvania (Capt. William A. Corrie)

1st Rhode Island [two companies] (Capt. Joseph J. Gould)

Third Brigade (Col. J. Irvin Gregg)

District of Columbia Volunteers [one company] (Capt. William H. Orton)

1st Maine (Lt. Col. Charles H. Smith)

10th New York (Maj. M. Henry Avery)

4th Pennsylvania (Lt. Col. William E. Doster)

16th Pennsylvania (Lt. Col. John K. Robison)

Third Division (Brig. Gen. H. Judson Kilpatrick)

First Brigade (Brig. Gen. Elon J. Farnsworth, Col. Nathaniel P. Richmond, Col. Othneil De Forest)

5th New York (Maj. John Hammond)

1st Ohio [two companies] (Capt. Noah Jones)

2nd Pennsylvania (Col. R. Butler Price)

18th Pennsylvania (Lt. Col. William P. Brinton)

1st Vermont (Col. Edward B. Sawyer, Lt. Col. Addison W. Preston)

1st West Virginia [ten companies] (Col. Nathaniel P. Richmond, Maj.
   Charles E. Capehart)
Second Brigade (Brig. Gen. George Armstrong Custer)
   1st Michigan (Col. Charles H. Town)
   5th Michigan (Col. Russell A. Alger, Lt. Col. Ebenezer Gould, Maj.
   Crawley P. Dake)
   6th Michigan [ten companies] (Col. George Gray)
   7th Michigan [ten companies] (Col. William D. Mann)

*Horse Artillery Division**
First Brigade (Capt. James M. Robertson)
   9th Michigan Battery (Capt. Jabez J. Daniels)
   6th New York Battery (Capt. Joseph W. Martin)
   Batteries B/L, 2nd United States (Lt. Edward Heaton)
   Battery M, 2nd United States (Lt. Alexander C. M. Pennington)
   Battery E, 4th United States (Lt. Samuel S. Elder)
Second Brigade (Capt. John C. Tidball)
   Batteries E/G, 1st United States [four guns] (Capt. Alanson M. Randol)
   Battery K, 1st United States (Capt. William M. Graham)
   Battery A, 2nd United States (Lt. John H. Calef)
   Battery C, 3rd United States (Lt. William D. Fuller)

---

*Except where noted, each battery—including combined units—mounted six cannon.

The Cavalry
at Gettysburg

[1]
The "Beau Sabreur" and His Cavaliers

CAVALRY served the mid-nineteenth-century army in a variety of tactical and strategic roles. It provided a battlefield commander with speed, mobility, the power of perception, and a unique combat punch. Able to strike unexpectedly and with intimidating rapidity, it could deal blows both physical and psychological. Its mobility permitted it to hold positions in the face of a larger but less agile enemy, purchasing time for infantry and artillery to reach the front. Most important of all, it gave antennae to its army—a form of vision and hearing—through its ability to discern the strength, dispositions, and intentions of the foe.

More specifically, cavalrymen could function six ways in aiding the fortunes of an army in combat. They could participate offensively, adding their weight to that of foot soldiers and cannoneers. They could perform reconnaissance. Troopers could also engage in counterreconnaissance, preventing enemy scouts from spying on the main army. They could delay enemy advances by falling back slowly from point to point, redeploying wherever terrain permitted further resistance. They could pursue and harass a retreating opponent, consolidating gains won in battle and preventing the foe from regrouping or counterattacking. And they could raid enemy positions and communication lines either independent of or in conjunction with a movement by the main army. In noncombat roles, cavalry could also serve as messengers, escort troops, and as garrisons for posts apart from the principal strength of the army.

By mid-1863, the majority of Union and Confederate commanders understood the importance of cavalry power. In the eastern theater of operations, however, only the Confederates seemed able to exploit it. From its inception, the Army of Northern Virginia projected an aggressive role for its horse soldiers, employing them offensively, in mass, and often far afield of the main army. As a result, Major General J. E. B. Stuart's troopers attained a record that far outshone their enemy's.

They won it largely by default. In contrast to the South's imaginative ways, the generals of the Army of the Potomac seemed bent on wasting cavalry's potential. For tactical use, they preferred to fragment their regiments (each theoretically composed of 1,200 troopers but soon whittled down to 50 percent of authorized strength) into 100-man companies, squadrons (two-company units), or battalions (two-squadron units). This practice served to deny the Union horsemen strength, cohesiveness, and a corporate identity. Their morale was also lowered by the high command's propensity to relegate them to unnecessary labor such as picketing infantry and artillery camps.

The South's better perception of cavalry's potential derived from its traditional interest in horsemanship. The region had been led to war by men born to the equestrian tradition or who had gained familiarity with the art through daily necessity. Many had served in mounted militia outfits such as those raised out of fear of slave revolts.[1] (A proportionally smaller number of Northern militia outfits served on horseback; they seemed to stress parade ground drill over horsemanship.) A region rife with open spaces and poor roads but handicapped by a severe shortage of wheeled transportation, the Southland had long produced in abundance material by which horsemen plied their trade. Many of the steeds ridden to war in 1861 were the offspring of thoroughbreds noted for endurance, strength, and speed. And many of those who rode such animals into battle came from generations of horse-breeders or from the families of blacksmiths, farriers, and veterinarians.[2] As one soldier wrote of the Confederacy, years after its demise, "probably no nation ever went to war richer in its cavalry raw material."[3]

The belief that Southern horsemen made superior fighters prevailed on both sides of the Mason-Dixon Line both before and after the Fort Sumter crisis. Also generally accepted was the notion that the South enjoyed a superabundance of born leaders, many of whom had gravitated to the mounted ranks. To be sure, cavalry generals were much more closely identified with their troops, and could better inspire them with their personal qualities, than commanders of infantry or artillery. One factor was the mounted leaders' immediate involvement in combat, in contrast to the more remote participation of infantry generals (many of whom directed operations from the rear) and artillery commanders (most of whom were treated as administrators or staff officers). In 1865 the nation's leading military journal examined this phenomenon, concluding that "the nature of cavalry service makes their [commanders'] presence a necessity, as in all formations for attack they *lead* their columns. They are supposed to possess those rare personal qualities that impart inspiration of invincibility to the squadrons they lead, and magnetize with individual daring each trooper."[4]

In the eastern theater, no cavalry officer possessed more "rare personal qualities" than James Ewell Brown Stuart. Thirty years old by mid-1863 (he attempted to hide his youth behind a cinnamon-colored beard), Stuart had already proved himself proficient in both reconnaissance and combat. Two years' worth of heroics performed with the élan of a character out of Thomas Malory or Walter Scott had earned him the appelation "Beau Sabreur of the

Confederacy."[5] Surely the title was fitting, for Stuart worked tirelessly to fill a dual role as votary and high priest at the altar of Southern chivalry. He seemed eager to project himself as a cavalier or as a warlord leading knights-errant into Arthurian combat. The regal allusions may have had some basis; family lore made reference to Stuart's direct descent from hard-fighting Scottish royalty.[6]

Despite such a psyche, Stuart was personable and approachable. By his simple good nature he commanded the affection and respect of his officers and men, as well as of many others. One trooper remarked that "a franker, more transparent nature, it is impossible to conceive [of]." An artillery officer regarded Stuart as "decidedly one of the very best officers we have . . . and is generally looked upon with much confidence." As for Stuart's personal life, the artillerist added: "he neither drinks [n]or smokes & is the plainest, most straightforward, best humoured man in the world." Stuart's aide, John Cooke, described him as "ardent, impetuous, brimming over with the wine of life and youth, with the headlong courage of a high-spirited boy, fond of bright colors, of rippling flags, of martial music, and the clash of sabres." Another observer pronounced him "a remarkable mixture of a green, boyish, undeveloped man, and a shrewd man of business and a strong leader."[7]

Virginia-born and -bred, the Beau Sabreur had attended Emory & Henry College, then the U.S. Military Academy, graduating from the latter in 1854. He made a creditable record as a young subaltern in campaigning against the Plains Indians. He also served as aide to Colonel Robert E. Lee when Regulars and state troops crushed John Brown's attempt to capture Harpers Ferry in 1859. Shortly before civil war developed, Stuart solidified his position in the Old Army by wedding the daughter of a prominent dragoon, Philip St. George Cooke, and by earning a captaincy in the 1st United States Cavalry.[8]

When war came, Stuart's fealty to the Old Dominion impelled him to cast his lot with secession, while other Virginia-born officers including his father-in-law opted to remain with the Union. His early reputation in mounted operations brought him command of the 1st Virginia Cavalry, which became notable for its fighting quotient as well as for the many Tidewater patricians in its ranks. During the first summer of the conflict the regiment performed brilliantly in containing the advance of a Union army in the lower Shenandoah Valley and preventing it from gathering intelligence about its opponents. Soon afterward, at Bull Run, the 1st Virginia helped turn Union defeat into rout with a vicious, panic-inducing pursuit of the enemy.

Stuart's early contributions were rewarded in mid-1861 when he was elevated from lieutenant colonel to brigadier general and received a brigade of horsemen. He quickly cultivated a bumper crop of able subordinates—including General Lee's son "Rooney" and Rooney's cousin Fitzhugh Lee—and with these men he honed his command to a deadly edge. During the winter of 1861–62 he also acquired a reputation as the finest reconnaissance commander in the Army of Northern Virginia.

Stuart improved upon that reputation—and also won new laurels in battle— early in 1862, during the invasion of the Virginia peninsula by Major General

George B. McClellan's Army of the Potomac. While the Confederates scrambled to protect Richmond, Stuart guarded their flanks, rear, and communication lines, deflecting blows aimed by blue-clad horsemen and preventing them from scrutinizing Lee's dispositions.[9]

By mid-June, Lee was anxious to gather like information about his adversary. The length of McClellan's lines made this impossible from the Confederate commander's present vantage point; thus, Stuart cut loose from the army with 1,000 troopers culled from his Cavalry Division, Army of Northern Virginia. From the twelfth to the fifteenth, he made a 150-mile circuit of the Union position, gathering facts about Yankee defenses, supply bases, detachments, and outposts. Of especial importance to his commander, Stuart determined the location and composition of McClellan's right flank along the Chickahominy River. Meanwhile, he and his cavaliers outraced or outfought scores of Federals sent to run them to earth, many led by General Philip St. George Cooke. After leaving his father-in-law far to the rear, Stuart returned to base with some of the most valuable intelligence an army leader could have desired. Realizing this, the enemy took radical measures to prevent a repeat performance of the raid, which altered the nature of their offensive and helped consign it to failure.[10]

More than any other exploit, the "Chickahominy Raid" made Stuart's reputation. Even the Yankee press gave it breathless coverage, the *New York Times* admitting that it "excites as much admiration in the Union army as it does in Richmond. . . . we regard it as a feather of the very tallest sort in the rebel cap."[11]

From that hour, Stuart rushed toward glory and promotion with irresistible momentum. Less than two months after bedeviling McClellan, he swooped down upon the army of another mediocre commander, Major General John Pope, in upper Virginia. Marching ahead of a 25,000-man force under Stonewall Jackson, he sneaked around Pope's upper flank and struck his supply base at Catlett's Station. There, on 23 August, Stuart's troopers captured three hundred opponents, destroyed much materiel, and carted off spoils ranging from lobster salads and champagne to General Pope's dress uniform.[12] Pope came nowhere close to bagging the raiders or revenging his embarrassment. Distracted and demoralized, he blundered headlong into Confederate infantry and artillery, losing the battle of Second Bull Run and, subsequently, his command.

Having disposed of one adversary, Major General Stuart acted promptly to arrange the retirement of George McClellan as well. After "Little Mac" removed his army to western Maryland early in September, Stuart again made the circuit of its lines, this time sacking supply bases in Chambersburg, Pennsylvania. A few weeks later, Abraham Lincoln forced McClellan into the growing ranks of the Union unemployed.[13]

That winter found Stuart not content with new-won fame. Shortly after the December 1862 battle at Fredericksburg, he mounted an expedition against McClellan's luckless successor, Major General Ambrose E. Burnside. Stuart's snow-pelted offensive carried him to Dumfries, Virginia, within a few miles of

Washington, where he appropriated the contents of supply bases under the noses of Federal officials. To cap his feat, the Beau Sabreur twitted Quartermaster General M. C. Meigs, to whom he wired a complaint about the "bad quality of the mules lately furnished, which interfered seriously with our moving the captured wagons."[14]

Stuart's critics—more than a few of them his colleagues—pointed to such exhibitions as examples of grandstanding, of playing up to newsmen and image-makers. Such observers also looked distastefully upon the gaudy affectations in which Stuart reveled: the scarlet-lined cape that covered his tunic, the ostrich plume and gilt-star clasp that adorned his hat, the flowers and ribbons he wore in his lapels, the golden spurs and elbow-length gauntlets he favored, and the banjoists and fiddlers who accompanied him on the march. Even one of Stuart's defenders, who wrote off such trappings as harmless frivolities, admitted that by flaunting them "he sometimes incurs ridicule."[15]

Stuart was capable of effective performances shorn of extravagance. At Chancellorsville, 2 May 1863, his quiet behind-the-scenes reconnaissance led to the sighting of an exposed Union flank, one mangled by Jackson's infantry and gunners that evening. When Stonewall went down soon afterward with a mortal wound, Stuart stepped in to direct his friend's corps with a low-key competence that consolidated Jackson's gains and enabled the Army of Northern Virginia to ruin "Fighting Joe" Hooker's career in much the manner it had ruined Burnside's, Pope's, and McClellan's.[16]

By the late spring of 1863, then, J. E. B. Stuart possessed a reputation backed by effective showings in command of all arms, one that appeared destined to add newer and even brighter triumphs. That reputation, plus an equally well-publicized regard for his soldiers' welfare, ensured that a large crop of horsemen awaited his call to action. And the myths that had enveloped his prowess continued to place his foes at a psychological disadvantage, thus increasing the tactical odds in his favor. All of this boded well for Stuart's successful participation in the invasion of the North which Robert E. Lee was planning for the coming summer.

Stuart's ranking subordinates, many chosen for qualities that complemented his own, also seemed to ensure a continuation of his success in combat. In the earliest days of his regime Stuart had made inspired decisions in securing three brigade leaders to translate his strategic vision into tactical reality. Two years later, he saw no reason to regret the choices.

His senior brigadier, forty-five-year-old Wade Hampton, a bearded, towering son of South Carolina aristocracy, was reputed to be the largest slave-owner in the South. Son of a War of 1812 officer, Hampton was himself destined for military fame, although he had had no training as a soldier. Much like Stuart, however, he had proven himself a born leader. In '61 he had gone to war at the head of a small army all his own—six companies of infantry, four of cavalry, and one of cannoneers, known as the "Hampton Legion" and clothed and equipped at his expense. After inspiring these natty but untutored warriors to give a strong performance at First Bull Run, Hampton won command of an infantry brigade, which he led gallantly at Seven Pines at the outset of McClellan's Peninsula campaign. Wounded in both battles in which he participated, Hampton, while convalescing from Seven Pines in July 1862, decided to accept a berth under Stuart.[17]

From the first he and his superior worked in tandem—professionally. Perhaps, however, because of the disparity in their ages and in their educational and social backgrounds, the pair never achieved an intimate personal association. Still, they shared many ideas on tactics and discipline, while radiating confidence in, and respect for, each other.

By mid-'63 Hampton had accumulated a record nearly as noteworthy as his commander's. He served ably during the Chambersburg and Dumfries raids, and in November and December of 1862 he led three expeditions of his own against the rear of Burnside's army, gathering three hundred captives and much booty.[18] He also comported himself with skill and fortitude at Fredericksburg and Chancellorsville—so much so that as the summer of 1863 approached, he loomed as Stuart's heir apparent, and not merely by seniority. Stuart had unbounded faith in the South Carolinian's abilities and in those of his well-disciplined brigade—two Palmetto State regiments and one from North Carolina, plus three regiment-sized legions of horsemen out of Georgia, Mississippi, and Alabama. Stuart knew that if he was taken out of action, he could not pass the division into better hands than Hampton's.

Directly below Hampton in seniority (though seventeen years his junior) was Fitzhugh Lee, Stuart's warm friend and Old Army colleague. A West Pointer like Stuart, Fitz Lee had made a less distinguished academic record; at the Academy, where he developed a compact, muscular physique and a hail-fellow manner, he seemed chiefly interested in gaining a reputation for conviviality, good horsemanship, and athletic prowess. A close acquaintence recalled "the strain of jollity pervading him. . . . he had hosts of friends, and no end of enjoyment." Another companion remarked: "he had a prevailing habit of irrepressible good humor which made any occasion of seriousness in him seem like affectation." Fitz was described as having "a square head and short neck upon broad shoulders, a merry eye, and a joyous voice of great power; ruddy, full-bearded, and overflowing with animal spirits."[19] As a tactician, he had performed successfully both in semi-independent operations and under Stuart's direct supervision. Although no strategic genius, he was a strong shoulder upon whom Stuart leaned in times of peril and doubt.

It seemed a pity that his talents would be denied to the Cavalry Division, A.N.V., for a time this summer. Late in May, Fitz had come down with inflammatory rheumatism, which prohibited him from exercising command for an indefinite period.[20] In his absence, his five Virginia regiments were led by his senior colonel, the sternly competent Thomas T. Munford. Another native Virginian (an alumnus of its military institute) and an antebellum planter, Munford had entered the war as an officer of mounted rifles. For some months he had served under Jackson in the Shenandoah Valley—during part of that period as Stonewall's commander of horse—and thus he brought to Stuart's command experience in mounted operations of various styles. To this background Munford soon added notable service under Stuart on the Virginia peninsula, at Second Bull Run (where twice wounded), Antietam, and Fredericksburg. Throughout, the white-maned, black-mustachioed officer, now thirty-two years old, had become known as a reliable sort who eschewed the flamboyance of his superior.[21]

Brigadier General William Henry Fitzhugh (Rooney) Lee, who led Stuart's third brigade—four regiments from Virginia and one from North Carolina—was the second son of Robert Lee and first cousin to Fitzhugh Lee. Militarily akin to the low-key, steady-going Munford, he was, physically, an expanded version of Fitz Lee. The same acquaintence who had characterized the latter described Rooney as "an immense man, probably six feet three or four inches tall. . . . I remember that I wondered, when I first saw him, how he could find a horse powerful enough to bear him. . . . His hands and feet were immense, and in company he appeared to be ill at ease. His bearing was, however, excellent, and his voice, manner, and everything about him bespoke the gentleman."[22] At Harvard, where he had been an indifferent student but a skilled oarsman, Rooney had exuded, in the phrase of a classmate, "the Virginia habit of command," a quality that had served him well ever since. Commissioned directly into the army following college, he had served two years as a frontier dragoon, in 1859 resigning and until the war farming on his estate, "White House," along Virginia's Pamunkey River.

Like his cousin, Rooney was not a brilliant strategist. Still, as colonel of the 9th Virginia Cavalry he had won Stuart's praise for tactical aptitude. Late in 1862, after participating in the Chickahominy Raid and taking a wound at Antietam, he had been named a brigadier, an honor justified by later service at Fredericksburg and during Hampton's and Stuart's expeditions at the close of the year.[23]

For several months prior to the late spring of 1863, Stuart had made do, very nicely, with the brigades of Hampton and the cousins Lee—a total of perhaps 6,000 horsemen.[24] This number he deemed sufficient to handle any assignment, either in concert with operations by the main army or on an independent mission. Now, however, Robert E. Lee's invasion plan dictated a temporary increase in the mounted arm. Four brigades of horsemen would be transferred from other theaters to bolster Stuart's command. Some of these units would not come under his authority until the latter stages of the coming campaign, and only indirectly even then. But all would provide reinforcements for Stuart's organic division at some point during that time.

Stuart played a passive role in selecting his supports. Given the opportunity, he might well have chosen otherwise. Of the four brigade commanders, none was his bosom comrade (he was in fact on poor terms with one), and he had grave reservations about the qualifications of two others.

One of three brigades to be drawn from the Shenandoah Valley for Lee's offensive was led by Brigadier General William Edmondson Jones, Stuart's least favorite colleague. Profane, disputatious, eccentric, Jones was so quarrelsome that he had received the nickname "Grumble." Thirty-nine years old and bald, with a grizzled beard and a penchant for rumpled attire, he was a learned tactician (an 1848 graduate of West Point) and he could instill in his troops his feisty spirit; hence his long tenure in brigade command despite his flaws as a human being. Particularly adept at reconnaissance far from the main army, he was touted by many, Stuart included, as the finest outpost officer in the Army of Northern Virginia. His "Laurel Brigade," composed of four regiments, a battalion, and a battery, all from Virginia, had gained experience in light cavalry tactics at the outset of the conflict but since that time had served as mounted infantry amid the mountain-strewn, river-swept Shenandoah.[25]

In the Valley, Jones had sometimes teamed with a physical opposite: dark-haired, dark-complected, patrician-looking John D. Imboden. The pair's most famous collaboration had come early in 1863 when raiding a strategic stretch of the Baltimore & Ohio Railroad in western Virginia. A soldier of average ability—with enough perception and objectivity to realize the fact—the forty-year-old Imboden did not share Jones's pyrotechnic temper or his idiosyncratic conduct. On the other side of the ledger, his command lacked the discipline and experience of Jones's; its potential contribution to the army was difficult to gauge. In time General Lee would come to regard Imboden's people as "unsteady" and "inefficient."[26]

Owing to Lee's timetable, it would prove impossible for Imboden to leave western Virginia and join the A.N.V. before the coming campaign got under way. Thus, at least in the early phases of the invasion, Imboden's motley command—one regiment of cavalry, one of mounted infantry, a company of partisan rangers, and a horse artillery battery, all recruited in Virginia—would operate independently. Lee wished Imboden to move parallel to the army off its western flank, threatening the B & O, distracting the attention of Yankees in the lower Valley, and gathering up remounts, rations, and materiel needed by the main army.[27]

A third body of Virginia horsemen would be detached from the western part of the state and given to Lee: three regiments and two battalions of so-called cavalry, plus a horse battery. Stuart received the news warily. The contingent's commander, Brigadier General Albert G. Jenkins, was not noted for soldierly ability, average or otherwise, though he had acquired a reputation for terrorism as a raiding leader. Like Imboden a prewar attorney and lawmaker (a member of the House of Representatives, 1857–61), the long-bearded, thin-faced, sad-eyed, thirty-two-year-old Jenkins was Northern-bred and -educated, having attended Pennsylvania's Jefferson College and the Harvard Law School. Inexperienced in the sort of cooperative operations that General Lee favored, and only recently brought together as a brigade, Jenkins's soldiers, most of them residents of the hill country of western Virginia, were of doubtful value in the role of a conventional cavalry force. Aware of this, Stuart was relieved to learn that, in the early going at least, they would not serve in his division. Due to its quasi-infantry status, its convenient position in the Valley, and Stuart's dearth of confidence in its ability, Jenkins's brigade was chosen to accompany the vanguard of the invasion, the corps of Lieutenant General Richard S. Ewell. It would be bolstered by the temporary addition of Major Harry Gilmor's six-company 1st Maryland Battalion (later to become a part of Fitz Lee's brigade), plus Captain William H. Griffin's 2nd Baltimore Battery, on loan from Stuart's horse artillery.[28]

The fourth brigade to augment Stuart was headed by yet another officer whose tactical ability Stuart held suspect: Brigadier General Beverly H. Robertson, one-time leader of the Brigade now commanded by Rooney Lee. Detached from the defenses of North Carolina for the invasion, Robertson— bald, gray-bearded, pop-eyed, perpetually scowling—would bring with him two of the five regiments in his new brigade, "fresh from the camp of instruction," while the rest remained in the Tarheel State or lower Virginia. In addition to the questionable quality of his command, Robertson's checkered combat career played hob with Stuart's peace of mind. One of the latter's aides described the thirty-seven-year-old brigadier as "an excellent man in camp to train troops, but in the field, in the presence of the enemy, he lost all self-possession, and was perfectly unreliable." Though committed to using the general to maximum advantage in the weeks ahead, even Robert Lee admitted: "What to do with Robertson I do not know."[29]

Among the commanders of the twenty-two field regiments, seven battalions, and various partisan units fated to serve under Stuart during the drive north, several were noted for qualities that promised them higher rank and authority. These included Colonels Laurence S. Baker of the 1st North Carolina; Richard L. T. Beale, 9th Virginia; Matthew Calbraith Butler, 2nd South Carolina; John R. Chambliss, Jr., 13th Virginia; Milton J. Ferguson, 16th Virginia; Asher W. Harman, 12th Virginia; Lunsford L. Lomax, 11th Virginia; Thomas L. Rosser, 5th Virginia; Williams C. Wickham, 4th Virginia; and Pierce M. B. Young, Cobb's (Georgia) Legion; plus Lieutenant Colonels Elijah V. White and Vincent A. Witcher of the 35th and 34th Virginia Battalions, respectively. Before the end of the war, Butler, Chambliss, Lomax, Rosser, Wickham, and Young would win command of cavalry divisions. While planning his summer campaign R. E. Lee even considered promoting some of them to head additional brigades carved from Stuart's enlarged command. Eventually he rejected the idea because of Stuart's depleted supply of troopers and the unwieldy number of general officers that would have resulted.[30]

In addition to so many valuable cavalrymen, Stuart, until recently, had benefited from the outsized talents of his horse artillery chief, Major John Pelham. In his early twenties but possessing the poise and intellect of one twice his age, the Alabama-born Pelham had won notice on several fields, and renown at Fredericksburg. There his handling of guns along the Confederate right had prompted Robert Lee himself to exclaim: "It is glorious to see such courage in one so young!" Three months later, however, the "Gallant Pelham" had taken a mortal wound in battle against Yankee cavalry and his expertise had been forever lost to the Army of Northern Virginia.[31]

Pelham's successor was a quietly capable Virginian, Major Robert F. Beckham. West Point-educated, he enjoyed experience as a topographical engineer and an infantry officer, as well as in artillery operations. To him Pelham had bequeathed a battalion of four batteries, three composed of Virginians and the other a Maryland unit. Each battery mounted four light cannon; 6- and 10-pounder rifled howitzers and 12-pounder "Napoleon" smoothbores predominated.

By June 1863 Beckham had found a comfortable berth in Stuart's division, his administrative skills winning special praise. Early on, one of Stuart's staff had described him as "a very nice fellow . . . [who] will go as far as any one to fill a place which can never be filled in the hearts of those who had the pleasure of knowing Pelham." This indicated the shadow that hung over the hard-working young artillerist, who realized that the coming campaign would reveal whether he could win widespread acceptance as Stuart's chief cannoneer.[32] At least he had the comfort of knowing he could depend on a complement of able battery commanders, Captains James F. Hart of South Carolina and James Breathed of Virginia being the most gifted.

In many respects, J. E. B. Stuart's relations with his cavalry and artillery subordinates were only as smooth as his staff made them. He had hand-picked the members of his headquarters family to combine administrative skill with the ability to exercise command in his name whenever conditions warranted. Major Henry B. McClellan (a Philadelphia-born cousin to George B. McClellan), Stuart's new adjutant general, shouldered primary responsibility for committing Stuart's wants and needs to paper. The twenty-three-year-old former schoolteacher would prove diligent in the discharge of every duty, from helping his superior grapple with campaign-report prose to safeguarding his sleeping privileges. Privy to every consequential event in Stuart's career from this spring onward, he would publish the most detailed memoir of his commander's career.[33]

Even more closely linked to Stuart—his devoted friend as well as his long-time subordinate—was his chief engineer, Captain William W. Blackford of Virginia, who doubled as the cavalry division's cartographer. Another well-bred young man of aesthetic proclivities, he too would pen a postwar account of service at Stuart's right hand.[34]

A third staff officer, Captain John Esten Cooke, possessed marriage ties to his commander. A Virginia lawyer, poet, essayist, and novelist as well as Stuart's brother-in-law, Cooke found his post as divisional ordnance chief a valuable vantage point from which to gather notes for a memoir of his own. This he

would add to a body of writing, already bookshelf-size, which included a lauda-
tory portrait of another superior, the *Life of Stonewall Jackson*.[35]

The most visible member of Stuart's military family was Major Johann August Heinrich Heros von Borcke. Prussian-born, fiercely mustachioed, of great
girth, and standing six feet four in his stocking feet, Heros von Borcke combined the functions of cavalry chief of staff, foreign military adviser, drillmaster, tactician—and court jester. In the latter capacity, he sought novel ways to
lighten Stuart's headquarters atmosphere, a duty he refused to entrust to
fiddlers or banjoists. On one occasion, appearing at a dance in Stuart's honor,
the hulking German took the floor clad in a veiled bridal gown. To the delight of
his commander, von Borcke and his escort, a fellow cavalry officer, capered
about with ludicrous abandon. As a former subordinate to the Prince of Prussia,
however, the blonde, blue-eyed "Von" also nourished combat ambitions; he
viewed the summer's campaign as an opportunity to gain a line commission
under his revered superior.[36]

***

The tactics that Heros von Borcke and other European drillmasters sought to
teach Stuart's cavalry lacked soil conducive to growth. The problem was that no
one in authority, including J. E. B. Stuart, admitted the fact.

The wide expanses of the Continent had engendered the development of
shock tactics by which cavalry, heavily armed and borne on large horses, delivered mounted charges with sabers and lances against troops of all arms. Advances in firearms during the early nineteenth century should have relegated
this mode of warfare to obscurity; mounted attacks against foot troops wielding
rifles and gun crews working rifled artillery had become perilous and uncertain
by 1861. Still the open terrain, which facilitated cavalry's maneuverability, and
the importance of horsemen in delivering the psychological blows so much a
part of Napoleonic warfare, perpetuated the theory of cavalry's effectiveness in
an offensive role.[37]

European observers of the Civil War believed that the wooded and broken
ground characteristic of American battlefields would severely limit cavalry employment. So too would the American military's aversion to using cold steel in
battle. They assumed that Unionists and Confederates alike regarded the horse
as a means of reaching the front, where riders dismounted to fight afoot with
carbines, rifles, and pistols. As this process did occur with regularity early in
the war, theorists refused to identify American cavalry as such. One visiting
Briton wrote that "the cavalry here is very differently organised from the same
branch of the service in Europe. They are, in fact, mounted infantry." Another
remarked with disapproval that "the cavalry on both sides . . . are not taught to
use the sword at all. . . . They are armed with rifles and revolvers, [and] the
consequence is that they never charge or get amongst the infantry, (the only

chance for cavalry) but dismount and skirmish, and of course get beaten as all cavalry must, in that sort of work. . . ."[38]

With reference to Confederate horsemen, such observations were only partially valid. It was true that the average Southerner considered his saber more efficacious as a camp tool than as a weapon.[39] While on horseback, he preferred to fight with his revolver; it seemed to answer better in close-quarters fighting and somehow appeared a more polite instrument of death. In battle, Rebels who encountered saber-wielding Federals sometimes shouted: "Put up your sabres, draw your pistols and fight like gentlemen!"[40] It was likewise true that upon occasion Confederate troopers fought on foot—and effectively—against forces of all arms.[41]

But the theory that the Rebel horsemen in the East fought primarily as mounted infantry evaporates upon scrutiny. In point of fact, those who served under Stuart learned to imitate European light cavalry. Only those units that fought in the Shenandoah and in western Virginia fit European observers' descriptions. As one of Stuart's troopers explained, the brigades of Jenkins and Imboden "were called cavalry but were essentially mounted infantry and only effective as such. . . . The Confederate cavalry proper hardly considered those forces as actually belonging to the army, but rather as a species of irregular auxiliaries." As these brigades wielded inappropriate firearms—smoothbores and even shotguns—and because they often encountered Federals sporting faster-loading carbines and rifles, they labored at a great disadvantage. They could be overwhelmed by an enemy who drew their fire at long range, then charged before they could reload. Noting Jenkins's and Imboden's handicaps, the troopers under Stuart had long since come to doubt the effectiveness of dismounted tactics.[42]

Indeed, the Stuartian brand of mounted warfare had a classic-cavalry flavor. Stuart personally favored the mounted attack, particularly when opposing other horsemen but also when facing incoherent infantry and unsupported artillery. Massed power in motion appealed greatly to his dramatic notions of warfare. It also possessed psychological advantages he could appreciate: he would have concurred with one postwar theorist that "in a mounted charge the element of fear, of caution in the heart of the soldier is largely eliminated."[43] Beyond its shock value and morale benefits, the mounted offensive fit the cavalier image that underlay the "Virginia habit of command."

As also befitted that image, Stuart was partial to the saber. He strove to inculcate in his squadrons the value of tempered steel in close combat. Above all, he drove home the lesson that when used on horseback, any firearm delivers ragged accuracy, no matter how near its target.

Stuart's lieutenants (with the exception of Colonel Munford and the few other mounted infantry veterans in the Cavalry Division, A.N.V.) echoed his thinking. Years later, Fitz Lee recalled the disapproval of nontraditional mounted operations that pervaded the officer corps. He stressed the dictum that a hybrid warrior such as a dragoon or a mounted rifleman usually proved inferior to a cavalryman, the worst elements of both arms resulting from efforts to combine the characteristics of foot soldiers and horsemen. His colleague Thomas Rosser agreed, insisting that "cavalry in this country . . . is worthless except in the charge, and should never be used for any other purpose. The cavalry soldier should never be dismounted to fight . . . but be educated to the belief *that nothing can withstand a well-executed charge* of cavalry."[44]

The majority of Stuart's rank and file fought by these precepts. If few troopers placed as much faith in edged weapons as Stuart, almost all echoed his preference for fighting mounted. One of his men put it succinctly: "Dismounted fighting was never popular with the Southern trooper, who felt that he was only half a man when separated from his horse." When compelled to fight afoot, the only happy Confederate was the one in four detailed to lead his own and his comrades' animals to the rear. Indeed, this fondness for mounted combat was a major preservative of Rebel morale.[45]

If always pitted against opponents equally committed to the classic tradition, Stuart's cavaliers—thanks to their native agility, their experience in horsemanship, and their boundless self-confidence—would have emerged victorious every time. Early in the war, when they encountered an enemy committed to no tactical model at all, they were victorious. But the extent to which the Confederates relied on old tactics limited their effectiveness in battle. For one thing, Stuart and his subordinates failed to appreciate (or to admit) the fundamental shortcoming of a mounted offensive: that no cavalry attack, however massive or energetic, could influence combat situations for long. Unless braced with infantry or artillery, as one Union general remarked after the war, a mounted charge "was out of control from the moment it began" because it generated an ungovernable momentum.[46] Since an attack could not be precisely directed, neither could it be timed to match the duration of infantry operations. And once it lost power due to the exhaustion of the horses or the interposition of enemy troops, its participants would always be repulsed by a counterattack that prevented them from securing captured ground.

An even more serious drawback was the lack of versatility among Stuart's horsemen. By 1863 tactical theory had become so fixed and rigid that the brigades of Hampton and the Lees served to advantage only as cavalry proper, while the men under Jenkins and Imboden were "only effective" as mounted infantry. Since neither class seemed comfortable in the other's role, each would find it difficult to withstand an enemy who combined both roles to advantage. Fortunately for J. E. B. Stuart, no such enemy had materialized—at least not by early June 1863.

***

Lee's plan for a thrust into the North met with Stuart's wholehearted approval. Stuart approved because he appreciated the motives behind its conception.[47] Originally, the campaign had been proposed as a means of diverting Union forces in the West—particularly in the hope of forcing Major General

U. S. Grant to lift his siege of Vicksburg, Mississippi. This objective now seemed only remotely attainable and Lee had other, more promising goals in view when, in late spring, he presented his blueprint of operations to his civilian overlords in Richmond.

Lee had come to view the invasion as a way to deal with Hooker's army, ensconced in an almost untouchable position at Falmouth. A movement northward would draw the enemy into an engagement on more favorable ground and would also foil Hooker's apparent intent to wage a summer campaign in Virginia. Lee realized that in abandoning his lines above Richmond he would invite his enemy to seize the Confederate capital; should Hooker make that effort, the offensive would have to be aborted. Yet Lee also knew that his adversary had been enjoined to cover Washington at all costs and that the Lincoln government considered the Army of Northern Virginia, not Richmond, Hooker's objective.

Lee further believed that a campaign in the North would draw to Hooker's side other forces that, left unattended, might menace strategic sectors of the Confederacy. Then, too, a move north would relieve ravaged Virginia—at least temporarily—of the enemy's presence, while permitting the poorly fed, poorly clothed, and poorly equipped Confederates to subsist for an indefinite period in a land of natural riches. Given even a few weeks to roam such a region, Lee could cure many of the supply problems that, through a dearth of distribution facilities, had hampered his army for over a year and a half. Recently, in fact, the Confederate commissary general had replied thus to critics of his supply efforts: "If General Lee wants rations let him get them from Pennsylvania."

The army commander had indeed fixed his gaze on the lush farming lands of the Keystone State. As early as February he had ordered his cartographers to prepare maps depicting the country as far north as Harrisburg, the state capital, and as far east as Philadelphia. According to one of his subordinates, Lee predicted a penetration to the Chambersburg-York-Carlisle area before Hooker overtook him. If the enemy moved more slowly, Lee aimed to seize Harrisburg and then sort out further options involving Philadelphia, Baltimore, or even Washington City. Of course, any objective would be attainable should Hooker be whipped on Northern soil as soundly as he had been beaten at Chancellorsville. In that event, the Lincoln government would surely collapse under opposition pressure, while peace-party agitation and the influence of foreign governments would dictate a speedy, negotiated triumph for the Confederacy. And even should the worst occur and the Army of Northern Virginia be thrust back south as it had after Antietam, it could occupy Pennsylvania long enough to cut rail, canal, and telegraphic communication between the East and Northwest. It could also lay waste to bridges, roads, mines, and mills, while disrupting operations at training camps, supply bases, and seats of government. Blows to Union prestige and morale might alone be worth the cost of an invasion.

For Stuart and his cavaliers, each of these potential benefits had allure, but the opportunity to remount and resupply in Pennsylvania was the most attractive. The war that had assaulted Virginia now threatened to dismount the Cavalry Division, A.N.V. Already it had occasioned an alarming depletion of manpower, and its effects were aggravated by a Confederate policy whereby each trooper furnished his own mount, being reimbursed at the rate of forty cents per day. While a substantial sum was paid to any whose animal died in service, the owner had to make good the loss if he expected to remain in the cavalry. Such men were forced to return home to secure a replacement, while those unable to obtain a remount were transferred to infantry or artillery service. Either way, Stuart's command shrank.[48]

A growing scarcity of weapons and equipment (a large percentage of which had been furnished early in the war by foreign contractors whose access to the Confederacy had since been restricted by the coastal shipping blockade) also bedeviled Stuart. Available materiel was shoddy. Lee himself complained about the cavalry's saddles and carbines: "the former ruined the horses' backs, and the latter were so defective as to be demoralizing to the men." Meanwhile, Unionists benefited from a greater supply of horseflesh, were armed with quality breechloaders and revolvers, and drew on a seemingly inexhaustible fund of equipment and ammunition.

Beyond these considerations, Stuart had a personal interest in revisiting the North. He wished to slake his thirst for adventure and publicity by returning his troopers to combat and his name to Northern as well as Southern newspapers. In particular, he yearned to give his record the luster he felt it had been denied at Chancellorsville (an injustice about which he complained, rather petulantly, to General Lee).[49] An invasion seemed to promise independent mounted operations of the sort that elevated his spirit. And should no such opportunity develop in natural course, Stuart might find a way to manufacture one.

***

Stuart was also pleased by the mechanics of Lee's offensive. Though never committed to paper, they were disseminated among Lee's ranking subordinates well before the movement began. The plan called for Lieutenant General Richard S. Ewell's 2nd Corps to leave the Culpeper Court House vicinity on the morning of 9 June and march northwestward, screened by Jenkins's horsemen (who had grouped in the Shenandoah Valley near Strasburg and Front Royal) and, farther west, by Imboden's brigade. Ewell's initial objectives were Winchester and Berryville, Union garrisons in the lower Valley which, if left unmolested, might batter the western flank of the invasion column. Once these were neutralized, Lieutenant General James Longstreet's 1st Corps, along with Stuart's reinforced division, would move north from Culpeper to cover the army's right flank. Foot soldiers and horsemen would move along the eastern side of the Blue Ridge Mountains. Longstreet would hold the several gaps and passes via which the enemy might seek to split the Rebel forces. Stuart, meanwhile, would advance through the Loudoun Valley, just east of the Blue Ridge, fending off attempts by Union calvary or other arms to scout the main army or slash its communications.

Longstreet's disposition would screen the movement down (i.e., northward

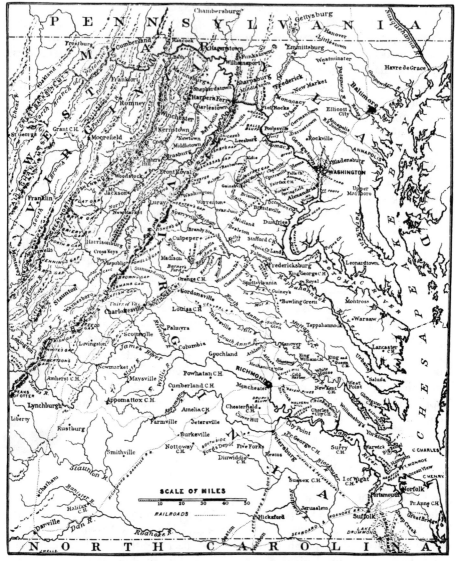

Virginia, Maryland, and Southern Pennsylvania. (Map from Battles and Leaders of the Civil War.)

through) the Shenandoah Valley by the 3rd Corps of Lieutenant General Ambrose P. Hill. When Hill had moved northwest of him, Longstreet would pass through the gaps and bring up the Rebel rear. Stuart would then take over the chore of holding the Blue Ridge entrances, evacuating them only after learning that Hooker had moved above the Potomac in full pursuit. By that time the forefront of the invasion, Ewell and Jenkins, would be in Pennsylvania, with comrades close behind. Stuart might then take the rear or move by a roundabout route to join Lee's vanguard.[50]

The preliminary phases of the movement had already gotten under way. On 11 May, Lee had ordered Stuart to mass at Culpeper Court House, within range of the upper (i.e., the southern) reaches of the Shenandoah. There the brigades of Hampton and the Lees would be joined by those under Robertson and Jones, and all could refit and plan for the work ahead.[51]

Because of delays common to concentrating so large a force in as unostentatious a manner as possible, Stuart's organic division, some seven thousand strong, was not in place at Culpeper till the third week in the month. The local accommodations pleased his people. A horse artilleryman noted that the courthouse town was "pleasantly situated on the gently rising slope of a hill in a rather rolling and diversified section of country." He and his cohorts appreciated the abundance of worm-and-post fences, enclosing fields lush with clover, wheat, corn, and oats. Within hours of the cavalry's arrival the fences had vanished—reappearing as fuel for campfires—while the crops had become the contents of numerous feedbags.[52]

Soon the plains above and below Culpeper took on the appearance of a parade ground. Stuart was inspired: on the afternoon of 22 May he led his troops about a half a mile northeastward and staged a review not far from the Orange & Alexandria Railroad depot of Brandy Station. The result was a scenic and military triumph not only by Stuart's criteria but in the minds of many locals who turned out to watch.

Such was its success, in fact, that the pageant-loving cavalryman called another review two weeks later. By then Robertson's demi-brigade had come up from North Carolina and part of Jones's had marched in from the Valley to boost divisional strength to nearly ten thousand.[53] To share the honor of the occasion, Stuart sought the attendance of General Lee and Confederate officials including ex-War Secretary George W. Randolph. The event was scheduled for 5 June, the evening before being given over to a ball at the courthouse, with Secretary Randolph as principal guest. A "gay and dazzling scene" ensued, with entertainment and victuals—wine, punch, and choice tidbits—served by Stuart's headquarters family. The tinkle of goblets raised in toast, the hum of genteel conversation, and the music of banjoists and fiddlers flowed through the evening. At the height of the festivities, officers in dress uniforms and longgowned belles from Richmond traced eccentric circles upon the courthouse lawn, their movements swathed in the light of candles strung above their heads.[54]

Next morning, the enemy, from his camps near Falmouth, had the ill grace to launch a reconnaissance in force against Lee's positions at and around Fredericksburg. The ensuing fracas compelled Lee to stay close to his headquarters instead of joining the units at Culpeper. Though the army leader missed Stuart's show, George Randolph and the other guests from Richmond did their utmost to fill his place.

They were treated to a grand spectacle. Beginning at 10:00 A.M., a two-mile-long column of cavalrymen and horse artillerists marched in review across a wide, level plain. As did each of his officers, Stuart, at the point of the column, sported his best attire, including a new slouch hat, cocked at a rakish tilt, a black ostrich plume jutting from the brim. Behind him came his staff, trailed by sixteen cannon and four brigades of horsemen, a guidon rippling in the van of each regiment. As the procession moved forward, damsels left the audience to scatter flowers across its path while, on the sidelines, three bands thumped and tootled away. The effect was imposing in the extreme—expecially to the participants. Wrote Heros von Borcke: "Our little [headquarters] band presented a gay and gallant appearance as we rode forth to the sound of our bugles, all mounted on fine chargers. . . ." Others in the column termed the procession "a grand sight" and the event "a great day among the cavalry." Most of the spectators clapped, cheered, and shouted in agreement.[55]

After the march-past, Stuart called for maneuvers by regiments and brigades, which drew forth even louder exclamations of praise. To cap his spectacle, he presided over a sham battle, his cannon firing blank rounds from half a dozen positions and his horsemen thundering past the guns, raised sabers jutting toward an invisible foe. The effect, concluded one horse artilleryman, was "inspiring enough to make even an old woman feel fightish." Many females in attendance clasped their hands and sank into the arms of their escorts "in a swoon."[56]

Stuart would have considered the day a perfect success had Lee been on hand. The army leader did not reach Culpeper, at the head of Ewell's corps, until Sunday morning, the seventh. Unwilling to see his commander deprived, Stuart hastily organized a third review, to be held early the next day on a field just east of the courthouse.

This time few citizens turned out, the novelty of the event having waned, and most of the 5 June guests were back home. Even so, a substantial audience was on hand: Alabama, Arkansas, Georgia, and Texas infantrymen from the division of Major General John Bell Hood, recently transferred from Fredericksburg to Culpeper for the invasion march. Hood alone had been invited to the affair, but Stuart had casually suggested that he bring "any of his friends" with him. Considering every member of his division a friend, Hood brought all six thousand of them, realizing they would appreciate the opportunity to deride the antics of their cavalry comrades, whom they considered comic-opera warriors out of Auber and Donizetti.

Stuart did not disappoint them. Again clothed in fine attire, he also displayed gigantic wreaths draped over his saddle and his horse's neck, gifts from adoring females. General Lee wrote next morning to his wife: "Stuart was in all his glory." Conversely, the army leader appeared to John Esten Cooke worn and pallid, an impression heightened by "his grizzled beard and old gray riding-cape." Another cavalryman, however, gloried in his "first sight of the great chieftain. Even his personal appearance indicates great mental endowment and nobility of soul."[57]

Unlike the pageant of the fifth, today's did not include a mock battle. Even so, fast-paced activity held spectator attention. As Lee looked on, the head of Stuart's division "moved at a walk until it came within some fifty or one hundred paces of the position occupied by the reviewing general, when squadron by squadron would take up first the trot, then the gallop, until they had passed some distance beyond, when again they would pull down to the walk." In their rear Stuart's batteries again fired blanks, this time in one barrage.[58]

The spectacle drew divided reviews. One onlooker proclaimed it a "splendid military pageant, and an inspiring scene, such as this continent never before witnessed." Another considered it "a most glorious and soul-stirring sight," while a third termed it "grand" and reflected that Lee "evidently witnessed with pride and satisfaction this incomparable body of mounted men." Less complimentary comments came from Hood's people, whose only satisfaction had derived from making trophies of hats blown from the heads of galloping troopers, from jeering the failure of Grumble Jones to conform his recently arrived brigade to the formation of Stuart's other units, and from treating the passing riders to frequent cries of: "Mister, here's your mule!"[59]

Once the pageant ended, Stuart accepted General Lee's compliments on the appearance of his troopers. The commanders then discussed details of the next morning's march. Exchanging hopes for its success, they parted, Lee retiring to his new quarters near Culpeper and Stuart leading his still-saddled division to its new camp near Brandy Station. At his headquarters on Fleetwood Heights, a long ridge just above the depot, he made dispositions with a view to a dawn crossing of the Rappahannock River.

Stuart placed three of his brigades north of the station; they could cross next day at nearby Beverly Ford. The northernmost position was assigned to Fitz Lee's brigade. Colonel Munford placed the command in bivouac above Hazel River, almost eight miles northwest of Brandy. Below Munford—two miles southwest of the confluence of the Hazel and Rappahannock and four miles above the depot—the main body of Rooney Lee's brigade, plus Breathed's Virginia battery, bivouacked near the home of a family named Welford, its advance guard posted at Oak Shade Church. And Grumble Jones's camp (as well as that of Beckham's gunners) was pitched in dense woods just above St. James Church, about two hundred yards west of the main road to Beverly Ford; Jones's pickets ran northeastward to Beverly and south to Rappahannock Bridge.

Below Brandy Station, Hampton's and Robertson's brigades camped between Fleetwood Heights and the westward hamlet of Stevensburg, many units bedding down on the spacious Barbour farm. Hampton's picket line extended southeastward to Kelly's Ford, then down the river as far as the tributary of Mountain Run, with a squadron posted along the road to Rappahannock Station. Finally, Robertson's videttes covered the ground between Jones and Hampton, including Kelly's, Wheatley's, and Norman's Fords.[60] In all, Stuart's division patrolled a perimeter more than ten miles long—a dangerously vast area, considering that relatively few troopers had been placed on picket. Stuart desired the great majority of his people to slumber peacefully until shortly before dawn. They would need all the shut-eye they could get, for in the future the opportunity to sleep for an extended period would prove elusive.

Early in the evening, with most of his men asleep, Stuart retired to one of the two tent-flies standing on Fleetwood Heights—the rest of his headquarters baggage had been packed for travel—and left an early-hour call. Given his parade-ground exertions, the general must have drifted quickly into unconsciousness.

[2]

The "Knight of Romance" and His Dragoons

WHILE the Confederate cavalry appeared to spring full-blown into existence, Union mounted forces in the East underwent a lengthy, arduous, and painful evolution. By June 1863 this evolution was coming to a close.

From the outbreak of war, the Federal cavalry in all theaters had been hobbled by the shortsighted, fossilized thinking of the officials who supervised mobilization. Well into 1861 the high command—most notably the seventy-five-year-old commanding general, Winfield Scott, and Simon Cameron, the secretary of war—continued to believe (at any rate, to hope) that the conflict would prove too brief to require the raising of more than a handful of mounted regiments. According to the popular wisdom, cavalry was too expensive to organize and maintain on a large scale; estimates held that every twelve companies mounted and outfitted at public expense would rob the Treasury of over $300,000 a year merely to cover upkeep on animals, remounts, weapons, and equipment—a proportionally greater amount than required to keep infantry and artillery in the field.[1] Another expense was a government statute that fixed pay for cavalry officers above that bestowed on officers in other arms. An entirely different concern was that cavalry tactics were too complex to be assimilated in proper time by civilian-soldiers, many of whom had never sat a horse, let alone fought aboard one with pistol, sword, and carbine. Finally, in common with colleagues abroad, Federal tacticians considered the seat of war in Virginia too broken and wooded to permit large-scale operations of the type popularized by European horsemen.

For these and other reasons, the War Department originally decreed that the five mounted regiments in the Regular Army (two of them originally designated as dragoons, one as mounted rifles, and each comprising ten companies) would meet the needs of the wartime army.[2] Put aside was the realization that these units had been depleted by officers gone south after Fort Sumter, while many of those who remained would jump to volunteer units to secure higher rank, pay, and prestige. Finally the hierarchy decided that all problems could be solved by recruiting a sixth Regular regiment, twelve companies strong, and by raising the others to like size.[3]

Clearer hands could have predicted the outcome. During the earliest combined-operations campaign in the East, the Federals met defeat at least in part through a scarcity of mounted forces. In the Shenandoah Valley, Major General Robert Patterson's handful of cavalrymen revealed their inability to deal with the 1st Virginia and other Confederate mounted units. Patterson was thereby prevented from detecting the withdrawal of his enemy eastward to Bull Run in mid-July 1861. And once the Rebel armies combined to oppose the invasion force of Brigadier General Irvin McDowell, Stuart and his associates easily outmaneuvered and outfought the five-hundred Regular troopers McDowell employed at First Bull Run. The latter were unable to make their presence felt at any point in the battle, while Stuart's riders and those in the "Black Horse Cavalry" won fame by lashing Yankee fugitives with cold steel and carbine fire, precipitating a rout.

Within days of the debacle at Bull Run George McClellan superseded McDowell. A few months later "Little Mac" replaced Winfield Scott as well. And early in 1862 Edwin McMasters Stanton succeeded Cameron in the War Office. Both newcomers, as well as a now-enlightened Abraham Lincoln, sought a much larger role for the Union cavalry. They actively sought six-squadron, twelve-company regiments of volunteers.[4]

Since the life of the mounted soldier was perceived to be more glamorous than that of the infantryman or the cannoneer, the volunteer recruitment program went smoothly. Unlike their predecessors, McClellan and Stanton did not discourage offers by prominent civilians (many seeking high rank) to furnish units of employees, friends, or constituents who fancied themselves cavalry material. Moreover, they implemented plans to secure from private industry enough materiel to upgrade the Regulars and to supply equipment-poor volunteers. They called to Washington most of the Regular troops scattered along the frontier on garrison duty. They established throughout the North stables, remount depots, and blacksmith's shops. In the summer of 1863 their efforts would culminate in the establishment of a Cavalry Bureau, a War Department agency charged with tending to the special needs of the arm.

Training programs were hastily organized for the thousands of recruits who had opted to ride to war. Many enlistees, however, proved resistant to learning the lessons required by the arm. Though an axiom proclaimed that two years' service was required to develop a competent trooper, drillmasters in the East swore that, given the material at their disposal, such a timetable was too optimistic.[5]

Inevitably, considering the Union cavalry's awkward start, it was consistently outshone and occasionally humiliated during the early going. Time after time the erstwhile day laborers from Ohio and store clerks from Massachusetts were surprised, routed, and pursued by the scions of Virginia and Carolina planters. A few months of such adversity made the Yankee horsemen pariahs in their own army. Recalled one trooper of his service branch: "The infantry men sneered at it, and the universal opinion was that cavalry was useless except for outposts and orderly duty—in fact, to look at the enemy and run away." So many ran that derisive expressions gained currency with foot soldiers. While disdainful Confederates greeted their cavaliers with "Here's your mule!" their Federal counterparts would exclaim: "There's going to be a fight, boys; the cavalry's running back!" and "Whoever saw a dead cavalryman?"[6]

The plight of the horse soldier was worsened by field commanders who shared Winfield Scott's obtuseness. Even McClellan—who was touted as a military genius, perceptive in the care and use of all arms—repeated his predecessor's mistakes. Little Mac failed to appreciate the advantages of coordinating the tactical strengths of cavalry with those of infantry and artillery. He followed the evil course of reducing mounted regiments to their smallest components for operational use. He wasted cavalry's potential and depressed its morale by employing its people as couriers, bodyguards for his subordinates, pickets for encampments, and wagon train escorts, instead of as combat troops.[7] More seriously, he failed to provide his horsemen with capable leaders.

McClellan met a deserved fate when his 1862 Peninsula campaign featured few contributions by his mounted wing. In fact, except for brief apearances in the May and June engagements at Hanover Court House and Gaines's Mill, the Union troopers were denied offensive roles in combat. Their most publicized contribution was their too-little, too-late effort to nab Stuart's Chickahominy raiders. Later in June, however, they did a fine job of covering the withdrawal of McClellan's army from Richmond to the James River.[8]

The next bright star in the Northern firmament, John Pope, waned more quickly than McClellan: his tenure embraced a bit more than two months that summer. Inept at handling troops of any arm, Pope managed his horsemen with inspired incompetence. He scattered his mounted forces, failed to heed their reports, and frittered away the talents of two of the finest cavalrymen any commander ever possessed, Brigadier Generals George Bayard and John Buford. Like Little Mac, Pope refused to commit his troopers to decisive work in any of the major engagements he directed, including Second Bull Run in late August. In consequence, he was bested by Lee, Jackson, and Longstreet—and embarrassed by Stuart.

Mercifully, Pope was relieved early in September. His Army of Virginia was absorbed into the Army of the Potomac and McClellan regained command of the latter. Little Mac promptly demonstrated that he had learned nothing from Pope's travail. On 17 September, he presided over the bloodiest day's fighting of the war, turning back Lee's invasion of Maryland. But, as though forgetful that he commanded horsemen, he failed to use his cavalry in an important sector of the battlefield. Even so, the troopers and horse artillerymen in Brigadier General Alfred Pleasonton's division turned a minor operation into a gallant feat by charging through a storm of cannon fire to seize and hold a contested bridge opposite the Confederate center.[9] Although he did not deserve the honor—he sat comfortably in the rear while his men carried out the attack—Pleasonton grabbed the credit in his battle report and exploited it in the newspapers. His reputation climbed.

In November, after his timidity and poor judgment prevented an effective pursuit of Stuart's Chambersburg raiders, McClellan left the field for good. His successor, Ambrose Burnside, did even worse by his horseman than had Little Mac. During his ill-conducted Fredericksburg campaign and the "Mud March" that followed, Burnside weighted down his cavalry with picket, reconnaissance, and skirmishing duties in wretched weather; for months afterward, the arm suffered every evil horseflesh is heir to, in the form of equine diseases. In battle, Burnside made less use of his troopers than had his several predecessors. On 13 December, while Stuart and Pelham demonstrated what cavalry and horse artillery, properly used and ably led, could do in combat, Burnside's mounted units acted as spectators of a bloody debacle in which thousands of their infantry comrades fell before impregnable defenses.

In January 1863, Stuck-in-the-Mud Burnside was replaced by Fighting Joe Hooker, and for a time—in the mounted arm at least—a new and better era had dawned. The next month Hooker formed the first corps of cavalry and removed the horsemen from the jurisdiction of other corps commanders, thus increasing cavalry's power, cohesiveness, and morale. Unfortunately, he placed all 1,400 troopers under Major General George Stoneman, a dragoon with seventeen years of Regular Army experience and who had been McClellan's chief of cavalry. Despite his prewar record, Stoneman was everything a mounted leader ought not to be: slow, ultraconservative, and unequal to handling large bodies of troopers. He also lacked the personality so vital to an officer in his branch. Not the least of his troubles was hemorrhoids—an acute affliction that threatened to disable him.[10]

Under Hooker the rejuvenated cavalry showed an early flash of brilliance. On 17 March a 2,100-man detachment under Brigadier General William W. Averell and Colonel Alfred N. Duffié swept down on Fitz Lee's camp along the Rappahannock, seeking to avenge the latter's recent surprise attack on Union pickets east of the river. The upshot was a ten-hour engagement near Kelly's Ford in which Lee absorbed a pummeling, John Pelham took his mortal wound, and a regiment or two of Virginians fled in panic from the troopers they had so long derided. Averell and Duffié retreated only after gaining the Army of the Potomac's first triumph in a mounted battle. Given the respectable number of casualties suffered, "dead cavalryman" jokes lost much of their popularity.[11]

The Federals' new-won success failed to endure. In subsequent campaigning both Averell and Duffié proved mediocre officers, their troopers found no opportunity to distinguish themselves further, and their adversaries saw cause to regard Kelly's Ford a fluke. The Chancellorsville campaign seemed to bear this out. In the first week in May, while Hooker's main army suffered defeat in the Wilderness at the hands of Lee and Jackson, George Stoneman and ten thousand of his men rode south to damage communication lines between Fredericksburg and Richmond. Intended to outshine any expedition mounted by Stuart, the raid achieved no strategic benefits. Undoing the good Hooker had accomplished by forming the corps, Stoneman split it into detachments which he expected to wreak havoc on Rebel supply depots "like a shell" and its fragments. The pieces had minimal impact. Though inflicting some damage to secondary objectives, they missed primary targets despite easy access to them. Some of Stoneman's parties, notably Averell's, did virtually nothing.[12]

Most of Stuart's horsemen disdained to pursue, realizing that the critical field of action lay in the Wilderness. Left free to maneuver by Stoneman's absence, Stuart bounded forward into the forest, spied Hooker's open right flank, and ensured its demolition. Soon afterward, the Army of the Potomac staggered back to its camp outside Falmouth. Learning of the retreat, Stoneman grew fearful, recalled his detachments, and scrambled back across the Rappahannock. On his return he found that Hooker had declared the raid a miserable botch and had made the cavalry a scapegoat for the failure of the campaign. Hooker relieved William Averell for incompetence, replaced him with Pleasonton, and hinted that the latter might succeed Stoneman as well.[13]

While Stoneman thrashed about in the Rebel rear, Alfred Pleasonton had remained with Hooker's main command. On the evening of 2 May, shortly after Stonewall Jackson turned the Union right, Pleasonton led a mounted brigade against a smaller band of enemy infantry which, in the dark, had frightened some of Hooker's people into retreat. Hooker and many of his subordinates believed this force consisted of Jackson's corps, and Pleasonton saw no reason to disillusion them—then or afterward. After stopping the advance with a mounted charge, the cavalry leader rounded up enough artillery to disperse the enemy. Later he announced that he had singlehandedly blocked a massive effort to close Hooker's route of retreat. Desperately searching for a positive note to the battle just concluded, Hooker accepted this story at face value. A few days later, when Abraham Lincoln visited the vanquished army at Falmouth, Hooker produced the cavalry leader and exclaimed: "Mr. President, this is General Pleasonton, who saved the Army of the Potomac the other night!"[14]

Not long after his return from raiding, Stoneman hobbled off to Washington to seek treatment for his piles. At once Hooker announced Pleasonton as his "temporary" replacement—though he had no intention of recalling Stoneman.[15] The promotion overjoyed Pleasonton, who had been on less than cordial terms with Stoneman dating from their attempt to nab Stuart following his sack of Chambersburg. In the aftermath of that bungled pursuit, Pleasonton had sought to place blame on Stoneman's shoulders, which the latter greatly resented. As an indirect result, Stoneman had demoted Pleasonton to brigade command. And by leaving him with the main army during the recent expedition Stoneman had intended to deny him participation in a glorious feat of arms.[16]

***

With officers such as Stoneman and Averell gone, the Cavalry Corps had improved its lot. Still, even as the men of the corps neared the close of their two-year probationary period, they were led by almost as many erratic, lackluster, and inept commanders as by soldiers of promise and performance. As the personal attributes of cavalry leaders meant so much in tactical terms, this seemed to bode ill for the command's performance in the crucial weeks of summer 1863.

The new man at the top embodied some of the best and many of the worst traits a soldier can possess. Like his predecessor, Pleasonton seemed to own a record of professional competence, embracing operations on the Peninsula and at Antietam, Fredericksburg, and Chancellorsville. Even his poor showing in pursuit of Stuart had been overshadowed by the ineptitude of McClellan, Stoneman, and Averell. Moreover, Pleasonton was active and energetic. He exuded self-confidence and a get-things-done attitude, suggesting that if given a free hand and a little time he would activate the full potential of his new command. Despite his short stature and slight build, he swaggered about as though he feared no one and conceded nothing to be impossible. He worked hard to instill these same traits in his troopers and to fix in their minds a picture of Alfred Pleasonton as someone they could follow, without qualm, on any occasion.

The Pleasonton image featured physical affectations such as dapper uniforms, stylish accoutrements, a carefully waxed mustache, a straw skimmer in place of the usual slouch hat, white kid gloves, and a cowhide riding-whip. To one of his officers, he was a "nice little dandy," while a more caustic critic felt that "his vanity is over-weening." Something of an epicure, Pleasonton treated his palate, whenever possible, to champagne, oysters, and other delicacies that his headquarters mess stocked even during active campaigning. In manner he was personable, witty, often charming (especially around the ladies, though destined for lifelong bachelorhood), and he made small talk without effort. A newspaper correspondent described him as "polished and affable, and thoroughly a man of the world."[17]

Perhaps his chief characteristic—exhibited with such force after Antietam and Chancellorsville—was a determination to advance his rank and standing by any expedient. In this he was aided by strong political and journalistic connections. Perhaps his most valuable contact was Republican Congressman John Franklin Farnsworth of Illinois, a friend and supporter of Lincoln and a former cavalry brigade leader under Pleasonton.[18]

Pleasonton's undisguised ambition, plus his reputation as a coldblooded martinet, antagonized many of his officers, who soon yearned for his predecessor's return. Even before Pleasonton's rise to power, a cavalry surgeon had written: "Poor little pusilanimous Pleasanton [sic] wants to . . . have Stoneman's place— & he is about as fit for it as any 2d Leutenant [sic] in the command." A captain in the 1st Massachusetts elaborated: "Stoneman we believe in. We believe in his judgment, his courage and determination. We know he is ready to shoulder responsibility, that he will take good care of us and won't get us into places from which he can't get us out. Pleasonton . . . is pure and simple a newspaper humbug. . . . He does nothing save with a view to a newspaper paragraph."[19]

Others felt he lacked integrity. Another Massachusetts officer wrote that "it is the universal opinion that Pleasonton's own reputation, and Pleasonton's late promotions are bolstered up by systematic lying." At least one cavalry officer believed that he stood for "tyranical [*sic*] & illegal exercise of military authority" and was a brutal disciplinarian. Late in 1862 a critic had warned army headquarters that "I sincerely believe that somebody will be wanted, before long to prefer charges against him."[20]

But none had done so, enabling Pleasonton to ascend the ladder of rank with speed disproportionate to his ability. Though a capable desk officer (for many years he had been an adjutant), he had never proved himself an outstanding leader in combat. Nor was he adept at reconnaissance; his dispatches to army headquarters were full of sound and fury, signifying nothing. His penchant for hearsay, speculation, and fancy would prompt postwar writers to dub him "the Knight of Romance." In battle he had become "notorious" for lack of bravery among those of his men "who have served under him and seen him under fire." Despite such failings, Hooker had promoted him over the multi-talented infantry division commander, Major General Winfield Scott Hancock, whom others had promoted for the Cavalry Corps post. Instead, Hancock took over the II Army Corps; higher command and greater responsibility would follow.[21]

To some extent, Pleasonton's flaws would be offset by the talents of two of his three ranking subordinates. West Point–educated and Regular Army–trained, Brigadier Generals John Buford, who led the 1st Cavalry Division,[22] and David McMurtrie Gregg, commander of the 3rd Division, were similar in personal and physical characteristics. Both were quiet, sober, self-reliant, and untouched by fear—soldiers highly respected by peers and subordinates. Relatively young (Buford was thirty-seven, Gregg thirty), each seemed much older, a legacy of professional maturity and facial disguise—a walrus mustache and leathery skin in Buford's case, and a patriarchial beard in Gregg's.

Buford was the more seasoned campaigner. He had established his reputation in the summer of 1862, when John Pope plucked him from staff duty and named him chief of cavalry of the Army of Virginia. During that season's campaigning, the Kentucky-born brigadier demonstrated talent at reconnaissance as often as Alfred Pleasonton revealed inadequacy. Time and again Buford's horsemen burst through the enemy's counterreconnaissance screen, providing headquarters with intelligence so timely and accurate that, had Pope not ignored much of it, Lee and Jackson could not have teamed to crush him at Second Bull Run.[23]

In the finale of the campaign in upper Virginia, Buford suffered a near-fatal wound that laid him low for a lengthy period. Even now it sapped his energy. He possessed a few military as well as physical weaknesses, including a tendency to move slowly when speed was necessary and a sometimes overprotective attitude toward his division. Yet his talents in training and leadership—especially in teaching his troopers the advantages of fighting afoot as often as in the saddle—far outdistanced his limitations. He was, as one colleague remarked, "straight-forward, honest, conscientious, full of good common sense, and always to be relied on in any emergency"—in short, "decidedly the best cavalry general" in the Army of the Potomac. Buford's men agreed. Wrote a member of the 8th Illinois: "He is kind, and always on hand when there is fighting to be done. . . . he don't put on so much style as most officers." His lack of ostentation was reflected in his choice of attire, usually an old hunting shirt "ornamented with holes" and ancient blue corduroy breeches "tucked into a pair of ordinary cowhide boots."[24]

Pennsylvania-born David Gregg had won notice as a regimental and brigade commander before reaching his present level as successor to George Bayard, mortally wounded at Fredericksburg. The same newspaper that had called Pleasonton urbane described Gregg in much the same way: "His heavy blue eye and regular features bear English characteristics. . . . Put him in peg-tops and a round hat, and he would typify the class of well-drawn thoroughbreds seen frequently in *The London Punch*." Not often did Gregg receive attention from journalists, for he disliked the breed and barred them from his command ("I do not propose," he once told an aide, "to have a picture reputation"). Like Buford, who also scorned to cultivate media connections, Gregg remained in the background of public consciousness while publicity hounds such as Pleasonton got the ink.[25]

Gregg possessed an unswerving calmness that amazed all around him. Once, when his headquarters in the saddle became the target of Rebel cannon, he trotted—not galloped—to safety, puffing unconcernedly on his meerschaum. When his aides pounded to the rear with unseemly dispatch, he called after them: "Be calm, gentlemen—no occasion for haste!" In the same quiet, deliberate tone, he attended to every matter of business, personal and military. One of his officers wrote that "I was more or less in awe of him . . . [but] one could not have been under a more considerate and finer commander."[26]

Pleasonton's third divisional leader never merited such praise. Another old-line professional, Colonel Alfred Duffié (pronounced DOOF-yea) had graduated from St. Cyr rather than West Point. The twenty-eight-year-old Frenchman was one of three foreign-born brigade and division leaders in the Corps—and the least talented of the trio.

It had not always appeared so. A veteran of mounted service in Algeria, Senegal, and the Crimea (during the period collecting four medals and eight wounds), Duffié had done a masterful job of training the 1st Rhode Island early in the war. Within weeks of his taking command, the once-chaotic regiment "breathed order, neatness and a perfect understanding of the last details of the service." Later the colonel had demonstrated skill in brigade command, especially at Kelly's Ford. Even so, the short, goateed, and well-tanned Duffié had been promoted beyond his ability (and rank) when in mid-May 1863 he received command of the 2nd Cavalry Division, two brigades strong. In quick time his men concluded "that Colonel Duffié, Commander, might be a good man, but he could not run a Division."[27]

Ironically, Duffié's impressive military background helped unfit him for service in America. He seemed a slave to European heavy-cavalry tactics, with their elaborate battlefield evolutions and inflexible rubrics of mounted warfare. Then, too, he adhered rigidly to Old World notions of deportment and decorum, which made him unpopular among many subordinates and superiors. One who disliked him was Pleasonton: Duffié's promotion had been Hooker's idea, not his. Pleasonton regarded foreign-born soldiers as inept mercenaries ("I conscientiously believe that Americans only should rule in this matter & settle this rebellion—& that in every instance foreigners have injured our cause"). Thus he hoped that Duffié would furnish grounds for his own relief.[28]

Of the seven brigades under Buford, Duffié, and Gregg, four or five were commanded by officers of tested merit. The other brigade leaders were inconsistent performers equally liable to cover themselves with glory and to embarrass themselves and their men. John Buford had raised the finest crop of subordinates: a pair of reliable West Pointers, one still in the Regulars, plus an unusually gifted civilian-soldier. His first brigade—one New York and one Illinois regiment, plus a half-dozen companies of Hoosiers—was headed by Alabama-born and Mississippi-reared Benjamin F. ("Grimes") Davis. An ex-dragoon who carried scars from Apache battles, the thirty-six-year-old colonel was known for rough manners and an even rougher approach to discipline. One volunteer considered him "a proud tyranical devil" as likely to be killed by his own soldiers as by his ex-countrymen. Old Army comrades regarded Davis as essentially kindhearted, especially in tutoring young subalterns; they admitted, however, that he was determined to keep enlisted men "on the jump." The army's provost marshal general declared him, simply, "our best Cavalry officer" and even his most critical troopers applauded his fighting spirit. Wrote a member of his 8th New York: "When Colonel Davis found the rebels he did not stop at anything, but went for them heavy. I believe he liked to fight the rebels as well as he liked to eat."[29]

The leader of Buford's second brigade, Colonel Thomas C. Devin, had come into the volunteers from civil life, where he had been a partner in a New York City paint, oil, and varnish firm. For years a militia officer, Devin acquired an early reputation as a superior cavalryman. When the War Department sent an old Regular to quiz the New Yorker on his acumen, the veteran came away amazed: "I can't teach Col. Devin anything about cavalry; he knows more about the tactics than I do!" By early 1862 Devin's 6th New York was "the best drilled Regiment in the service."

Though older than the average mounted leader, Devin could act as quickly and energetically as officers half his age. Still, he often emulated John Buford's careful bent, taking all steps and precautions necessary to secure success. So reliable a subordinate was the balding, ruddy-faced Irishman that he had won the sobriquets "Old War Horse" and "Buford's Hard-Hitter." During especially able service at Antietam and Chancellorsville he demonstrated that the command given him by Buford—one New York regiment, two battalions of a second, a regiment from Pennsylvania, and a squadron from West Virginia—

deserved a title all its own, as the hardest-fighting brigade in the Cavalry Corps.[30]

Thanks to its third component, the "Reserve Brigade," permanently assigned to it on 6 June, Buford's division enjoyed a source of elite talent. Formed by McClellan as a nucleus of professionalism, this brigade comprised the only Regular mounted units in the Army of the Potomac: the 1st, 2nd, 5th, and 6th United States Cavalry. Its lone field officer and current commander was Major Charles J. Whiting, an eight-year veteran with a West Point education, a background in civil engineering, and a tendency to derogate his civilian superiors. That his rank was not commensurate with his position indicated how badly the Regulars had been depleted since the oubreak of war. In point of fact, they were never the bulwark McClellan had envisioned. Weakened by lax recruiting during prewar years, they had been reduced further by Southern officers gone home, by sickness and battle casualties, and by members serving on detached duty. As of the spring of 1863, forty-eight commissioned officers were estranged from the brigade through staff duty or service with volunteer outfits.[31]

To compensate for the losses, the Regulars had been brigaded with the larger 6th Pennsylvania, perhaps the most distinctive volunteer unit in the Union cavalry. Organized by Richard Rush, grandson of Colonial America's foremost physician, a signer of the Declaration of Independence, it had been organized as a gentleman's regiment, seeking the sons of Philadelphia's social, athletic, and cultural elite. They had gone to war lugging nine-foot-long lances with eleven-inch blades—weaponry suggested by the Europhile McClellan. By mid-1863 "Rush's Lancers" had jettisoned the arm as inappropriate to service in Virginia, and Colonel Rush had been invalided out, bequeathing the regiment to Robert Morris, Jr., great-grandson and namesake of the "Financier of the Revolutionary War."[32]

Himself descended from Old American stock, Major Whiting had faith in the ability of his patricians in uniform. Their numbers and Whiting's experience, however, would go only so far in balancing out the brigade's general manpower shortage. Then, too, in a few months Whiting's expertise would be lost to the Reserve Brigade, the result of his publicly questioning the competency of Abraham Lincoln as commander in chief.[33]

Scrutiny of the 2nd Cavalry Division revealed that Colonel Duffié's six regiments had been divided between brigade leaders of contrasting temperament. One was passionate, excitable, impetuous; the other was low-key, unflappable, reliable. Either seemed better qualified than Duffié to lead the division.

The impetuous one was Colonel Luigi Palma di Cesnola, who led one Massachusetts and one Ohio regiment, plus Duffié's old 1st Rhode Island. Son of an Italian count who had fought for Napoleon, Cesnola had studied briefly for the priesthood before entering the Royal Military Academy of Turin. Since age seventeen, when he fought for Sardinia against Austria, Cesnola had put his military training—if not his religious education—to continuous use. Service in the Crimea in the late 1850s had given him a gleaming reputation, which in 1860 he carried to America. When the Civil War erupted, he was twenty-eight, happily married to the daughter of an American naval officer, and the director of a 700-pupil military school in New York City.

Welcoming an opportunity to return to arms, Cesnola raised, trained and assumed command of the 4th New York, an urban regiment stocked with French, German, Italian, Hungarian, and Spanish immigrants. With most of his men the colonel could converse fluently, and he barked drill instructions in an astonishing array of tongues. His erudition ranged beyond languages and military science: in postwar life he would gain renown as an archaeologist and a museum director.[34]

The leader of Duffié's second brigade was a practical man of business rather than a stalwart of learning. A former iron merchant from Centre County, Pennsylvania, John Irvin Gregg—older cousin of David McMurtrie Gregg— was as solid as the metal from which he had earned his living. Memorably tall, with a piratical beard (his men called him "Long John"), the thirty-six-year-old colonel had seen action in the Mexican War, rising from private to captain of volunteers. His soldierly qualities gained him a postwar berth in the Regulars, in which he spent ten years prior to entering commercial life. Shortly before the South seceded, he rejoined the service, and by the spring of 1861 he was a company commander in the 6th U.S. Cavalry as well as colonel of a volunteer infantry regiment. Late in 1862 he took command of the 16th Pennsylvania Cavalry and led it with marked success if little fanfare. Now leading two other Pennsylvania regiments, as well as the 16th, Gregg appeared destined to win the rank and recognition already bestowed on his cousin.[35]

David Gregg himself was saddled with a pair of ranking subordinates of uneven talents. His first brigade, composed of two regiments from New York, one from Maine, and a company of District of Columbia volunteers, was in charge of an officer whose ambition, cunning, and gall matched Alfred Pleasonton's. Although the physical antithesis of the military and political hero— meager of stature, shrill of voice, and looking like a weasel in sideburns— Colonel Judson Kilpatrick had devoted himself to attaining great goals. These included a major generalship, the governorship of his native state, New Jersey, and the presidency. Though sometimes erratic and unstable, and so insensitive toward his men and their mounts that he had won the nickname "Kill-cavalry," the twenty-seven-year-old West Pointer had recently ascended to brigade command, no mean feat for a soldier trained as an artilleryman and who had entered the conflict as an infantry officer. Already his record in cavalry service included noteworthy participation in the Second Bull Run campaign and in Stoneman's raid. Then, too, his unctuousness and glad-handing had placed him in the good graces of his corps leader, despite Pleasonton's occasional suspicion that Kilpatrick was after his job. All of which hinted that the first of Kill-cavalry's aims was not unreachable.[36]

Yet, skeletons rattled in his closet. For some weeks in 1862 he had languished in prison under suspicion of having confiscated Virginia livestock and government provisions and selling them for personal gain. Later he had anticipated Charles Whiting by defaming government officials during a drunken spree in Washington, again landing in jail. He had even been implicated in a scheme to extort bribes from brokers wishing to sell horses to his brigade.[37]

While such conduct would have ruined most soldiers, Kilpatrick had survived. Nor had his career been sidetracked by flaws of character. In addition to lacking honesty and stability, he was a devotee of prostitutes and camp followers, though supposedly happily married (and an expectant father). Whenever possible, he slaked a thirst for hard liquor, all the while professing temperance. He roamed the realm of fiction when recounting his feats in battle and the number of casualties he had inflicted upon the enemy. One officer remarked disgustedly that Kilpatrick's campaign reports were "great in 'the most glorious charges ever made,' 'sabering right and left,' and such stuff." Another observer called him a "frothy braggart, without brains," while a third saw him as an "injudicious boy, much given to blowing and who will surely come to grief." But others had predicted as much back in 1861 and two years later Kilpatrick's star was still ascending.[38]

Akin to Kilpatrick in impetuosity, though a man of grace and integrity, was the British knight who commanded Gregg's second brigade. Colonel Sir Percy Wyndham, twenty-nine-year-old leader of a New Jersey, a Pennsylvania, and a Maryland regiment, was the son of an officer in Her Majesty's 5th Light Cavalry and his baroness wife. From the age of fifteen a warrior in the English, French, Austrian, and Sardinian armies, Sir Percy sported a row of decorations almost as long as his incredible mustache. He kept his flowing side whiskers combed and waxed and, like Stuart and Pleasonton, he favored well-cut uniforms, capes, jackboots, and gauntlets.[39] One subordinate, amused by his foppishness, compared him to a bouquet of flowers: "You poor little lilies, you! You haven't the first chance with the glorious magnificence of this beauty. He's only been in Camp for two hours, and he now appears in his third suit of clothes!" But Sir Percy was also an expert pugilist and swordsman, traits that caused offending colleagues to fear for their lives; his tinder-dry temper more than once prompted him to challenge other officers to duels.[40]

In addition to most of his brigade and division leaders, Alfred Pleasonton could rely on the majority of those officers who commanded the two dozen regiments that made up the Cavalry Corps, Army of the Potomac. Foremost among these were Colonels George H. Chapman, of the 3rd Indiana; Calvin S. Douty, 1st Maine; Josiah H. Kellogg, 17th Pennsylvania; John B. McIntosh, 3rd Pennsylvania; and William Sackett, 9th New York; as well as Lieutenant Colonels Virgil Brodrick, 1st New Jersey; Henry E. Davies, 2nd New York; William E. Doster, 4th Pennsylvania; William L. Markell, 8th New York; and Willam Stedman, 6th Ohio. Of the lot, Chapman, Davies, and McIntosh were destined to lead brigades or divisions later in the conflict, as were several associates who by June 1863 had yet to attain regimental command.

The Cavalry Corps contained four organic batteries of horse artillery, three being Regular units. Because they were parceled out to Pleasonton's divisions as circumstances dictated, they had no overall commander, although loose authority was exercised by the senior battery officer, James M. Robertson, a military version of Santa Claus, with his white hair, florid face, and pipe-parted beard. A soldier since 1838, Robertson had received his captain's bars only in May 1861; from long service as an enlisted man he knew the horse artillery business from roof to cellar.

By the first week in June 1863, Pleasonton had disposed of the horse batteries thus: Robertson's combined Battery B/L, 2nd U.S. Artillery, was attached to Buford's division, as was Lieutenant Samuel S. Elder's Battery E, 4th U.S. (the latter specifically assigned to the Reserve Brigade); Lieutenant Alexander C. M. Pennington's M, 2nd U.S., served with Duffié; and the volunteer unit, the 6th New York Independent Battery under Captain Joseph W. Martin, was a part of David Gregg's division.[41]

A second horse artillery command constituted a four-battery brigade within the army's Artillery Reserve. Available to any mounted division when battle loomed, the brigade consisted of Batteries E/G and K of the 1st Artillery, commanded respectively by Captains Alanson M. Randol and William M. Graham; plus the 2nd Artillery's Battery A and Battery C of the 3rd, under Captains John C. Tidball and William D. Fuller. As senior officer, the thirty-eight-year-old Tidball—tall and lean, with a hawkish face and an austere demeanor—exercised command over the brigade.[42]

Before the coming campaign was half over, Robertson and Tidball would each be assigned to lead a brigade of horse artillery made part of the Cavalry Corps. Additions to and subtractions from the original complement would give Robertson five batteries, Tidball four. All but one of these units consisted of six cannon mounted on lightweight carriages (Randol's battery, recently converted from light to horse artillery, temporarily had four guns). Each battery was composed exclusively of 3-inch ordnance rifles, highly maneuverable cannon with an extreme range of 4,000 yards.

The coming reorganization would recognize Robertson's and Tidball's expertise as well as seniority: by all accounts, they were the ablest horse artillerists in the ranks. This was high distinction indeed, for the artillery of the Cavalry Corps had long enjoyed an advantage over its adversary not only in the quantity of its ordnance and equipage but also in the quality of its personnel. The most talented of the battery leaders were Captains Randol and Martin and Lieutenants Elder and Pennington. This elite group also embraced a pair of lieutenants who would rise to battery command during the campaign: John H. Calef, Tidball's replacement as head of the most famous horse artillery unit in the army; and Edward Heaton, of Robertson's combined battery. Many of these officers would rise to higher station before the war closed; Randol and Pennington were destined to attain cavalry brigade command.[43]

To facilitate his dealings with these cavalry and artillery subordinates, Alfred Pleasonton depended upon a band of young staff officers. With some he had established an almost paternal relationship—especially with George Armstrong Custer, a twenty-three-year-old West Pointer with Ohio and Michigan roots who held a lieutenancy in the 5th United States. The headstrong, opportunistic Custer, whose penchant for derring-do would advance him more quickly than anyone suspected, boasted that no "father could love his son more than Genl. Pleasanton [sic] loves me." He aped the ways of his superior, strutting about in uniforms flooded with gilt lace and silver piping and cultivating a crop of yellow hair which he curled around candles while he slept. One who met him for the first time wrote that he "is one of the funniest-looking beings you ever saw . . . like a circus rider gone mad!" A West Point comrade, observing him in mid-1863, described Custer as "careless, reckless," but also as "a gallant soldier, a whole-souled generous friend, and a mighty good fellow."[44]

Two other captains in their early twenties occupied favored positions at corps headquarters. Elon J. Farnsworth, favorite nephew of Pleasonton's Congressional friend, owed his post as much to his uncle's connections as to his own abilities. Nevertheless, the dark-complected and mustachioed youth was regarded highly by the men of his regiment, the 8th Illinois, among whom his "shrewdness and wit were proverbial." Plagued by a troubled past (including expulsion from the University of Michigan in 1858 following a prank during which another student was killed), he had started over as a civilian forager in the prewar army and, when war came, as a subaltern who accompanied his regiment in forty-one battles and skirmishes. Devoted to the Union, young Farnsworth won notoriety in 1862 during occupation duty in Alexandria, Virginia, when he hauled from his pulpit an Episcopal rector who had omitted from services the prayer customarily offered for the welfare of the president and Congress. Such impulsive behavior had not prevented him from becoming one of Pleasonton's most trusted aides.[45]

The other young captain on the corps staff, Wesley Merritt (West Point 1860 and thereafter the 2nd U.S. Cavalry), was one of the toughest disciplinarians in the cavalry. Though hardly fitting the physical image—he had a beardless, boyish face—Merritt was an old Regular in deportment and philosophy, if not in years.[46] Some citizen-soldiers considered him an unfeeling martinet (one termed his disposition "miserable"), while others, more perceptive, wrote of his "genial, though rather . . . reticent demeanor." One volunteer officer praised his "modesty which fitted him like a garment, charming manners, the demeanor of a gentleman, [and] cool but fearless bearing in action." Even more significantly, Merritt was regarded highly by the older, more experienced officers in the army.[47]

A third young captain with cavalry contacts would be attached to Pleasonton's staff during portions of the coming campaign—on loan from Hooker's military family. Like Elon Farnsworth, twenty-one-year-old Ulric Dahlgren enjoyed fortunate family connections; he was the son of Admiral John A. Dahlgren, inventor of naval ordnance and future commander of the South Atlantic Blockading Squadron. And like George Custer, the slim, blonde, pale-eyed Dahlgren craved adventure and scorned high risks. Already he had conducted several perilous intelligence-gathering missions, sometimes leading detachments, sometimes scouting alone through hostile territory. On one occasion he had perched for hours in a treetop, counting Rebel troops passing beneath. Late in May 1863 he had unsuccessfully sought Hooker's permission to lead a daylight raid into Richmond, to destroy military and industrial facilities. Despite the magnitude of the project and its prospective obstacles, the captain had planned to conduct it with a single regiment of Regular cavalry. Hooker's veto failed to kill Dahlgren's interest in the undertaking; in 1864 he would convince another superior to allow him to accompany Judson Kilpatrick on a raid against the enemy capital. The mission would fail, costing Kill-cavalry his command and Dahlgren his life.[48]

***

By this midpoint of the conflict, the horsemen of Hooker's army were striving to reconcile two schools of mounted tactics. In prewar years, the American cavalry had developed a tradition of fighting afoot and of relying on firearms rather than edged weapons. This was brought about by the forest-covered terrain east of the Mississippi and the demands of Indian fighting on the western frontier. During the Revolutionary War, the guerrilla tactics employed in the swamp- and canebrake-infested South by Francis Marion, Casimir Pulaski, and "Light-Horse Harry" Lee had reinforced the concept that a soldier used a horse mainly as transportation, not as a platform for weaponry.[49]

As the nation aged and acquired additional elements of civilization, European influences swept military as well as social, political, and economic circles. Shock tactics popularized in western Europe in the early nineteenth century made inroads into domestic military thinking. The War of 1812 and the Mexican War of 1846–48 featured more than a few mounted attacks, some against infantry, artillery, and field works. In later years saber charges were even employed against hostile Indians. When in 1853 mounted tactics were added to the West Point curriculum, they were based heavily on the European model. At the same time, the army patterned its cavalry training on a body of tactics of French origin, first published in America in 1841. Attempts over the next two decades by Philip St. George Cooke and other theorists to adapt this system to American needs failed to keep the Union armies of 1861–63 from helping perpetuate the foreign influence.[50] Early in the war, this influence was strengthened by refugees from German, French, British, and Italian armies who instructed the American volunteers in the same tactics they had fought by on the Continent. From the first, saber practice and mounted training took preference over target shooting and dismounted drill.[51] European-tutored commanders and like thinkers such as McClellan encouraged such training. It is not surprising that lances were furnished to the 6th Pennsylvania in 1861.

Almost two years of warfare were required to demonstrate the limitations of such training. By mid-1863, enough charges in the classic style had met defeat that even the most zealous traditionalist had grown discouraged. As one New York veteran trooper admitted: "Our regiment was one of the best drilled and most efficient bodies of mounted men in the service; but for all that . . . set us across country at any such gait as is understood by a cavalry charge, and out of our ten troops there would not have been so much as a corporal's guard left at the end of six hundred yards." Such a charge was certain to be overcome by a counter-charge, whereupon even greater chaos resulted. Observed a New Jersey trooper of such an event: "Pressing upon one another, strained to the utmost of their speed, the horses catch an infection of fear which rouses them to frenzy. The men, losing their places in the ranks, and all power of formation or hope of combined resistance, rush madly for some point of safety upon which it may be possible to rally. Each check in front makes the mass behind more dense and desperate, until horses and men are overthrown and ridden over, trampled on by others as helpless as themselves to rescue or to spare. . . ."[52]

Ironically, one of the most disastrous mounted charges was the work of the officer who had labored to modify European tactics. At Gaines's Mill, 27 June, 1862, General Cooke, then commanding the brigade of Regular cavalry under McClellan, spied hordes of Confederate infantry closing in on a brace of Union cannon. Placed in an exposed position to buy time for a partial withdrawal, the artillery appeared doomed to mass capture. Without authorization, Cooke ordered 600 members of the 1st and 5th United States and the 6th Pennsylvania, under then-Captain Charles Whiting, to charge with the saber against the Rebels. The horsemen obeyed with dash and determination but were broken to bits at first contact—not so much by overwhelming opposition as by the confining terrain and the uncontrollable power of their charge. Within minutes, fifty-eight troopers had been shot from their saddles and survivors were scrambling to the rear. Afterward Cooke's superiors blasted his tactics, claiming that the cavalry's advance and retreat had blocked and demoralized the artillery, and had caused the loss of many of the guns Cooke had hoped to save. The latter was relieved and held no field command through the remainder of the war, and cavalry commanders long remembered the lesson he had taught them at such personal expense.[53]

By spring 1863, following dismounted service in the campaigns of Second Bull Run, Antietam, and Fredericksburg, the Federal horse soldiers in the East had rediscovered their roots as dragoons. Most now fastened their scabbards to the side of their saddles, so that sabers would not impede their progress afoot. They placed more reliance than ever on their firearms and adhered to the dictum that "one carbine in the hands of a dismounted man under cover is certainly worth half a dozen in the hands of men on horseback." They retired their lances and fancy hussar unifirms, put aside their pretentions to the cavalier tradition, and looked beyond the limits of early-war tactics. "Cavalry, as such," they believed, "only capture and turn over [objectives] to infantry. Well-drilled dragoons will both capture and hold."[54]

This return to first principles was the handiwork of old dragoons elevated to positions in which they could exert widespread influence—men such as Pleasonton, David Gregg, and Buford (Buford being known as "perhaps more than any other a typical . . . Dragoon"). Such pragmatic officers rejected the value of weight in motion, stressing instead staying power, tenacity, and endurance. Even so, their tactics were not inflexible. They advocated the employment of mounted tactics whenever geographical, strategic, psychological, and other considerations favored them. They realized that the effort to build an eclectic school of tactics was a continuing process. But they sensed that when final results were in, the Cavalry Corps of the Army of the Potomac would hold a substantial advantage over those enemy troopers who had been touted as their superiors since the genesis of war.

Not only the generals felt that a new era was coming. Wrote Captain Charles F. Adams, Jr., 1st Massachusetts Cavalry, in mid-June 1863: "As for the cavalry, its future is just opening and great names will be won in [it] . . . from this day forward."[55]

***

In advance of their flowering as combat troops, Joe Hooker's horsemen enjoyed great advantages (in both quality and quantity) of ordnance, equipment, ammunition, and animals. The industrial abundance of the North resulted in troopers taking the field in 1861 so overburdened with equipment and weapons that their horses could barely carry them. The same soldiers who learned to discard old-world notions of fighting gradually disposed of all but essential baggage, thus facilitating individual and collective mobility. By this third spring of the war, the average trooper retained a saber and scabbard, a carbine fastened to a shoulder-sling, one or two revolvers with removable, preloaded cylinders, a rawhide "McClellan" saddle and underpad (often a sleeping blanket did double duty as a saddle cushion), with forage, rations, and ammunition carried in saddlebags, a haversack, and a cartridge box, respectively. Ideally, this paraphernalia weighed less than sixty pounds.[56]

By this point in the conflict, it was especially important not to overtax one's animal. Although horseflesh was abundant in the North, transportation facilities were limited. Moreover, the ravages of the previous winter, exacerbated by the arduous campaigning under Burnside and Hooker, had left the Army of the Potomac's horses in short supply and fragile health. Since the outset of the war the government had furnished over 284,000 cavalry mounts for the Union armies, an average of almost five horses per trooper. Late in May, however, Alfred Pleasonton had reported his corps so short of healthy animals that it "is not fitted to take the field" for extended service. Owing to the effects of rain, snow, mud, "hoof-rot," "scratches" and "grease-heel," Duffié's and Gregg's divisions could mount only half their combined force of 6,000, while Buford's command required more than 2,000 remounts. Thus, 40 percent of the 12,000 troopers carried on the rolls of the corps were on inactive duty or had been shipped to depots in the rear to await remounts from Washington. During the last days of May and the first weeks of June, most of these men—including the Reserve Brigade in its entirety—would be remounted. Nevertheless, for months the effectives on hand would not match the corps's paper strength.[57]

If he temporarily lacked a horse, the average trooper did not want for weaponry.   As a legacy of his early education, he carried a light saber with a slightly curved blade which was rarely kept as sharp as a European drillmaster would prefer. Some Continental-minded soldiers might lug a Prussian saber with a long straight blade, but the typical cavalryman preferred the less cumbersome English model or its model-1860 American counterpart. The trooper also wielded a pair of American-made percussion revolvers, normally the Colt six-shooter in either the .44 Army or the .36 Navy version, or the .44 Remington. Less conventional comrades carried Starr, Whitney, or Rogers & Spencer pistols.[58]

As for carbines, Federal troopers were issued a variety of brands and models, most being single-shot breechloaders with barrels ranging from thirty-six to forty inches long and with firepower accurate at distances of 150 to 200 yards. By 1863 the .52 Sharps (Model-1859) was generally regarded as the most reliable arm and saw the most extensive use. Next in preference and prevalence was the .54 Burnside, designed in the mid-1850s by Ambrose Burnside, then a Rhode Island arms manufacturer. Other carbines of note included the Ballard, Gallager, Merrill, and Starr, all .54; and the .52 Smith & Joslyn. Still others, of various caliber, saw more limited service: the Ball, Cosmopolitan, Gibbs, Greene, Gwyn & Campbell, Howard, Jenks, Lindner, Maynard, North-Hall, Palmer, Perry, Sharps & Hankins, Smith, Terry, Warner, and Wesson.[59]

A few squadrons of troopers employed repeating rifles rather than single-shot carbines, enduring extra length and weight and decreased range in order to gain greater muzzle velocity. Favorites of this class were the .56 five-shot Colt's Revolving Rifle and the .56 Spencer, which discharged a tube of seven cartridges as quickly as its owner could pull trigger and eject spent shells. The Spencer was the more sought after, but because the infantry had cornered the market on this arm only a handful of mounted units were supplied with it. All told, fewer than six hundred members of the Cavalry Corps possessed a Spencer rifle; they were scattered through the 8th and 12th Illinois, 3rd Indiana, 8th New York, and 1st West Virginia regiments. Not till midsummer would the first carbines roll off the assembly line at the Spencer Repeating Rifle Company, New Haven, Connecticut. A few months later they would become available in quantity to the cavalry, in whose hands they would win a reputation as the most effective small arm of the war.[60]

***

On 27 May 1863 General Hooker received a report from his intelligence chief, Colonel George H. Sharpe, that inaugurated the service of the cavalry under Pleasonton. Sharpe's scouts had learned that three brigades of Stuart's horsemen, under Hampton and the Lees, had moved from Fredericksburg to Culpeper, there to recruit strength and prepare for an expedition of unknown destination. Additionally, said Sharpe's people, Robert E. Lee had recalled detached infantry commands and had placed his entire army under marching orders. A movement against or around the Union right flank seemed probable.

This intelligence, added to reports recently received from other sources, should have alerted Fighting Joe that his opponents were stirring from their post-Chancellorsville inactivity. Hooker, however, did not take the hint. He was not alone. Neither Secretary of War Stanton nor Major General Henry W. Halleck, the General-in-Chief in Washington, believed that the Army of Northern Virginia was preparing to move in force. Hooker and the War Department remained skeptical even after Major General Robert H. Milroy, commanding the Shenandoah Valley outpost of Winchester, upheld Sharpe's pronouncement of a massive effort against Hooker's right.[61]

Though in command of the cavalry for less than a week, Alfred Pleasonton held the confidence of Stanton and Halleck, whom he had flattered by sending them intelligence in advance of informing Hooker. Most of Pleasonton's information seemed to confirm the War Department's preconceived opinion that a movement by Stuart alone (perhaps supported by a small force of infantry) was in the offing. This view appeared verified by a report sent in on 28 May by David Gregg, whose division patrolled the Orange & Alexandria Railroad near Bealton Station, fifteen miles northeast of Culpeper Court House. Gregg's dispatch conveyed subordinates' findings of Rebel horsemen above the Rappahannock in the direction of Sulphur Springs, astride the 3rd Cavalry Division's line of communications. Pleasonton interpreted this as evidence that Stuart was scouting in advance of a move north on an independent expedition—this bound for Washington or an industrial center such as Pittsburgh. On 1 June Pleasonton's case for a raid was shaken when a more thorough reconnaissance of the Sulphur Springs area by John Buford located no enemy trooper north of the river. Nevertheless, the Knight of Romance continued to predict a mounted raid.[62]

At first comforted by his cavalry chief's opinion, Hooker soon grew uneasy, and with good reason. On 29 May, Major General Julius Stahel, a Hungarian immigrant commanding the 3,600-man cavalry division of Major General Samuel P. Heintzelman's Department of Washington, provided new support for the Sharpe-Milroy theory. Though a lackluster field leader, the thirty-seven-year-old Stahel occasionally relayed credible intelligence about enemy movements outside his departmental confines. His new communiqué, conveying information from a spy inside Rebel lines, detailed a recent high-level conference in Richmond. At this council a "forward movement" by Lee's army had been decided upon, to take advantage of a manpower loss recently suffered by Hooker when several two-year regiments had left his army, their enlistments ended. And the next day, General Milroy again warned Washington (in a dispatch relayed to Hooker) that Lee was about to move north in strength. One of Milroy's scouts had penetrated enemy lines, returning with word that Lee's recently bolstered command would soon cross the Rappahannock en route to Washington. According to Milroy's informant, "Lee will risk all in this fight."[63]

During the first days in June, Hooker learned from his own signal officers, some carried aloft by observation balloons, about the disappearance of a few Rebel camps opposite Falmouth. Uncertain whether this heralded an offensive or merely indicated a shift of positions, the army leader ordered part of his VI Corps to probe the enemy left—where the missing units might have moved—and to take prisoners from identifiable units. But the demonstration of 5–6 June proved inconclusive: all fifty Rebels captured were from A. P. Hill's corps, known to have occupied the vicinity for some time. Further attempts to ascertain Lee's movements were no more successful. This gave Hooker no cause to discredit Pleasonton's theory that, in the words of the *New York Times*, Stuart's division, "the largest body of cavalry that the enemy has ever got together," was about to push into Maryland and Pennsylvania "in a very few days." The *Times* (whose reporters often parroted Pleasonton's opinions) advised that "the only way to effectually interfere with this dashing arrangement is to pitch into him [Stuart] where he is. . . ."[64]

On this point Hooker and Pleasonton concurred, although they attributed conflicting objectives to such strategy. Later Hooker claimed that he ordered Pleasonton, with as many men as he could mount, to smash Stuart, thereby preventing him from carrying out his expedition. Pleasonton would contend that Hooker directed him to engage the Rebel cavalry in an effort to determine its size, position, and intentions.

In either case, Pleasonton on 7 June was commanded to depart his headquarters at Warrenton Junction and place his corps below Bealton, opposite Beverly and Kelly's Fords on the Rappahannock. His former posts along the railroad would be taken up by Stahel's division, which Hooker had appropriated while Stahel marched through O & A territory early in June en route to the Shenandoah Valley for a scout.[65]

As a veteran dragoon, Pleasonton understood the weakness of an offensive devoid of infantry support. To ease his concern, he was granted command of two brigades from the V Corps, which had been helping the cavalry patrol the river. Hooker then advised Pleasonton to launch a two-pronged movement, Buford's division to cross the river at Beverly Ford and Duffié's division (temporarily under Gregg), plus the latter's command, to ford at Kelly's. Buford would enjoy the close cooperation of Brigadier General Adelbert Ames's 1,300 infantrymen plus an extra battery of horse artillery, while 1,500 infantry under Brigadier General David A. Russell would accompany Duffié and Gregg. The aggregate strike force would number 11,000 officers and troopers and twelve cannon.[66]

Unknown to Pleasonton, who supposed he possessed enough men and arms to land a mighty blow, his troops only slightly outnumbered Stuart's 9,500 horsemen, who also enjoyed an advantage in artillery strength. Furthermore, the Union cavalry leader was ignorant of the precise location of his enemy. Having learned of Stuart's recent reviews near Culpeper Court House, he assumed that the Rebels lingered there, far from infantry support. Predicated upon such ignorance, his plan of attack called for his columns to close upon their foe in pincers fashion, meeting at Brandy Station. From that depot, four miles southwest of Beverly Ford and almost eight miles northwest of Kelly's, the Yankees would proceed to the courthouse village. Yet only Buford and Gregg would join forces as soon as across the river; Duffié's small division would penetrate westward and southward to Stevensburg, clearing the left flank of potential obstacles, before joining its comrades.

Pleasonton's plan was now inoperable: given Stuart's bivouac positions near Brandy Station, the Federals would find themselves trying to concentrate in the midst of the enemy. Hooker's suggestion that Pleasonton combine two lines of operations without first reconnoitering the area to be occupied constituted a major blunder.[67]

Blissfully unaware of the fact, Pleasonton's people eagerly marched toward the Rappahannock, arriving about half a mile from the fords by 11:00 P.M. on the eighth. They unsaddled but did not unbridle, and they sought repose without campfires to tame the chill of morning. Cavalrymen fell asleep with reins looped over their arms, while foot soldiers and horse artillerymen slept with equipment well secured and battery trace-chains muffled.

A certain number of soldiers could not sleep. Aware that the first great trial of the reborn cavalry was at hand, they waited impatiently for the dawn. The majority, however, seemed confident that, given their four months' experience as members of a full-fledged corps, they would acquit themselves well in the morning. As a member of the 8th New York recalled, the psychological wounds received at Chancellorsville had scarred over, "and the shadow of the fearful loss of life suffered on that field was fading. . . . Our own troops were alert and determined." A New England trooper agreed: he and his comrades intended "to have a good square fight with the famous Gen Stuart," going after him "for all we were worth."[68]

Before 2:00 A.M. on 9 June, cavalry, infantry, and artillery were prodded out of their bedrolls. Within an hour, breakfast eaten, both columns were in motion, Buford moving off for Beverly Ford, Duffié seeking the path to the downstream ford. At this point there was error and confusion. A local guide whom Duffié employed led his command onto the wrong road, with the result that the Frenchman, after much delay, had to countermarch. Unable to move until he did so, Gregg's men looked on in disgust, angered not only by the warped timetable but because they had been awakened so early to no purpose.[69]

When Duffié found the right path, Gregg's division at last lurched forward. One of the last men to climb into the saddle was the leader of the column's rear brigade, Judson Kilpatrick. Provoked by the cold air and the long delay, the professed teetotaler pulled a flask of "whiskey punch" from a saddlebag and, after a few pulls, passed it among his officers. Even those of the 1st Maine, a regiment known as "the Puritans" for the cold-water pledge it had taken en masse, did not refuse his offer. In fact, when Kilpatrick suggested a toast in honor of the day's significance, one Puritan responded: "Here's hoping we will do as well at Brandy Station . . . as we are doing at whisky station." Kilpatrick grinned: "Good, blamed good!"[70]

Minutes later, the general and his men heard gunfire at Beverly Ford. The Cavalry Corps's baptism of fire had begun.

[3]

Brandy Station

LUTHER Hopkins, a sixteen-year-old fresh from the farm, had just been relieved from picket duty at Beverly Ford and was trotting southward when the shooting began. Turning in the saddle, he saw bluecoats galloping out of the pines that separated his detachment of the 6th Virginia from their relief at the riverbank. Even a pea-green recruit knew what to do now: in an instant, Luther was pounding toward St. James Church, crouching low as blasts of gunfire sounded in the near distance.

"I was riding with the captain in the rear," he recalled years later. "We were not aware that the Yankees were so close to us, and the captain was calling to the men to check their speed. I looked behind, called to the captain and told him they were right on us, and just as I spoke two bullets went hissing by my head. The captain yelled to his men to move forward, and bending low on the necks of our horses, we gave them the spur." Only by desperate riding did they make it to Grumble Jones's bivouac near St. James Church.[1]

Even before reaching the camp, Hopkins and his squad were crowded off the road by elements of Jones's "grand guard," the 7th Virginia under Lieutenant Colonel Thomas Marshall. Marshall's men had responded so promptly because they had awakened to reveille shortly before the ruckus at Beverly Ford had begun. Even so, many troopers were shirtless and without boots or hats. Similarly disheveled were the 150 men of Hopkins's regiment, hastily assembled by Major C. E. Flournoy, who passed to the front of Marshall's men on the way to the ford. Behind this motley command came Grumble Jones himself, screeching curses as he too fought his way to the head of the column.[2]

To the rear, confusion swept through Jones's bivouac and that of Major Beckham's horse artillery. Although most cavalrymen were now awake—fumbling into essential attire, strapping on cartridge boxes, slinging rifles and muskets over their shoulders—Beckham's men were experiencing the rudest of awakenings. One cannoneer recalled that "just as we were rounding up the last sweet snooze for the night, bullets fresh from Yankee sharpshooters came from the depth of the woods and zipped across our blanket beds." Then "such a getting up of horse artillerymen I never saw before."[3]

By the time the artillerists were in motion, the bulk of Jones's troopers had ridden off and the increased volume of rifle fire to the north and east indicated they had struck the enemy. Beckham realized that if the Federals beat down the opposition, they would come swarming over the artillery park, where dozens of guns lay ripe for the taking. Hoping time had not run out, the major set his men to fetching limbers, hitching up teams, and trundling cannon out of harm's reach.

***

John Buford had taken pains to preserve the element of surprise, crucial to such an operation as his. Shortly before 4:30 A.M., a couple of squadrons of New Yorkers from Devin's brigade had forded the river, capturing several pickets, some ensconced in rifle pits protected by sharpened-log abatis.[4] A handful of Virginians scrambled through the trees before they could be gobbled up, but their escape did not diminish the attackers' advantage. At about five o'clock, Buford's vanguard descended the east bank and entered the stream, "the plunging horses throwing the spray high in the air."[5] Their movements shrouded by morning fog and muted by the roar of water at a dam just above Beverly Ford,[6] the troopers cut through the river, water lapping at their saddle-skirts. In the van of the column rode the 8th New York, Grimes Davis at its head, an old poncho thrown over his tunic. Close behind came the 8th Illinois, followed by the two battalions of the 3rd Indiana, then by the battery under James Robertson, Devin's and Whiting's brigades, and Elder's battery, with Ames's infantry bring up the rear.

Even before they reached shore, the lead riders could hear Rebel bugles and shouts of alarm. Anticipating opposition, Colonel Davis passed the word along the ranks: "Stand ready, men, and begin firing as soon as you see anything!"[7] Then the fog dissipated and solid earth loomed up. The Federals discerned enemy troops in the near distance, swinging aboard their animals and scattering into the shoreline woods. Rifle shots spattered from out of the trees; some Rebels had lingered in an effort to permit comrades to escape.

His sword drawn, Davis ordered his brigade forward at the gallop. His advance echelon ran down the nearest, slowest Confederates, trampling them under or downing them with pistol shots and saber thrusts. Some of the New Yorkers plunged into the pines in pursuit of fugitives as a firefight broke out all along the river. An enthusiastic Federal recalled that resistance multiplied and "the fight grew beautifully larger & larger." One of Davis's officers spied a runaway horse "dragging the body of his rider by the foot hung in the stirrup. This seemed to promise a hot reception for the troop following. . . ."[8]

Undaunted, the colonel cantered into the woods. On the other side he and his men reached a cleared plateau, several hundred yards long, on the far side of which began another neck of trees that ran almost to St. James Church. Ahead of them the 6th Virginia pickets retreated across the clearing, some toppling from their mounts in response to gunfire. Then the Federals spied a more tempting target: at the far edge of the open ground were several cannon, unlimbered, their half-dressed crews laboring frantically to haul them to the rear. Envisioning an unprecedented coup—none of Stuart's guns had fallen to the enemy—Davis's men charged Hart's South Carolina battery, which occupied the most exposed position.[9]

They almost reached their objective. They were within grasp of it when met by Rebel cavalry bursting out of the trees—the 150 members of Major Flournoy's regiment on the right of the ford road, Marshall's troopers to the left of it and farther to the rear. Flournoy's men spurred forward, and, as ever, countercharge broke charge. Struck head on with great force, the bluecoats reeled backward, many falling with saber and small arms wounds.[10]

One Yankee refused to fall back. Sitting his horse in quiet defiance of the Rebel advance, Grimes Davis challenged all comers to combat. From beneath the poncho his Colt revolver blasted away, while he twirled his saber menacingly with the other hand. His pistol emptied, he devoted full attention to the sword, swiping at any Virginian who ventured near.

Lieutenant R. O. Allen of Flournoy's regiment was not intimidated. Brandishing a pistol, he closed in on Davis, hugged his horse's neck to evade a saber slash, then bobbed up and fired three times at point-blank range. The third shot struck his opponent in the forehead, killing him instantly and flinging his body to the ground. To avenge his fall, the adjutant of Davis's 8th New York charged up, singled out a Rebel sergeant whom he took for the colonel's assailant, and with a sword blow laid open his skull "midway between eyes and chin."[11]

For a time leaderless, the 8th New York seeped into the woods, where it mixed with the advance guard of the next unit in Davis's column, the 8th Illinois. Stymied by the New Yorkers' retreat, the Illinoisians found it impossible to reach the open ground until they sorted themselves out. As they regrouped, many dismounted, drew carbines, and peppered away at the 6th Virginia from behind trees, while Robertson's Regular artillery unlimbered in a narrow clearing to apply muscle to the stalled offensive.

Gradually the energy faded from Flournoy's counterthrust. Strung out by its charge, having lost thirty casualties to sharpshooters, the lead regiment of the Laurel Brigade fell back to the edge of the plateau, where it joined a skirmish line formed by a part of the 7th Virginia. Lieutenant Colonel Marshall, with the balance of his outfit, then spurred toward the 8th New York's supports, led by Grimes Davis's successor, Major William S. McClure of the 3rd Indiana. (Major Alpheus S. Clark of the 8th Illinois had taken command upon Davis's death but had fallen almost immediately with a mortal wound. Originally in temporary command of the single battalion of his own regiment, plus a squadron of the 3rd West Virginia and a battalion of the 9th New York, McClure assumed the higher position because three other brigade officers who ranked him—Colonel Chapman of his own regiment and Lieutenant Colonels Markell of the

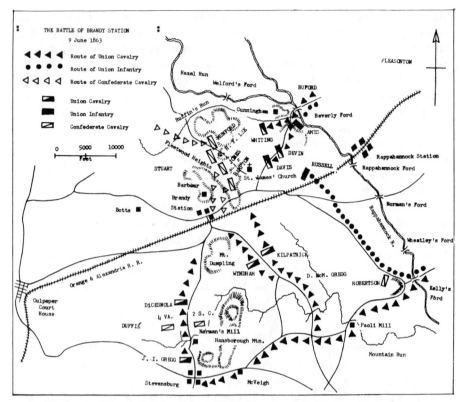

The Battle of Brandy Station, 9 June 1863. (Map drawn by Lawrence T. Longacre.)

8th New York and David R. Clendenin of the 8th Illinois—were on furlough or detached service this morning.)[12]

The 7th Virginia, in column of squadrons, slammed hard aground against McClure's larger, more cohesive force, which had been reinforced by a portion of Devin's brigade in its rear. Colonel Marshall's troopers bounced backward and broke into detachments capable of little staying power. After a few defiant rounds, the detachments scurried rearward.[13]

The survivors joined with the 6th Virginia to build a wall around Beckham's camp, buying time for the cannoneers to find safer ground. Then additional protection materialized as Grumble Jones reached the scene with the balance of his brigade. Keeping Marshall and Flournoy on the advanced line, he secured their rear and flanks with Lunsford Lomax's 11th and Asher Harman's 12th Virginia regiments, plus the 35th Virginia Battalion of E. V. White.[14]

Beckham's guns were not yet out of danger. Barely had Jones arrived when the Federals overran a part of his newly formed line and made for a pair of howitzers that Beckham had failed to draw into the woods. When about to become enemy property, the snub-nose cannon let loose with the first Confederate barrage of the day. To Private Luther Hopkins, the "roar . . . in the woods at that early hour in the morning was terrific."[15] It was also deadly, tearing jagged holes in the assault column. To evade its wrath, the blue-clad horsemen fanned out to either side, finding vantage points from which to pick off crew members. The cannon proved unable to fire in an arc wide enough to even the contest; again they seemed destined for capture.

Observing the gunners' plight, Jones sent forward the 12th Virginia, charging on either flank of the howitzers. It soon collided with the Yankees, forming what one artilleryman called "a mingled mass, fighting and struggling with pistol and saber like maddened savages."[16] Because it had assaulted half again as many troopers, Harman's regiment, like Marshall's before it, could hope to gain only temporary advantage. His troopers did, however, enable the little cannon to limber up and move to the rear, crew members lashing their teams into a frenzy. Seeing their prize elude them, McClure's and Devin's men took their revenge on the artillery's mounted supports. Under the Federals' pressure, several members of the 12th Virginia fell dead or wounded, while the rest withdrew in disorder.

Praying that Stuart would soon appear with reinforcements, Jones committed his remaining troops. Shouting warwhoops, the "Comanches" of the 35th Virginia Battalion thundered forward, Lomax's 11th Virginia on their flank. Ramming into the enemy, the attackers forced McClure's men back on Devin's, the Union lines telescoping upon one another. Eventually, Grimes Davis's erstwhile brigade turned about and headed toward the river, where the rest of Buford's column awaited a clear road to the front.[17]

One Federal caught up in the withdrawal was George Armstrong Custer. The young staff officer had crossed the river in company with Grimes Davis, hoping for an opportunity to command during the coming fight. Now mobbed by McClure's fugitives, Custer's horse took fright and bounded, not toward the rear but into a fence alongside the road to the ford. There it huddled in fright, neighing madly but budging not an inch, though carbine and pistol balls whizzed past its rider's head. Cursing violently, Custer scrambled out of the saddle, hauled on the reins, and by nerve-wracking exertion turned the animal toward the river. He jumped aboard only seconds before the beast took off like a shot. Confronted by a stone wall, horse and rider topped it awkwardly, horse stumbling atop it and Custer flying head over heels through the air. Dazed but unhurt by his landing, the lieutenant remounted and this time was carried to safety.[18]

During Custer's ordeal, the attack by the Comanches and the 11th Virginia lost impetus and cohesion. At an opportune moment, Devin's brigade—Colonel Kellogg's 17th Pennsylvania (today only ten companies strong), the eight-company 6th New York of Major William E. Beardsley, and the three remaining battalions of the 9th New York under William Sackett—charged through McClure's line and struck the Virginians. The newcomers came on with such verve that they convinced Lomax and White to retire toward the west.[19]

Watching his Laurel Brigade fall back, and realizing that Beckham's guns could not support his men for fear of striking them as well as the enemy, Grumble Jones suddenly doubted that reinforcements would reach him in time to prevent disaster.

***

Enjoying his morning coffee when the fighting began at Beverly Ford, J. E. B. Stuart—still groggy with sleep—was not in ideal shape to plot battle dispositions, especially defensive ones. Still, even before couriers from Jones reached Fleetwood Heights, he had sent aides to hasten Hampton, Robertson, Munford, and Rooney Lee toward the threatened sector.

Soon, however, bad news multiplied. From Robertson, near Kelly's Ford, came word that two regiments of Yankee horsemen had forced their way over the river in his front, while additional cavalry and some infantry readied a crossing. To safeguard his lower flank, Stuart now instructed Robertson to hold his ground, preventing the enemy from moving inland. To aid in that endeavor the cavalry commander sent toward Kelly's the 1st South Carolina under Colonel John Logan Black, a regiment of Hampton's that had spent the night near division headquarters. At the same time, to guard his rear and to keep open communications with Lee's infantry near Culpeper, Stuart ordered Hampton to detach Colonel Butler's 2nd South Carolina and send it to the depot at Brandy.

These dispositions completed, the major general pounded off to St. James Church. In his rear came what remained of Hampton's brigade—the 1st North Carolina and the Jeff Davis, Cobb's, and Phillips Legions—guided by members of Stuart's staff. Soon only the faithful Major McClellan was holding the fort on Fleetwood Heights.[20]

As Stuart rode toward the fighting, his other subordinates reacted to his orders with various degrees of promptitude. Like Wade Hampton, Rooney Lee responded quickly and precisely, leading his four regiments and his section of Breathed's battery to the battle area. By no fault of his own, Colonel Munford was much less responsive. Through a mistaken sense of protocol, Munford's order to proceed to St. James Church was given to Fitz Lee, who was convalescing some miles from the brigade bivouac. Marked 7:00 A.M., this order did not reach Munford until about ten o'clock, five hours after the fight began. Nor did it call the colonel to the battlefield; it merely directed him to move "a little farther" south, alerting his pickets to a possible advance. Later orders from Stuart's headquarters required Munford to send one regiment to Stuart's side and with the rest to hurry "this way." Dutifully, the colonel dispatched Williams Wickham's 4th Virginia to Fleetwood Heights;[21] but because Stuart's courier rode off before explaining which direction was "this way," the brigade leader was left in a quandary. Though he surely heard the fighting near St. James Church, Munford decided that his job was to guard the upper reaches of the Rappahannock. Instead of turning south, he marched east to Welford's Ford, where he remained for several hours.[22]

While Munford dithered, Stuart, with Hampton's brigade, reached the woods and clearings where Grumble Jones stood embattled. Minutes before, Lomax's and White's advance had fallen back under Union pressure, after permitting Beckham's howitzers to evade capture. Following the Virginians' withdrawal, the Federals had not pressed their advantage, deferring an offensive till they completed new dispositions. During the lull that ensued, Stuart whipped Hampton's men into line on Jones's right, connecting with the 6th Virginia and facing east. Noting the substantial number of horsemen massing in his front—with foot troops reportedly in supporting range—Hampton dismounted 100 riflemen and deployed them in advance of his main body to dislodge Federals from nearby woodlots. Laters he bolstered this force to 200 and added still others when Colonel Black's regiment, recalled from Kelly's Ford, joined him. [23]

Meanwhile, Rooney Lee brought his brigade into line on Jones's left, linking with the 7th Virginia and extending as far north as a farm owned by a family named Cunningham. There some of his troops took position in a tree-bordered field, others behind a stone fence that afforded excellent cover. Saber-wielding reinforcements stood to horse toward Lee's rear; still farther back, Captain Breathed's two guns had unlimbered atop a small ridge. [24] Lee's line was well anchored; Stuart found no fault with the Harvard man's dispositions. Since Hampton's position enjoyed similar strength, only the center of the line concerned the cavalry chief: Jones's troops, forced to shift position again and again during the early fighting to take advantage of what cover the plateau provided, now faced generally northward, their line pitched at nearly a right angle to that of Hampton and Lee. [25]

Despite its awkward appearance, the entire front proved mighty enough. Soon after Hampton's and Lee's arrival, the Federals launched a series of small, dismounted attacks against many positions. They met strong resistance everywhere, especially near the Cunningham farm, where R. L. T. Beale's 9th Virginia aborted several advances with volleys of rifle fire. When the last attack gave way, detachments of Colonel Solomon Williams's 2nd North Carolina and Colonel J. Lucius Davis's 10th Virginia staged a mounted pursuit, covered by Beale's sharpshooters and by John Chambliss's 13th Virginia. Once they felt their foe had been sufficiently chastised, the horsemen wheeled about and returned. [26]

By this point both Alfred Pleasonton and John Buford had reached the front. They scrutinized the field, probing for weak points in the recently extended enemy line. Now that their plan to link near Brandy Station with Gregg and Duffié had broken down, the Union leaders determined to retain whatever advantage they had gained at St. James Church, holding the ground till they could establish communication with the lower column. [27] While couriers sped off to communicate with Gregg, Buford brought forward Major Whiting's Reserves as well as Ames's command—the 2nd and 33rd Massachusetts, 86th and 124th New York, and 3rd Wisconsin Infantry. Placing Whiting's troopers in line of battle alongside McClure's and Devin's brigades and deploying the foot soldiers on the flanks, Buford also made room for his artillery. [28]

For some time the opposing gunners carried on the fighting, while Pleasonton, Buford, and their subordinates solidified their positions. When dismounted skirmishing resumed in force, the Federals held an initial advantage, thanks to their infantry support. Then, however, Beckham's gunners got the range of their enemy, disabling some of James Robertson's cannon and forcing other batteries to flee from positions in forest clearings.[29] Then, at about 10:00 A.M., Hampton's dismounted troopers advanced and pressed the Union left so heavily that Buford's forward lines gave way, threatening the stability of the entire position. Buford redeployed rapidly to counter the threat but failed to neutralize the Confederates' momentum.[30]

Finally—doubtless with Pleasonton's approval if not by his order—Buford resorted to tactics rarely favored by commanders bred in the dragoon tradition. Calling on Whiting's men, he sent forward as skirmishers a few companies of Captain T. F. Rodenbough's 2nd United States Cavalry, supported by Lieutenant Elder's battery of the 4th Artillery. Then he brought up the rest of Whiting's command, the 6th United States under Captain George C. Cram, and the 6th Pennsylvania of Robert Morris. This was the extent of the Reserve Brigade today, for Captain Julius W. Mason's 5th United States was on detached duty and the 1st Regulars of Captain Richard S. C. Lord had been left on the eastern side of the river, at Pleasonton's orders, to guard Buford's communications.[31]

Captain Rodenbough's skirmishers moved ahead a short distance, fanning out north and south and opening an avenue of advance for their comrades. Minutes later, as the 6th U.S. fell in on their flanks, five companies of the 6th Pennsylvania started forward at the trot, in column of squadrons.[32] In their front, perhaps eight hundred yards off, stood a bank of guns supporting Hampton's flank drive. Riding knee-to-knee, the erstwhile lancers broke into a limited gallop, then, as buglers blared the charge, into an extended gallop, angling toward the point at which Hampton's brigade joined Jones's.[33]

Rebel riflemen shredded the Pennsylvanians even before they covered half the distance. Mounted members of the 12th Virginia then piled into their flanks, and close-quarters combat flared along the path of the assault. The attackers had still other obstacles to face. Recalled Morris's executive officer, Major Henry C. Whelan: "As we flew along—our men yelling like demons—grape and cannister [sic] were poured into our left flank. . . . We had to leap three wide, deep ditches, and many of our horses and men piled up in a writhing mass in those ditches and were ridden over." Among those caught in the pileup was Major Morris; injured in the melee, he was unhorsed and taken prisoner. Soon he was on his way to Richmond's Libby Prison, where he would die of disease and malnutrition.[34]

His subordinate continued: "I didn't know that Morris was not with us, and we dashed on, driving the Rebels into and through the woods, our men fighting with the sabre alone, whilst they used principally pistols. Our brave fellows cut them out of the saddle and fought like tigers, until I discovered they were on both flanks, pouring a cross fire of carbines and pistols on us. . . ."

Outgunned and losing momentum, Whelan's mounted supports gave way and raced for their own lines. Many of the Pennsylvanians joined them; others forged onward alone. Rallied by Captain Dahlgren—who, like Custer, had accompanied Buford's column in hopes of seeing action—the volunteers reached the cannon in their front and grappled with gun crews, who swiped at them with rammer staffs and blasted them with pistols. Mounted Rebels including Colonel Harman's men swarmed over the volunteers, most of whom at last turned and fled.[35] There followed, in Major Whelan's words, "a *race for life*." As during their advance, the ex-lancers encountered ditches and stone walls; again their mounts "got jambed [*sic*] and piled up in a horrid, kicking mass. . . . It seemed hours of horror, to be pinioned and fettered by a writhing mass of heavy horses, and the murderous Rebels coming up to shoot or stab us in the back."[36]

The few hundred survivors of the charge regained the safety of Buford's line, where comrades covered them by lashing the plateau with minié balls and shells. Though tactically unsuccessful, the Pennsylvanians' assault had restored the status quo around St. James Church; Hampton's dismounted men had retreated, and no countercharge followed their withdrawal. The aristocrats in uniform had also contributed a dramatic display of pluck and determination impressive to all observers. General Buford thereafter called them his "Seventh Regulars."[37]

Another lull followed the 6th's repulse. Pleasonton and Stuart made new deployments, shifting units through the trees toward opposing flanks and advancing others into forward positions while also removing dead and wounded men from the cleared ground.[38] Stuart considered resuming the contest by maneuvering Lee's brigade in a manner similar to Hampton's, but he resolved to move slowly and carefully.

By now it was noontime and the sun was a red-hot ball directly overhead. At this point, suddenly, combat erupted on a front not far from St. James Church. Stuart learned of it after meeting a courier sent by Grumble Jones. The latter had gotten word that the lower column of Union horsemen, about which Robertson had alerted Stuart early that morning, was marching north from Brandy Station.[39] Preoccupied with the fighting near St. James and thinking the new warning overstated, Stuart barked a reply to the subordinate who had relayed it: "Tell Gen. Jones to attend to the Yankees in his front, and I'll watch the flanks!"

The courier did as told. When he received Stuart's response, Jones flew into one of his towering rages: "So he thinks they ain't coming, does he? Well, let him alone; he'll damned soon see for himself!"[40]

***

Not until after 6:00 A.M. did Duffié begin his crossing at Kelly's Ford.[41] In brief order, Gregg's division, accompanied by Martin's New York battery and followed by Russell's division of infantry, waded the cool stream, clambered onto shore, and poised on the road that ran northwestward to Brandy Station.

By then Duffié was moving westward with a speed that seemed an effort to compensate for earlier tardiness and which belied his weary hours of marching and countermarching. A battalion of the 6th Ohio under Major Benjamin C. Stanhope led Duffié's advance, intending to seize Stevensburg and to hold it "at all hazards." Then followed the rest of Cesnola's brigade, the brigade of Irvin Gregg, the six-gun Regular battery under Lieutenant Pennington, and a line of supply wagons.[42]

With Duffié gone, General Gregg faced a situation that required a change of plans. Thus far opposition had been slight—almost nonexistent. The nearest Rebels, pickets from Robertson's demi-brigade, had been gobbled up in advance of Duffié's crossing by two troops under Captain P. Jones Yorke of the 1st New Jersey.[43] Other North Carolina cavalrymen had come up to challenge Duffié's crossing, but they proved so unaggressive that when Gregg reached shore he paid scant attention to them. Still, in an effort to avoid time lost to enemy delaying action, Gregg declined to force a passage on the direct road to Brandy. The division leader decided to leave a large body of Russell's men at the river to prevent Robertson from pursuing, while other infantry passed up the direct road to the depot. Meanwhile, Wyndham's troopers, followed by Kilpatrick's, would march on Duffié's track. Gregg's scouts assured him that after crossing Mountain Run and passing Paoli Mill, he would meet a road that led to the railroad depot from the south. The new route would place the 3rd Division in a better position to meet the demands of the day. Couriers from Pleasonton plus the sounds of fighting from the north told Gregg that Buford had met unexpected opposition above Brandy. A move directly north from the depot would enable Gregg to flank the troops generating that opposition.[44]

Gregg's decision to change route was the proper one, as was his desire to march directly to Buford's aid. He erred, however, in leaving his powerful infantry support behind. Possibly the decision was not his; given his preoccupation with lines of communications and routes of retreat, Pleasonton may have instructed Gregg to detach at least a part of Russell's command to guard them.[45] But Gregg compounded the error by delaying until many of the foot troops deployed. This was proven unnecessary by the weak opposition of Robertson. Soon after Gregg started west, Russell's 2nd and 7th Wisconsin and 56th Pennsylvania easily overawed the North Carolinians, who had elected to remain on the Brandy Station road instead of following the 3rd Division. Robertson spent the day falling back before the Union infantry, rendering Stuart little service beyond notifying him of the enemy's movements. Later in the day Robertson's two regiments were called north to aid Rooney Lee, but they arrived too late to do much good. All in all, Robertson's performance this day would only confirm the opinion of his critics.[46]

Once he left Robertson behind, David Gregg's path was clear and his progress rapid. Beyond Paoli Mill, as anticipated, the Brandy Station road appeared, and Wyndham's column veered onto it. Shortly before noon—with the sounds of Buford's fight temporarily waning—the Federals drew within sight of the rail depot and the heights north of it, where Stuart's tent-fly remained standing. Everything there looked quiet and still, indicating that the advance had gone undetected.[47] In fact, the game lay in the invaders' hands. By continuing north a couple of miles, two thousand men would come up behind Stuart's back. The giant pincers envisioned by Hooker and Pleasonton, though bent out of shape, would close on the foe as intended.

At the last minute, the arm of Colonel Sir Percy Wyndham shot up and his brigade shuddered to a halt below the Orange & Alexandria. Through his field glasses, the British soldier of fortune had spied a cannon being trundled into position atop Fleetwood Heights to sweep his approach. He feared this indicated the proximity of other cannon; perhaps a trap was being baited. Minutes before, a courier from Pleasonton had called David Gregg to a hastily arranged conference east of St. James Church,[48] so the decision to halt or proceed lay with Wyndham, the senior officer in the division.

Normally aggressive in the extreme, Wyndham decided to play the prudent man on this occasion. Before proceeding farther, he brought up his own guns— a section of Martin's battery—supported by skirmishers from his lead units. It took several minutes for the two cannon under Lieutenant M. P. Clark to move into position below the heights, and as time seeped away the enemy in Wyndham's front made good use of his uncertainty and hesitation.[49]

***

For Major McClellan, as for everyone on Stuart's staff, it had been a bad day already. His peace of mind shattered by attacking Yankees, the division adjutant had been further discomfited when forced to remain at headquarters while Stuart and the rest of his military family charged northward into the fray. A bit later, the staff officer had been ordered to send the only nearby troops—Butler's South Carolina regiment—to Stevensburg to meet Duffié's advance. And soon after Butler left, McClellan experienced the worst moment of his day (perhaps of his life) when he saw the head of yet another enemy cavalry column trotting toward him from the south: "They were pressing steadily forward upon the railroad station, which must in a few moments be in their possession. How could they be prevented from also occupying the Fleetwood Hill, the key to the whole position?"

The major proved equal to the crisis. Collaring the few orderlies remaining on Fleetwood, he sent them galloping north with a plea for immediate reinforcement. Even as they departed, however, McClellan realized that any aid from Stuart would come too late. Searching about for a miracle, he found the next best thing: a 6-pounder howitzer from Chew's battery, under Lieutenant John W. Carter, which, its ammunition nearly exhausted, had retired from the fighting near St. James Church and had halted at the base of Fleetwood Heights. Scrambling down the hill, McClellan shouted out his plight to the gun crew, which manhandled the piece up the slope and toward its forward crest, in plain view of the enemy now drawing up near the railroad tracks.

At McClellan's urging, Carter opened a slow fire with "a few imperfect shells and some round shot." This had the desired effect: it compelled the Federals to throw out dismounted skirmishers and to return the fire with their own guns. Despite the odds facing him, Lieutenant Carter succeeded in disabling one of the opposing cannon. This seemed to reinforce the enemy's unwillingness to advance in force before neutralizing the howitzer. For a time at least, the Confederates had staved off disaster at Brandy Station.[50]

***

In point of fact, J. E. B. Stuart had resolved to investigate affairs at the depot even before McClellan's couriers reached St. James Church. Following the repulse of the 6th Pennsylvania and its supports, the Confederate leader felt able to turn toward the sector already brought to his attention by Jones and Robertson. Despite rebuffing the earlier warnings, Stuart had been nagged by doubt about the safety of his rear; this prompted him to send Captain Hart, temporarily detached from his battery, to "see what this foolishness is about!" But before that officer could report back, Stuart was met by one of McClellan's couriers, who shouted that the Yankees were swarming over Brandy Station. For the first time, Stuart saw the trap closing on him.[51]

Perhaps it was now, as John Esten Cooke later wrote, that "the tiger was aroused in him. His face flushed; his eyes darted flame; his voice grew hoarse and strident."[52] Whatever his physical reaction, he responded to the news with immediate action, sending messengers in many directions to detach engaged units that might relieve the pressure toward the south. Fortunately, the lull caused by Buford's decision to bring up his infantry and artillery seemed likely to endure for some time. Thus permitted to disengage, Stuart withdrew from the center of his line three of Jones's units—the 12th and 6th Virginia regiments and the 35th Virginia Battalion—as well as some of Beckham's batteries. Soon the outfits were racing south, the gaps they left quickly filled by the rest of the Laurel Brigade and by Rooney Lee, whose men sidled down from the Cunning-ham farm. After instructing Wade Hampton to follow Jones to the depot as soon as the road was clear, Stuart charged after the detached units, straining to overtake them in time to lead them against Brandy.

Jones's people covered the two-mile distance in a furious, extended gallop, guidons flapping sharply in the breeze, cannon under Captains Chew and William McGregor bouncing and rocking in rear of the column. When the artillery cleared St. James Church, Hampton fell in behind. In his vanguard rode the Cobb Legion, Pierce Young in command; in echelon to the left followed Black's 1st South Carolina, Baker's 1st North Carolina, and the Jeff Davis Legion under

Lieutenant Colonel J. F. Waring. Abreast of the relief force rode Hart's battery, his men lashing the horses in an effort to keep pace with the cavalry.[53]

***

Before Stuart and his cavaliers reached Fleetwood, David Gregg returned from his conference with Pleasonton and Buford, rejoining Percy Wyndham below the depot. Rapidly interpreting the situation, the division leader concluded that no substantial force held the crest in his front. At his command, bugles squalled and Wyndham's 1st New Jersey—troopers the Briton had transformed from undisciplined malcontents into model cavalrymen—broke across the railroad tracks and made for the western spur of Fleetwood Heights, known as Barbour House Hill.[54] As the Jerseymen gained the forward slope on the dead run, General Gregg himself, aboard his sprightly mare "Pretty," joined them. "It was a very thrilling sight," observed one of his staff officers, "to see these troops going up the slope in the bright June sun, their sabres glistening. As they neared the enemy General Gregg showed an enthusiasm that I had never noticed before. He started his horse on a gallop . . . swinging his gauntlets over his head and hurrahing. . . ." For the reserved and dignified commander, this was an amazing display.[55]

Thundering up the incline, the 1st New Jersey swerved to the left, straining to flank Carter's howitzer, which, out of ammunition, was being pulled to the rear of the crest. Because this piece had done its job so well, Wyndham's troopers never reached it. Just short of the summit, they found a mob of riders hurtling down upon them. Colonel Harman's 12th Virginia, Stuart's lead regiment, had hit the opposite slope barely fifty yards ahead of the Federals.

Aware that a critical moment was at hand, Stuart had directed Harman's men into action without allowing them to shift from a column of fours into a line of battle. The result was inevitable: the Federals cut through the Virginians like a hot knife slicing butter.[56] Flailing away with their swords, the New Jersey riders ignored the familiar challenge the Virginians shouted to them: "Put up your sabres; draw your pistols!" At such close quarters, the revolver-wielding Rebels were at a disadvantage, which, added to the disarray of their formation, made defeat certain. At first contact the regiment shattered, its pieces flying every which way, Colonel Harman falling severely wounded.[57]

The 35th Virginia Battalion, its ranks better aligned, now gained the heights and spurred ahead to even the contest. "Lige" White's troopers, however, suffered the same fate as their predecessors. Shoved aside by the momentum of the Union attack, the Comanches split into small detachments, most of which raced back down the hill in the wake of Harman's troops. Not until Jones's third regiment reached Fleetwood did Wyndham's riders give way. Cut in two by the hard-charging 6th Virginia, and menaced on the flanks by the first of Chew's and McGregor's guns to unlimber behind the hill, the Britisher's troopers scattered for their lives. Sir Percy joined them, having taken a wound in the right leg that left him weak from loss of blood. Even so, the mustachioed colonel refused to leave the area till the outcome of the fighting was known.[58]

The succession of charge and countercharge continued when the 6th Virginia found itself facing the rest of Wyndham's brigade, now clambering up the slopes to the rear, right, and left of the 1st New Jersey. Outmanned by Colonel John P. Taylor's 1st Pennsylvania and the 1st Maryland of Lieutenant Colonel James Deems, the Virginians were forced to flee to safety. A demoralized Confederate recalled the pell-mell rush downhill: "As the enemy poured an incessant fire at my back, I felt as if lizards and snakes were crawling up my spine, and expected to be perforated every moment."[59]

At this juncture at least, David Gregg was the victor on Fleetwood Heights. His Pennsylvania and Maryland regiments swept over its wide crest, charging through the remnants of Stuart's headquarters and almost gobbling up Lieutenant Carter and Major McClellan as well. Then Lieutenant Clark's section of Martin's battery shelled the Barbour House, near which dozens of Grumble Jones's survivors continued to resist the attackers. Meanwhile, at the base of the heights, Stuart and his staff—notably Heros von Borcke—were striving desperately to rally the rest of the Laurel Brigade and return it to the fight.[60]

Although these efforts had no immediate effect, Confederate reinforcements again reached the ridge at a crucial moment. As the Yankees prepared to take full possession of the disputed ground, Wade Hampton, aboard his charger, "Captain," led the advance of his brigade up the back slope. Seeing them ascend, Stuart let loose a cry of welcome: "Give them the sabre, boys!"[61]

Most of the new arrivals preferred six-shooters but they fulfilled the spirit of their commander's injunction. The Cobb Legion drove straight across the crest toward the nearest Federals, while the rear units passed to the flanks and swept over neighborhing spurs. Given new heart by Hampton's appearance, men of the three regiments that had preceded him returned to the summit. The combined Confederate force thudded into the troopers of Taylor and Deems with what Captain Blackford of Stuart's staff called "a shock that made the earth tremble."[62]

Hampton's first victims were the remains of the 1st New Jersey, under Lieutenant Colonel Brodrick. The Jerseymen were inundated by the Confederate wave; dozens went down dead or wounded. Brodrick himself slumped over with mortal wounds, as did his executive officer, Major John H. Shelmire. Those who fled unharmed escaped down the rear slope of Barbour House Hill and at its base pounced on McGregor's battery, which they found bereft of mounted support. Still, the battery was able to defend itself; with well-placed volleys it laced the 1st New Jersey's shattered ranks. Those troopers who escaped the torrent of shells were content to recross the railroad and take refuge on the flanks of Judson Kilpatrick's brigade, now coming up in Wyndham's rear.[63]

Before Kilpatrick could strike, Hampton's regiments uprooted the rest of

Wyndham's brigade, including the men of Pennsylvania and Maryland, and scattered them like chaff in a whirlwind. While the Cobb Legion and the 1st South Carolina met the Union riders in front, the 1st North Carolina and Jeff Davis Legion cannoned into their flanks. Quickly, most of the Yankees abandoned Fleetwood and fell back toward the depot. A few remained to support Captain Martin's three guns, which had unlimbered at the base of the ridge.[64]

Martin decided to make a stand there, although most of his cavalry comrades seemed bent on getting to the rear in record time. By firing double rounds of canister—each round containing twenty-seven iron balls packed in sawdust—he persuaded Hampton not to pursue Wyndham. However, Lige White, who had rallied his Comanches on the side of the ridge, was not intimidated by the trio of guns. Sweeping in from the west, two of his companies chased off the New Yorkers' supports, then mixed with the cannoneers in hand-to-hand fighting. Taken by surprise, the artillerymen quickly went under. Thirty of Martin's three dozen men crumpled with wounds; around them, an uncounted number of horses fell dead in their traces. Unable to pull the guns to safety, Martin spiked them by wedging shells backward down their barrels, before escaping on foot with his surviving crewmen.[65]

At this moment, Kilpatrick's brigade reached the line of the Orange & Alexandria in Martin's rear. Envisioning a do-or-die assault to retrieve Gregg's lost advantage, the young colonel gave a disinterested glance at the abandoned battery. When one of Gregg's aides rushed up with a plea to rescue the cannon, Kill-cavalry snorted: "No! damned if I will!"[66] His heart was set on a climactic charge up the hill—the success of which would bring him enduring fame—and nothing would deter him from it. Tilting his saber toward Fleetwood Heights, he ordered an advance by his leading regiment, Lieutenant Colonel William Irvine's 10th New York.

Kilpatrick's quest for immortality began badly. First, he failed to place his own detachment of Martin's battery, two guns under Lieutenant J. Wade Wilson, in a position to give his brigade maximum support. By sending the section too close to the front, Kilpatrick exposed it dangerously. As a result, Wilson's guns were overrun by re-formed elements of the 6th Virginia. Unable to seize the pieces, the 6th did compel Wilson to follow Martin's lead by taking flight—though without leaving his pieces behind.[67] More significantly, Kilpatrick failed to reach the crest of the ridge before Hampton's troopers swarmed over the 10th New Yorkers, breaking their formation and wounding and capturing their commander. Major M. Henry Avery collected the outfit's remnants and led them in a wild race to the rear. Rushing back to the low ground, Kilpatrick placed himself at the head of his 2nd New York, the "Harris Light Cavalry"—the regiment he had led as a lieutenant colonel in the war's early days—and ordered another charge.[68]

Even under his leadership and that of Lieutenant Colonel Davies, the Harris Light fared no better than Irvine's men had. As they surged across the railroad line and up the Barbour House Hill, the New Yorkers were taken in flank by some of Hampton's men, who had diverged from his main column to sweep around the west side of the ridge. Despite the urging of their officers, the 2nd New York swerved to the right, broke, and fled in utter rout. Its panicky retreat disordered elements of the 10th New York, which had been trying to re-form, and ensured that regiment's flight as well.[69]

By now, as one onlooker observed, Judson Kilpatrick was "wild with excitement."[70] With Hampton's men shouting a victory cheer atop the heights, the brigade leader called up his last outfit, the Puritans of the 1st Maine. (Kilpatrick's company of District of Columbia cavalry, under Captain William H. Orton, was being held farther south as a rear guard.) Galloping up to the Maine commander, Kilpatrick took some minutes to indulge his love of oratory.[71] After calling on the newcomers to save the day by a heroic feat of arms, Kilpatrick barked: "Colonel Douty, what can you do with your regiment?" The hulking, heavily bearded officer replied: "I can drive the rebels to Hell, sir!" At that, wrote one of Douty's troopers, Kilpatrick "hollard [sic] for us to charge."[72]

The Puritans sustained their commander's boast. Rising in their stirrups, holding sabers aloft, they raced forward in what proved to be the most successful Union attack of the day. Obliquing to the right, they butted into Hampton's flank, slightly wounded the brigade leader, and siphoned off the strength of his attack. The men of Maine sheared through the Rebel column, riding over the summit of Fleetwood Heights and cutting a path of withdrawal down the backslope. They too lost heavily: ravines, fences, ditches, plus the pressure of Hampton's rear regiments, broke their formation, isolating a large group of riders under Lieutenant Colonel Charles H. Smith and savaging it with saber and pistol blows.

During its frantic charge, the regiment experienced some wild adventures. One of its sergeants, chronically nearsighted, reached the base of the hill and took refuge with what he believed to be Captain Martin's battery, only to discover he had ridden into the hands of Virginia cannoneers. The horse of another sergeant stumbled over the railroad tracks en route to the heights and fell down the gradient in a series of somersaults. An observer noted that "first the sergeant, then the horse appeared in rapid succession. . . . Every time the sergeant appeared on top a terrible volley of invectives, mixed with sand, poured from his mouth, until suddenly shut off by his rapid disappearance under the horse and sand again, and instantly resumed upon his coming up on the other side."[73] A third member of the regiment was pursued across a part of the Barbour estate by howling Confederates. Failing to negotiate a critical turn, animal and rider crashed through an icehouse and tumbled down the deep hole inside. The horse died but the trooper was hauled to the surface by his captors.[74]

The 1st Maine's assault succeeded in thrusting Hampton from Fleetwood Heights, but only temporarily. After retreating in the direction of St. James Church, the Carolinian halted the flight of his command. Rallying the men and absorbing reinforcements from some of Jones's regiments that had been chased from the heights, Hampton realigned his column and led it back to Fleetwood at a gallop.[75] There it again collided with Kilpatrick and Douty, and this time it carried the day. Thanks to an especially vigorous attack by Pierce Young's Cobb Legion, the Rebels hurled the already splintered 1st Maine from Barbour House Hill and its neighboring peaks.[76] As the New Englanders retreated, J. E. B. Stuart sealed his triumph by sending Lunsford Lomax's 11th Virginia, only recently detached from the Laurel Brigade near St. James Church, to join the Cobb Legion in overrunning Martin's battery once again. The Virginians also broke up final pockets of Union resistance near Brandy Station and chased away troopers they found wrecking Confederate supplies stored at the depot.[77]

Stunned by this series of blows, David Gregg called it quits. It was now midafternoon; his division was fought out; he could send up no reserves worthy of the name; and he had heard that Confederate infantry had moved within supporting distance of Stuart. As he collected his scattered regiments, the division leader, coincidentally, was ordered by Pleasonton to withdraw over the Rappahannock.[78] His pullback went uncontested; a mix-up in orders by Stuart and Hampton kept two regiments from pursuing, while others were stymied by an inadvertent shelling from their own cannon atop the heights.[79]

In falling back, Gregg could only count his losses, second-guess his handling of the fight, and bewail the lack of assistance he had received from Buford and Duffié. Either might have turned the tide at Fleetwood Heights in his favor. But Buford had been strangely inactive for the past few hours—and Duffié, though repeatedly ordered to leave Stevensburg and aid the 3rd Cavalry Division, had arrived only minutes before Gregg's retreat—much too late to render assistance.[80] It appeared the Frenchman had some explaining to do.

***

At perhaps ten o'clock that morning—some six hours before Gregg's repulse near Brandy Station—Stanhope's 6th Ohio battalion reached Stevensburg and continued beyond to check the number and condition of the roads running to Culpeper. Duffié's main body moved with much less speed. This may have been inevitable; Pennington's battery and the division's train of supply wagons and ambulances were substantial impediments. Still, at least one officer in the column thought the march unconscionably slow.[81]

The upshot was that when Stanhope returned east and found trouble at Stevensburg, he had no comrades within supporting range. The trouble appeared in the guise of Butler's 2nd South Carolina, which came down cautiously from the north soon after Stanhope reached the village. The majority of Butler's horsemen, uncertain of the size of their opposition, seemed content to oppose the Ohioans at long range. But soon a fourteen-man detachment under Lieutenant Colonel Frank Hampton, younger brother of Stuart's ranking subordinate, charged Stanhope's men as the latter passed through the town. Despite its superior strength, the Union battalion took fright and sped eastward in search of friends.[82]

As his enemy raced off, Hampton established an outpost amid the ruins of an abandoned seminary south of town. There he was joined by forty men under Major T. J. Lipscomb, who had moved cross-country to pursue Stanhope's detachment, falling back upon the approach of Duffié's main body. Hampton commandeered about half of Lipscomb's men and sent him, with the remainder, to report to Colonel Butler. When Butler assimilated the major's detachment, his line extended for a mile above Stevensburg, across the stream known as Mountain Run. Hampton's position constituted the right flank and Butler himself held the center (most of his troops having dismounted among woods on the east side of the Stevensburg–Brandy Station road), while Lipscomb was the ranking officer on the left. The total force numbered fewer than two hundred, though at that hour one of Stuart's aides, Captain W. D. Farley, was leading Wickham's 4th Virginia down from Brandy Station to reinforce the South Carolinians.[83]

Before Wickham could arrive, Alfred Duffié drew up east of Stevensburg and surveyed his opposition. It took him more than half an hour to identify Frank Hampton's outpost as the key to the position and to determine to strike it with Cesnola's brigade. By then, Duffié's men had taken the decision to attack out of his hands. Cesnola's advance regiment, Lieutenant Colonel Greely S. Curtis's eight-company 1st Massachusetts, had been forced to wait on the left of the road to Stevensburg while Hampton's dismounted sharpshooters popped away at them with carbines, rifles, and muskets. Likewise discomfited was the regiment on the other side of the road, Lieutenant Colonel John L. Thompson's 1st Rhode Island, and the troops between the New England outfits, the eight companies of Stedman's 6th Ohio. Finally, unable to withstand the fusillade any longer, some of the Massachusetts troopers made an unauthorized charge alongside the road to town, covered by Thompson's and Stedman's men, the 4th New York of Lieutenant Colonel Augustus Pruyn, Pennington's battery, and, in the rear, two regiments of Irvin Gregg's brigade.[84]

Seeing the Yankees coming on, Frank Hampton mounted thirty-six of his men and rushed east to meet them. The opposing forces crashed together on and off of the road. The superior weight of the Federals—the squadron of Captain John Tewksbury, supported by other members of Curtis's outfit—decided the outcome in a few minutes. Wade Hampton's brother received a mortal pistol wound and his brave little band disintegrated and dispersed.[85]

The victors did not slacken their pace after Hampton's overthrow. Reinforced by skirmishers from Thompson's and Stedman's regiments, the Bay Staters raced up the road to Brandy Station and into Butler's main body. With spitting pistols and slashing swords the Federals not only cut their way through the 2nd South Carolina but through the newly arrived 4th Virginia as well. They caught Wickham's regiment at a disadvantage, while trying to change formation on the narrow, tree-lined road from column of fours to a battle line. To add to the Virginians' plight, demoralized troopers from the 2nd South Carolina surged through their ranks, stampeding horses and riders. By the time the Union riders reached Wickham's original position, the 4th Virginia was in full retreat, most of its men heading toward Culpeper and the safety of General Lee's infantry. Observing from the rear, one of Irvin Gregg's troopers noted that his comrades drove the Confederates "through the thick woods and it was a regular steeple chase, through ditches, over fences, through underbrush. . . ."[86]

After his men had fled almost half a mile, Wickham rallied many of them and ordered a counterattack. The enemy, having halted in the road to receive the Rebels' thrust, began to waver at their approach. Before reaching the line, however, a majority of the 4th Virginia again scattered in panic and this time resisted all efforts to re-form. Mortified and disgusted, Wickham halted and with ten men who remained carried on the fight with carbines and pistols at long range.[87]

Although he had reinforced Tewksbury, Duffié made no attempt to follow up his success. When Butler reformed his Carolinians above Mountain Run, the Frenchman hesitated to commit himself to a further offensive without making new dispositions and softening up the enemy with his artillery. Pennington's battery came up, unlimbered, and promptly beat down the fire of the single cannon that Stuart had sent Butler. Pennington even put a shell squarely in front of the spot where Butler and Captain Farley were observing the fight. The explosion mangled the right legs of both men, Farley's being severed and Butler's nearly so. The staff officer died of his wound; the colonel would be incapacitated for several months.[88]

About midafternoon, Duffié finally nerved himself to clear away Butler's and Wickham's remnants and to link with Buford and Gregg at Brandy Station. Just as he prepared to cross Mountain Run, he got word that Gregg required his presence at the depot immediately. For some time Duffié had heard the sounds of the 3rd Division's battle and had suspected he might soon be called north. Having delayed his operations so long, he could not lose additional time by cutting his way through the Rebels. At Gregg's stipulation, he turned east and retraced his steps along the route he had taken that morning.[89]

Not until five o'clock did Duffié clear Stevensburg, and when he reached Gregg's sector he found the battle at Brandy Station over and the army in retreat to the Rappahannock. Though Duffié had inflicted many casualties and had captured some sixty Rebels, several of his men considered his fight at Stevensburg an exercise in futility, an example of hard work without strategic benefit—a day marked by indecision and delay, poor judgment, and opportunities not exploited.[90]

***

While Duffié and Gregg prepared to retreat, their fighting done, John Buford, his troopers, and their infantry and artillery supports made a final push from St. James Church toward Brandy Station. For unknown reasons, the commander of the 1st Cavalry Division had failed to make inroads against his opposition following Stuart's detaching of Hampton's brigade and much of Jones's. No doubt at Pleasonton's behest, Buford had spent the early afternoon on the defensive. And when he renewed the contest at about 3:00 P.M., it was largely for defensive reasons—primarily to neutralize a threat to his communications and his retreat route.

That threat was posed by Rooney Lee, whose brigade, following Hampton's and Jones's departure, had fallen back to a more formidable position on high ground, covered by Breathed's battery. From there dismounted skirmishers had continually moved forward, as though seeking to skirt Buford's upper flank and gain his rear. Of particular concern to the Union leader was a phalanx of sharpshooters on Lee's left, protected by stone walls and other barriers. They furnished some work for Ames's foot soldiers. Riding his gray horse up to the infantry's position, Buford caught the attention of officers of the 2nd Massachusetts and 3rd Wisconsin Regiments. "Do you see those people down there?" the brigadier asked, motioning toward the walls. "They've got to be driven out." When one officer remarked that the enemy appeared to have a force double their own, Buford responded, "Well, I didn't order you, mind; but if you think you can flank them, go in, and drive them off."

Though not accustomed to taking directions from cavalry officers, whom they regarded as poseurs and fops, the foot soldiers admitted that in his hunting shirt and dirty corduroys the plain-spoken Buford did not fit the stereotype. Impressed by his air of command, one company from each regiment started westward, passed around an elevation that screened them from enemy view, crawled through hedges and clover fields, and came up on the left rear of Rooney Lee's northern flank. On a signal the infantrymen rose above the walls sheltering troopers of the 10th Virginia and 2nd North Carolina and blasted away at the other side. Many Confederates died before realizing what had hit them; the survivors raced away. Under a retaliatory fire from the rest of Lee's brigade, the snipers then made their way back to Buford.[91]

Emboldened by the infantry's success, the 6th Pennsylvania Cavalry, which had suffered so heavily in its earlier charge, made a second mounted attack on Lee's line. Led by Major Whelan, the 6th charged the main body of the 10th Virginia "through a perfect tempest of shell, grape, canister, solid shot and rifle bullets." Though a member of Lucius Davis's regiment admitted to being "hard pressed and slowly pushed back," supports including the 7th Virginia, the only element of Jones's brigade still on the ground, turned the path of the attack into what Whelan called "decidedly the hottest place I was ever in. A man could not show his head or [even] a finger without a hundred rifle shots whistling about. . . . the air [was] almost solid with lead."[92]

Reaching the Cunningham farm, the Pennsylvanians were met head-on by Colonel Beale's 9th Virginia, sent in by Rooney Lee. There followed a frantic melee that gyrated back and forth over plowed ground, "the dust and smoke and steam from the heated horses making the air dark and obscuring the vision." One whose vision was obscured was Wesley Merritt. Having recently relinquished staff duties, the young Regular was now riding in support of the Pennsylvanians along with comrades in the 2nd United States. Assisted by well-placed shots from Robertson's artillery, the Regulars took Beale's people in flank and slowly pressed them back. Individual combats broke out everywhere, and Merritt found himself engaged in swordplay with a tall officer of high rank (quite possibly Rooney Lee himself, riding with the regiment he had led to war in 1861). Merritt's opponent deftly parried his every blow, then inflicted on him the indignity of losing his hat to a saber slash and the pain of a gash in the leg. A moment later the Rebel vanished in the battle smoke and in his place a bevy of lesser-ranking officers challenged Merritt. Characteristically, the captain called on them to surrender. Perhaps startled by his audacity, the Confederates held back, permitting him to hew a path of retreat eastward.[93]

For a time the Pennsylvanians and their Regular comrades held sway, cutting off and capturing dozens of Beale's troopers: "Those who surrendered were told by a motion to go to the rear . . . and those who resisted were sabered or shot till they reeled from their saddles, the victor never pausing to see how well his work was done but rushing madly on to engage a new foe."[94] Then Rooney Lee threw in Solomon Williams's 2nd North Carolina, backed by the regrouped 10th Virginia; the positions they vacated were quickly occupied by Lee's only uncommitted outfit, John Chambliss's 13th Virginia. Soon afterward, the advance units of Munford's brigade finally reached the battlefield from Welford's Ford and added their weight to the contest. With this, the Federals gave ground rapidly. Still, they exacted a heavy toll: Colonel Williams was shot dead and General Lee suffered a leg wound that took him out of the fight and ultimately brought him months in a Northern prison camp, he being captured during his convalescence.[95]

Following the loss of their leaders, the Confederates did not press their advantage. Bedeviled by Buford's artillery and sharpshooters, they returned in triumph to their original position, where they found that Colonel Chambliss had relieved the stretcher-borne Rooney Lee.

Their fallback effectively ended the day's combat. As early as 12:10 P.M., Pleasonton had received authority from Hooker to recross the river if conditions warranted; two and a half hours later he had stated his intent to withdraw.[96] Now, at about five o'clock—realizing that Gregg as well as Buford had been fought out, and that Duffié could not play a significant role this late in the day— he saw no reason to prolong the operation. Moreover, he considered his job well done: his men had captured some official papers (probably from Major Beckham's field desk, which had fallen into Union hands early in the fight), and these, Pleasonton claimed, heralded a coming raid into Maryland. This was just the sort of intelligence the cavalry leader believed his superior had sent him to obtain.[97] Then, too, reports from Gregg and other subordinates about the presence of Confederate infantry skirmishers between Culpeper and Brandy Station made Pleasonton believe he had fulfilled another important part of his reconnaissance mission. Lee had indeed sent the 2nd Corps brigade of Brigadier

General Junius Daniel to within supporting distance of Stuart after the latter reported himself facing enemy foot soldiers as well as horsemen. Honoring Lee's wish that they not be used except in an emergency so as not to publicize their location so far west of Fredericksburg, Stuart had kept Daniel's troops in his rear as a reserve.[98]   ·

Covered by Ames's infantry as well as by Russell's (the latter having come up from Kelly's Ford after overawing Robertson), Buford's men recrossed the Rappahannock at Beverly Ford. Their exhausted opponents offered little resistance beyond a desultory cannonade. Soon thereafter, Gregg's command moved eastward from Brandy Station then north to a better crossing site at Rappahannock Ford. During the maneuver its rear was covered by the still fresh division of Duffié. Both fording operations were completed by nine o'clock. The Federals then continued north and east toward the Warrenton–Catlett's Station area. They bivouacked about three miles from the river on some of the same ground they had occupied the previous night.[99]

Throughout, the troopers retreated slowly, deliberately, and defiantly. Though worn and torn, covered by blood, dust, and grime, to a man they considered themselves victors, not vanquished. In virtually every sector of the field they left behind, they had held their own against the Rebel cavaliers, gaining the upper hand more than a few times. At the same time, few would have denigrated the power of the resistance their offensive had met at the hands of Stuart's surprised, hard-pressed, and harrassed squadrons. Such an acknowledgment was the Confederate cavalry's due, for the armies had shared equally in making Brandy Station the most spirited clash of horsemen in North American history.

[4]

Advance to Pennsylvania

THE legacy of Brandy Station—its significance to the cavalry forces of the opposing armies—was difficult to assess. Tactically a draw, it ended with the Confederates holding the field and an edge in statistics. Of the almost 8,000 troopers (and 3,000 infantry) led into battle by Alfred Pleasonton, 866 had become casualties—a great many of them listed as missing, only to rejoin their outfits in subsequent days. In contrast, Stuart had suffered fewer than 500 casualties out of approximately 9,500 effectives on hand. The Rebels had also seized 3 cannon, 142 carbines, 223 pistols, and over 150 sabers left behind by their enemy.[1]

In two of the three major sectors, Stuart's men had given somewhat better than they got; only at Stevensburg had the Federals emerged victorious— mainly through Alfred Duffié's numerical superiority—and even there they had gained no strategic advantage. Moreover, Stuart's legions had prevailed despite being forced on the defensive, despite lacking active infantry support, and despite having to fight dismounted almost as often as in the saddle. Most important, Stuart's stubborn opposition had prevented Pleasonton from fulfilling what Hooker considered to be his main objective. Having suffered 5 percent casualties, the Confederates were neither crippled nor scattered, Pleasonton's claims to the contrary notwithstanding.[2]

Perhaps the most enduring result of the twelve-hour contest was the revelation that the Union cavalry was coming of age, was becoming capable of standing up to its vaunted opponent. It had made Stuart's cavaliers, and the Beau Sabreur himself, look bad more than a few times on 9 June. Numerous Confederate observers took note of this phenomenon and tried to discern its repercussions. General Lee, who on the tenth visited the battlefield to see his wounded son and confer with Stuart, deemed the latter's dispositions "judicious & well planned . . . skillfully managed."[3] Others, in high places and low, voiced different opinions.

Perhaps inevitably, given the height to which a fickle public had raised Stuart, a torrent of criticism and abuse descended upon him in the battle's aftermath. Some reaction was restrained but fraught with anxiety. Wrote a Confederate War Department clerk: "The surprise of Stuart, on the Rappahannock, has chilled every heart. . . . The question is on every tongue—have our generals relaxed in vigilance? If so, sad is the prospect!"[4] Other observers were harsh, even brutal. One Virginia woman sent an indignant letter to Jefferson Davis, in which she called Stuart "nothing more or less than one of those fops, devoting his whole time to his lady friends' company," to the detriment of his military responsibilities.

A greater volume of criticism came from the Fourth Estate. The *Richmond Dispatch* growled about Stuart's ignominious surprise and near rout, the latter avoided by the sheerest of luck. The *Charleston Mercury* took him to task for the very traits that had long amused Confederate sensibilities, including "rollicking, frolicking and running after girls." This journal even converted the prebattle festivities at Culpeper Court House into a night of drunken revelry and attributed the near-defeat of 9 June to its aftereffects.

The Confederate press was just warming up. In its 12 June edition, the *Richmond Examiner* alluded not only to Brandy Station but to Kelly's Ford, claiming that "this puffed up cavalry of the Army of Northern Virginia has been twice, if not three times, surprised. . . . such repeated accidents can be regarded as nothing but the necessary consequences of negligence and bad management. . . . the country pays dearly for the blunders which encourage the enemy to overrun and devastate the land." Even the *Richmond Whig*, one of Stuart's most consistent supporters, blamed him for laxity and overconfidence and suggested that he recoup lost prestige by renewing combat with Pleasonton as quickly as possible.[5]

For his part, the cavalry leader made a public show of unconcern. He possessed far too much pride to admit to himself and his men that they had been outfought at Brandy Station. Two days after the fight, in a congratulatory address to his division, he strove to convince everyone that a lopsided victory had been won: "Comrades! two divisions [*sic*] of the enemy's cavalry and artillery, escorted by a strong force of infantry, tested your mettle and found it proof-steel. Your saber blows, inflicted on that glorious day, have taught them again the weight of Southern vengeance. . . ." His theme continued through numerous purple paragraphs.[6]

It is doubtful that Stuart's experiment in thought control had the desired effect. As one of his officers wrote a few days after the fight: "Brandy Station can hardly be called a *victory*. Stuart was certainly surprised and but for the supreme gallantry of his subordinate officers and the men in his command it would have been a day of disaster and disgrace."[7] Presumably the officer exempted from his praise subordinates such as Beverly Robertson and Thomas Munford, who had performed poorly on the ninth; his comment would then appear valid. So too would the observation of a Virginia trooper that at Brandy

Station the Yankees had proved themselves "foemen worthy of our steel." Much later Major McClellan rendered the famous pronouncement that the battle "*made* the Federal cavalry," in that it gave Pleasonton's men "that confidence in themselves and in their commanders" that permitted future success to come more easily.[8]

To be sure, the cavalrymen now camped about Warrenton and Catlett's Station saw things in the same light. Although they had been handicapped by faulty reconnaissance and ill-timed delays, had failed to bring their maximum weight to bear on any part of the field at a crucial time, and had neither broken up Stuart's division nor sapped the strength it needed for future operations, the booted and spurred youngsters under Pleasonton were jubilant over their recent showing. "We had a great many narrow escapes," a member of the 8th New York wrote his family, "but we gave them the worst of it." A captain in the 3rd Pennsylvania rejoiced that "the Cavalry begins to hold up its head," adding that even Hooker's infantrymen now treated it "with as much respect as they have at [their] command for anybody." And a trooper of the 1st Maine reported that "I never felt so gay in my life as I did . . . at Brandy Station." Many men professed to be mystified by Pleasonton's decision to withdraw. "The enemy seemed badly beaten & did not want to see another fight," thought Ulric Dahlgren.[9]

Favorable reactions to the cavalry's performance soon circulated through the army. "Brandy Station certainly did a great deal to improve the morale of our cavalry," remarked an artillery colonel, "so that they are not now afraid to meet the 'rebs' on equal terms." An infantry surgeon, who had long disparaged horse soldiers, now realized that "the Cavalry is beginning to do good service. . . ." And a grizzled, hawk-nosed corps commander named George Gordon Meade wrote his wife that Brandy Station had been "a very brilliant affair," and that the Union troopers had treated their opponents "pretty severely."[10]

While the newspapers of the South defamed J. E. B. Stuart, the Northern press waxed ecstatic over his adversaries. The *New York Tribune* crowed: "The Confederates begin to find that their boasted cavalry is being overmatched by the Union horsemen. Our troops . . . will make as fine cavalry as can be found in the world." Even the enemy advanced extravagent claims for the horsemen in blue: the *Richmond Examiner* believed that they were "daily learning to despise the mounted troops of the Confederacy."[11]

Some who lauded the cavalry for its performance on 9 June excluded one person from their praise. While several newspapers hailed Alfred Pleasonton's leadership, a number of his own troopers give him no credit at all. The acerbic Captain Adams, writing two days after the fight, declared that "I am sure a good cavalry officer would have whipped Stuart out of his boots; but Pleasonton is not and never will be that." The next day a young Pennsylvania officer, in a letter to a friend, castigated Pleasonton's leadership, called him a "humbug," and wished that "Stoneman was back again." Other members of the army, including Hooker's provost marshal general, felt that the Knight of Romance was returning to first principles by making exaggerated claims about Stuart's destruction. It was significant, however, that even this critic—given to carping about his army's shortcomings—did not deny that Pleasonton's men had won their spurs on 9 June. [12]

* * *

Despite Pleasonton's assertions that the Rebels were no longer in a condition to raid the North—assertions he repeated after the cavalry's return to Warrenton and Catlett's Station on 10 June—General Hooker doubted that a Rebel raid had been preempted at Brandy Station. [13] In fact, the army leader decided that Lee was preparing to encircle his right flank by crossing the river above Fredericksburg—the same move Hooker had made late in April when inaugurating the Chancellorsville campaign. The pity was that Fighting Joe could not count on Lee's effort failing as signally as had his own.

Hooker's first inclination, he told the White House, was to march on Richmond should Lee abandon the Fredericksburg line. Lincoln promptly killed the idea. [14] He did not relish the prospect of Lee moving unmolested through the North; furthermore, he believed the cracking of Richmond's defenses would prove to be a more formidable task than Hooker envisioned. Thus, the latter was left no alternative but to monitor his enemy's movements, and to follow those movements, as closely as possible. [15]

To do this, he required the services of Pleasonton's tired if jubilant troopers. On the eleventh he relieved the cavalry pickets along the Orange & Alexandria east of the Rapphannock with the III Corps. He then sent the horsemen upstream to patrol sectors through which invasion-minded Rebels might pass. [16]

In complying, Pleasonton showed the darker side of his character. Unbeknownst to his superior, he determined to obey only a part of his orders. Convinced that his battle-weary horsemen must remain in camp for renewal and refit, and unwilling to stray far from Stuart's presence near Brandy Station, Pleasonton extended his lines only as far as Waterloo Bridge, some ten miles above Beverly Ford. From there he sent Hooker a series of dispatches that gave the impression his scouts were scanning an area three times as long. On 12 June he resorted to a blatant lie, telling the army leader that he had placed pickets as far west as Chester Gap in the Blue Ridge Mountains—a defile Confederate infanty was passing through that same day! [17] Finally, unable to ignore a flood of reports from local Unionists that Rebels had been seen moving much farther to the north and west (the same rumors bothered Hooker), Pleasonton went as far as to suggest that Stahel's cavalry, now back at Fairfax Court House within view of Washington, be sent to take sightings beyond the Bull Run Mountains. But when the Hungarian complained that he had recently done just that and had found no Rebels, both Pleasonton and Hooker dropped the subject. [18]

Therefore, Pleasonton got the time he wanted to reorganize and refurbish his command. One of his first moves, completed on the eleventh, was to merge Duffié's tiny division into Gregg's, the latter's now being designated the 2nd. Ostensibly he did this in an effort to streamline administration and facilitate tactical maneuvering. But his animus against Duffié—intensified by the Frenchman's poor performance on the ninth—undoubtedly played a part in the change. Dropped to brigade command was the colonel whom Pleasonton would conspicuously omit from his campaign-report list of subordinates worthy of high honors—a list lengthy enough to include Lieutenant Custer and Captains Merritt, Dahlgren, and Farnsworth (the last-named had ably commanded his old outfit, the 8th Illinois, during the early fighting near St. James Church).[19]

Pleasonton demoted Colonel di Cesnola as well. On 11 June the Italian's brigade passed out of existence, its regiments being absorbed by other brigades and he returning to the command of his original outfit, the 4th New York. With Duffié and Cesnola reduced in authority and Percy Wyndham in Washington on convalescent leave, Pleasonton's campaign to rid his corps of foreign-born commanders was progressing well.

Three newcomers rose as the immigrants fell. Two days after Brandy Station George Chapman returned from sick leave to find himself successor to the lamented Grimes Davis.[20] On 13 June, however, Colonel William Gamble of the 8th Illinois also came off leave to rejoin the brigade and by seniority assumed command of it. A native of County Tyrone, the forty-five-year-old Celt did not stir in Alfred Pleasonton the resentment that other foreign-born officers activated. For one thing, he had lived in America since early youth and possessed several years' experience as sergeant major of the 1st U.S. Dragoons. Having left the army in 1843 to practice civil engineering in Chicago, Gamble, with his military background, frizzy sidewhiskers, and florid, beefy face, fit well the image of the old cavalryman. But although he had been active enough to win plaudits on several fields (and had taken a chest wound while leading a charge on the Peninsula), Gamble seemed to lack the aggressiveness, the drive, the love of combat that had made his predecessor, Davis, so formidable in brigade command.[21]

The second new leader, John B. McIntosh, who took Wyndham's brigade, seemed better equipped to handle enlarged responsibilities. Formerly a midshipman, later an officer in the 2nd Dragoons, he belonged to a fighting family with Southern ties and a glorious heritage. Son and great-nephew of military heroes, he was also the brother of General James McQueen McIntosh, killed at Pea Ridge the previous year while commanding Confederate horsemen. John McIntosh had made an enviable reputation of his own in both the Regulars and the volunteers, especially during the Peninsula campaign and at Kelly's Ford. But his roots, his conservative politics, and his continuing friendship with his old commander, the deposed and discredited William Averell, may have worked to deny him a brigadier's star. Now elevated above his permanent position as commander of the 3rd Pennsylvania Cavalry, he finally seemed in a position to win that promotion in name as well as in fact.[22]

The third change in command placed Major Samuel H. Starr of the 6th U.S. Cavalry, a twenty-year veteran of the Mexican and Seminole Wars and frontier service, at the head of the Reserve Brigade. Having rejoined his Regular outfit immediately after Brandy Station following a two-year leave and command of a volunteer infantry regiment, Starr displaced Charles Whiting, whom he ranked by a year's seniority. Though he lacked Whiting's West Point education, Starr possessed an Old Army reputation for dependability without flashiness. Another Irish-American with long experience in dragoon service, "Old Paddy" Starr was known for a violent temper which he was just as likely to unleash against his own men as against the enemy.[23]

While making personnel changes, Pleasonton formally designated John Buford commander of the 1st Division (till now known as Pleasonton's own even though the Kentuckian had effectively asssumed its leadership three weeks ago). At the same time the Reserves became an organic part of the command, officially its 3rd Brigade. The division's composition remained intact with the exception that four companies of the 12th Illinois, recently returned from York-town (their base since the close of Stoneman's raid), were added to Gamble's brigade. Chapman took direct command of them, adding them to the six companies of his own 3rd Indiana.

David Gregg's division took on a new look, its brigades now led by McIntosh, Duffié, and Irvin Gregg. McIntosh was given Wyndham's three regiments, plus his own 3rd Pennsylvania, formerly in Duffié's division. The first three had been so ravaged at Brandy Station that they were soon on their way to the cavalry depot at Alexandria, Virginia, for a wholesale refit, McIntosh accompanying them; they would not return to the corps till 22 June. Duffié, meanwhile, received those regiments recently under Cesnola, plus the 2nd New York, led by another erstwhile brigade leader, Judson Kilpatrick. Irvin Gregg retained his 4th and 16th Pennsylvania while adding the 1st Maine, 10th New York, and Orton's independent company.[24] This shuffling about reduced the bulkiness of the corps and distributed its strength more equitably.

On 11 June Pleasonton also revamped the horse artillery. He sent Robertson's battle-scarred brigade to the Artillery Reserve to replace lost or worn guns, ammunition, equipment, and horses. It proved to be in such poor shape (Martin's battery, for example, had been virtually destroyed at Fleetwood Heights) that it was transferred to Washington for a complete overhaul. To fill in during its absence, Captain Tidball's 2nd Brigade, Regular Division, Artillery Reserve, was attached to the Cavalry Corps. Tidball would prove so indispensable that his command would remain after Robertson's return on 28 June, serving with Buford's division while the latter fought with Gregg's and others' commands.[25]

When not busy with personnel and unit changes, Pleasonton distributed quantities of small arms, sabers, and horse equipments required to offset recent losses. He even managed to exchange inferior carbines (many had fouled or burst from rapid firing on 9 June) for more reliable models sent down by the Ordnance Department. As if not sufficiently occupied, the cavalry leader engaged in sundry ventures including an improbable effort to bribe the Confederate partisan leader John S. Mosby into turning Union spy. This endeavor failed; Mosby, if indeed informed of Pleasonton's overture, spurned it.[26] Though he was inept at operational command, these activities demonstrated that Pleasonton was an organizer, an administrator, and a visionary of the first rank.

***

Pleasonton would have been surprised and chagrined to learn that his enemy's plans had been little affected by Brandy Station. The battle merely persuaded Robert E. Lee not to call on Stuart to escort his main army from Culpeper. While realizing his horsemen would require time to recover from the effects of combat, the army leader saw no reason to postpone his invasion more than a single day. By the morning of the tenth he felt certain that Pleasonton's attack had not signified a general offensive. Early that afternoon he instructed the leader of his invasion vanguard, bald, one-legged Dick Ewell, to resume his arrested movement from Culpeper toward the Shenandoah Valley. A few hours later, the long-awaited march got under sail, the 2nd Corps moving in two columns to Woodville and Gourd Vine Church, then to Sperryville and Gaines's Crossroads, well beyond Pleasonton's right flank. As Ewell started, Longstreet's corps shifted north from Culpeper to cover Hill's move to the latter point from Fredericksburg.[27]

While the infantry marched, Stuart's battered but intact division remained in camp near Brandy Station. Realizing that their refit would not take long, many troopers speculated that they were being held in place as a screen for Ewell. Some fretted over their inactive status, longing to return to action against an enemy to whom they owed a thrashing. No one fretted more than Stuart, who wrote his brother that "I am standing on the Rappahannock, looking beyond . . . and feel not unlike a tiger pausing before its spring. . . ."[28]

During that pause he tended to his wounded as well as to those of the enemy who had fallen into his hands; he culled unfit horses from his command and sent their owners in search of remounts; he distributed captured weapons and materiel to his most underprivileged; and he revamped his command staff to fill gaps recently created. He handled in a routine manner the vacancies caused by the death of Sol Williams and the disabling of Calbraith Butler; those next in seniority received promotions. The only change required in the upper echelon had been made with the elevation of John Chambliss—a darkly handsome thirty-year-old West Pointer, a prewar planter and militia officer, and the son of a Confederate Congressman—to replace the already missed Rooney Lee.[29]

These changes consumed at most a few days. But it would be a full week before Lee would call Stuart from the Rappannock to serve with the marching army. Until that time Stuart could only watch the Union troopers across the river and plot revenge.

***

As Ewell's infantry crossed the river on the tenth and marched northwest toward the Blue Ridge, Lige White's 35th Virginia Battalion provided it with mounted support. Like the rest of Stuart's people the Comanches had passed through a rough time on the ninth. But Ewell, who valued the battalion's services from past association with it, had personally requested its attachment for his march. Colonel White had assented and had refit his unit in record time.[30]

The Comanches constituted the extent of Ewell's cavalry for the first two days of the march, as his columns passed through such locales as Flint Hill, Sandy Hook, and Chester Gap. Not until the twelfth, after the gray vanguard reached Cedarville, in the Shenandoah Valley three miles above Front Royal, did a substantial body of horsemen join "Old Bald Head": the 2,000 men of Albert Jenkins, most of them armed with Enfield rifles and pistols. Along with Jenkins came a single horse battery as well as the cavalry of the "Maryland Line," the 1st Maryland Battalion of Major Harry Gilmor, which, encamped at Fisher's Hill, had been awaiting Ewell's coming.[31]

Ewell met with his new cavalry officers, listened to their reports of local affairs, and determined that no word of his advance had preceded him. The way seemed clear to strike at the first tactical objectives of the invasion—the Union garrison at Winchester (held by 12,000 troops of all arms under General Milroy), plus its eastern and northern outposts at Berryville (1,800 men under Colonel Andrew T. McReynolds) and Martinsburg (Colonel Benjamin F. Smith's 1,200 infantry and horsemen). It was decided that Ewell, with two-thirds of his infantry—the divisions of Jubal A. Early and Edward Johnson—would move against the largest post, a major communications hub and a strategic link between the Eastern and Western Theaters. To ensure that the satellite garrisons did not reinforce Milroy before Ewell's arrival, Jenkins and Gilmor, with the infantry of Major General Robert E. Rodes, would move directly against them. If all went as planned and the garrisons fell, Ewell would remain at Winchester to appropriate spoils and wreck communications while Rodes pushed on to Williamsport, Maryland, along the Potomac River; Ewell would rejoin him there. Jenkins would also move to Williamsport but would continue into Pennsylvania, raiding the Cumberland Valley as far north as Chambersburg. There—unlike Stuart during his raid of the previous autumn—the horsemen would gather foodstuffs and livestock for Lee's army rather than destroy enemy materiel.[32]

Late on 12 June, as Ewell's rear closed up at Cedarville, Rodes and the cavalry marched off to put their commander's strategy to the test. They forged northeastward toward Millwood, fighting off heat and clouds of choking dust. Before evening fell they met their first opponents on the road to Berryville, and the encounter did not augur well for their endeavor. Mildly concerned by rumors of intensified enemy activity in his bailiwick, General Milroy had sent two forces to investigate. Trooping down the Valley Turnpike from Winchester, two squadrons of Colonel James A. Galligher's 13th Pennsylvania Cavalry happened upon Rodes's advance guard—a company from Colonel James Cochran's 14th Virginia, Jenkins's brigade, and one of Harry Gilmor's Maryland companies. Jenkins had failed to provide the detachment with strength sufficient to protect his temporary camp below Middletown. But Major Gilmor, a mustachioed dandy in a gold-spattered uniform, had a reputation as a reckless fighter. He upheld that reputation by opening a fire on the Union column from a tree- and rock-fringed hill alongside the pike.

Galligher's men refused to accept the challenge, as though fearing themselves outnumbered. Leaving behind some dead and wounded, they retreated northward in the fading light. Not content with so easy a victory, Gilmor led his company toward a ridge beyond which the enemy had fled. Not till he topped the rise did he see his error: his opponents had lured him into a trap, set by dozens of deployed comrades and two cannon. Unable to halt in time, several Marylanders were shot out of their saddles by carbine and shell fire. Four were killed and thirty wounded, many being captured; the rest, Gilmor among them, escaped by the sheerest of margins. One of those who fell into Union hands later vowed that "I may be darned ef I'm goin' to foller that thar feller with the spang new yaller clothes any more!"[33]

Fortunately for the Confederates, their captured came from units that had long served in the Shenandoah. When their identity was conveyed to Winchester, Milroy was none the wiser about Ewell's approach. It appeared that the Union commander wished to remain ignorant, for he played deaf to other reports that ought to have alerted him to danger. When the leader of a second scouting force from Winchester, Major Darius Titus of the 12th Pennsylvania Cavalry, informed him of large enemy concentrations in other locales, Milroy dismissed his findings out of hand.[34]

Ewell could not have hoped for a more favorable situation. By late on the thirteenth, when he made contact with Milroy's detachments below the garrison town, it was too late for the Federals to be reinforced. In fact, just as Milroy telegraphed his plight to his superior, Major General Robert C. Schenck, commander of the VIII Corps, his enemy cut the telegraph. From this point on, Ewell's job was easy. That night elements of his infantry, plus attached cavalry from Jenkins's command—Major James H. Nounnan's 16th Virginia—drove Milroy's detachments into his works west of Winchester. There, next day, Early's and Johnson's divisions attacked from the east, south, and west, simultaneously. As infantry and cannon pounded his works, Milroy saw the extent of his helplessness. That night he managed to flee north with about four thousand men, mostly members of his three cavalry regiments. But an equal number of Federals had been killed, wounded, or captured in a futile attempt to defend the town.[35]

Ewell made little effort to run the escapees to earth. This was a mistake, for the War Department detained many of Milroy's troops in southwestern Pennsylvania to resist further Confederate encroachments (though their commander was relieved from duty and his conduct at Winchester investigated).[36] The majority of Ewell's troops remained in the vicinity of their victory, confiscating supplies, wrecking rail and telegraph lines, and paroling captives.

Meanwhile, his subsidiary operations proceeded apace—if not as smoothly or as successfully as those against Milroy. On the thirteenth, Rodes and Jenkins moved from Middletown toward Berryville, via Millwood. Though enjoined to move stealthily, the cavalry's outriders failed to prevent the enemy from detecting their approach and spreading the alarm to Berryville. When Jenkins reached Colonel McReynolds's alert garrison at midday on the thirteenth he drove the forward pickets inside their works and skirmished actively with them. But when Rodes's main body closed up on Berryville one hour later, the division leader found the cavalry fighting a skeleton force holding trenches below the town; McReynolds's main force had massed for a retreat northward, and was no longer engaged. At Rodes's terse command, Jenkins passed to the west while the infantry attacked the opposite side of the place. Again, however, the horsemen moved so clumsily and slowly that the enemy divined their intentions and cleared out. McReynolds's men, together with a long supply train (just the sort of prize for which Ewell hungered), followed for a time roads leading north but then swung west to Winchester, as per a previous arrangement with Milroy. After halting to repulse the forefront of the Rebel pursuit—Jenkins's 36th Virginia Battalion, under Major James W. Sweeney—the fugitives reached Milroy's garrison at dusk. Thus they became part of the force beleaguered and overrun on the fourteenth by Ewell. The only unit from McReynolds's command to escape Winchester before the enemy arrived was a company of the 1st New York Cavalry, under Captain William H. Boyd. This proved costly for the Confederates; in coming weeks Boyd's little band would cause no end of trouble for the invaders of Pennsylvania and Maryland.[37]

After failing to overtake McReynolds's runaways, the troopers under Jenkins compounded their poor performance of 13 June. Late that afternoon, chasing McReynolds's wagon train, they reached the settlement of Bunker Hill, halfway between Martinsburg and Winchester, and found a small local force—four infantry companies under Major W. T. Morris—huddling behind stone walls and breastworks outside town. Allowing himself to be distracted from his quarry, Jenkins determined to bag the garrison. Despite outweighing their opponents twenty to one, however, his men failed to crack Morris's defenses in a series of dismounted assaults. Finally they retreated, unable to pry the enemy out of two churches they had converted into blockhouses and allowing them to join Milroy's garrison at Winchester.[38]

Jenkins also gave up his attempts to capture the train of provisions out of Berryville. With Rodes, he headed north to Martinsburg instead. Infantry and horsemen converged on that vicinity on the morning of the fourteenth. Upon their arrival, the cavalry skirmished with the outpost troops of the town, while Jenkins sent a surrender demand to Colonel Smith and his recently arrived superior, Brigadier General Daniel Tyler. Spurning the demand, the Federals evacuated the town that evening via roads running southeast toward Shepherdstown and Harpers Ferry, losing five cannon and some 150 prisoners. Jenkins pursued almost as far as the Potomac but managed to nab few additional captives.[39]

Though his subsidiary operations had not gone according to blueprint, Dick

Ewell, by nightfall of the fourteenth, had cleared away opposition to his operations in the Valley and to the movements of the troops to follow him. He now gave the go-ahead for Rodes and Jenkins to venture into the Union heartland.

Though Rodes expected Jenkins's advance troops to proceed swiftly to Chambersburg, he was disappointed to learn that the horsemen, after crossing the Potomac at Williamsport early that day, moved like a tortoise on the Maryland side. To some extent, their slowness was attributable to Captain Boyd and his forty-man company of New Yorkers. Having taken up a position to resist the Rebel advance from Winchester, Boyd deployed his men Indian-fashion in front of Jenkins's brigade and employed hit-and-run tactics against it throughout the day.

Reaching Hagerstown, Maryland, about midday, Jenkins was pleasantly surprised by his cordial reception. Though represented by a star in the Confederate flag, Maryland was a border state whose people had given a cold greeting to the Army of Northern Virginia during the Antietam campaign. After partaking briefly of the local hospitality, the Rebels pushed across the Pennsylvania line toward the village of Greencastle. There, despite his past residency in the Commonwealth, Jenkins met a less friendly reception. Still, though braced for an encounter with militia or embattled-farmer types, he was opposed only by stragglers from Milroy's command, retreating through the village. When Jenkins's advance loosed a few rounds from their Enfields, the Federals hastened their flight, though one luckless officer, slow to withdraw, fell captive.

Although advance word of his coming had enabled farmers to spirit away goods and livestock, Jenkins sent detachments to scour the countryside for beef on the hoof. In and near Greencastle, he also confiscated farm and carriage horses for use as battery animals and wagon teams; then his men torched rolling stock on a nearby railroad. These first blows of the campaign gave great satisfaction to his Virginians, who had seen their own state ravaged by two years of war.[40]

Their work well done, the invaders took leave of the good folk of Greencastle, and, driving a small herd of cattle before them, moved northward toward Chambersburg, seat of Franklin County. The five-mile ride took the troopers through rich pastureland and past rolling hills dotted by whitewashed barns, some of which bore hex signs and the image of that legendary fowl, Distelfink. The rigors of the march were eased by side-trips by detachments seeking pigs, hams, chickens, geese, and any homemade delicacies they might extort from the populace.

At 11:30 in the evening, Jenkins's advance reached the environs of Chambersburg. Having been warned by local Paul Reveres that "the Rebels are coming," the townspeople were prepared for his entrance. As the general's point riders trotted down the dark streets, someone with a pistol fired on them, and townspeople burst from their homes and captured a pair of Rebel lieutenants. Infuriated, Jenkins charged into the town under a heavy escort and freed his subordinates. Then, reported one villager, his "angry voice was heard, up and down Main Street, proclaiming in thunder tones that with any more firing on the part of the citizens, he would instantly burn the town." Soon his provost marshals were bustling about to enforce his decree; by the time his main body rode in, suspected assailants had been apprehended, stores and houses had been placed under guard, and the main street had been cordoned off. Since the shooting had injured no one, the troopers passed through town without harming it, bivouacking in clover fields two miles to the north. Making himself as comfortable as conditions permitted, Jenkins settled back to await Rodes's and Ewell's arrival.[41]

While in Chambersburg some of the invaders plundered private property, not only ransacking homes in search of items of use to the army, but hunting for "fugitive" blacks they might return to slavery in the South. Such items as they felt obliged to purchase from local merchants they paid for in Confederate currency. One realistic inhabitant, the editor-politician Alexander K. McClure, remarked with tongue in cheek: "True, the system of Jenkins would be considered a little informal in business circles; but it's his way, and our people agreed to it perhaps, to some extent, because of the novelty, but mainly because of the necessity of the thing."[42]

Despite such conduct, the visitors were well tolerated by the natives, some of whom professed to find Jenkins just, prudent, even amiable—a better man than a soldier. On his part, he enforced, more or less strictly, prohibitions against looting and carousing. No woman or child was molested during his stay and most citizens were allowed—within obvious confines—to go about their daily business.

Even with these prohibitions, by the morning of the seventeenth Jenkins had amassed a considerable body of plunder. He had even wrung $900 from the municipal treasury to compensate troopers whose horses had been "stolen" by locals. (In a cunning maneuver, the irony of which must have tickled him, the burgesses voted to pay Jenkins in the same depreciated money with which his men had papered the town.) Jenkins had also wrecked local transportation facilities, including the Cumberland Valley Railroad bridge at Scotland, almost four miles northeast of Chambersburg. And he had downed telegraph cable to slow the spread of news about his presence in Franklin County. This, however, had not prevented residents from alerting the rest of the valley to his operations. Tales that magnified his numbers and ferocity sent a wave of panic rolling through southern Pennsylvania but also pricked the curiosity of less nervous residents.[43]

As a result, on the morning of the seventeenth Jenkins's pickets advised him of the approach of a large, unidentified force from the north. Rumor had it made up of militia from neighboring localities, or even elements of the Army of the Potomac, come to rid Pennsylvania of the invader.

Jenkins was wont to lose his head in a crisis, and he did so now. Yanking in his detachments and gathering up his booty, he led his brigade through town at a rapid gait, heading for the Maryland border.[44] By departing so abruptly, he

left behind numerous head of cattle and horseflesh. Not until he reached Greencastle after nightfall did he consider himself beyond harm's range. There, he felt
safe enough to dispatch a 250-man unit under his senior regimental commander,
the battle-scarred Colonel Ferguson, to move west of Cove Mountain and search
the McConnellsburg region for additional spoils.[45]

This expedition proved nearly as successful as the foray into Franklin
County. Reaching McConnellsburg on the nineteenth, Ferguson's men
confiscated an array of spoils including shoes, clothes, and hardware. Of more
interest to Jenkins, on their return to Greencastle the raiders drove before them
a herd of cattle worth an estimated $11,000, plus 120 horses. En route, Fergu-
son stopped at Mercersburg, nine miles east of McConnellsburg, his men entering the town "with pointed pistols and drawn sabres." During their brief
occupation, the horsemen added to their haul, while their commander debated
politics with a professor at the local theological seminary. Their depredations
completed, the raiders departed town in a haughty, defiant mood that left
Ferguson's host "deeply humbled and ashamed" by his government's inability
to protect its people.[46]

While Colonel Ferguson cut a swath to the west, Jenkins decided that he was
not safe enough in Greencastle, after all; thus he resumed his retreat, moving
back to Williamsport. There he linked with Rodes's troops, to whom he relayed
the plunder obtained in Franklin County. Rodes accepted the booty without
comment, though obviously displeased by Jenkins's fallback. The division
leader grew even more disgusted when it became known that the cavalry had
not been chased out of Chambersburg by armed opponents. The mob seen
advancing there two days before had contained only curious locals, wishing to
observe the fearsome Rebels at close range. The majority were old men and
boys, not one of whom carried a weapon.[47]

***

For three days after Ewell departed Culpeper, Alfred Pleasonton remained
on the Rappahannock, certain that no Rebel had left his front. He was as-
tounded, therefore, when credible informants brought him word on 13 June
that Ewell had flanked the cavalry by marching north and west toward Sperryville. Relaying the news to army headquarters, he was ordered by Hooker to
"post us very quickly when and where they went."[48] Pleasonton could not or
would not do so; for one thing, he did not entirely credit the report. Stuart's
continued presence across the river militated against the theory that Lee's army
was in motion westward; surely the cavalry would have screened such a movement. The extent of Pleasonton's response was his renewed suggestion that
Stahel be directed to scout the Shenandoah Valley for the enemy; the Cavalry
Corps, he implied, had more important work to do.

Pleasonton's do-nothing attitude rankled his superior, especially later that
day when Hooker learned from the War Department that Milroy had called for

help against Ewell. At once Hooker issued orders to move the right wing of his army—the I, III, and V Corps, under Major General John F. Reynolds—northward; attached cavalry, with a light battery, would then range as far westward as Thoroughfare Gap in the Bull Run Mountains. Soon Fighting Joe decided to relocate his entire army along the Orange & Alexandria line in the vicinity of Manassas Junction.[49]

While his men concluded their seven-month residency at Falmouth, Hooker determined to pitch his headquarters at Fairfax Station, a point equidistant between the Rebels known to remain on the Rappahannock and the assumed location of Ewell's people. To spearhead the shift, Buford's division was hauled out of its camp at Catlett's Station very late on the thirteenth and much of it was shoved toward Thoroughfare Gap as Hooker had ordered. Then David Gregg's recently enlarged command hit the road, on the fifteenth reaching the vicinity of the Bull Run battlefields, where Buford joined it.[50] The littered ground that marked the site of past Union defeats seemed a gloomy omen, but it also held a macabre fascination for Gregg's men. A trooper from Maine noted that "the bones of those who had been killed . . . were all sticking out of their graves—skull bones, old knapsacks and cannon balls lay in great confusion. . . . oh how desolate that place looks. I shuddered while we were on it."[51]

On this ground and nearby, Buford and Gregg spent forty-eight hours searching westward for traces of their adversaries. As Hooker joined them and set up his supply base, trains rolled in from Alexandria with rations and materiel. From their contents Pleasonton completed the refit begun immediately after Brandy Station by doling out ordnance stores. Much of Buford's division was outfitted with the highly prized Spencer rifle.[52]

Hooker sought additional work for his horsemen early on the sixteenth, after Washington notified him that Rebels had been sighted in central Pennsylvania, destroying and stealing. Circumventing Henry Halleck, who had miffed him by pooh-poohing his earlier suggestions that Lee might march, Hooker asked Lincoln if he ought not send Pleasonton across the Potomac to strike the head of the Rebel vanguard; Stahel could guard the army's flanks and rear in the interim. The president replied as Hooker feared Halleck would have: the army must continue to screen the capital and the population centers of the North. Perceiving Halleck's hand in the president's rejoinder, Hooker acquiesced grudgingly.[53]

He soon found another job for Pleasonton's men. Late on the sixteenth, with much of the army closed up near Fairfax Station, the remainder of it en route, Hooker ordered Gregg, followed by Buford, to proceed west to Aldie Gap.[54] This was a Bull Run Mountain pass that gave access to the Loudoun Valley, a direct corridor to the Shenandoah. From Aldie, some thirty miles northwest of army headquarters, the troopers could fan out toward Winchester and other suspected Confederate points of call. If they could not find Ewell, they might at least locate his line of communications with Lee. That line cut, Ewell would probably fall back south. Could he accomplish this, Pleasonton would largely atone for his recent sins of omission and commission.

***

When Lee at Culpeper saw Hooker pull northward on the thirteenth and fourteenth, he realized the time had come to send Longstreet, Hill, and Stuart on their way. At dawn on the fifteenth, having positioned units so as to permit Hill to disengage from Fredericksburg, the army took to the road.[55] By late in the day, Hill's rear guard cleared its old campgrounds and closed up on the right of the 1st Corps, already in motion. The corps moved north and west, Hill's in the wake of Ewell's column, Longstreet's some twenty miles farther east. By temporarily marching east of the Blue Ridge, Longstreet would not only screen Hill but would confuse enemy countermovements by masking the objective of the invasion until the campaign was well advanced.

Now that Pleasonton had abandoned the Rappahannock, Stuart made last-minute preparations to join his infantry friends. Though originally intended to guard the advance of Longstreet's corps, the cavalry was blocked by wagon trains that clogged the parallel roads, forcing it to wait till early on the sixteenth to depart Brandy Station. Even then, only a part of the division forded the river twenty miles beyond the most recent location of Hooker's right flank. The brigade under Munford (Fitz Lee accompanying it in an ambulance) crossed at Rock Ford, while those of Robertson and Chambliss splashed over the Hazel River near Hinson's Mill. Left behind were Jones and Hampton, the former to picket Hazel River for another day, the latter to hold the line farther south until the twentieth, then to join Stuart as his rear guard. Also lost to Stuart (in addition to Lige White's Comanches) was Major Charles R. Collins's 15th Virginia, Chambliss's brigade, which would remain on the lower Rappahannock, guarding the army's old base of operations, throughout the campaign.[56]

Although at less than maximum strength, J. E. B. Stuart was again in motion, heading north on a journey that would furnish the most significant service of his military career. After a week of clawing at his bars, the tiger had sprung into action.

[5]
Aldie and Middleburg

BY the morning of 17 June Stuart's division, as well as the majority of Lee's infantry, formed a discontinuous line thirty miles long from the Rappahannock to Salem, Virginia, in the heart of the Loudoun Valley. Having ridden hard through the previous day to reach the head of this line, the Beau Sabreur now moved to block gaps by which the Yankees east of the Bull Run Mountains might pass into the Shenandoah, there to spy on the moving columns of Confederate foot troops. Stuart had decided to form a two-ply counterreconnaissance screen, neither layer of which the enemy should be able to penetrate.

Stuart realized that, although no contact had been established, Pleasonton's corps must be moving toward him. Early that day John Mosby had brought him word, based on careful scouting by his partisan rangers, that the Yankees were marching parallel to Lee's columns, but far to the east. Mosby added that thus far only small mounted bands had reached the Loudoun Valley, part of what was known as "Mosby's Confederacy."[1] Stuart foresaw, even so, that a clash of arms was imminent. Thus the cavalry commander prepared to take a place in the background, from which to observe the capabilities of his new subordinates—Chambliss, Munford, Robertson, and Jones—who would supervise the screening and the fighting. Much would depend on how well these leaders did in semi-independent command; Stuart needed to acquaint himself better with their strengths and weaknesses so as to activate the former and suppress the latter during the balance of the campaign.[2]

He rode with Munford's command as far as Middleburg, a picturesque village in Virginia's horse-breeding country adjacent to Aldie Gap, at the northern terminus of the Bull Run Mountains. There he pitched camp, while sending Munford toward the pass's namesake village, a logical route of enemy approach. Simultaneously he ordered Chambliss's brigade toward larger and more accessible Thoroughfare Gap, about a dozen miles below Aldie. Robertson's demi-brigade he ordered to Rectortown, approximately equidistant from the mountain defiles, from which it might aid either of its comrades in a crisis.

The seventeenth was fair and mild, a light breeze penetrating the springtime heat, and Munford's riders passed westward across land abounding in wheat, clover, and gentle ridges crowned with oak and pine. The colonel's men, many of them natives of this region, swore that the Shenandoah, for all its legendary splendor, boasted no greater beauty.

The lush pasturage invited troopers to replenish haversacks and feed bags. Munford's brigade having had, as Stuart admitted, "very little food" since leaving Brandy Station, Stuart permitted it to send pickets ahead to Aldie while it moved northwest of the village to partake of a corn crop which a farmer named Carter had agreed to sell Stuart.[3] A second detachment, Colonel Wickham's 4th Virginia and the 1st Virginia of Colonel James H. Drake, along with the battery of Captain Breathed, proceeded along a valley road to Dover Mills, a mile and a half due west of Aldie. Near the granary, troopers and cannoneers found tall grass and a clear stream, at which their horses slaked hunger and thirst. While this took place, a third detachment, Tom Rosser's 5th Virginia, moved toward Aldie to bivouack west of it, just inside the valley.

After sighting a fertile glen that would do for a camp, Rosser, about 4:00 P.M., continued the march to Aldie Gap, Wickham, Drake, and Breathed to meet him there when finished at Dover Mills. Less than a mile after starting out, however, Rosser was brought up short by the crack of carbines and the sight of gray-clad troopers charging toward him. Munford's advance detachment had been driven through Aldie by enemy troopers who had muscled their way past the gap from the east.[4] The confrontation in Loudoun Valley had come sooner than expected.

***

"Put the main body of your command in the vicinity of Aldie," Hooker had ordered Pleasonton that morning. For a change, the cavalry leader complied quickly and fully. Even today, however, he carried out his orders in a manner that portended failure.

At botton, Pleasonton did not understand what Hooker required of him. This was his own fault, for the army commander had tried to impress on him the importance of finding Lee's main army and determining its direction. This required Pleasonton to locate and shatter Stuart's counterreconnaissance barrier, but he acted as though expected to smash Stuart in battle. Even now, as he moved north on the right side of the mountains, Pleasonton was planning another lesson in violence for the troopers he felt he had bested at Brandy Station. But he did not expect a clash just yet; like Hooker and just about everyone else at army headquarters, Pleasonton supposed that Aldie and vicinity—in fact, the entire Loudoun Valley—was free of Rebels. They blithely assumed that none of Lee's people was east of the Blue Ridge.[5]

When moving out of the Fairfax–Bull Run area, Pleasonton sent detachments ranging west toward the Shenandoah. But their small size suggested the relative unimportance he assigned to the mission—as did his choice of leaders. Early on the seventeenth, for example, he sent Colonel Duffié toward Thoroughfare Gap, thence to Middleburg, to scout the Loudoun Valley. After spending the evening at Middleburg, Duffié was to march toward the Shenandoah, sniffing about Snicker's and Ashby's Gaps for Lee's scent. The Frenchman was then to curl north, rejoining the corps near Noland's Ferry, along the Potomac, by the evening of the eighteenth. Duffié must accomplish all of this with the three hundred sabers of his 1st Rhode Island, to the command of which he had been dropped on the fourteenth. His replacement as brigade leader was Judson Kilpatrick, who had just been appointed a brigadier, largely as a result of the notice he had won on Stoneman's Raid and at Brandy Station.[6]

It seems astonishing that Pleasonton expected Duffié, with such a slim force, to cover so many miles of unknown territory, so far from his support forces. It is no less astonishing that Pleasonton took for granted his own ability to cut through two mountain chains and perhaps also enemy forces in time to meet the Frenchman next evening. The timetable set for Duffié to rejoin the corps was absurdly rigid, given those factors beyond the control of either officer likely to intervene. Manifestly, Pleasonton's animus had resulted in Duffié's assignment to a suicide mission. As soon as Pleasonton sent the colonel on his way, he forgot about him and made no attempt to cover his operations.[7]

Gregg's division led the march toward Aldie through dust that lay inches deep on the road. Just shy of noon, Pleasonton directed him to send another scouting force to the gap in advance of the main force. It would pass through Loudoun in a southwesterly direction toward Front Royal, thence (like Duffié) northward to Noland's Ferry. For the mission Gregg told off the newly minted general, Kilpatrick, and his men. The latter included Kilpatrick's old 2nd New York, which aimed to make the most of the assignment. The regiment was downhearted over its repulse on Fleetwood Heights; supposedly, its men had urged Kill-cavalry to employ them in front-line combat as soon as possible, so they might make amends.[8]

The 2nd New York, leading Kilpatrick's advance, found an early opportunity to prove its sincerity. Drawing within sight of Aldie Gap about 4:00 P.M., the New Yorkers spied Rosser's pickets marching toward them less than a mile off. The regimental commander, Lieutenant Colonel Otto Harhaus (Henry E. Davies, promoted colonel the previous day, had left the regiment on sick leave, not to return till August),[9] sent the squadron of Lieutenant Daniel Whittaker to challenge the Rebels. Sabers and pistols raised, Whittaker's people chased the outnumbered enemy through the gap onto the Little River Turnpike, the lower of two roads that forked westward toward the Blue Ridge. Shooting past the dozen houses that comprised the town of Aldie, the Confederates made for the safety of their comrades near Dover Mills.[10]

The New York squadron never reached its quarry. Just inside Loudoun Valley Whittaker halted to meet the counterattacking 5th Virginia, Thomas

Rosser at its forefront. Countercharge repulsed charge, regiment overwhelmed squadron; after a flurry of swordplay, the New Yorkers fell back on the main body of their regiment.

When Rosser failed to pursue, Kilpatrick caught up to his old outfit, which gave way before his attached artillery: two guns from Alanson Randol's E/G, 1st U.S. Artillery. To protect Randol's 3-inch ordnance rifles, which he placed along the more northerly Snickersville road, Kilpatrick chose not the 2nd but the 4th New York, under Colonel di Cesnola.

As the polyglot regiment fell in on the cannon's flanks, the 5th Virginia backed out of range. Rosser then dismounted part of Captain Reuben F. Boston's squadron and deployed it behind some haystacks to the east and west of the DiSierga farm, which sat just above the turnpike, about three-quarters of a mile west of Aldie. The bulk of the regiment, under Rosser's supervision, trotted even farther west, and later moved crosscountry to the end of the road on which Randol had unlimbered.[11]

His view constricted by the high ground between him and Rosser, Judson Kilpatrick believed the Snickersville road free of the enemy but for a few forward pickets. This route seemed the best way to flank Rosser's dismounted troopers to the south. So thinking, the young general called up one squadron of Colonel Curtis's 1st Massachusetts and advanced it 350 yards along the road. At that point, the sixty-man unit was to halt and await supports.[12]

Instead, thanks to the squadron commander, Kilpatrick's strategy fell apart. Captain Lucius M. Sargent, Jr., regarded by fellow officers as sometimes lacking in sound judgment,[13] ranged beyond his assigned position to pursue the enemy pickets in his front. His squadron broke into the same sort of unauthorized charge another element of the regiment had made at Stevensburg on 9 June. Topping the rise to the west, the Bay Staters were suddenly scorched by the fire of Rosser's marksmen, hiding behind a stone wall north of the road. Realizing his error, Sargent too late tried to flee. Only minutes before, the head of Wickham's 4th Virginia had reached the field from Dover Mills, with Colonel Drake's 1st Virginia in its rear. Now Wickham placed the 1st just above the Little River Turnpike about a half-mile west of the DiSierga farm; with his own regiment, plus two Blakely rifles of Breathed's battery, he raced north to the Snickersville road to smite the men of Massachusetts.[14]

Sargent's men were overtaken before they reach the security of Randol's cannon. They turned about and the result was one of the fiercest saber battles of the war. Watching from the rear, Count Ferdinand von Zeppelin, German military observer at Pleasonton's headquarters, was impressed by the "brandishing and slashing of swords on all sides." After a few minutes the outnumbered Federals broke free and galloped eastward, many with head wounds.[15] Those slashed or shot included Sargent, Lieutenant George Fillebrown, and Major Henry Lee Higginson, the latter having been sent by Curtis in a vain effort to extricate the squadron. Then the squadron of Charles F. Adams, Jr., was thrown in to rescue Higginson. Predictably, it too was cut up, as were still other detachments of the regiment, sent to support it. The captain lamented that "my poor men were just slaughtered and all we could do was to stand and be shot down, while the other squadrons rallied behind us. The men fell right and left and the horses were shot through and through." His unit lost forty of its ninety-four men. Though Adams himself escaped injury, almost every other officer of his regiment engaged went down severely wounded; many, Sargent included, fell into Rebel hands.[16]

Their enemy sufficiently bloodied, the 4th Virginia drew off toward the west. Instead of sending fresh troops to follow the withdrawal, Kilpatrick shifted his attention to the Little River Turnpike. Deciding to pry Boston's sharpshooters from the DiSierga farm, the new brigadier sent two companies of the 2nd New York out that road to draw their fire. He then gave the rest of the Harris Light its chance to atone for Fleetwood Heights. As he had done on the latter occasion for benefit of the 1st Maine, Kilpatrick (the valedictorian of his West Point class) orated to the New Yorkers. Enjoining them to cleanse the stain from their record in one dashing, determined stroke, he jabbed his saber toward DiSierga's place and cried: "Go! Take *that position!*"[17]

This was a tall order, but if pluck counted for anything there was room for optimism. Tearing down rail fences that blocked the way, a fresh squadron of the regiment charged gamely up the pike, absorbing a stiff fire from Boston's men as well as from the third and fourth guns of Breathed's battery, which had unlimbered to the rear near the 1st Virginia. The combination proved so formidable that after suffering many casualties the squadron raced back short of its objective.

Kilpatrick tried again—with new strategy—but again he used a fragment of his force. Five companies of the 2nd New York, Captain Henry Grinton leading, went up the Snickersville road a short distance before veering south into Boston's left flank. While they occupied the sharpshooters' attention, William Stedman's 6th Ohio bounded along the lower road, cut between Boston's main force and the line of haystacks, and advanced against the Rebel left.[18] Dismounting and crawling through the wheat, part of the Ohio regiment surrounded the haystacks, while the remainder confronted Boston's main position. His force already depleted by errant rounds from Breathed's guns, Captain Boston surrendered with forty of his men (he himself broke loose and fled to freedom). In the melee, the 6th Ohio suffered almost as heavily as he, including the mortal wounding of Major Stanhope.[19]

No sooner did the fighting on the turnpike tail off than Kilpatrick resumed the fight along the upper road. He did so by calling up the only unused squadron of the 1st Massachusetts, that of Lieutenant Charles G. Davis, and by moving the 4th New York to its support.[20] With the appearance of these units, the advantage returned to the Federals. So it must have seemed, at least, to Thomas Munford, who had just arrived to take command of the Confederate line. His grip on the turnpike broken, he must hold the Snickersville road by any strategem. But the fighting had nearly exhausted his regiments on hand, who had battled a seemingly endless succession of Yankees attacking their front and flanks. Two other outfits from his brigade, Lieutenant Colonel James W.

Watts's 2nd and Colonel Thomas H. Owen's 3rd Virginia, had not reached the scene. Munford's only uncommitted unit on the field was Drake's 1st Virginia (J. E. B. Stuart's original outfit), but this he wished to reserve as a means of securing a retreat route. Watching the new Federals make preparations for a charge, Munford must have envisioned ending his first battle in brigade command by being swept from the field.

At that minute, however, the colonel swung about in response to activity farther west. Relief flooded over him when he saw Watts's and Owen's regiments hastening up the Snickersville road.

When the new arrivals came abreast of the walls occupied by Rosser, Munford bolstered his men with two dismounted companies of the 2nd Virginia, supported by a squadron of the 3rd. Afterward, he ordered Lieutenant Colonel Watts to lead the rest of his outfit in a charge downhill against Kilpatrick's front. Watts spurred forward, even as Lieutenant Davis did the same at the other end of the road. The result was the bone-jarring crunch of columns colliding head-on.

Though Watts held a heavy advantage in manpower, the impact stunned his leading ranks. Wounded Confederates, including Watts himself, staggered off into fields on either side of the road. Others rallied and finally shoved back Davis's men, while the 3rd Virginia's main body passed to the flanks and shot and sabered the Federals' supports, aided by Rosser's marksmen.[21] "In a moment," recalled the historian of Davis's regiment, "the road was full of dead and dying horses and men, piled up in an inextricable mass. . . . All who were not killed were captured, except a very few of those in the rear of the squadron." When the dust cleared, the 1st Massachusetts had suffered seventy-seven members killed and wounded, the most to be lost in combat by any Union cavalry regiment during the campaign. Captain Adams attributed the loss not to enemy tenacity but to the "incompetence or jealousies of [our] Generals."[22]

As Davis's survivors limped eastward, Munford's frame of mind improved. H. B. McClellan speculated that Munford "now felt that his position was secure against an attack of cavalry, and there was nothing he more desired than that the enemy should wear himself out against it. His flanks were secured by the Little River and its tributaries. The enemy must necessarily attack his front. . . . Munford felt that unless his cavalry failed in their duty his dismounted men were perfectly secure."[23]

Judson Kilpatrick did see the necessity of striking his foe head-on, and soon: the day was drawing to a close and darkness would halt operations. In an almost desperate effort to regain the upper hand before too late, he sent in the 4th New York, unsupported. Though at last willing to attack with an entire regiment, he was still fighting piecemeal. This was unnecessary, for the rest of Gregg's division was now massing in his rear. For his part, David Gregg did not attempt to persuade Kilpatrick otherwise; he merely lent him the lead regiment of Irvin Gregg's brigade, the 1st Maine.[24] Having employed the latter at the eleventh hour at Brandy Station, Kilpatrick planned to use it in a similar role today if Cesnola's regiment failed in its effort.

It did fail, but through no fault of its leader. When called upon to attack up the Snickersville road, Cesnola was not with the outfit. Recently placed in arrest—apparently the result of a clash of temperaments with his new brigade leader—the colonel could not bear the sight of his men riding into combat without him. Flanked by provost guards, he rode up to his superior and begged to be permitted to lead the charge, with or without the sidearms Kilpatrick had stripped from him. Abashed, then regretful, the younger officer handed Cesnola his own saber, remarking: "Colonel, you are a brave man; you are released from arrest" (the *New York Times* heard him add, staring at the sword: "Bring it back bloody!")[25]

Even with his comforting presence, Cesnola's regiment was not equal to such a forlorn-hope assault as this. Soon after starting up the road past signs of earlier carnage, it lost cohesion, its men peeling off to right and left. Unlike Williams Wickham at Stevensburg, the regimental commander completed the charge alone, racing into the waiting arms of the 2nd Virginia. He was rewarded with ten months' confinement in Libby Prison. Presumably, Kilpatrick never saw his sword again.[26]

As if its squeamishness was not embarrassing enough, the 4th New York, in its race for the rear, blundered into units of the 1st Massachusetts that had regrouped farther east. An even greater panic and a larger stampede ensued, placing Kilpatrick's upper flank on the verge of collapse. To hasten events, Munford sent Colonel Owen's regiment, supported by parts of the 2nd and 5th Virginia, against the fugitives. The regiment responded so boldly that he termed the result "the most spirited charge of the day." Hearing the clang of doom, Kilpatrick galloped back to the 1st Maine, borrowed a sword from someone, and led Colonel Douty's men into the fight.

Answering his fervent wish, the 1st Maine swept all before it. Beyond easy support, its energy drained from pummeling Davis's men and then Cesnola's, the 3rd Virginia barely resisted as Douty's people surrounded and slashed at it in the gathering shadows.[27]

One of the slashers was George Armstrong Custer, who had received Kilpatrick's permission to enter another battle as a combatant. As at Brandy Station, he was troubled by a skittish steed. Unnerved by the thundering force of Douty's charge, "Harry" stampeded, carrying Custer to the forefront of the fray. This time the lieutenant turned the predicament to his advantage, slamming into two enemy riders and cutting them out of their saddles with his long Toledo blade. As his horse continued its gallop, the staff officer charged through the rest of the enemy outfit, seeking an exit. At last gaining control, he burst out the other flank, circled the field, and returned to Kilpatrick's headquarters. Overserving his gyrations—and unaware that they were uncontrolled—admiring newspaper correspondents depicted Custer as a hero of the battle.[28]

Having taken enough punishment, the 3rd Virginia emulated Custer's rapid retreat. In its wake, elements of the 2nd New York and 1st Massachusetts aided the men of Maine in driving the sharpshooters of the 5th Virginia from their stone wall. When parts of 4th Virginia and other units, all under Captain William B. Newton, came up to help Owen withdraw, the Federal units, tired but exhilarated, made no protest.[29]

Watching from the rear, General Gregg let the enemy go without further molestation. The darkness deterred further combat, and he was concerned by the three-hundred-odd casualties Kilpatrick and the 1st Maine had suffered; they included Colonel Douty, who had been killed during the final spate of fighting at the stone wall. In his battle report, Colonel Munford claimed that "I have never seen as many Yankees killed in the same space of ground in any fight." In fact, the 1st Massachusetts had been so severely battered that for the next ten days it was not used in active campaigning.[30]

Having sustained only 119 losses, Munford had reason to consider himself the victor, not the vanquished as he had feared.[31] He had fought most of the battle with only a portion of his widely scattered brigade against a more numerous enemy with reinforcements within range. He could also claim to have retired not because overwhelmed but in response to a dispatch from Stuart recalling him to Middleburg. Throughout the fight both he and Rosser had displayed a greater tactical ability than Kilpatrick or Gregg, artfully shifting troops to cover exposed points on an extended line. They had escaped destruction mainly because their adversaries fed in units piecemeal rather than in powerful combinations. This practice, followed by Union commanders since First Bull Run, indicated that the Cavalry Corps, Army of the Potomac, had not quite come of age, tactically.

Even so, Kilpatrick, Gregg, Pleasonton, and other observers including Count von Zeppelin viewed Aldie as a Union victory, another sign that the horsemen in blue had attained parity with Stuart's best. Unlike Brandy Station, the Confederates had retreated from this field, after absorbing a terrible beating. Next day Pleasonton announced in a letter to Congressman Farnsworth that "we smashed Fitz Hugh Lee's [sic] brigade considerable," doubtless closing out Stuart's part in Lee's invasion.[32]

The Knight of Romance had already bragged too much. On the evening of the seventeenth and early on the eighteenth, based on his short-range reconnaissance missions of recent days, he had declared to Hooker that no Confederate infantry worth mentioning lay east of the Blue Ridge. But at that very hour Longstreet's corps was encamped in Stuart's rear, in the heart of the Loudoun Valley. It had reached there prior to the combat at Aldie and it would not pass into the Shenandoah until next morning.[33]

***

The 275 Rhode Islanders under Colonel Duffié who left Manassas Junction that morning were unaware of any enemy presence in Loudoun. Therefore they started toward the Bull Run Mountains in high spirits. "They whistled and sang," a bugler recalled, "they bantered [with] one another, they jested. . . ."

The beautiful weather and the interesting country conspired to keep the mood gay until late in the morning, when the whistling and joking died out.[34]

About 9:30 A.M., entering Loudoun Valley via Thoroughfare Gap, Duffié's point riders met opposition from an equal number of Rebel cavalrymen, members of Lieutenant Colonel William H. F. Payne's 2nd North Carolina of Chambliss's brigade. Formed in skirmish lines near the town of Salem, just west of Thoroughfare, the Rebels created little trouble for the invaders but worried them a great deal. Required by his rigid timetable to hasten to Middleburg, Duffié threw one company toward the west, dismounted it in a wheatfield near Payne's position, and left it to occupy him. Shortly before noon, Duffié led his main force north to Hopewell.[35]

As the New Englanders feared, Payne's detachment indicated Stuart's nearness to them. The bulk of Chambliss's command, only a few miles in Payne's rear, would have attacked Duffié had not Chambliss refused to believe that the Union command would send a single unsupported regiment into this no-man's land. Expecting other Yankees to appear in its rear, he remained to receive them.

For Duffié, bad news accumulated quickly. Just shy of Hopewell, his advance guard captured a Rebel scout who boasted that two thousand horsemen and four cannon under Stuart were in the area. Though the colonel did not credit the tale, he moved warily through the village. He marched so slowly that he did not reach the Middleburg vicinity until 4:00 P.M. There he learned that his informant had spoken the truth.[36]

***

Early that morning, after leaving Robertson's brigade at Rector's Cross Roads and sending Munford's toward Aldie Gap, Stuart had proceeded to Middleburg, setting up headquarters in an area that had seen several skirmishes between his men and Pleasonton's the previous autumn. He began to coordinate operations among his scattered forces, tended by his staff and two squadrons of Chambliss's troopers—the only line units within several miles of the town.[37]

The escort proved its value by shielding the Beau Sabreur from his adoring public. Barely had he dismounted in the main street than the citizenry mobbed him. So many pretty girls flitted about Stuart, wrote Heros von Borcke, that "the scene looked like a dance around a maypole." Stuart's four companies proved even more valuable when, shortly after four o'clock, the happy scene was darkened by the arrival of pickets, shouting word of Duffié's approach. The warning almost came too late: Stuart and his band jumped aboard their horses and raced out the east end of town just as Captain Frank Allen's squadron of the 1st Rhode Island charged in from the south, scattering residents in its path. Unable to clear the town in time, the rear of Stuart's escort fought a desperate delaying action, enabling their charge to escape with hide intact.[38]

As Duffié's regiment flooded into the village, Stuart raced toward Rector's

Cross Roads, his anger boiling over. For the second time in eight days he had been surprised and harassed by the enemy—and this time forced to flee for his life! Vowing retaliation, he dispatched gallopers to recall all three of the brigades near him this day, including Munford's at Aldie. When the first reached him, Stuart would return Duffié's visit.

As soon as ensconced in Middleburg, Colonel Duffié perceived it to be a trap. He realized that he would soon find himself surrounded by Rebels of the sort encountered near Salem. His men were equally prescient. Duffié's bugler observed that they "became somewhat quiet . . . feeling a sense of impending disaster."[39] Another commander would have looked at once for an escape route, such as Aldie Gap. But Duffié's inflexible European notions of obedience to orders allowed him no alternative but to spend the night in Middleburg unless forced out. Thus he deployed his men for battle, barricaded the streets, and placed scouts on all roads out of town.[40]

He did send a few men, including a detachment under Captain Allen, to bring Pleasonton word of their predicament, but nothing came of it. Allen managed to reach Kilpatrick's headquarters near Aldie at nine o'clock that night, after some hair-raising travel over a roundabout route through enemy lines, but he found "Kill-cavalry" unwilling to exert himself in Duffié's behalf. After a hard day's fight with Munford, the brigadier considered his men too tired to go anywhere till the morrow. Nor did Pleasonton himself, to whom Allen relayed word of Duffié's plight, respond helpfully. Not till early on the eighteenth did he send troops toward Thoroughfare Gap and even then the would-be rescuers moved slowly and unconcernedly. In effect, Duffié and his men were abandoned to their fate.[41]

They did not have long to wait to learn the result of this decision. About 7:00 P.M. Duffié heard that Rebels were coming in from the west—Robertson's 900-man brigade, Stuart in command. Soon afterward came the news that advancing from the south were the men of John Chambliss. Now at last, with disaster staring at him, Duffié tried to pull out by the way he had come in. It was too late. Only a few of his men had mounted when Stuart and Robertson charged in, evading Duffié's barricades and pursuing his dismounted troopers out the Aldie road, overtaking and cutting down or capturing them. Finding no exit in that direction, Major Preston M. Farrington and twenty-five Rhode Islanders huddled in a wooded field enclosed by stone walls beyond the village, where they escaped detection.[42]

With shadows descending, Stuart charged Duffié's main body, capturing over seventy-five men. The rest, however, stood firm against three attacks. Their obstinate resistance resulted in numerous Confederate casualties, including the severe wounding of Major James H. McNeill of the 5th and Lieutenant Colonel Edward Cantwell of the 4th North Carolina.[43] The doomed Federals stood their ground so well that the battle dragged on through the early hours of the eighteenth. Only then did Stuart copy his enemy's tactics by dismounting much of Robertson's brigade and sending it into fields flanking the Yankees. As the Confederates moved in for the kill, the Rhode Islanders considered an every-man-for-himself retreat, "but such was the discipline of the men' that officers and enlisted men seemed to strive to avoid a panic" and thus rejected the tactic. Instead they grouped about their colonel, who at a critical moment remounted them and led them through a crease in Robertson's line.[44]

The Federals had galloped barely two miles southward, Robertson's men in pursuit, when Chambliss charged in to foil their escape. The Yankees reared backward as the new arrivals struck them in front along a gullied mountain road. Realizing their enemy faced annihilation, the Rebels cried: "Surrender! It's no use!" Most of Duffié's men agreed, throwing their weapons down and their hands up. Thirty-two others, including the colonel, crossed Little River southeast of the town, hid in riverbank underbrush, and after sunup on the eighteenth escaped Loudoun Valley through Hopewell Gap. Four other detachments, totaling sixty-one troopers, hid in the trees throughout the night and for most of the next day as well, till able to sneak away after dark on the eighteenth. By then nearly one hundred members of the outfit had been killed or wounded and as many others had been started off for Rebel prisons.[45]

Having repaid his opponents for their latest audacity, Stuart returned in triumph to the streets of Middleburg. For an hour he tended to the casualties on both sides, interrogated his captives, and supervised a half-hearted pursuit of Duffié's escapees. He then rode back to the vicinity of Rector's Cross Roads where that evening he celebrated his success to the music of Sam Sweeney and friends.[46]

Early on 19 June, Duffié and his ragged band of fugitives staggered into army headquarters at Fairfax Court House. With tears in his eyes, the colonel reported to Hooker: "Here is all I have of my fine regiment. I obeyed the order. We went. They cut me up. But my men did well; they fought hard. . . ."[47]

To recuperate from their ordeal, his survivors—whom an observer described as "haggard and emaciated as if suffering from recent fever"—were ordered to Alexandria to refit and recuperate. Though two companies would be returned to the field before the end of July, the regiment would not see service at anything approaching full strength until fall.[48]

Considering the impossibility of his situation, Duffié had done well to bring off any of his regiment. So thought Hooker, who appointed the Frenchman a brigadier general a few days after the affair at Middleburg. The irony in this amazed Duffié. Reflecting on Brandy Station, he mused: "When I do well, they take no notice of me. When I go make one bad business, make one fool of myself, they promote me. . . ."[49]

In the end, his new rank counted for little, as Hooker allowed himself to be influenced by Alfred Pleasonton. The man who had sacrificed Duffié and his troopers charged that the colonel had failed to obey orders while in Loudoun Valley, allowing the enemy "to obtain such a position as to be able to kill, wound, & capture a large number of his men & officers." He recommended

Duffié be court-martialed for "not fighting his men properly" at Middleburg, adding that he had proven himself "totally unfitted to command a Regiment."

Hooker seemed to endorse this patently unfair assessment of Duffié's performance. He held no court-martial or official inquiry, but neither did he provide Duffié an opportunity to answer Pleasonton's charges. At the latter's urging, he sent the new general to Washington for reassignment. Duffié would never again serve in the Army of the Potomac.[50]

General Wade Hampton.
(Photograph courtesy of the Library of Congress.)

General J. E. B. Stuart.
(Photograph courtesy of the Library of Congress.)

General Fitzhugh Lee.
(Photograph courtesy of the Library of Congress.)

General W. H. F. ("Rooney") Lee.
(Photograph courtesy of the Library of Congress.)

114

General Beverly H. Robertson.
(Photograph courtesy of the Library of Congress.)

Colonel M. Calbraith Butler.
(Photograph courtesy of the Library of Congress.)

General John D. Imboden.
(Photograph courtesy of the Library of Congress.)

General William E. ("Grumble") Jones.
(Photograph courtesy of the Library of Congress.)

Colonel Thomas T. Munford.
(Photograph courtesy of the Library of Congress.)

Colonel John R. Chambliss, Jr.
(Photograph courtesy of the Library of Congress.)

General Alfred G. Jenkins.
(Drawing courtesy of the Library of Congress.)

Left, *General George Armstrong Custer*; right, *General Alfred Pleasonton. (Photograph courtesy of the Library of Congress.)*

Seated, *General John Buford and staff.*
(Photograph courtesy of the Library of Congress.)

Seated, third from right, *General David McMurtrie Gregg and staff. (Photograph courtesy of the Library of Congress.)*

General H. Judson Kilpatrick. (Photograph courtesy of the Library of Congress.)

[6]

Middleburg Again and Upperville

THE eighteenth of June was intolerably hot: ninety-eight degrees in the shade, 112 under the Virginia sun.[1] Despite the conditions, the horsemen of both armies were kept busy throughout the day consolidating the strategic success each side felt it had gained on the seventeenth.

The Federals were more active. While Stuart conducted some short-range scouting missions (he was more intent on grouping his brigades and absorbing that of Grumble Jones, coming up from the Rappahannock),[2] Pleasonton sent out four long-range expeditions and laid the groundwork for a fifth. Yet only one accomplished anything of value.

The first began as a belated effort to rescue Duffié at Middleburg. That part of the 1st Pennsylvania which had not gone to Alexandria for remounting was dispatched to Thoroughfare Gap, where it found neither Duffié nor his antagonists. Next day it was joined by the rest of what remained of McIntosh's brigade, under Colonel Taylor, which moved through the gap to Haymarket and picketed that vicinity till the twenty-first.[3]

The second mission sent Devin's brigade of Buford's division to approximately the same locale. It remained there in observation of Rebel movements near the Bull Run Mountains until the twentieth, returning to home base with as little to show for its efforts as the Pennsylvania regiment had gained. Since fighting, not scouting, was Tom Devin's strongpoint, it was perhaps understandable that he failed to detect Jones's passage through that sector en route to Stuart's headquarters.[4]

The third expedition saw Irvin Gregg's brigade, plus an artillery section, move toward the Blue Ridge via Middleburg, near which elements of Chambliss's and Robertson's commands lingered. Gregg detected the Rebels' presence and mustered enough energy to thrust them aside and seize Middleburg. He spent the balance of that day behind the barricades the 1st Rhode Island had erected on the seventeenth, skirmishing listlessly until 6:00 P.M., when recalled to Aldie. Upon his departure, Stuart reoccupied the village. Gregg had not gotten close to his assigned objective, Ashby's Gap, through which he might have scanned Lee's dispositions beyond the Blue Ridge.[5]

As part of the day's fourth movement, Colonel Gamble, accompanied by Lieutenant Calef's Battery A, 2nd U.S. Artillery, ranged toward Snicker's Gap, some ten miles above Ashby's and only a few miles east of Robert E. Lee's newly established headquarters at Berryville. Gamble's mission miscarried when Munford's brigade, fresh from its fight at Aldie, brought him up short at Philomont, some miles short of his destination. Gamble contributed an inauspicious maiden effort in semi-independent command by deciding that Munford outnumbered him. After sending a few detachments down the roads from Philomont but short of the mountains, he withdrew timidly to cavalry headquarters.[6]

The final mission of the day involved not Pleasonton's but Stahel's horsemen from the Washington defenses. Not wishing to be distracted from his confrontation with Stuart, Pleasonton convinced Hooker that his corps was too busy to fulfill an assignment given them: a reconnaissance back toward Warrenton and Rappahannock Station, to determine if Rebel infantry lingered there and thereabouts. Fearing he had been too hasty in supposing that the whole of Lee's army was in the Shenandoah, the Union commander wondered if Ewell's movement might not have been a feint for a larger march through Manassas and Thoroughfare Gaps to the Bull Run vicinity. As a result, General Heintzelman, for the second time in a week, was prevailed upon to lease part of Stahel's division to the Army of the Potomac.

Late on the seventeenth, as the fighting died out near Aldie Gap, Stahel obligingly sent two of his regiments, under Colonel Othneil De Forest, to pass through an area that Hooker had vacated a few days ago. At the same time, the division leader pushed a small force toward Leesburg, hard by the northernmost gaps in the Bull Run Mountains, to hunt for Rebels in that sector as well.[7]

The smaller band found nothing of note, but Colonel De Forest—consistently praised by his superiors as an energetic, intelligent officer[8]—gained the sort of information Hooker desired. In the Warrenton vicinity, his men found Confederate troopers—Hampton's 1,500-man brigade—in force. Flanked and forced to fall back, De Forest greatly exaggerated the size of his opposition but ascertained that only cavalry remained along the Rappahannock. This should have proved to Hooker that his worry about a Confederate movement in his rear was groundless.[9]

***

The eighteenth proved a good day for J. E. B. Stuart, primarily thanks to his subordinate and friend, John Mosby. During the previous two years, the partisan chieftain had performed service of incalculable value to the Confederacy, especially when operating in his home region of Staunton, Loudoun, and Fairfax Counties, Virginia. But few of his previous feats matched that which he performed for Stuart on this day. Early on the eighteenth the slight, thirty-year-old ex-attorney rode into Stuart's camp near Rector's Cross Roads to show him the fruits of his previous night's work. He had swept down on a way-station near Fairfax Court House, departing with two captives, staff officers carrying orders from Hooker's headquarters. The dispatches, intended for Pleasonton's eyes, outlined the positions of every major element of the Army of the Potomac and indicated the movement each was to make on the eighteenth. Specifically, the papers revealed that Hooker was moving his headquarters to Fairfax Court House, that most of his army was camped along the O & A, and that it would remain there until Pleasonton brought new information on Lee's whereabouts. The documents also detailed Pleasonton's activities about Aldie and mentioned De Forest's pending reconnaissance toward Warrenton.[10]

Realizing the magnitude of Mosby's coup, Stuart forwarded the papers to General Lee, while relaying word of Colonel De Forest's movement to Warrenton so that Hampton would be prepared to receive him. The dispatches also enabled the cavalry commander to revamp his plans for resuming combat against Pleasonton. As he later wrote: "I therefore concluded in no event to attack with cavalry alone the enemy at Aldie. As long as he kept within supporting distance of his infantry at that point [on this day, Meade's V Corps was camped near Gum Springs, less than ten miles southeast of Aldie], my operations became necessarily defensive, but masking thereby the movement of our main body by checking the enemy's reconnaissance and by continually threatening attack."[11] So deciding, he ensured that Loudoun Valley would remain a cavalry battleground for days to come.

***

After dark on the eighteenth Hooker reiterated his desire that his cavalry attempt to scout beyond the Blue Ridge. Pleasonton took the hint and instructed Gregg's division to move from Aldie to Middleburg at dawn. If unopposed, Gregg was to proceed farther west to Upperville by way of the direct road to Ashby's Gap.[12]

A sudden shower struck Aldie before sunrise on the nineteenth, cutting the heat and laying the dust but forcing the troopers to make a sodden, muddy march. Despite the rain, Gregg's column—Irvin Gregg in advance, followed by Kilpatrick's brigade, then Gamble's (the latter on loan from the 1st Division)—made good progress. After an hour on the road, Irvin Gregg spied the outskirts of Middleburg through the gray haze. At about this point, as per their orders, Gamble's men filed off to the north, heading for the town of Union, where they might flank the Rebels Gregg encountered in front, before gaining their rear.

At about 7:00 A.M., pickets whom the defensive-minded Stuart had placed east of town sent a spattering of shots at the Federals. They withdrew, however, before the brisk advance of Gregg's lead regiment, the 4th Pennsylvania of William Doster. A few more minutes of riding brought the blue vanguard into the village, from which they evicted some stragglers. A volley of rifle fire beyond Middleburg told the invaders that Stuart and his main force had taken position a mile west of the place, guarding the mountain gaps.[13]

David Gregg made a strategic error by not attempting to flank these troops and gain access to the passes. As though his mission were to smash Stuart instead of gathering information of value to Hooker, the brigadier decided to mount a saber charge along the road from Middleburg to Upperville. But what seemed a good idea to him held no appeal for his cousin; after moving forward to set up the assault, Irvin Gregg worried about the enemy's dispositions. Through his field glasses he could see Chambliss's brigade holding a rugged crest north of the pike, supported by Hart's battery atop a higher spur beyond. Some of Chambliss's troopers had dismounted behind a stone wall, ready to sweep the road with rifles, carbines, and pistols. On their right, Robertson's North Carolinians were deployed on commanding ground south of the pike. A detachment held a timbered crest to the front, and the rest of the brigade had massed farther to the rear. Behind all of these troops, Chambliss's main force— mounted, ready to charge if the opportunity offered—formed a bulwark.[14]

On the defensive or not, Stuart inaugurated the fight in midmorning by having Hart's guns send some rounds into Irvin Gregg's midst, in an effort to get the Federals' range. Despite the shelling, Colonel Gregg made his dispositions slowly and deliberately. He placed a skirmish force at the edge of a wheatfield just below the turnpike, perhaps a quarter of a mile east of Stuart's fortified crest. Adjacent to the wheat he stationed half of the 4th Pennsylvania, dismounted. At the southernmost point of the line he placed a battalion of the 10th New York under Major Avery, some of its men afoot, some on horseback. And on open ground above the turnpike, the rest of Doster's regiment went into position, with Lieutenant Colonel Harhaus's 2nd New York as rear guard and Colonel Stedman's 6th Ohio as guardian of the far right flank—the latter two outfits supplied by Judson Kilpatrick.[15]

Opposed by Hart's shelling and a hail of rifle fire from Chambliss's troopers at the stone wall, Colonel Gregg became increasingly reluctant to order the charge. He temporized so long that the usually calm David Gregg came up to investigate. To his cousin's concern over the enemy's positions, the division leader responded with extraordinary vehemence: "The attack *must* be made, and at once!" He did, however, send forward Lieutenant Fuller's Battery C, 3rd United States Artillery, to try to neutralize Hart.

Somewhat relieved, Irvin Gregg resumed his dispositions by bringing up Lieutenant Colonel John K. Robison's 16th Pennsylvania and dismounting it inside a woodlot between the 10th New York and the lower half of the 4th Pennsylvania. Gregg completed the preliminaries by placing the mounted 1st Maine—now led by Lieutenant Colonel Smith—behind the 4th and 16th Pennsylvania, just south of the road.[16] At about six o'clock, the assault at last went forward. Robison's outfit and the lower portion of Doster's made the main effort on foot, just below the road; above them, the 1st Maine galloped up the pike at the same time, pistols cracking.

As Gregg had feared, Hart's battery sliced up his battle line before it could make its numbers felt. His men also absorbed a destructive barrage from Chambliss's and Robertson's sharpshooters. At last, however, Fuller's gunners found Hart's range and, with heaping doses of roundshot and shell, put the battery out of the fight. The Union's superiority in horse artillery, rarely evident at Brandy Station and at Aldie, was again on display.

Chambliss's men north of the pike held their position tenaciously; their fire curtailed the assault in that sector. But on the left, the 1st Maine and the Pennsylvania outfits raced across the intervening ground, leapt the crest of the ridge, and slid down the backslope, shouting in triumph. Only when they pushed past the timber did they halt. Before them loomed Chambliss's mounted reserves, sabers and pistols held high.[17]

To meet the crisis, Irvin Gregg threw in his own reserves, the remaining two battalions of the 10th New York. Starting at a trot up the pike, one squadron failed to get up steam before Chambliss's sharpshooters raked it. Many of its officers down, the unit whirled to the rear. By the time it reached safety, only five of its eighty members remained unwounded. Another squadron then attempted to make headway westward. It gained an appreciation of the odds against it when Chambliss's main force swept down the wooded rise, driving a mass of Yankees before it. Cowed by the spectacle, the squadron emulated the comrades who had gone—and fled—before it.

Two factors kept the Rebel counterassault from full success. Many of the Federals driven from the ridge rooted themselves to level ground and held it to the last. One sergeant in the 16th Pennsylvania blasted the charging enemy with carbine and pistol till out of ammunition, then pelted them with rocks before saber strokes laid him low. Secondly, the narrow pike funneled Chambliss's ranks together and slowed their advance to a crawl.[18] Since Stuart had had ample time to reconnoiter the ground, this said little for his tactical perception.

Though stymied, the Confederates refused to quit. Chambliss dismounted his men and led them on foot against their enemy. Munford's and Robertson's men plunged into the wheatfield after them, bagging a Union squadron left isolated by retreat-minded supports. Buoyed by this success, Stuart, watching from the ridge, anticipated not merely Gregg's repulse but his utter rout. When Heros von Borcke expressed doubt, the cavalry leader replied: "You're mistaken for once, Von; I shall be in Middleburg in less than an hour!"[19]

It was Stuart who was mistaken. Minutes after the Prussian spoke, Chambliss's men came rushing back for their horses. Behind them came the third battalion of the 10th New York, led by Major Avery, followed closely by Harhaus's 2nd New York, also mounted. Once in the saddle, Chambliss's people made a brief show of resistance, but their commander, fearing this advance portended an offensive by Federal reserves beyond Middleburg, pulled his brigade back to the high ground. Avery and Harhaus, realizing that their foe had deserted the front, turned back to their starting point.[20]

Stuart let them go. His chance of overthrowing the enemy ruined by Chambliss's pullback, he withdrew a short distance to the west and kept his men in defensive positions for the balance of the day. When darkness came without further enemy thrusts, he considered his stay near Middleburg over. Unit by unit, he hauled his lines farther westward, deploying on another ridge about half a mile closer to Upperville. This position would make Union attempts to flank him away from the Blue Ridge gaps even more difficult than before.[21]

During the withdrawal, Yankee skirmishers crept forward through the trees and brush, some coming within range of Stuart's field quarters. One of them mistook the tall, plume-hatted von Borcke for the Beau Sabreur himself and drilled the Prussian through his bull neck. The wound nearly proved fatal; it relegated its victim to a long convalescence and cost Stuart the services of his most versatile aide.[22]

By the time Stuart had established his new line, another bloody battle had closed under the canopy of night. The cavalry leader was in lofty spirits. He had fallen back of his own volition and only after ensuring Pleasonton's inability to enter the Shenandoah. Nevertheless, Stuart realized that the enemy had gained much ground in the direction of the Blue Ridge as well as new confidence in its ability to contest him on even terms. In fact, both sides had fought hard and skillfully under the torrid sun. Each had suffered casualties approximating 10 percent of the troops engaged—about one hundred for each side.[23] It seemed certain that heavier losses would accumulate in the near future.

***

While the fighting raged near Middleburg, a sideshow took place along the road to Union, three miles to the northwest. In advance of Gregg's movement toward Stuart's position, Buford had told off Colonel Gamble's brigade to reconnoiter along the Rebel upper flank. By this end run, Gamble hoped to gather the information Hooker needed about Lee's infantry. But Stuart detected the flank march and some time that afternoon sent Rosser's 5th Virginia, backed by part of the recently arrived command of Grumble Jones, to stop Gamble short of Ashby's Gap.[24] When the Rebels reached Gamble's position, they found him deployed near a wooded crossroads beside an old pottery kiln, picketing the roads toward Union, three miles farther north. Rosser easily drove the pickets back on their main force, which he found formed in dismounted skirmish lines behind fences of stone, with three cannon atop a tall rise in the rear.

Undaunted, the 5th Virginia moved against the town—and made no headway. Sent in on Rosser's right, Lieutenant Colonel Marshall's 7th Virginia of Jones's brigade did no better, stymied by the fire of troopers hidden behind the first fence. Replying in kind, Marshall dismounted some of his men and sent them thrashing through tall grass toward Gamble's position—only to find that the Yankees had fallen back to another fence line. By the time the 7th Virginia had passed the first barrier, it was absorbing not only carbine fire but canister from the well-positioned artillery. Flustered, the Virginians rejoined their horse-holders.

Content to deflect Stuart's blow, Gamble held his position as a stepping stone for a further advance by Buford. But he himself made no further progress west; the Confederates had moved north to Union, where they continued to block access to Ashby's Gap.[25]

***

A thunderstorm swept the Middleburg-Union vicinity on 20 June, precluding a quick renewal of the fighting.[26] Both sides shifted positions slightly and set up a long-range skirmish fire. Essentially, however, the day was given over to devising new strategy.

For Alfred Pleasonton, this meant a new method of besting Stuart in battle. Though reconnaissance should have been uppermost in his mind, he was preoccupied by his inability to land a knockout blow against the horsemen in gray. Thus, he plotted a climactic confrontation with his adversary in which he would destroy him unit by unit.

Yet Pleasonton was not confident enough to attempt this on his own. At midday on the twentieth he asked Hooker to loan him enough foot troops to give his assault the kind of staying power he felt that cavalry alone, even on foot, could not generate. Troubled by Stuart's recent reliance on dismounted skirmishers in commanding positions, Pleasonton felt that only infantry could neutralize the advantages of such tactics. As a further reason for desiring support, the Knight of Romance told his superior that Stuart led twice the troops previously attributed to him. This estimate was derived from dubious sources: the rumors of local secessionists and the power Stuart had displayed at Middleburg.

Though doubtless skeptical that the enemy's cavalry could be annihilated, even with infantry assistance, Hooker approved of Pleasonton's pugnaciousness, a happy contrast to the timidity of his predecessors. The army leader directed Brigadier General James Barnes's division of Meade's V Corps, then camped west of Gum Springs, to report to Pleasonton early on the twenty-first.[27]

By 7:00 A.M. on that day, the cavalry chief had called in his outlying detachments and was moving toward the position that Stuart had occupied late on the 19th and had strengthened next day. For the first time since Brandy Station, the Cavalry Corps was going into battle en masse, almost 12,000 strong.[28]

Pleasonton's tactical plan seemed relatively simple, though it contained features that would make it more complex than he envisioned. Buford's division, which had been thrown north of the Middleburg-Upperville Pike, would lap around the Rebel left (upper) flank just below a meandering stream known as Goose Creek, following up that flank as far as it would go. To enable him to do this, Gregg's division, to which the infantry brigade of Colonel Strong Vincent was attached (the rest of Barnes's division would remain in reserve near Middleburg), would mount a limited assault to hold Stuart's right and center in place. If Buford enjoyed success, Gregg and Vincent would forge westward in an all-out thrust toward Ashby's Gap.

As at Brandy Station, however, Pleasonton had based his plans on faulty reconnaissance. His lack of knowledge about the enemy's position showed in his failure to take into account Jones's newly arrived brigade, which, along with Chambliss's, occupied positions above Goose Creek. This prolongation of the Rebel left meant that Buford's offensive, instead of being a flank drive, would strike the median of Stuart's line. Once again, Alfred Pleasonton was about to stumble blindly into combat.[29]

***

The twenty-first of June being a Sunday, Stuart, devout Christian that he was, intended to pass the day in quiet contemplation. "Not so the enemy," he noted, "whose guns about 8 a. m. showed that he would not observe it."[30]

The cannon that spoke were those of Captain Fuller, still attached to David Gregg's command. Planted in the road west of Middleburg, they were charged with clearing a path for the first troops to engage Stuart—Vincent's brigade. Supported by marksmen of the 16th Michigan, 44th New York, and 20th Maine Infantry, the horse artillery did an exemplary job, enabling the 83rd Pennsylvania to pass through a belt of woods south of the road and gain an enfilading position along the Rebel right. As the Pennsylvanians came on, bayoneted rifles tilted forward, Stuart's flankers galloped toward Upperville, short of which their leader had pitched his headquarters. From the rear, Pleasonton looked on in satisfaction: as he had hoped, foot troops and cannoneers had emptied the road for the 2nd Cavalry Division.[31]

At David Gregg's order, Judson Kilpatrick's men led out. Despite the recent decimation of the 1st Rhode Island and the weakening of the 1st Massachusetts, the brigade moved forward with verve, the 6th Ohio galloping along the right of the road, the 2nd New York charging up the left, and the 4th New York, under Lieutenant Colonel Pruyn, holding the rear.[32]

Then James Hart's battery of Blakely rifles, posted on a ridge east of Upperville, showered the Union column with canister, draining its momentum before it could reach the village. Fuller's gunners, who had won a similar confrontation two days before, accepted the challenge. Firing incessantly, Fuller finally placed a shell among Hart's caissons, one of which detonated with an unearthly roar, damaging a cannon. Standing near the impact point, Wade Hampton barely escaped death, but his only reaction was a quiet remark to an aide: "Well, I am afraid Hart has lost a gun this time."[33]

This was so. Plagued by such accurate fire, plus the renewed advance of Kilpatrick's three regiments, Stuart pulled back to another position farther west. In doing so, he was forced to leave behind the damaged cannon. Its loss pricked Stuart's pride; in his campaign report he italicized his chagrin: this was *"the first piece of my horse artillery which has ever fallen into the enemy's hands."*[34]

Leapfrogging toward the rear, the Confederates conducted delaying actions on foot. Along Goose Creek, midway between their initial position and Upperville, they held off Kilpatrick and his infantry comrades for almost ninety minutes. There Hart's truncated battery unlimbered on a steep ridge north of the creek and fired effectively enough to foil a charge by Vincent's forward regiments and Kilpatrick's 2nd New York. Finally, the 16th Michigan Infantry rushed the Rebel-held bridge over Goose Creek under a blizzard of rifle and cannon balls. Their movement pried loose Hart's gun crews as well as their dismounted cavalry support—some of Robertson's men, who had held a stone wall that commanded the approach to the stream. The bulk of Robertson's brigade rushed up from the west to enable their embattled comrades to withdraw without further loss. With Hart's retirement, the rest of Stuart's units still in contact with the Federals fell back stubbornly, careful to maintain battle formations as much as possible. Their leader watched approvingly: "Nothing could exceed the coolness and self-possession of officers and men in the movements, performing evolutions with a precision under fire that must have wrung the tribute of admiration from the enemy, even. . . ."[35]

Unwilling to subject the citizens of Upperville to a battle in their streets, Stuart pulled his troops through the town without delay. But Judson Kilpatrick ("true to those reckless and inhuman instincts," wrote Stuart) could not resist the opportunity to strike Robertson's rear as it coiled through the village, hemmed in by trees and buildings. Accelerating to top speed, his men left their infantry cohorts behind. In minutes, the 2nd and 4th New York and 6th Ohio overtook Peter Evans's 5th North Carolina. Routed almost immediately, the Carolinians sought refuge in side streets and back alleys, where saber and pistol battles broke out in profusion.[36]

Part of Stuart's main body hastened to the rescue. First to reach the scene was Hampton, who, with Lieutenant Colonel Waring's Jeff Davis Legion, made for Kilpatrick's left flank along the south side of Upperville. A Rebel trooper observed Hampton at the point of the counterattack, "seemingly angered, looking a veritable god of war" as he "drew his saber [and] . . . plunged into the charging column of the enemy."[37]

Stunned by Hampton's fury, the 2nd New York fell back, though able to break free only after the 4th New York charged up to eradicate the stain its reputation had received at Aldie. It did so by blasting back the Davis Legion and the outfits now behind it, the 1st North Carolina and the Cobb Legion, under Laurence Baker and Pierce Young respectively. Both New York regiments, free of pressure, scurried eastward, where they re-formed and launched a second offensive. Simultaneously, Hampton rallied his regiments. Heedless of his superior's concern for the safety of the village, he charged through Upperville and piled into the head of Kilpatrick's column.[38] The result was the chaos common to cavalry-versus-cavalry engagements. Some troopers singled out opponents for individual combat, while others slashed and jabbed wildly at faceless antagonists. At the same time, Rebel and Yankee artillery returned to work. This time Hart's gunners took the honors by shelling Kilpatrick's rear with masterful precision. Under the cannonade, numerous Federals fell wounded, including David Gregg, who also saw his horse shot away beneath him.[39]

After several minutes, the opponents broke free of their embrace and staggered off. They retired to realign on either side of town, leaving dead horses and mangled riders piled in the streets.

The Federals quickly returned to the fight. Soon after Hampton disengaged, his men observed the 6th United States—sent down from Buford's position by Alfred Pleasonton[40]—advancing briskly along both sides of the road to Upperville. Their opponents could not have deployed in time to meet them; thus Hampton was relieved to see the 6th's horses halt, winded, while trying to negotiate the uphill terrain in front of his position. Cut up at Brandy Station, led by junior officers lacking battle experience, the Regulars had begun their charge too soon and had exhausted their momentum short of their objective. Then, too, the route chosen by Captain Cram had been broken by marshes, plowed fields, and two "almost impassable" ditches that so scattered his men they could not have landed a solid blow. When Hampton sent a single fresh regiment to challenge them, the Regulars turned about and sheepishly retraced their steps. Once safely behind the wall at the starting-point of their charge, the 6th's officers received a tongue-lashing from Major Starr, who had witnessed their sorry effort from the rear.[41]

Another observer disgusted by the 6th's performance was Alfred Pleasonton, who had sent in the Regulars out of concern that Gregg was moving too slowly to reinforce Kilpatrick. Now the corps commander called down the rest of Starr's brigade, dismounting most of the 2nd and 5th United States and sending them along the Upperville road under Wesley Merritt's supervision.[42]

Having failed to see the newcomers dismount, Wade Hampton believed them to be Vincent's infantrymen. Holding the power of foot troops in high regard, the Confederate brigadier called up Major Lipscomb's 2nd South Carolina to cover his rear. He then abandoned the field, falling back behind Upperville, Lipscomb following.[43]

While Hampton and the Regulars were confronting each other, Kilpatrick, late in the afternoon, renewed his encounter with Robertson's brigade. This time he led not his own troops but two regiments on loan from Irvin Gregg. Having noted the fagged-out condition of Kilpatrick's brigade, Gregg had reciprocated Kilpatrick's gesture of two days before, when the latter had tendered his troops to "Long John" in a crisis. Leading Lieutenant Colonel Smith's 1st Maine, Kilpatrick again spurred through Upperville, evading downed men and horses. On the other side of the village he dismounted a portion of Smith's regiment and sent it against the carbineers of Colonel Dennis D. Ferebee's 4th North Carolina, who were hugging walls on top of two ridgelines.

Before the Federals could strike, the rest of the Maine regiment was assailed by the 5th North Carolina, which had recovered its composure after fleeing during the initial Union attack. Rushing in from the west, Colonel Evans's men overwhelmed Smith's, shoved them through the town, isolated their vanguard, and briefly held Judson Kilpatrick prisoner.[44] The 4th Pennsylvania, the second regiment lent Kilpatrick by Gregg, then arrived to rescue him. Again surrounded by troopers in blue, Kilpatrick regained the offensive along with his freedom. "Swearing and brandishing his sabre," he led Colonel Doster's Pennsylvanians forward, forcing the two North Carolina outfits to retire.

Though Ferebee's men did not immediately rally, Evans's regrouped on the western outskirts and wheeled about to meet Kilpatrick's thrust. Seeing the Rebels stand firm, the Union brigadier attempted to halt and form the 4th Pennsylvania. As Colonel Doster realized, however, "there is no stopping five hundred wild and infuriated men with drawn sabres." Instead of slowing his regiment, Doster guided it against Evans's flank.[45]

This assault—aided by the Maine troopers who had assailed Ferebee—ripped the life out of the 5th North Carolina. Struck on their weak side, Evans's riders spun about and flew out of control—whereupon the rear squadrons of the 4th Pennsylvania hit them head-on with crunching force. Evans took a mortal wound; many of his men fell with him, others surrendering before becoming casualties. The colonel's rear guard made a game but unsuccessful effort to save him. With unaccustomed gallantry, Judson Kilpatrick risked his life to take up Evans on his own horse—preventing him from being trampled in the road.[46]

Finally the fighting petered out, both forces falling back, clearing the road as if by prearranged signal. By now the sun had touched the horizon, and Stuart felt the enemy lacked the necessary light to peer into the Shenandoah toward Lee's camps. Therefore he led his brigades at a deliberate pace toward Ashby's Gap, carrying off a number of wounded men and captives.

Neither Pleasonton nor Vincent attempted a pursuit. They feared the reported proximity of Confederate infantry in strength greater than their own. Additionally, the cavalry needed a refit before able to renew combat. The day's losses had been relatively light considering the duration of the action (Kilpatrick, Gregg, and Starr reported a combined total of 136 casualties, Vincent 21, while Stuart's greatest loss was his 250 captured).[47] Still, the Union troopers had had little time to regroup and reorganize since Aldie, and the combined losses of 17–21 June had exacted a heavy toll.

Whether or not they had whipped Stuart as thoroughly as Pleasonton envisioned, the Union horsemen had given another stout account of themselves, forcing their enemy to quit the field. Years later, David Gregg turned lyrical in recalling that "the retreat of the enemy . . . as the sun was sinking behind the nearby mountain, made a glorious ending to a day filled with the incident and excitement of battle."[48]

***

While the twenty-first had been a day of vacillating fortunes for David Gregg, it had been one of fatigue and frustration for John Buford. Even Buford's day, however, closed with an accomplishment that seemed to make his travail worthwhile.

For the leader of the 1st Cavalry Division, troubles began early. At midnight on 20–21 June, when Pleasonton relayed his order for the main attack above Upperville, Buford found he had only two hours to prepare for the march. This was insufficient to feed men and horses (neither had enjoyed regular meals for two days), let alone to orient his subordinates to the details of tactics and strategy. Thus the Kentuckian's people left the Aldie vicinity shortly after daylight, hungry as well as fatigued. They then suffered the discomfort of marching through a steady drizzle toward Middleburg. About 7:00 A.M., a gray dawn having broken, the advance of the division came within sight of the field of the nineteenth. It then forged northward toward the presumed location of Stuart's left, while Gregg pressed westward along the road to the town.[49]

Several minutes of marching brought Buford to Goose Creek. He struck west along its lower bank in conformance to orders. Soon afterward—as Gregg's men readied their secondary assault—the 1st Division bogged down on muddy bottomland before Grumble Jones's pickets. A glance at his position told the Union leader that if he had found the Rebel left, it was so well anchored at the stream that it could only be turned from above. Buford cursed his luck and the time constraints that had prevented a preliminary reconnaissance.

As Pleasonton was riding with Gregg, Buford alone must decide how best to comply with the general plan. After some deliberation, he made a time-consuming countermarch till he reached a site at which he could cross Goose Creek to the north. He did so against an intermittent fire from some of Jones's men above the stream. Patiently he thrust his assailants westward, following them in hopes of looping around the enemy flank by recrossing to the south near the hamlet of Millville. When reinforcements from Jones reached the scene, much of the 11th and 12th Virginia—Colonel Lomax in overall command—opposed Buford's advance. Buford's progress became correspondingly slower.[50]

Sometime in early afternoon, the 1st Division reached Millville. By then Buford decided that his steady if slow march had availed him nothing. He still could not find Stuart's upper flank, and by now he was so late and so far afield of Gregg that he doubted he could contribute anything to the planned offensive.

Considering further progress uncertain, he sent a courier to inform Pleasonton that his operation was a shambles. He suggested instead that Gregg make the primary assault; Buford would assist him in any way possible. In fact, Buford lent help almost immediately, after a courier brought Pleasonton's order that Starr's brigade, minus the 6th Pennsylvania, was to be sent to Gregg's front.[51]

About the time he learned of Buford's crossing of Goose Creek, Grumble Jones received a communiqué from Stuart near Upperville. Already pressed by Kilpatrick and his supports and contemplating a full withdrawal, Stuart had determined to recall both Jones and Chambliss to his main position. Though probably disappointed by his superior's decision, Jones obeyed with good grace. Keeping Lomax's skirmishers in place, the brigadier backed off with the majority of his brigade. Coming down from the north, Chambliss's men joined him. Both commands moved west, then directly south toward Upperville. The troopers rode on either side of the road, their artillery and a long supply train crowding the space between.[52]

In their wake, Lomax's rear guard unleashed a skirmish fire, fell back, then stood and fired again, preventing Buford from striking the disengaging units. At a few points Lomax attempted limited assaults, but these fared poorly. As a member of Lieutenant Colonel Thomas B. Massie's 12th Virginia explained, the Yankees "were too many for us."[53]

Finally losing his patience, Buford attempted to evade Lomax by angling southwestward toward Upperville. Almost all the way, however, his advance was "disputed pretty warmly" by the Virginian; every mile or so the column would grind to a halt and deploy for a fight. Several times Buford replied with his attached section of Graham's Battery K, 1st United States. Then, reaching elevated ground less than two miles from Upperville, he altered course again. Now within sight of Gregg's embattled division, the Kentuckian decided to aid it with the bulk of his force. Thus he left the road he had been traversing and struck off across farm fields and open land toward the 2nd Division's position. But the rough, muddy ground so disordered his advance that he halted a half-mile from his objective in rage and frustration.[54]

Casting about for a new avenue of approach, Buford spied the wagons and artillery vehicles in Jones's column, passing down the road to Upperville. At the general's signal, the point riders in Gamble's brigade raced across the fields, aiming for the train. A mile and a half of riding brought Gamble within cannon range of the enemy-held road—whereupon the four Napoleons in the battery of R. Preston Chew dosed Gamble's men with canister, blowing the colonel's own mount to pieces. Despite the vicious hail, his Indiana and Illinois outfits managed to reach a stone wall that shielded the Rebel gunners and by firing atop and around it forced them to abandon their pieces. But before the Federals could seize the prizes, Lieutenant Colonel O. R. Funsten led the 11th Virginia through a hidden gap in the wall and into their midst. A frenzied saber and pistol duel raged over the muddy ground alongside the road on which Jones and Chambliss had been brought to a halt. During the melee, Chew was able to recover his guns and remove them to safer ground.

When Grumble Jones fed in elements of his 6th and 7th Virginia, Gamble's men broke off the fight and raced eastward. The three Rebel regiments responded with a vigorous attack on the Federals' stone wall, a few hundred yards off. They might have flanked that barrier on both ends had not Tom Devin's brigade and the artillery come up at the double-quick to aid Gamble. The combined force slowed Jones's offensive to a standstill, then wrecked it with cannon and rifle fire.

With the retreat of Funsten and his supports, Jones withdrew westward by a side road, Chambliss's brigade in his rear. Having suffered over seventy casualties and still pressed by his antagonists, Jones decided not to continue to Upperville but to make a quick march to Ashby's Gap. Buford, who had absorbed forty-odd losses, followed Jones but with the intention of scouting enemy infantry dispositions, not to renew battle.[55]

Shortly before sundown, Buford's advance reached the mouth of Ashby's Gap. The Rebel cavalry stood defiantly to the west, four of their batteries occupying the defile itself. Behind them, though shielded to enemy view, lay the bivouacs of Major General Lafayette McLaws's infantry division of Longstreet's corps. His trail thus blocked, Buford sent scouting parties up to the nearest ridge. From atop it, one of Gamble's troopers noted, "our company . . . could see all over the Shanendoah [sic] valley on the other side."[56]

Visibility was hampered by coming night and a thick haze. Still the twilight provided just enough light—Stuart's expectations to the contrary notwithstanding—to discern McLaws's camps, close by the western rim of the mountain. This told Buford that at least two of Lee's corps were in the Shenandoah, part of the first already in Pennsylvania, the second within easy marching distance of the Keystone State. Pleasonton relayed the information to Hooker the following day, but Fighting Joe did not act on it. Until the twenty-fifth the Army of the Potomac sat idle along its railroad far to the east—testimony to Hooker's indecisiveness and lethargy.[57]

Certain that Stuart would remain in Ashby's Gap for the near future, Buford withdrew to Upperville. There he linked with Gregg and Vincent, neither of whom had moved much beyond the village once the enemy departed. Cavalry and infantry congratulated each other not only for gaining important intelligence but for forcing Stuart to quit his third battlefield in as many engagements. An Illinois trooper exulted to his parents: "We drove the Rebs eight miles. . . . It was the prettiest fight I ever saw. . . . You ought to have seen us run them and heard us yell at them." For once, Alfred Pleasonton was more cautious in his self-praise and even gave Stuart his due; he called the day's work "splendid—but the rebels were as stiff as pokers, & disputed every inch. I never saw them so hard to move before." Reciprocating, one Confederate letter-writer referred to his enemy as "certainly the bravest and boldest Yanks that ever fought us on any field."[58]

The fervor with which the antagonists had struggled was indicated by the ghastly plethora of bodies and carcasses in and around Upperville. Writing his father, a Maine boy recounted his walk over the field: "The road where we charged was literally covered with blood and to see the dead piled up was perfectly horrid." To a great degree, statistics told the story. In the period 17–21 June, Stuart's division had suffered almost 500 casualties, Pleasonton's corps about 860. Adding the losses at Brandy Station, the toll mounted to over 1,000 Rebels and 1,700 Yankees killed, wounded, or missing.[59]

Following Upperville, both cavalries felt weary but in good spirits, Stuart's because it had held Pleasonton's scouts in check for several days, Pleasonton's because it had proved conclusively that it could match the born horsemen of the South under almost any battle conditions. With some exceptions, both leaders had also gained a high appreciation of the skill, tenacity, and combativeness of their ranking subordinates.

Still, the heavy toll of horses and riders worried the commanders. With the most crucial days of the campaign still ahead, many men were already exhausted from almost constant marching and fighting. "We have had a right busy time of it for a couple of weeks," wrote a laconic member of the 2nd Virginia. "We have been marching nearly all the time," complained a Georgian of the Phillips Legion on 23 June. He added that in recent days almost as many of his comrades had been incapacitated by fatigue and heat prostration as by bullets.[60]

Their adversaries agreed. A New York trooper noted that he had been in the saddle so long that he could no longer tell one day of the week from another. And a concerned member of the 6th Pennsylvania worried that "all the fighting since the battle of Chancellorsville has been done by cavalry . . . and if they keep this up much longer that branch will be almost extinct."[61]

[7]

Jenkins's Expedition—Williamsport to Petersburg

BY Thursday, 18 June, Ewell's corps lay along the Potomac River and also stretched north from Winchester, Virginia, to Williamsport, Maryland. It continued to assimilate the supplies that Jenkins's horsemen had brought it, while taking a final rest before proceeding en masse into the enemy's country.[1]

That afternoon, Ewell left his headquarters above Martinsburg—even as his subordinates at Winchester scrawled paroles for over three thousand Yankees—and rode north to give final orders to the commanders of his advance echelon. Crossing the pontoon bridge that his engineers had thrown across the river at Williamsport, the corps leader met with Rodes and Jenkins on the upper shore and directed them to push on to Chambersburg in the morning. On the way, they would be joined by Edward Johnson's infantry division. Meanwhile, Early's division—supported by Colonel William H. French's 17th Virginia, Jenkins's brigade—would feint towards Harpers Ferry, to hold its garrison in place, then move northeastward along the base of South Mountain, the Blue Ridge extension that formed the eastern rim of the Cumberland Valley. A third column—one of Johnson's brigades—would march toward the west, to guard the left flank of the main command. All three forces would fulfill Lee's wish that they scour the valley along as broad a front as possible, confiscating every resource—animal, vegetable, or mineral—of utility to the Army of Northern Virginia.[2]

With Hooker's army known to be lingering along the Orange & Alexandria Railroad, the route of invasion looked open and free. The only other major defense force the Federal government could muster was that of General Schenck's Middle Military Department, and most of Schenck's troops lay too far afield to worry the invaders. From his headquarters in far-off Baltimore, Schenck was responsible for protecting the territory between the Delaware and Ohio Rivers, which took in parts of six states. His infantry and artillery were scattered from Philadelphia to Wheeling, West Virginia, concentrated at communications hubs such as Winchester and Harpers Ferry; while his horsemen were so few—one regiment, one battalion, and a dozen separate companies—that Schenck's ability to cover even a small portion of his territory was minimal. His inability to reinforce Winchester and its satellite garrisons on 13–15 June had proved as much.[3]

The burden of defending Pennsylvania had fallen to militia and short-term volunteers. Governor Andrew G. Curtin, who had predicted a raid by Stuart into Pennsylvania's western reaches, had recently called out state forces. Recognizing its limited ability to aid him, the federal government quickly approved his actions and helped him resolve legal and political entanglements. On the tenth the government created two military districts charged with protecting western and southern Pennsylvania. These were the Department of the Susquehanna, commanded at Chambersburg (and later at Harrisburg) by Major General Darius N. Couch, formerly Joe Hooker's senior subordinate; and the Pittsburgh-based Department of the Monongahela, under an erstwhile VI Corps division leader, Brigadier General William T. H. Brooks.[4]

The generals had stocked their departments with as many militia, national guardsmen, and "emergency forces" as they could get their gloves on. Pennsylvania herself contributed several thousand citizen-soldiers, most of whom agreed to serve for up to 120 days or until the crisis abated. A few neighboring states also helped out, but only New York did so in volume, Democratic Governor Horatio Seymour sending Curtin almost 10,000 organized militia and 2,000 volunteers. Various other units augmented these forces; Couch and Brooks pressed into service any troops who happened to be in their bailiwick, including newly recruited regiments bound for Virginia; ambulatory convalescents from state military hospitals; members of the so-called Invalid Corps; and any private citizen who flocked to the colors, with or without weapons. Those lacking rifles shoveled earth to build the breastworks thrown up at Harrisburg, Pittsburgh, and at various strategic locations in between.

Even with these resources, Couch and Brooks were in poor shape to defend the Commonwealth. Though expressing faith in the minute-man concept, Governor Curtin would find that not until Rebel infantry set foot in Pennsylvania would volunteers come forward in force. By mid-June, the Department of the Susquehanna was defended by barely 20,000 troops, many of them ignorant of the basics of soldiering. For all the obstacles they could impose, Lee's 80,000 veterans might be trooping through Harrisburg before the month ended.[5]

***

Early on the nineteenth, as Pleasonton and Stuart prepared for their encounter at Middleburg, Rodes's infantry and Jenkins's horsemen left Williamsport for Hagerstown and Boonsboro, Maryland. Infantry and cavalry made an easy, loping march of it, confident they were so far ahead of any pursuers that they could not be overtaken before gaining their objectives. Three days later they crossed the Mason-Dixon Line, amid outbursts of exultation. Most of the celebrating was done by Rodes's men, whose knowledge of Pennsylvania derived only from tales told by Jenkins's troopers.[6]

That same day, no longer stymied by rain-swollen waters at Shepherdstown, Early's division forded the Potomac, shook itself dry, and moved in the general direction of Waynesboro, Pennsylvania. By then Johnson's column had crossed the river at Boteler's Ford, joining Rodes and Jenkins in Governor Curtin's state.[7]

Leading Rodes's march, the cavalrymen of Jenkins's brigade renewed their efforts at confiscating Pennsylvania crops and livestock. They sent their prizes to the rear, where Rodes stored them aboard forage wagons or relayed them to Virginia. On this jaunt, however, Jenkins found slimmer pickings than he had a week ago; many farmers, bypassed by the horsemen the first time around, had secreted their horses and cattle in the mountains in anticipation of the Rebels' return.[8] The shortfall caused by their foresightedness was only partially offset by the plunder taken by Company D, 14th Virginia Cavalry (Captain Robert B. Moorman), which Jenkins had sent east of his column through lush areas in Maryland.

On the twenty-second, three days after he crossed into Pennsylvania on his foraging expedition, Captain Moorman precipitated the first sustained clash of arms above the Mason-Dixon Line. By then his men had already encountered snipers and roadblocks, signs that greater trouble awaited them. That afternoon, while marching east on the Chambersburg Pike near Monterey, they sighted mounted men ahead of them—members of three Pennsylvania units. These were Captain Robert Bell's Adams County Cavalry, Captain David Conaughy's company of home guards from the same county, and a seventy-seven-man detachment of the 1st Troop, Philadelphia City Cavalry, under Captain Samuel J. Randall. The latter, a prestigious militia outfit that dated from Revolutionary times, had come over one hundred miles by rail and highway to assist General Couch.

Noting that the Yankees seemed willing to fight, Moorman's men formed a line beside the pike and for several minutes engaged the civilian-soldiers in a carbine and revolver duel that inflicted no casualties. When he realized he was outpositioned as well as outnumbered, Moorman led his band, plus their bovine and equine booty, by a roundabout route to rejoin Jenkins. They reached him without further incident.[9]

Shortly before Moorman's return, Jenkins's brigade had moved from its latest bivouac, south of Greencastle, toward the village from which it had fled so ignominiously on the seventeenth. On the way, it shared some of Moorman's experiences. Only a mile below Greencastle, the cavalry's advance guard, Captain J. A. Wilson's Company I, 14th Virginia, observed a body of blue-coated horsemen about five hundred yards ahead, sitting their mounts astride the road to town. Believing them to be militia, Wilson at once retreated, intending to lure them into a trap formed by the bulk of his regiment. Agreeably, the Yankees followed in haste.

But the trap failed to spring, because the oncomers were the New York veterans under Captain Boyd. Having escaped from Martinsburg and Winchester, the little band had fallen in with McReynolds's supply train, escorting it all the way to Harrisburg and handing it over to General Couch. From the state capital Boyd and his men had returned to the field as temporary additions to the Department of the Susquehanna, with orders to scout the head of the invasion force, impede its movements as much as possible, and menace its communication lines. A prudent man with keen intuition, Boyd sensed the proximity of a large enemy force even as he drove in Wilson's men. Thus he halted his pursuit just short of a bend in the road toward Greencastle, around which Wilson had disappeared. Tall wheat blocked Boyd's view of Jenkins's main force farther west, but through field glasses he discerned Rodes's infantry marching along a ridge in rear of the cavalry.[10]

While noting Rodes's dispositions, Boyd and his company became a target for Jenkins's sharpshooters hidden near the bend in the road. The captain pulled his men out of range and hustled them back to Chambersburg, informing the local commander, Brigadier General Joseph F. Knipe, of the enemy's approach. Knipe, commanding 800 New York militia recently dispatched to Franklin County, shocked Boyd by abandoning the town and leading his troops to Carlisle, over thirty miles to the northeast. The minutemen departed so hastily they left behind a huge cache of equipment and ordnance, including a section of artillery. They also left a disgusted Boyd, who refused to be a party to such precipitate flight.

After debating his course, the captain also prepared to leave Chambersburg, but only to find a better position from which to monitor the Rebels' progress. He delayed long enough to fetch a doctor and an undertaker for two men who had been shot by Jenkins's marksmen near Greencastle. The victims—Sergeant Milton Cafferty, who had taken a minié ball in the leg, and Corporal William F. Rihl, shot through the skull—had become the first of 87,000 Federals and Confederates to fall dead or wounded in Pennsylvania during the war's pivotal campaign.[11]

***

Late on the twenty-third, Jenkins's brigade reentered Chambersburg, its band thumping and blaring away in salute to "The Bonnie Blue Flag." The troopers happily appropriated the items Knipe had left for them—those that remained following the descent of local looters. Forewarned of his enemy's hasty exit, Jenkins had regained the nerve he lost during his first visit to the town. As one resident remarked: "Unlike his former entrance . . . he this time came in slowly and confidently."

Not content to seize Knipe's picked-over gifts, the cavalry leader again levied a quota of spoils—this time only rations and forage—on the citizenry. By threatening to send his provost marshals to take what they wanted from homes and stores, he got enough donations to satisfy his needs. After a fashion, he rewarded those who piled their offerings in the middle of Main Street: "As flitch after flitch [of bacon] . . . with a sprinkling of bread, cakes, and pies, were deposited in the pile, in front of the courthouse, the name of the unwilling contributor to the stomach of the Southern Confederacy was taken down, by which his residence would be exempted from search in case enough was not voluntarily brought in."[12]

Next morning General Ewell, riding in a buggy at the head of Rodes's division, entered the village to view the local reaction to this program of donation or confiscation. Later he wrote his niece: "The people look as sour as vinegar, & I have no doubt would gladly send us all to kingdom come if they could."[13]

On the twenty-fourth, with Edward Johnson's division fast closing up in Rodes's rear, Ewell freed Jenkins from tribute collecting and sent him seven miles toward Harrisburg, to picket the Shippensburg vicinity. Quickly Jenkins was reminded of how preferable was foraging to scouting. That evening, while patrolling the roads toward Carlisle, his pickets were fired on by the roving troopers of Captain Boyd. As on 17 June, Jenkins was pushed toward panic by the unexpected opposition. The brigadier fell back from the roads he had been commanded to hold and called frantically for help from Chambersburg. Not till Ewell dispatched an infantry brigade to his side did Jenkins's anxiety subside. By then, of course, Boyd's men had fled into the night, planning to fight again another day.[14]

***

Dick Ewell, shortly before reaching Chambersburg, received a few hundred additions to his mounted wing: Lige White's 35th Virginia Battalion. Having been detached from the main body of the 2nd Corps a week ago, the Comanches had made inroads into Union territory along the lower Potomac. They had done so without regard to the size of their opposition—"marching careless of our cavalry," in the words of Hooker's chief of staff.[15] By their boldness and energy, the Virginians had cleared away further potential opposition to Lee's invasion— while also settling scores with some old antagonists.

Following Ewell's victory at Winchester, White had won the corps leader's permission to take 125 men on a raid against the Baltimore & Ohio Railroad depot at Point of Rocks, a Potomac River site about a dozen miles east of Harpers Ferry. Ewell had long ago decided to bypass the latter, considering its troops too few and not aggressive enough to menace his march. Still, he admired White's plan to wreck track and materiel at Point of Rocks and to cut the communications of the river garrison.

By hard riding, the Comanches neared their objective on the evening of 17 June. They found waiting for them three companies of Union horsemen, two having been dispatched from Harpers Ferry in response to reports of their approach. The reports also confused and frightened the Yankees into thinking the oncomers consisted of Stuart's entire division. Fearing themselves greatly outnumbered, the defenders took fright when White's force burst out of the gloom to challenge them. After brief resistance, they were "overpowered and whipped" and forced to fall back. Having lost dozens of casualties to rifle- and pistol fire, the Yankees retreated northeastward.[16]

From captives, Colonel White was pleased to learn that his victory had come at the expense of three units that had long opposed him in this vicinity: Captain George D. Summers's mounted Company F, 2nd Maryland Home Brigade; Captain George W. F. Vernon's Company A of Major Henry A. Cole's Maryland Cavalry Battalion; and the "Loudoun Rangers" (Company F, 3rd West Virginia Cavalry), under Captain Samuel C. Means.[17] White was also gratified by the success of a detachment from his command, under Lieutenant Joshua R. Crown. This band had taken a side road to Point of Rocks, striking a blow against Union horsemen stationed a few miles southeast of the post. Crown's opposition embraced the bulk of Cole's battalion, which outnumbered the attackers two-to-one. In the dark, however, the size of Crown's force was so magnified that it scared the wits out of the Maryland Unionists, who, according to a Confederate officer, "fled like sheep from hungry wolves."[18]

All told, the Comanches bagged over a hundred prisoners, while shooting up thirty-one others, four fatally. Resistance ended, the battalion spent several hours destroying material at Point of Rocks, including miles of trackage and telegraph wire, army storehouses—and a multi-car freight train, which they torched, then sent careening down the track with throttle wide open.

Thanks to White and Crown, the Federals at Harpers Ferry would have to restore broken communications instead of attempting to block Ewell's way. Their path lighted by the blazing warehouses, the Comanches proudly rode off to meet Ewell in upper Maryland, via Loudoun County. The countryside for miles around mobilized to pursue, but the battalion rode so fast and yet so carefully that it rejoined its army without loss of man or animal.[19]

***

By Wednesday, 24 June, Brigadier General George H. Steuart's brigade of Johnson's division, the left flank of Ewell's corps, had crossed into the Keystone State. That day the foot soldiers marched westward out of Greencastle via the base of Cove Mountain. Bound for McConnellsburg, they aimed to meet a pilferage quota of their own.[20]

A few miles short of McConnellsburg, Steuart was overtaken by the 150 horsemen of the 1st Battalion, Maryland Line, under Major Harry Gilmor, that man in the "new yaller clothes." Since his ill-considered charge near Middletown twelve days ago, the major had made efforts to cleanse his record while serving Dick Ewell on detached service. On the twenty-first Gilmor had seized and occupied the supply center of Frederick, Maryland. Despite being temporarily evicted by a portion of Cole's cavalry, he and his men had confiscated and destroyed materiel earmarked for the Army of the Potomac. The battalion had then been sent to Steuart as his advance guard.[21]

Thus, Gilmor led the way through the area that Colonel Ferguson's Virginians had so recently visited. The major's ride, however, was not as obstacle-free as his predecessor's. Nearing McConnellsburg, he encountered three enemy forces aiming to slow Steuart's march. The first was a part of Milroy's force of 1,700 fugitives which, under Colonel Lewis B. Pierce of the 12th Pennsylvania Cavalry, had taken refuge in General Couch's department near Bloody Run.[22] Essentially, it consisted of Pierce's own regiment, under Lieutenant Colonel Joseph L. Moss. The second source of opposition was a regiment of Pennsylvania emergency infantry under Colonel Jacob Szink. Although both forces held strong positions—Moss's among tree- and boulder-strewn ground east of McConnellsburg and Szink's atop Cove Mountain, south of town—neither offered much resistance to the invaders. Gilmore came on so quickly and confidently that Moss and Szink lost their nerve and fled their positions long before their enemy reached McConnellsburg. Only the third Yankee band—a company of Huntingdon County militia under Captain William W. Wallace, bolstered by a few local veterans from the 125th Pennsylvania Volunteers—remained to contest Gilmor's advance. Appropriating the position abandoned by Szink, Wallace's men fired down on Gilmor's rear guard as it passed a gap in Cove Mountain. The Marylanders lashed out in retaliation, and with "bullets striking the rocks and bushes like hail," Wallace's band was forced to abandon its perch. The Rebels then scrabbled up the mountainside to try to flush out the defenders from boulders and underbrush. Wallace's men nevertheless raced to safety, having suffered only one officer wounded.[23]

Their path now clear, the 1st Marylanders passed the mountain gap and continued west at a moderate pace. Suddenly they spurred into a charge that carried them through McConnellsburg after dark, frightening the locals half to death. Encountering no resistance in the village, Gilmor bivouacked his men until Steuart's infantry arrived to impress the citizens by their motley but fierce appearance. Infantry and cavalry remained in the vicinity for the next two days, ranging as far west as Fort Loudoun in their hunt for any prizes of war that Colonel Ferguson had overlooked. Not till the twenty-sixth did they march toward Chambersburg, Shippensburg, and Carlisle.[24]

***

While Steuart and Gilmor moved to rejoin Ewell, Jubal Early's division marched eastward toward the Susquehanna River by way of Greenwood, Cashtown, and Gettysburg. Early's immediate objective was the city of York, twenty-two miles southeast of Harrisburg. There he was to break the Northern Central Railroad, connecting the state capital with points south. This would so isolate Harrisburg as to make its seizure a formality.

In addition to French's 17th Virginia, which joined him at Cashtown, Early enjoyed mounted supported from White's Comanches. The Virginia battalion had been assigned him on the eighteenth, following its fifty-seven–mile round-trip expedition against Point of Rocks. As soon as Early commenced his move toward York on the twenty-sixth, he directed both French and White to search for any militia, short-term volunteers, or gun-toting farmers who seemed likely to offer resistance. He particularly directed their attention to a force of unknown size and composition reported to be operating out of Gettysburg.

Such forces were capable of minimal opposition, but Early did not take chances. Intending to outmaneuver the troops at Gettysburg—to strike them in flank as well as in front—he sent one of his four brigades, under Brigadier General John B. Gordon, screened by White's horsemen, along the Chambersburg Pike and through South Mountain to the Adams County seat. Meanwhile, Early led the brigades of Brigadier Generals Harry T. Hays and William Smith and Colonel I. E. Avery toward the north and east via the road to Mummasburg, French's troopers in the advance.[25]

White and Gordon approached Gettysburg under a rain shower shortly after noon on the twenty-sixth. About three miles west of town they encountered the mounted units of Bell and Conaughy. Behind the horsemen lay the bivouac of the recently formed 26th Pennsylvania Volunteer Militia, Colonel William W. Jennings. Though the majority of the regiment's 743 men lacked military training (many were students at Gettysburg's Pennsylvania College or Lutheran Theological Seminary), the outfit was leavened by some veterans of the Army of the Potomac, including the twenty-five-year-old Jennings. Moreover, a Regular Army officer sent to Gettysburg by General Couch, Major Granville O. Haller of the 7th Infantry, exercised overall command of the defenders.[26]

Ironically, while the raw recruits seemed willing to make a stand at Gettysburg (one felt "the occasion required that what they were capable of doing, whether much or little, should be done"),[27] Major Haller was not. Though sent to block the South Mountain passes against such an advance as Early's, Haller decided to make a token show of resistance. His lack of faith in his troops was shared to some extent by Jennings. As soon as Lige White appeared west of town, the colonel hauled his infantry and Conaughy's scouts out of their farmfield camps and led them northeastward in retreat. Infected by their leaders' nervousness, the citizen-soldiers double-quicked cross-country toward the Mummasburg road, casting anxious glances over their shoulders.[28]

Bell's cavalry and a picket company of Jennings's outfit, holding the forwardmost positions, could not get such a head start on their enemy. Before they were able to withdraw, White's Virginians swept down on them, sabering and shooting them into headlong flight. After landing the initial blow, the attackers drew back to re-form and to scrutinize their opposition. Once convinced that only fifty amateurs stood between them and Gettysburg, Colonel White launched a second, more determined assault.

Bell's horsemen had spurred eastward along the Gettysburg Pike; the Comanches chased after them "with barbarian yells and smoking pistols." En route, they overtook Jennings's fleeing pickets, dispatching some with pistol balls, cutting down others with their swords. The Virginians' horses, however, were so blown from recent service they could not overtake the fresh mounts of the Adams County Cavalry, who raced into Gettysburg with the news that Rebel hordes were on the way.[29] Within minutes, Major Haller and most of his remaining troops were careening wildly through the streets, seeking exit. The fugitives included the Philadelphia City Troop, which fled its billet near Haller's midtown headquarters and galloped out York Street in a frenzy. Part of the troop halted and countermarched toward town, where it delayed White's advance by some stubborn dismounted fighting. Their pride restored, the Philadelphians then retreated in an orderly fashion. Later they entrained for home, returning on 16 July to a hero's welcome.[30] On his part, Major Haller led a mixed band of escapees to Hanover, then to two other towns, as though determined to maintain maximum distance between himself and the invaders of Pennsylvania.[31]

Jennings's emergency troops were not so fleet of foot. Marching eastward from Mummasburg late in the afternoon, they were relieved to find that White's Comanches had given up their pursuit. But just as the regiment lay down to rest in muddy fields four miles due north of town, French's Virginians galloped up from Mummasburg to take them in rear. Dismounting as skirmishers, some Confederates held their opponents' attention, while others galloped through Jennings' already broken ranks, giving the quasi-soldiers another lesson in violence. Because their powder cartridges had been rendered useless by the rain, few of the militia could have offered effective resistance. Stampeded by panic, most did not even try. "Such confusion I never saw," recalled one of them, "everyone gave orders and no one obeyed . . . and half the right [wing were] already skedaddling. . . ." After fleeing through woods, Jennings rallied much of the regiment along the west bank of Rock Creek, beyond which the Confederates declined to venture. After that, most of the emergency troops escaped cross-country, abandoning about 180 others wounded or captured.[32]

Not long after the shooting died out above Gettysburg, Gordon's foot troops and White's riders entered the village. Residents—curious, apprehensive, and resentful—congregated around the midtown Diamond to gawk at the invaders. Schoolteacher Sallie Robbins Broadhead found them "a miserable-looking set. They wore all kinds of hats and caps, even to heavy fur ones, and some were barefooted." A professor at Pennsylvania College likened them to "so many savages from the wilds of the Rocky Mountains."[33]

The savages would remain for one night only—long enough to parole Jennings's captives, to harangue the people with secessionist propaganda, and to demand of them a requisition in the form of 60 barrels of flour, 7,000 pounds of pork, 1,200 pounds of sugar, and large quantities of other staple goods (only part of which would be met).[34] Still, before a week passed, White's and Gordon's men—as though charmed by the local hospitality—would make a return visit in company with the rest of Lee's army.

***

The next morning, most of Early's division moved north and east from its bivouac near Mummasburg toward Dover, via Hunterstown, Hampton, and East Berlin. Lower down, Gordon, White, and French marched along the York Pike directly toward its namesake city. The latter reached New Oxford, on the western border of Adams County, from which point Gordon and French continued toward York while the Comanches curved to the right and made for the railroad that Ewell had directed to Early's attention.

Passing through McSherrystown late that morning, White's troopers reached the town of Hanover at about 10:30 A.M. Today marked the first time in a week that the battalion traveled alone in enemy country; uncertain of the situation ahead, the Comanches cast anxious looks down the streets of Hanover as they cantered in. "They seemed to be in a state of trepidation," a citizen noted. "Every man had his carbine in his right hand with his finger on the trigger ready for any emergency."[35]

No emergency developed, so White continued to the center square, where he addressed an assembled throng in a subdued, even soothing tone. After describing his troopers as "gentlemen fighting for a cause they thought to be right, but [who] would harm no one," the portly officer appropriated the obligatory spoils, especially remounts. In exchange for their dray, carriage, and riding horses, several residents received wornout nags, some almost dead of exhaustion; others were reimbursed in Confederate scrip.

After an hour given to horse swapping, the Comanches rode out York Street to visit Hanover Junction. They reached the depot at about 2:00 P.M., from which point squads proceeded to various stretches of the railroad marked for destruction. By day's end the Virginians had wrecked rails and ties, bridges, culverts, and telegraph cable, while chasing from trackside breastworks a frightened detachment of the 20th Pennsylvania Emergency Troops.[36]

Having ensured that aid could neither be wired nor hauled to Harrisburg from the south, the Comanches countermarched to Jefferson, then toward Spring Grove. Next day they rejoined Early's division on the road to York, their demolition efforts earning them a cordial reception.[37]

Prior to their return, Early's command, screened by the 17th Virginia, had marched east from Gettysburg toward the mouth of Conewago Creek, near York. En route, Colonel French chopped up several bridges on that stream and another between York and Hanover Junction, strewing new obstacles in the path of any pursuers. When the Comanches reached York, they found Early levying the now-standard tribute on the inhabitants—in this case $100,000 in cash ($28,600 was offered and accepted), plus all manner of supplies.[38]

In midafternoon, Early ordered White, along with Gordon's brigade, to run a mission to Wrightsville, a dozen miles off. Ewell had decided to cross the river there as well as higher up, directly across from Harrisburg. Although Ewell planned this movement as a feint for the main effort to the north, Early wished the mile-long covered bridge at Wrightsville to be seized intact, so he might cross to the suburb of Columbia, then move on the city of Lancaster before striking the state capital from the rear.[39]

But Dick Ewell had his way, after all. Arriving at Wrightsville late in the afternoon of the twenty-eighth, Gordon and White were stymied by an unexpectedly large force: two state emergency regiments, three others, a detachment of invalid troops, Bell's and Randall's companies, and several smaller units—all under Major Haller, the fugitive from Gettysburg. Although Haller duplicated his earlier performance by withdrawing in the face of the Rebel advance, he did fire the bridge in his wake, foiling Early's plan. When the span—reportedly the longest structure of its kind in the world—crashed into the Susquehanna, the Confederate invasion had suffered its first setback.[40]

Early the next day Gordon and White glumly retraced their steps to York, where they reported their failure. They had little time to brood over their misfortune, for on the thirtieth, in company with Early and French, they were ordered to march northwestward to keep a rendezvous with the rest of Ewell's corps at neighboring Carlisle. The latter had been chosen as the jumping-off point for the final push to Harrisburg.

Late on the twenty-ninth, however, one of Ewell's aides brought Jubal Early surprising news. The 2nd Corps, whose main body had entered Carlisle on the twenty-seventh, had received orders to join General Lee in the Cashtown-Gettysburg vicinity. To conform to the movement, Early was to hasten to Ewell's side at Carlisle (later the rendezvous was changed to Heidlersburg, between Carlisle and Gettysburg). Puzzled by any directive that would carry him away from Harrisburg, the division commander started off as ordered, White and French, as always, in the advance.[41]

***

Ewell, with the divisions of Rodes and Johnson and Jenkins's horsemen, had departed Chambersburg on the twenty-sixth, following a brief but profitable stopover. Driving a herd of confiscated cattle and hauling a train of well-stocked forage wagons, the corps commander moved northeast toward Carlisle with hopes and spirits high. Thus far all seemed to have gone according to blueprint and timetable—not only for him but for the entire invasion force. As the 2nd Corps neared Harrisburg, Lee, with A. P. Hill and Longstreet, was arriving at Chambersburg, within supporting distance of Ewell.[42] Meanwhile, as far as could be determined, the Army of the Potomac remained stationary along the Orange & Alexandria line.

Late on 26 June Ewell's column made a slow and cautious march through the Shippensburg vicinity—where Captain Boyd's ubiquitous New Yorkers struck the vanguard, inflicting several casualties, before speeding away toward Carlisle. Studying their route of retreat, Ewell suspected that another fight awaited him in the old garrison village. As it happened, General Jenkins found no Federals when he entered the city on the twenty-seventh, although Knipe's militia, driven from their most recent base at Shippensburg, had reached Carlisle only hours before—just in time to flee toward Harrisburg.[43]

As at Chambersburg, Gettysburg, Hanover, and their other ports of call, the invaders met with the officials of Carlisle, promised to do the latter's constituents no harm unless provoked, and requisitioned from the populace whatever was needed to fill the command's quota of plunder. Having disposed of these formalities, Jenkins repaired to the century-old cavalry depot below the town, whose 274-man garrison had scurried across the Susquehanna prior to Knipe's arrival, adding a Regular Army tint to the panic produced by Ewell's coming.[44]

At the depot barracks Jenkins camped his brigade and set up his headquarters. There, late in the day, Ewell joined him, to renew his association with a post at which he had served a stint of dragoon service twenty years before. In taking over Jenkins's headquarters, the corps leader evicted the cavalry, sending it westward to reconnoiter the approaches to Harrisburg.

Accompanied by Ewell's engineer officers, Jenkins got his men on the road with unusual celerity. They rode well into the night, heading for Mechanicsburg and other capital suburbs. By 9:00 A.M. on Sunday, the twenty-eighth, the horse soldiers had reached a road fork just west of Mechanicsburg. From here Jenkins sent a detachment under Colonel Ferguson—the latter's own 16th Virginia, Major Sweeney's 36th Virginia Battalion, and the four-gun battery of Captain Thomas E. Jackson—to flank any defense force along the Carlisle Pike, just north of the road occupied by the main body. With the latter—Colonel Cochran's 14th Virginia, Lieutenant Colonel Vincent A. Witcher's 34th Virginia Battalion, and an attached battery of Parrott rifles under Captain William H. Griffin of Maryland—the brigade leader continued northeast on the Trindle Spring road.

It was well that Jenkins took precautions. On his side-trip, Colonel Ferguson sighted Knipe's infantry, some home guard cavalry, and a Pennsylvania battery—part of a militia division under Brigadier General William Farrar ("Baldy") Smith, another former commander in the Army of the Potomac now serving Darius Couch. Smith's men held a line of defenses between Wormleysburg, on the Susquehanna opposite Harrisburg, and Sporting Hill, about four and a half miles to the west. Upon Ferguson's approach, Smith hunkered down behind his works at Sporting Hill as if determined to bar the way to the river, come what may.[45]

Near Sporting Hill, Ferguson ordered into action Jackson's battery, which had never fired a round in anger. Despite the artillerists' inexperience, their shelling was accurate enough to compel the militiamen to scurry eastward to heavier works at Oyster's Point, halfway between Sporting Hill and the river.

Fighting resumed at the new site late in the afternoon, by which time Jenkins had placed his main command in bivouac east of Mechanicsburg. After gathering intelligence from newspapers perused at a local hotel, the general accompanied most of his troops out the Trindle Spring road, where he watched as Griffin's Parrotts shelled the woods in front of Knipe's position. The fire was replied to by the militia battery—to the delight of residents of Harrisburg, who had climbed onto roofs to watch the fracas from across the river. The artillery duel petered out around dusk, Jenkins having decided not to attack until next day.[46]

Early on the twenty-ninth, part of Colonel Ferguson's regiment renewed the action by advancing on the Carlisle Pike against Oyster's Point. While his men kept the militia occupied, Jenkins, with Ewell's engineers, reached the shoreline beyond the southern flank of General Smith's works near Wormleysburg. From atop a ridge southeast of Shiremanstown, the Confederate officers spent several minutes inspecting the defenses along both sides of the Susquehanna.

Their notes taken, Ewell's emissaries rode back to Carlisle Barracks, where they reported so favorably on the prospect of taking the capital that Ewell drafted an order for Rodes's division to march on Harrisburg the next morning.[47]

But the farthest point of Confederate invasion had already been reached. Barely an hour after penning the directive to advance, Ewell received a courier from General Lee's headquarters at Chambersburg. The dispatch he carried recalled the 2nd Corps immediately to Gettysburg via Heidlersburg.

Only later would Ewell and his subordinates learn of certain recent events at the headquarters of the Army of Northern Virginia and the Army of the Potomac. Some seventeen hours ago, while preparing to send Longstreet to Harrisburg in support of Ewell, and Hill to Cashtown to cut the capital's communications from above, Robert E. Lee had been paid a visit by a civilian scout just up from Virginia. The spy, who had ridden around the Union army en route to Pennsylvania, conveyed the startling intelligence that the enemy was moving north rapidly to counter Lee's advance. He explained that Lee no longer faced the sluggish and indecisive Hooker, but his swift and savvy replacement, George Meade. Aware that the Philadelphian would move aggressively to defend his native state, Lee now determined to group his scattered forces around the little college and seminary town that was also a strategic road hub.

Ewell, though disappointed at losing the opportunity to cross the Susquehanna, obeyed Lee's order dutifully and without delay. By daylight on the thirtieth Rodes's and Johnson's men had evacuated Carlisle; from his carriage seat, the one-legged corps commander guided them westward into Adams County.[48]

Though Ewell sent word for Early, at York, to follow him, Albert Jenkins failed to get the message. The cavalry leader did not conform to the withdrawal until about 2:00 P.M., when he sent Colonel Cochran's regiment on ahead to Carlisle. Later, as the main body disengaged, another artillery exchange near Sporting Hill constituted the final action of Jenkins's command during its advance to the Susquehanna.[49]

With General Smith's artillery booming out a farewell, Jenkins's brigade—fatigued from long marching and intermittent fighting, enervated by the necessity of remaining alert for long hours, and reduced to ten rounds of Enfield ammunition per man—moved south to the hamlet of Petersburg. There, about 2:00 A.M., the troopers found longed-for rest, bivouacking beyond range of armed Unionists. While the main body of the brigade bedded down, foraging details scoured the countryside for items of value, especially feed and medical supplies.

Instead of roughing it with his men, Jenkins spent the night and part of the next day as a guest at the home of a local merchant named Hiteshaw. About midday of 1 July, soothed by a hearty dinner topped off by cigars and brandy (Mr. Hiteshaw was a Unionist but a politic one), the brigadier seemed to forget the fatigue of recent days. He turned loquacious, discussing military affairs and politics with his host. At one point, in response to an observation that the Union army must soon be at Lee's heels, Jenkins scoffed: "Oh, the Army of the Potomac is away down in Virginia; they will most likely cross the river about Shepherdstown and advance over the battle field of Antietam." Such a movement would take days, perhaps weeks: "We expect to remain here [in the North] all summer."

Later the two men strolled about the grounds, smoking their cigars. Cresting a rise that overlooked a valley, they suddenly heard the distant sounds of thunder—or cannon fire—coming from the southwest. As if on cue, a mounted messenger galloped through the yard, pulled up beside them, saluted Jenkins, and thrust a dispatch at him. Nonplussed, the general tore open the envelope. After scanning its contents, he looked up at his host.

"Mr. Hiteshaw," he said in a tone of profound disbelief, "the Army of the Potomac is at Gettysburg now!"[50]

[8]

Stuart's Expedition—Salem to Hanover

ALTHOUGH on 21 June Yankee troops had peered through Ashby's Gap into the Shenandoah, J. E. B. Stuart felt he had already accomplished his mission to screen Lee's infantry. No time remained for Hooker to halt the Confederate column short of Northern soil. That very evening, Longstreet and Hill moved within easy marching distance of Ewell's headquarters near Chambersburg. Within four days, both corps would cross the river into Maryland—long before the Army of the Potomac could concentrate, force the Blue Ridge gaps, and strike their rear.[1]

The morning after Upperville, as Pleasonton withdrew eastward, Stuart sent units in the same direction to certify that the Yankees were retreating, not feinting with the intention of striking Ashby's Gap. Annoyed by the pursuit, Pleasonton's rear guard wheeled about and offered battle near Middleburg. Both sides had artillery, and for much of the day cannon dueled at long range without decisive result. In the evening the Rebels returned toward the Blue Ridge. Now that his front was clear, Stuart placed his entire force in bivouac at Rector's Cross Roads.[2]

Gratified by the cavalry's success at counterreconnaissance, General Lee realized that the first phase of its participation in the invasion had ended. Now he must decide how to employ it as the campaign approached high tide.

As early as the twentieth, Stuart had suggested to Lee that he be allowed to make an independent campaign to slow Hooker's pursuit of the Army of Northern Virginia. He would dog the Yankees' heels, monitoring their movements as closely as possible. And if he found them about to cross the Potomac, he would retire from their front and join Lee's main body for the movement north.[3]

If Stuart viewed his plan as a means of duplicating his dramatic rides around McClellan (as his critics later charged), he also saw strategic utility in it. By operating far to the east of Lee's army he could confuse the Yankees as to its whereabouts and intentions, while harassing Hooker in rear and flank and cutting his communications. Then, too, by placing his men in the enemy's country Stuart could send his commander precise information on Union movements. Finally, a march around Hooker's army would permit the cavalry leader to secure the riches of a region untouched by Lee's infantry. Conversely, should Stuart at once move west of the Blue Ridge in conjunction with Longstreet and Hill (as Lee had originally envisioned), he would be impeded by having to detour around the infantry and their wagons and by the necessity of twice passing the mountains—at the outset of the march and again north of the Potomac.[4]

Many of Stuart's objectives appealed to Lee, who by the twenty-second developed the concept that the cavalry should pass around Hooker and link with Ewell's advance guard in Pennsylvania. That day he sent Stuart the first of two orders, informing the cavalry leader that "if you find that he [Hooker] is moving northward, and that two brigades can guard the Blue Ridge and take care of your rear, you can move with the other three into Maryland, and take position on General Ewell's right, place yourself in communication with him, guard his flank, keep him informed of the enemy's movements, and collect all the supplies you can for the use of the army."[5]

The next day Lee forwarded a second set of orders, dated 5:00 P.M., that confused the issue. Now Stuart could move around the enemy if he found Hooker inactive below the Potomac. On the other hand, Stuart should cross west of the Blue Ridge and proceed to Frederick, Maryland, should Hooker "not appear to be moving northward." The apparently conflicting set of conditions may have meant Lee feared that the Federals were preparing a southward march on Richmond, a movement Stuart might observe and oppose from a strategic location such as Frederick.[6]

At any rate, Lee left the crucial issue to Stuart's discretion: "You will, however, be able to judge whether you can pass around their army without hindrance, doing them all the damage you can, and cross the river east of the mountains." Stuart perceived this as a loophole: having parlayed as much latitude into dramatic success on two prior occasions, he felt confident in his ability to do so again. His first use of such discretion was to interpret his orders to mean that he might flank Hooker if the latter was either stationary or heading north. At the same time, he chose to overlook another, less ambiguous stipulation in Lee's orders: that he must curtail his expedition and return west of the mountains if he found his path obstructed and his travel impeded by the enemy.[7]

Stuart's interpretation of his orders—that whatever he deemed possible was permissible—was endorsed by James Longstreet, to whose command the cavalry had been assigned. Later Longstreet would claim that he made clear to Stuart his preference for the cavalry's moving on the west side of the Blue Ridge, remaining on the infantry's right flank at least as far as the Potomac—at which point Stuart could make a more informed choice as to his options. But in forwarding Lee's 22 June orders to Stuart, the corps leader remarked that "I think your passage of the Potomac by our rear at the present will, in a measure, disclose our plans. You had better not leave us, therefore, unless you can take the route in rear of the enemy."[8] Perhaps he was suggesting that Stuart ought not detach himself from the army at all. But because Longstreet's wording was as ambiguous as Lee's, Stuart cannot be blamed for failing to take the hint.

Details as to the route Stuart should take were not made clear in either of the orders Lee gave the cavalry leader. The route he ultimately followed was suggested to him early on the twenty-third by John Mosby, who rode into Rector's Cross Roads following a reconnaissance inside Hooker's lines. Some of the partisan leader's scouts, disguised in blue uniforms, had slipped into bivouacs and behind picket cordons, intercepting rumors and capturing and interrogating prisoners. The upshot was Mosby's conclusion that Hooker, instead of preparing to march north, lay idle and would remain so for the immediate future. Mosby also informed Stuart that the Army of the Potomac was stretched so thin—along a line twenty-five miles long, from Leesburg south to Thoroughfare Gap—that Stuart could ride *through* it without great difficulty. If he intended to do this, Mosby recommended a swing south and east via Hopewell or another gap in the Bull Run Mountains below Middleburg, points known to be lightly held by the enemy. Turning north, Stuart could cross the Potomac at Seneca Ford, twenty miles upstream from Washington, D.C., before sweeping into Union country. In addition to laying hands on Hooker's lines of movement and supply, the Confederate horsemen might scare the wits out of the denizens of the Yankee capital.

Here was a plan that warmed Stuart's heart. As Mosby repeated it, the cavalry commander had aides commit it to paper. Shown to Wade Hampton and Fitz Lee (the latter now recovered from his infirmities), it elicited favorable comment. Stuart personally conveyed it to army headquarters at Berryville and awaited Lee's reaction with high hopes.[9]

That evening, covered by a poncho, Stuart slept fitfully under a tree in a yard at Rector's Cross Roads, his repose challenged by thunder and rain. About midnight Major McClellan, slumbering on a porch nearby, was roused by a courier bearing a dispatch from Lee. After perusing it to determine its significance, McClellan shook his superior awake. By lantern-light Stuart read Lee's authorization for him to choose between joining the main army west of the Blue Ridge or moving eastward around the foe. The order was accompanied by Longstreet's endorsement recommending the latter route. This of course was what Stuart wanted to hear. It gave him ample authority to implement Mosby's plan and was sufficiently open-ended to suit him—even as to time of departure if not as to destination. Although there is no evidence that anyone ever mentioned the city, Stuart, according to Major McClellan, was told by General Lee that if he passed around Hooker, he was to link with Ewell's advance—the division of Jubal Early—at or near York, Pennsylvania.[10]

In preparing to put John Mosby's plan to the test, Stuart took steps to protect himself against criticism that he had failed to provide enough horsemen to support the main army on its movement north. Such troops would be crucial to the success of Lee's invasion, especially if the suddenly aggressive cavalrymen under Pleasonton took advantage of Stuart's absence to harass Longstreet and Hill. Although he believed his march would, instead, draw the Yankee horsemen after him, Stuart intended to comply fully with Lee's injunction that he leave 40 percent of his force behind.

By the twenty-fourth Stuart believed he and Longstreet had reached an understanding on this issue. The cavalry leader would leave the brigades of Jones and Robertson to cover the main army's rear and flanks. Though Robertson's brigade was tiny, Jones's was by far the largest in the division; the combined force of 3,000 effectives Stuart considered ample to ensure the army's security, especially given Jones's reputation as an excellent outpost commander.[11] Longstreet, however, would maintain that Stuart contrived to rid himself of his least favored and least efficient brigades, led by officers he disliked. Since both brigades had comported themselves inconsistently in recent fighting, he believed that Stuart did not trust them enough to accompany him on his expedition. Longstreet also claimed he had ordered Stuart to leave with him a more reliable subordinate such as Hampton. Perhaps he ought not to have supposed that Stuart would set off on such a mission without his senior lieutenant. Even so, Stuart failed to acquaint Longstreet with the composition of his mounted contingent. Such misunderstandings—which caused serious problems for the army in subsequent weeks—might have been averted had Stuart left behind a capable officer as a liaison between the infantry and the cavalry. Longstreet had specifically requested a go-between, but apparently Stuart ignored his wish.[12]

***

To accommodate those troopers holding the mountain gaps, who would have to travel far to reach him at Rector's Cross Roads, on 24 June Stuart moved his headquarters southwestward to Salem, two miles closer to the Blue Ridge. He spent most of that day assembling the brigades that would accompany him and culling out those horses and men not deemed able to withstand a rigorous campaign. The rain having ended, a balmy day aided Stuart's efforts to put his force into marching and fighting trim.

Determined to reduce impediments to speed, the cavalry leader assigned to Jones and Robertson every horse artillery unit except a six-gun battery, plus all but a few ambulances. The raiders would live off the land, even to appropriating wheeled transport as needed.[13] Stuart also decided to leave behind a few companies of the 2nd Virginia Cavalry, who would escort to the Rappahannock the Yankees captured in recent battles. And instead of taking Mosby and his guerrillas along, he sent them north toward Dranesville, to renew their watch over the enemy camps and to report their observations to him before he entered Pennsylvania.[14]

Preliminaries attended to, Stuart led the brigades of Hampton, Fitz Lee, and Chambliss, the guns and their appurtenances, out of Salem just after midnight on 24–25 June. The 6,000-man column wound south and east through farm and pasture lands until in early morning it neared Glasscock's Gap in the Bull Run Mountains. There, as Mosby had predicted, the Confederates found only a handful of Yankee pickets, easily dislodged. Without missing a stride, the raiders passed through the gap into the open country beyond—riding in the direction of Hooker's rear echelon.[15]

It was not long before Stuart's cavaliers, after spending several days flushed with the excitement of combat, had thoroughly reacquainted themselves with the fatigue and monotony of sustained marching. Close to noon, however, they were fighting again, along the Warrenton-Centreville Turnpike just east of the Bull run chain, near Haymarket. This time their opponents were infantrymen from Winfield Hancock's II Corps, moving northwestward toward the point at which Stuart had planned to check in with Major Mosby. Hancock's intervention meant that the Stuart-Mosby conference would never take place and that the partisan leader would not reach Pennsylvania this summer.[16]

Presumably, Hancock's intrusion also meant the end of Stuart's expedition. The Federals' course might bring them into contact with Lee's rear. This, as Stuart's orders stipulated, meant he must return to the other side of the Blue Ridge and rejoin the infantry.

Stuart rejected the idea at once. He refused to terminate such a promising operation, already well advanced—especially when countermarching would take so long that God alone knew when he might reach Longstreet's column. The discretion given him to proceed as he thought best seemed to override the rest of his instructions. He decided to make only a slight alteration of his route, swinging farther south than originally intended, until he bypassed Hancock's line of march.[17]

While so planning, Stuart resolved to make the most of his meeting engagement with the II Corps. As his rear echelon crossed over to a new road, he ran his six cannon to the front, where they unlimbered in a field west of Haymarket blocked from enemy view. The cannon then opened on the nearest infantrymen, causing consternation and damage. Stuart may have reflected that already he had carried out one of his recently assigned objectives, by inflicting injury on an enemy force that had crossed his path.[18]

Scrambling into defensive positions, Hancock's soldiers threw forward skirmish lines and brought up their own artillery. Soon Stuart and his staff came under a heavy shelling, while foot troops pressed forward on the cannon's flanks. Looking on with concern, John Esten Cooke decided that "when calvalry undertake to cut off infantry, the process is exciting, but not uniformly remunerative."[19]

Before Hancock could enfilade his position, Stuart departed Haymarket in company with his erstwhile advance guard—now the column's rear echelon. Quickly he passed to the front of the column, directing Lee's brigade toward the Manassas Gap Railroad depot of Gainesville. In nearby Buckland—well beyond the range of Hancock's artillery—he camped for the night with Hampton and Chambliss, whose horses needed rest and feeding.

After selecting a bivouac amid a field of clover ("the only forage procurable in the country"), Stuart discussed with his subordinates the logistics of their re-vamped route and how best to aid the main army. Already he had sent a courier to inform Robert E. Lee what he had learned from prisoners captured at Hay-market: that the II Corps was heading for Gum Springs and other points leading to the Potomac. Unfortunately for Stuart and his superior both, the message never reached its destination, leaving Lee ignorant of Hooker's rapid pursuit.[20]

Early on the twenty-sixth the march resumed in a direction that reflected Stuart's growing caution. Instead of turning north just short of Centreville, as originally planned, he decided to continue southeastward to Brentsville, then to Wolf Run Shoals on the Occoquan River, before moving north via Hooker's old headquarters at Fairfax Station. By nightfall he found that the detour had enabled him to make only thirty-five miles in forty-eight hours.[21]

After spending the night north of Bull Run—where darkness shrouded the grisly sights Pleasonton's men had recently observed—Stuart sent his main force toward Fairfax on Saturday morning, the twenty-seventh. Fitz Lee de-toured to the east to cut railroad track and telegraph lines at Burke's Station. After completing his visit to that depot—which he had plundered the previous December during Stuart's Dumfries raid—Lee would rejoin Hampton and Chambliss at or beyond Fairfax.[22]

Hearing that Fairfax Station was lightly held, if at all, the Beau Sabreur galloped ahead of Hampton's brigade, outdistancing even his personal escort. The upshot was a scene in some ways reminiscent of his surprise and near-capture at Middleburg on 17 June. Coming within sight of the depot, Stuart nearly ran into the arms of Companies B and C, 11th New York Cavalry, Major S. P. Remington commanding. The latter's eighty-six men had been sent from the Washington defenses on the twenty-sixth to watch over the army stores that Hooker had left behind and which Stuart was seeking.[23] The Confederate leader put spurs to "Virginia" and fled south aboard his fleet-footed charger.

As surprised as Stuart over their meeting, Remington's men had little time to speculate about the identity of the escapee before Stuart's advance guard swarmed over them. Although heavily outgunned, the Yankees charged the lead regiment, Baker's 1st North Carolina. The New Yorkers were tossed back but not before they killed Major John H. Whitaker and some of his troopers. Forced to take position in a gully near the station, twenty-six of Remington's men quickly became casualties, most of them as prisoners. The rest put spurs to their mounts and flew off through neighboring woods.[24]

While an unruffled Stuart sent a message informing General Lee of his victory (one that failed to find its destination, though a copy somehow reached the War Department in Richmond), the army leader's nephew was dashing into Annandale, above Fairfax Court House. Fitz Lee's brigade met little opposition there but found signs that the VI Corps of Major General John Sedgwick had recently encamped nearby. After burning abandoned sutlers' and medical supplies, Lee moved warily up to Dranesville.[25]

Rejoining the other brigades at that place, Lee saw that they too had found sutler's goods at the depot as well as at Fairfax Court House, where they had rested after the clash with the 11th New York. Many troopers sported white gloves, straw hats, and shiny boots. Others had gorged themselves on ginger cakes and lobster salad, wine, and ale.[26]

Well-fed and well-attired, Hampton's brigade soon resumed the march. The raiders' next objective should have been Seneca Ford on the Potomac, but the revamped route led Hampton instead toward Rowser's Ford, directly above Dranesville. En route, he chanced upon a civilian who recommended a crossing at Rowser's. Though recent rains had elevated the Potomac by two feet above normal height, that site remained crossable and free of Yankees. Accepting the advice, Hampton led onward to the ford, where his command waded across the mile-wide stream without notable difficulty. Late in the evening, Stuart followed with the main force. After Lee's and Chambliss's men forded, the artillerymen crossed with shells and bags of powder held on their heads. With hawsers they towed their dismantled cannon across aboard flatboats.[27]

Watching from the Maryland side in the dusk, Esten Cooke recorded the crossing of the rear guard: "The spectacle was picturesque. The broad river glittered in the moon, and on the bright surface was seen the long, wavering line of dark figures, moving 'in single file'; the water washing to and fro across the backs of the horses, which kept their feet with difficulty."[28]

Not till 3:00 A.M. did the last of Stuart's column get over.[29] Once on the northern bank, many raiders expressed satisfaction that they again had carried the fight into the enemy's homeland—an accomplishment that seemed to make the ordeal of getting there worthwhile. But their toil was far from over; before allowing his troopers to sleep, Stuart set them to destroying property along the Chesapeake & Ohio Canal, where they also assimilated more prisoners. By dawn the cavalrymen had mutilated boats, barges, and a sluice gate at one of the canal's principal locks. They had captured new quantities of quartermaster's and commissary stores ("some," remarked a member of the 1st Virginia, "very tempting to a hungry and thirsty soldier"—including several barrels of whiskey). The raiders had also nabbed perhaps three hundred Yankees en route by canal boat from Ohio and West Virginia to the Union capital. The captives, plus those gobbled up at Fairfax Station, were escorted to Rockville, Maryland, eight miles to the northeast.[30]

To reward his men for their exertions, Stuart did not resume the march until late in the morning of the twenty-eighth. From that point on, however, he resolved to lose as little time as possible. The prisoners taken at the river informed Stuart that Hooker yesterday had made his headquarters at Poolesville, Maryland, fifteen miles to the west, and was heading due north. The fact that the Yankee army had moved so far so fast made the cavalry leader appreciate the need to accelerate his own march.

Even so, the column slowed at various points to confiscate additional supplies. As Stuart had foreseen, the farmlands of lower Maryland were lush and unspoiled, in contrast to the barren country below the Potomac. "There is plenty of grass and grain here," a Virginia trooper wrote his father that day. "Thousands of bushels of wheat are standing about in stacks." As for the men's rations, "we have been getting plenty . . . and have no reason to complain."[31]

The spoils quickly multiplied. Near Rockville, barely eight miles northwest of Washington, Hampton's point riders flushed from roadside trees fugitives from the 11th New York and bands of the 2nd Massachusetts Cavalry, another element of the Washington defense force.[32] While pursuing the Yankees, Hampton's men happened upon undreamed-of riches along the Rockville outskirts. First, they became the focal point of attention from students at the local female academy. The damsels surrounded the young cavalrymen, chatting and flirting, pinning ribbons on them, taking locks of their hair as keepsakes. This demonstration of affection abashed and charmed the troopers, as did the edibles the young ladies thrust upon them. Esten Cooke rhapsodized over "the beautiful girls in their fresh gaily coloured dresses, low necks, bare arms, and wilderness of braids and curls. . . . Every eye flashed, every voice exclaimed; every rosy lip laughed; every fair hand waved a handkerchief or a sheet of music (smuggled) with crossed Confederate flags upon the cover."[33]

Other delights lay just ahead. Hampton's advance regiment, the 2nd South Carolina, sent back word that a long supply train was rumbling toward the town from the direction of the capital, apparently bound for Hooker's army. With a whoop of delight, the rest of the column tore free from their comely admirers and spurred after the wagons. They yelled and cheered in such a frenzy that their quarry panicked. Some teamsters turned off onto side roads, while those in rear of the train fled back toward Washington to evade capture, lashing their mules without mercy. The result was that some of the spanking-new wagons overturned and others collided, spilling foodstuffs and equiment onto the ground. Riding at the head of the pursuers, William Blackford wrote that for a long distance "you could see nothing but the long ears and kicking legs of the mules sticking above bags of oats emptied from the wagons." Farther to the rear, Stuart himself roared with delight: "Did you ever see anything like that in all your life!"[34]

When they overtook those wagons still upright, the Rebels brought the train to a stop by slashing halter reins or gunning down teams and drivers. A pileup at a narrow curve east of Rockville foiled further pursuit and allowed twenty-five wagons to escape. Still, 125 others had been overturned or overtaken. Chambliss's brigade rooted through the contents of many, filching ham, sugar, and whiskey. Other troopers helped right fallen wagons capable of being salvaged, torching those too badly wrecked or entangled. Still other Confederates made a futile effort at running to earth the escaping vehicles. Riding with them, Captain Blackford topped a ridge and was startled to find himself gazing across a valley at the unfinished dome of the Capitol Building.[35]

***

The city under Blackford's eye was running scared. Not since the earliest days of the war had Washington seemed so vulnerable to attack and capture. By slicing miles of telegraph wire at Rockville, Stuart had isolated the capital from communication with points west—and with the army charged with protecting it.[36] Local newspapers, which had predicted a Rebel raid in a far-distant locale, now foresaw an attack on the lightly held line of forts encircling the capital.

General Heintzelman mobilized to resist an onslaught. Under his supervision, a motley force of defenders—Regulars, volunteers, militia, home guards, disabled soldiers, government employees and other private citizens in temporary service—improved palisades and earthworks, erected barricades in the streets, scouted the countryside, packed government archives and artifacts in case their removal became necessary, and steeled themselves for the worst.[37]

Heintzelman's cavalry made the most energetic efforts to protect the city. As Stuart drew near on the twenty-eighth, horsemen under Colonel Charles Russell Lowell, Jr., once an officer in the 6th United States Cavalry and more recently commander of the 2nd Massachusetts, patrolled outlying roads, staffed picket posts, and sorted out rumors of enemy movements to the south and west. Meanwhile, Sir Percy Wyndham cut short his convalescence to try to raise, horse, and equip three thousand troopers—many of them dismounted members of Pleasonton's corps—at the cavalry depot at Giesboro Point.

Even so, these efforts were too feeble to deter Stuart if Stuart had decided to attack. The small size of Lowell's command led him to predict that if he did encounter Rebels "I presume I shall not harm them much."[38] Wyndham, despite best efforts, could not locate enough horses and equipments to accommodate his potential force (which an observer on 30 June found "in a heap"). And the capital's only substantial cavalry force, Stahel's division, lay too far afield to defend it, thanks to the Heintzelman-Hooker lend-lease program.[39]

Thus, had he wished to take the time, J. E. B. Stuart could have walked into the most politically important city in the land. But because he was guided by military and not political considerations, on the twenty-eighth he bypassed the capital ten miles to the west.[40] In the city along the Potomac soldiers and civilians alike shuddered with relief.

***

Largely because of its 125-wagon impediment, Stuart's column moved toward its next major objective, Westminster, Maryland, more slowly than it had at any point on the road to Rockville. This worried the cavalry leader, especially given the need for celerity in joining Ewell. On the other hand, he considered the captured train proof that he had fulfilled a major part of his orders: the requirement to confiscate enemy property of value to the A.N.V.

Soon after daylight on the twenty-ninth, following an all-night march, the Rebel advance struck the Baltimore & Ohio twenty-odd miles from its namesake city. There Hampton and Chambliss joined Fitz Lee, who had preceded them to get a head start at destroying what Stuart called "the enemy's main war artery." By the time the two brigadiers reached the depot of Hood's Mill, Lee had wrecked the bridge at neighboring Sykesville and was ranging westward, laying waste to track, rolling stock, and station buildings in the direction of Mount Airy. Now Hampton and Chambliss struck off to the right to do the same along a six-mile stretch; in the process they scattered Federal patrols near Cookesville. To do a thorough job, Stuart kept the troopers at work through the morning; when he retook the road north at noon, he felt certain he had incapacitated the North's most vital rail system.[41]

Such work had further slowed his pace, making a shambles of his timetable. So had his decision to parole the four hundred prisoners taken at Rockville—a time-consuming process his subordinates had begun last night and had not finished till this morning. Stuart tried to make amends by cutting the number of rest periods he allowed the men, but the effect was minimal: by 4:00 P.M. the column had progressed only thirty-five miles from Rockville. It should have been well into Pennsylvania by now.[42]

As he closed in on Westminster, the terminus of a branch line of the Northern Central Railroad, Stuart experienced his longest and most crucial delay. Entering the depot village via the Washington road, his advance guard, a company of Wickham's 4th Virginia, was sent reeling by a volley of carbine fire. Before the unit could re-form it met a squadron of blue-jacketed troopers charging around a street corner onto the Washington road. The Yankees bowled over a number of Wickham's men, wounding a few and hurling the rest back on Stuart's vanguard.[43]

The attackers proved to be ninety-five troopers of Companies C and D, 1st Delaware Cavalry, under Major Napoleon B. Knight. Members of Schenck's Baltimore-based VIII Corps, they had recently been sent to guard the railhead, which would soon become the main supply depot of the Army of the Potomac. Without ascertaining the size or identity of the force advancing toward him from the south, Major Knight had decided to take it on. That is, his men took it on. Knight, despite his name, was no warrior; after spending some hours in a local tavern, he mounted up rather unsteadily and weaved his way out of town just ahead of Stuart's arrival, leaving Captain Charles Corbit to welcome the raiders in his stead.[44]

Concerned, but not panicked, by the enemy's daring, Stuart sent scouts to surround the town and size up the opposition. When his scouts reported in, he discounted the notion that so few horsemen would stand against him, let alone attack. Eventually he saw this to be true and made plans to secure the town as quickly and as painlessly as possible. By then he had deployed fifty of Wickham's men, under Lieutenants St. Pierre Gibson and John W. Murray, at a road junction east of Westminster, while a larger detachment waited northwest of the town to cut off Corbit's escape.

But before Stuart could strike, his enemy again took the initiative. Charging east against Wickham's fifty men, Corbit's troopers slashed their way through them with a violence that led one of Stuart's men to compare them to wild Turks. Again, the Virginians were compelled to flee. Attempting to rally them, Lieutenant Gibson took a ball through the skull. And when Lieutenant Murray succeeded in returning some of his men to the fray, he too was shot dead.[45]

Inspired by the bravery of the young officers, and led personally by Stuart, the 4th Virginia counterattacked in force. Its weight forced the men of Delaware westward—whereupon the Rebel flanking party fell like a gray net over Corbit's men. In a brief but spirited battle with revolver and sword, sixty-seven Federals were killed, wounded, or captured, Corbit and two of his lieutenants among the prisoners. The survivors raced after Major Knight along the road to Baltimore.

Taking full possession of the town at about 5:00 P.M., Stuart made a crucial decision to remain there long enough to secure forage, parole many of his prisoners, and tend to the casualties on both sides, including all but two of the dead. At the request of townspeople sympathetic to the Confederate cause, he allowed them to inter Gibson and Murray.[46]

Soon night came on. The raiding leader spent part of it in the center of town, sleeping in a chair propped against a private residence. Slumbering near him, his command stretched five miles northward to Union Mills. Not all of Stuart's men slept, however; in the summer darkness, scouting forces roamed the countryside in advance of the column. One, a detachment of Cobb's Legion, Hampton's brigade, pushed as far north as Hunterstown, Pennsylvania.[47]

At daylight on the thirtieth, the column again rumbled into motion. Throughout the day its point riders looked and listened for signs they were nearing Dick Ewell's sector, but they came up dry. Not even the advance scouting parties received positive word of the 2nd Corps's whereabouts.

Stuart tried to assuage his concern by partaking of early morning hospitality at the Union Mills home of William Shriver. The patriarch of the clan—four of whose sons had gone to war in gray but whose staunchly Unionist brother lived just across the Westminster road—had his womenfolk provide Stuart and his staff with flapjacks, biscuits, coffee, buttermilk, and other breakfast victuals. Following the meal, the Shrivers joined the general and his staff around the family Steinway, passing a pleasant hour by singing "Annie Laurie," "My Old Kentucky Home," and that theme song of the Southern trooper, "Jine the Cavalry." To at least one family member, their guests seemed to have no care in the world as they "frolicked all over and around the home, singing, laughing, even cutting up like boys. . . ." Another Shriver critiqued Stuart's rendition of

"Jine the Cavalry": "He put as much enthusiasm in that song as I know he does into matters of a much more serious nature; his eyes sparkled; and he kept time with his foot, he was the very personification of fun and spirit. . . ."[48]

Fun and spirit halted abruptly when scouts entered the house to report the presence of a large body of horsemen—not militia or home guards, but veterans of the Army of the Potomac—seven miles to the north, near Littlestown, Pennsylvania. Suspecting this force had been dispatched for the express purpose of running him down, Stuart knew greater concern than ever before. Already a day and a half late for his rendezvous with the infantry, he now faced the prospect of losing more time by detouring around Littlestown. But detour he must; he could not afford to be drawn into another battle, especially while encumbered by so much impedimenta.

Pondering his dilemma, Stuart grasped at hope in the guise of sixteen-year-old Herbert Shriver, his host's youngest son. A mature youngster with a firm knowledge of local geography, Herbert volunteered to lead the column around the enemy by way of Hanover, Pennsylvania, eight miles north and east of Littlestown. At Stuart's inquiry, the boy's parents consented to his accompanying the command. In return, Stuart promised him a free education at the Virginia Military Institute and afterward a position on his staff. Thus, at 8:00 A.M., when the Rebel leader led his vanguard out of Union Mills, a teenager rode at his side, pointing the way.[49]

Five miles later, the column crossed the Mason-Dixon Line. Cheering spread through the ranks as Stuart's troopers began their second visit to the Keystone State in nine months. Luther Hopkins of the 6th Virginia, who crossed the border a few days later, doubtless spoke for Stuart's men when he remarked that "it gave us inexpressible joy to think that we were strong enough and bold enough to go so far from home and attack our enemy upon his own soil."[50]

A mile above the line, the point of the column waded Indian Run, climbed Conewago Hill, and met the road to Hanover precisely as Herbert Shriver had promised. Meanwhile, flanking parties probed toward Littlestown. They returned word that the enemy—ignorant of the raiders' approach—seemed content to remain to the west.

Just as Stuart began to feel more easy, his point riders struck a rise that offered a clear view of Hanover and the surrounding country. Before them, a long line of Yankee cavalry wended its way northeastward from Littlestown along a road that squarely crossed the path of the column.[51]

The raiders were about to pay for the time lost at Fairfax Station, Rockville, and, especially, Westminster.

***

At Cashtown, twenty-odd miles northwest of Hanover, Robert E. Lee paced about his headquarters tent, wondering aloud why he had heard nothing from

Stuart. With Meade's army drawing close, his need for mounted support was becoming critical. Frequently he asked his subordinates: "Have you heard anything about my cavalry? I hope no disaster has overtaken my cavalry. . . . Any news to give me about General Stuart?"[52]

[9]

Pursuit to Pennsylvania

FOR five days after the battle of Upperville, the cavalry of the Army of the Potomac marked time near Aldie. While Stuart planned his excursion into Pennsylvania, Pleasonton busied himself by plugging manpower gaps caused by the recent fighting and by extending his picket lines as far west as Middleburg.[1] He also spent a great deal of time politicking. Already his long-distance lobbying with movers in Washington had borne fruit: on the twenty-fourth, he received word of his nomination before the Senate as a major general of volunteers.[2] The news may not have elated him, as two-star rank was the due of a corps commander. Having enlarged his rank, however, he redoubled his efforts to play political contacts, this time to enlarge his command.

Specifically, Pleasonton wanted Julius Stahel removed from the field and his division added to the Army of the Potomac. On 23 June, the Knight of Romance wrote to his old patron, John Farnsworth, seeking assistance in bringing this about. In the confidential missive, Pleasonton berated Stahel for lacking the good sense and energy required of a cavalry commander. He spoke of the defeats and setbacks Mosby and his partisans had dealt the Hungarian during months of outpost and picket clashes. He also implied that Stahel was unfit because of his foreign origins.

Pleasonton was not above furthering his designs through family connections. He enclosed in his letter to Farnsworth a short note from the Congressman's nephew. Elon Farnsworth, whom Pleasonton had recently appointed to his staff, informed his uncle that "the Genl. speaks of recommending me for Brig[adier General]. I do not know that I ought to mention it for fear that you will call me an aspiring youth. I am satisfied to serve through this war in the line. . . . But if I can do any good anywhere else of course 'small favors &c.' Now try and talk this into the President and you can do an immense good. . . ."

Only five days later, by coincidence or design, the War Department summarily relieved Julius Stahel and added his division to Pleasonton's command. That

161

same day, Pleasonton jumped young Farnsworth from captain and company commander to brigadier general and brigade leader.[3]

***

Shortly before the axe fell, Stahel was again pressed into service to supplement the efforts of the man who would replace him. Still believing Pleasonton's corps too weary and too busy to spare for additional chores, Hooker worked out an agreement with General Heintzelman to use Stahel's division for yet another reconnaissance toward the Rappahannock. On the nineteenth the Hungarian was told to mass his 3,600 troopers and one battery at Fairfax Court House. The next day Hooker directed him to send two columns, totaling 500 men, toward the river via the Manassas Junction–Catlett's Station vicinity as well as by the Brentsville-Greenwood route, farther to the east.[4] On the twenty-first, as the fighting raged at Upperville, Stahel was told to send his main force to Warrenton, while also scouting points south and west including Waterloo, Sulphur Springs, Beverly Ford, and Rappahannock Station. Should Stahel find any Rebels there—Hooker thought that at least a brigade of horsemen (ostensibly Hampton's) lay at Warrenton—he was to drive them below the river. Stahel was also to fix the whereabouts of any foot soldiers in the vicinity; Hill's corps was still thought to be somewhere along the river. Obviously, Hooker had disregarded Colonel De Forest's recent report that no Confederate infantry lingered that far to the south. Moreover, he was asking Stahel to do the job of scouting that Pleasonton's corps had failed to do in Loudoun Valley.[5]

By the twenty-third, as Stahel went about his new mission, he found his orders suddenly changed. Having at last learned of the Rebel infantry's presence in force in the Shenandoah, Hooker called off the reconnaissance to the Rappahannock and ordered Stahel, then encamped at Gainesville, just east of the Bull Run Mountains, to return to Fairfax Court House. Stahel moved wearily to comply—only to be ordered on the twenty-fourth to march instead to Harpers Ferry, reporting to Major General William H. French, for the purpose of driving off or destroying the horsemen attached to Ewell's corps. Stahel reported his willingness to obey promptly, "although my command has not yet recovered from the fatigue of the last few days' march." In private, he expressed "feelings of bitter regret and disappointment" over his aborted movement.[6]

But Stahel's ordeal was not over. On the twenty-fifth he led his men, cannon, and a long supply train toward the Potomac, downstream from French's garrison. Early that day, however, Hooker instructed him to leave only an "escort" with French and to report with the rest of his force to John F. Reynolds, commander of the forward wing of the Army of the Potomac. The latter had already begun to cross into Maryland via two pontoon bridges at Edwards Ferry, about twenty miles east of Harpers Ferry. His movement north at the head of the I, III, and XI Corps was testimony to Hooker's belated resolve to pursue Lee beyond the Mason-Dixon Line.[7]

Crossing the river at Youngs Island Ford, a few miles below Reynolds's crowded bridgehead, Stahel's men found their work just begun. From the ford they were ordered to guard two South Mountain passes against the advance of the Rebels beyond. The long, weary march was made more uncomfortable by an intermittent rain as well as by the lack of a supply train. The same swollen waters that would force Stuart's raiders to cross the Potomac at Rowser's Ford compelled Stahel to leave his wagons on the south bank of the stream.[8]

On 25 June, as the northernmost unit in Reynolds's wing, the XI Corps, moved from the Potomac toward Middletown, Maryland, Stahel's men trotted east of it, toward Frederick. Rain and mud made the journey notable for its discomforts, but the next day the sun reappeared and that afternoon Stahel's men wended their way into Frederick, where townspeople gave them a hearty welcome. One trooper marveled at the "great demonstrations of Union feeling" and the "flags in the windows. . . . this is a beautiful place."[9]

Stahel allowed only a portion of his command to savor the greeting. In fulfillment of his orders, he moved the three-regiment brigade of Othneil De Forest westward to hold one of the most strategic defiles in South Mountain, Crampton's Gap, five miles beyond Middletown. One regiment of Colonel R. Butler Price's brigade he sent to guard Turner's Gap, a half-dozen miles farther north. And to occupy an advanced position above Frederick, from which to probe toward the enemy in south-central Pennsylvania, Stahel sent north his "Wolverine Brigade," three Michigan regiments under Brigadier General Joseph T. Copeland, a long-bearded, sad-eyed, fifty-year-old former lumberman and politician.[10] Instead of accompanying any of these forces, Stahel remained at picturesque Frederick, which he considered a central point between his forward sector and Reynolds's headquarters at Jefferson, eight miles to the southwest. By not personally ranging beyond Frederick, however, Stahel gave Reynolds the impression of a lazy and inefficient officer. This prompted the wing commander to complain to Hooker that he was not getting the support he required from his cavalry. A native Pennsylvanian, Reynolds would be difficult to please now that the enemy had defiled his state. Though exaggerated, his strictures would hasten Stahel's demise.[11]

At Hooker's behest, Stahel on the twenty-seventh ordered patrols to scour the land east of the Catoctin Mountains, within hailing distance of the Pennsylvania line. Two-thirds of Copeland's brigade moved north to Emmitsburg, then continued toward the road hub of Gettysburg, thus becoming the first body of Union horsemen to enter Pennsylvania.[12]

Early in the afternoon of Sunday, the twenty-eighth, the 5th and 6th Michigan loped into Gettysburg from the southeast. They entered amid the pealing of church bells and the cheers and songs of residents who regarded them as saviors. Only two days before, White's Confederates had come charging through the village, screaming like banshees, and the townspeople hoped the troopers would protect them against a recurrence.[13]

While his men partook of the local hospitality—pails of water, loaves of fresh bread, and tubs of apple butter were placed before them—Copeland listened to the citizens' tales of fear and woe. He also learned of Lige White's operations at Hanover Junction; that an enemy force was moving five miles to the north of Gettysburg; that another was reported to be marching from Carlisle toward York; and that Lee's headquarters lay at Chambersburg.

The brigade leader immediately forwarded the intelligence to Frederick, along with ample evidence to verify it. In a stroke of good fortune, his pickets west of Gettysburg had nabbed a courier riding from Ewell at Carlisle to Early at York. The papers he carried bore out most of what Copeland's informants had told him.

Copeland never learned whether the intelligence was relayed to Hooker; most likely it was, only to be overlooked during a hectic series of administrative changes that affected the Army of the Potomac on the twenty-seventh. Toward evening—to the chagrin of the townfolk—the general received orders to withdraw from Gettysburg. Next day, the chagrin was Copeland's: en route to Emmitsburg, he learned of Stahel's relief from command—as well as his own.[14]

The top floor of Stahel's house had been swept clean. The division leader had been ordered to Harrisburg to take over the minuscule cavalry force in Couch's department; Colonel De Forest had been sent on an extended leave of absence; and Colonel Price had been reduced to the command of his old outfit, the 2nd Pennsylvania. Copeland at first had hopes of retaining his command under Pleasonton. But when he met his new superior at Frederick, he learned that Pleasonton had been given carte blanche to appoint his subordinates. Since the general preferred young and enterprising officers "known to himself and who [were] affiliated with him," the fifty-year-old Copeland was soon relegated to a series of desk jobs in Maryland, Pennsylvania, and Illinois.[15]

***

At last attuned to the pleas of Pennsylvanians overrun by the enemy, Hooker left Fairfax Court House for points north on the evening of 26 June. Now certain that Lee's main body had pushed so far up the Shenandoah Valley that it posed no threat to Washington, the army leader hastened to Frederick, where he joined John Reynolds and his three corps on the twenty-seventh. He planned to remain there until the balance of the army came up from the Orange & Alexandria. By the twenty-ninth, he believed, his entire force would be available for a thrust into Pennsylvania.[16]

The cavalry was fragmented to assist the infantry, artillery, and support arms during the move north. Buford's men had guarded the rear of Reynolds's wing as it crossed the Potomac on the twenty-fifth and twenty-sxith, while Gregg did the same for the rest of the army and its supply train. The troopers could hardly wait to cross their army's namesake river. "Getting out of old Virginia," wrote one who passed over at Edwards Ferry, "was like getting out of a graveyard into Paradise." A second horseman also adopted a biblical metaphor: "It was like

Moses and Aaron turning their back upon forty years of wandering in the wilderness . . . to catch a glimpse of the promised Canaan."[17] The thought of waging war in the North, while frightening, had its psychological advantages. In addition to a warm reception from the populace, the cavalry believed that above the Potomac they would find the key to victory that had eluded them for so long. If they could not fight well in the face of so immediate a threat to home and hearth, they did not deserve to win the war.

Late in the afternoon of the twenty-seventh, Hooker's rear echelon crossed at Edwards Ferry and closed up in the direction of Frederick. Gregg's riders, the last to cross, trod the pontoons to the strains of "Maryland, My Maryland," performed by the band of a Pennsylvania infantry unit on the north shore. The scene was "beautiful to behold," in the eyes of one trooper. It grew even lovelier when the column reached Frederick, which an officer from New York found surrounded by "an almost intermimable stretch of beautiful rolling land, nearly every inch of which is not only arable but richly productive. . . ."[18]

When the army settled down in Frederick, however, administrative rather than aesthetic considerations monopolized its attention. Stahel's removal was only one facet of an upheaval that reached the highest ranks. On the twenty-eighth, following a conflict with the War Department over his demand that the garrison at Harpers Ferry be added to his field force, Hooker requested to be relieved. Since Lincoln, Stanton, and Halleck had lost confidence in Fighting Joe during the aftermath of Chancellorsville, they promptly accepted his resignation.[19]

Looking for a replacement, the government was forced to pass over Hooker's senior subordinate, John Reynolds, who had already made known his unwillingness to accept high command on any terms except his own. Thus Lincoln chose Reynolds's friend George Meade, who received word of his promotion while lolling in his V Corps's camp outside Frederick. Though reluctant to take the command, especially at such a critical juncture, Meade accepted it as "God's will."[20]

Reaction to his elevation was generally favorable, especially among the older, more conservative members of the officer corps. One of the few who regarded him doubtfully was Alfred Pleasonton. Unlike Hooker, Meade had never evidenced an appreciation of cavalry's skill and strength. Pleasonton may also have considered him too fusty and slow-moving to challenge the innovative, energetic Lee. Quite possibly, Pleasonton was also jealous that a soft-spoken leader who never promoted himself should have high command handed to him as if on a platter.

Whatever his reservations about Meade, Pleasonton was pleased when the new commander gave him free rein to reorganize his newly expanded corps. "Give me 15000 cavalry [and] let me place my own officers over it," Pleasonton had implored John Farnsworth, and soon he would have Lee's horsemen gasping for quarter. Now he had the opportunity to lead almost as many troopers as he had longed for: Stahel's additions gave him about 12,700 effectives, a total that outweighed Stuart's organic division four-to-three. Furthermore, Pleasonton enjoyed the chance to place in high positions "officers with the proper dash to command cavalry."[21]

Right away, he found three dashing officers. Barely twelve hours after Meade assumed command, Pleasonton drew up orders that announced the appointments of Captains Merritt, Farnsworth, and Custer (the last-named having won his bars only days before) as brigadier generals of volunteers. Another order issued the same day proclaimed that Merritt would replace Major Starr at the head of the Reserve Brigade, while Custer and Farnsworth divvied up Stahel's units. Farnsworth received command of most of the regiments under De Forest and Price, the 1st Vermont, 1st West Virginia, 5th New York, and 18th Pennsylvania; while Custer took over Copeland's 5th, 6th, and 7th Michigan (to which Price's erstwhile 1st Michigan was added, strengthening the identity of the Wolverine Brigade). Ironically, it was in Copeland's command that George Custer had unsuccessfully sought a regimental berth a few months before. Both Farnsworth and Custer received several veteran outfits as well as a couple that were pea-green; notable among the latter were the 18th Pennsylvania and the 7th Michigan.[22]

To head Stahel's old force, now known as the 3rd Division, Cavalry Corps, Army of the Potomac, Pleasonton tabbed Judson Kilpatrick. He had sung Kilpatrick's praises ever since Brandy Station, lauding particularly the Jerseyman's combativeness at Aldie and Upperville. Pleasonton thought of the younger officer as a kindred spirit and—as he did Farnsworth and Custer—a protégé. Still, since Kilpatrick was Pleasonton's youngest senior subordinate, it seemed fitting that he should command the smallest division in the corps. Some 3,500 strong, it was only 70 percent as large as Gregg's command.[23]

Pleasonton's appointments gave general satisfaction, though some subordinates, whether from jealousy or sincere misgivings, questioned the elevation of junior staff officers to brigade command. J. Irvin Gregg, for one, so objected to the promotions that he put his displeasure into a confidential memorandum perhaps intended for circulation inside political circles. Though hostile neither to Pleasonton nor to his new subordinates, Gregg doubted that "any reason can be assigned by the most favorably disposed to warrant these appointments."[24] He may have had a point in regard to their timing, for the prospect of a clash in Pennsylvania made this an awkward hour in which to shake up the corps. Still, not even Gregg could deny that the new brigadiers were vigorous leaders well versed in cavalry service through education and experience. If a couple of them seemed given to impetuosity and flamboyance, all exhibited the commendable trait of being willing, even eager, to fight.

The new appointees lost no time in assuming command. The day after winning his star, Merritt called on the Regular Army officers over whose heads he had been promoted, secured their pledges of support, then inspected the brigade's camps near Frederick. The same day, Elon Farnsworth rode out to look over the bivouacs and picket lines along the mountains west of Frederick;

he wore a brigadier's uniform borrowed from his patron, Pleasonton. George Custer improvised more elaborate raiment. As befitted his personality, he donned a sailor's shirt with silver stars at its collar points, a red cravat, a hussar jacket of black velveteen whose sleeves sparkled with lace, olive corduroy trousers, shiny jackboots, and a brown felt hat. Riding toward Emmitsburg to meet part of his brigade (the rest, on detached duty, would not join him till the thirtieth), Custer appeared to one of his new subordinates "showy like Murat" in his "fantastic" garb. A colleague later remarked that the attire made him look like "a circus rider gone mad."[25]

Also on the twenty-ninth, Judson Kilpatrick bade farewell to his old, battle-scarred brigade and rode to Stahel's headquarters. There he studied the size, condition, and dispositions of his new command. Much of what he saw firsthand and in Stahel's reports disturbed him. There seemed no reason to doubt the fighting caliber of these former members of the Washington defense forces. But their relatively small size did not match Kilpatrick's expectations; he had believed reports that put Stahel's effectives at more than four thousand. Then, too, the troopers and horses were worn down from continuous work—several days of marching twenty-five to fifty miles. This was less Stahel's fault than Hooker's. But Kilpatrick and his new subordinates would pay the price for the weariness of the command; by all indications, the respite it so badly needed would not be available for some time.[26]

While the new generals took hold, changes occurred within the horse artillery. On the twenty-eighth, Pleasonton added Robertson's brigade, just back from Washington, to his horse artillery. New, unassigned units were grouped into a reserve force; they included Captain Jabez J. Daniels's 9th Michigan Battery, recently attached to Copeland's brigade. Almost immediately, the combined force was fragmented for field service. Two of Robertson's five batteries (Elder's and Pennington's) were assigned to Kilpatrick's division, others (along with those in Tidball's five-battery brigade) to Gregg and Buford.[27]

By the twenty-eight, John B. McIntosh had also come in from Washington City, returning much of the 1st Brigade, 2nd Division, from Percy Wyndham's remount depot. As McIntosh settled back into the command, Colonel Pennock Huey's 8th Pennsylvania, most recently attached to Buford's command, joined the same division. Though he enjoyed a less-than-brilliant reputation (one colleague termed him "an overpowering damned fool"), Huey was named commander of Kilpatrick's old 2nd Brigade by virtue of seniority.[28]

While at Frederick, several units were detached from the corps for special service. All but one company of the 1st Pennsylvania were withdrawn from McIntosh's brigade to serve as escorts, couriers, and orderlies for the commanders of the VI Corps and the Artillery Reserve, respectively. Smaller units performed similar duties elsewhere. Two companies of the 6th Pennsylvania, as well as detachments of the four Regular regiments in Merritt's brigade, joined Price's 2nd Pennsylvania at Meade's headquarters. There they also served beside the independent New York company known as the Oneida Cavalry, which had done headquarters escort duty since early in 1862. Other units on escort service included a company of the 1st Maine, at the headquarters of the I Corps; a squadron of the 6th New York, with the II Corps; a 17th Pennsylvania squadron at V Corps headquarters; a company each of the 1st Pennsylvania and 1st New Jersey at the headquarters of the VI Corps, a squadron of the 1st Indiana with the XI Corps, and two companies of the 1st Ohio at Cavalry Corps headquarters, one serving David Gregg, the other Judson Kilpatrick.[29]

***

Though gratified that Meade had granted him the power to make so many command alterations, Alfred Pleasonton was taken aback by one change he had not counted on. As soon as his corps began its movement north from Frederick, he found it beyond reach of his immediate authority. This remained the case because he was not allowed to accompany it into the field.

The controlling factor seems to have been Meade's understanding of the duties of a cavalry commander. Rather than treating Pleasonton as a field leader, as Hooker had, Meade viewed him as a staff officer. Perhaps because of Pleasonton's Old Army experience as an adjutant, the army leader enlisted his aid in administrative and organizational matters. In fact, Meade probably regarded him as a future replacement for his chief of staff, Major General Daniel Butterfield, a holdover from Hooker's tenure whom the new commander disliked and mistrusted. In any case, Meade had Pleasonton pitch his tent next to his own on almost every leg of the trip to Pennsylvania and rarely let him out of eyesight or earshot. The only personal contact Pleasonton maintained with his field force was through roving members of his staff, especially his adjutant general and chief of staff, Lieutenant Colonel Andrew J. Alexander.[30]

Minus its ordained leader, the cavalry fanned out from Frederick in all directions, scouting far above the main army, while also guarding its flanks and rear. By virtue of the positions they had taken during Hooker's final operations, Kilpatrick covered the army's center, Gregg its right and rear, and Buford its left. From Frederick, Pleasonton exercised only the remotest supervision over the divisions.

Though holding the most vulnerable position, John Buford was not fazed by the demands of semi-independent command. On 27 June he marched from Edwards Ferry to Jefferson, Maryland, via Point of Rocks, Lige White's old stamping ground on the Potomac. Next day he moved farther north, scouring Pleasant Valley in an unsuccessful attempt to locate flank detachments from Lee's army. The 1st Cavalry Division then marched along the eastern base of South Mountain as far as Kilpatrick's bailiwick at Middletown. Nearby, Buford met the advance of French's garrison, moving toward Frederick. Though the War Department had barred Hooker's efforts to use French in the field, Meade's request to do the same had been granted within a few hours of his appointment.[31]

Early on the twenty-ninth Buford resumed his trek toward the northwest. With Gamble and Devin he moved from Middletown through Turner's Gap to Boonsboro, then sharply northeastward toward Fairfield, Pennsylvania. His ultimate objective was Gettysburg, where Pleasonton had ordered him to bivouack the next day. Meanwhile, Wesley Merritt led his new brigade, plus the divisional trains, northeast from Middletown to Mechanicstown, Maryland, guarding his comrades' right flank.[32]

The march of 29–30 June was an ordeal for both columns. They had to endure rocky, sloping terrain, a blistering sun, and clouds of dust so thick a man could not clearly discern those who rode beside or before him. Progress was aided, not slowed, by several rest halts. Buford and Merritt also ensured that their men partook of the food and drink dispensed by Unionists who turned out at every town and crossroads to greet them. Still, physical exertion took its toll. At night, men would topple from their horses as though shot, while "jaded studs . . . stood like mute sentinels over their riders dead in sleep."

Despite the heavy toll of fatigue, Buford's main body bivouacked only about ten miles southwest of Gettysburg late on the twenty-ninth. Though in friendly country, the division commander posted strong picket lines. He had encountered no Rebels more threatening than stragglers and foragers, but he was aware that large bodies of the enemy lay ahead.

By now Buford's march had taken on heightened importance, especially for the men of the 17th Pennsylvania, a regiment recruited in that part of the state occupied by the Confederates. Late that afternoon, the main column had wound around the base of South Mountain before striking for Fairfield, Pennsylvania, on the last leg of its journey north. As the line of march straightened, men in the rear spied a member of the 17th Pennsylvania sitting his horse alongside the road, his gloved fist enclosing the staff of the regimental guidon. At once the men realized the significance of the flag-bearer. Splitting their throats with cheers, they surged past him across the Mason-Dixon Line.[33]

***

At 2:00 P.M. on 28 June, Pleasonton informed David Gregg, near Frederick, that Stuart's "brigade" had crossed the Potomac, heading for the Baltimore & Ohio, several miles east of Meade's headquarters. Gregg was directed to send two brigades and a battery down the Baltimore Pike to New Market and Ridgeville. The units were then to move along the railroad toward Ellicott's Mills, near the eastern terminus of the B & O. At some point on this route, it was assumed that Gregg would find graybacks hard at work with levers and claw crowbars. As the Rebels were on a detached mission far from their army, Gregg should halt their demolition and also keep them apart from Lee.[34]

It took six hours for Gregg to ready his command. At about 4:00 P.M. he dispatched McIntosh's brigade to Ridgeville, from which McIntosh sent regiments to towns including Cooksville, Lisbon, and Poplar Springs. At the same time, detachments from Huey's brigade marched toward the B & O depot of Mount Airy, seeking the enemy. Next day, McIntosh thrust patrols as far east as Woodbine and Sykesville.

At Woodbine, McIntosh learned that Stuart's people were smashing property just to the east, at Hood's Mill. Fearing to march there alone, the colonel rejoined Huey and Irvin Gregg at Mount Airy, where the latter were feasting on the contents of the wagons that had escaped the Confederate raiders at Rockville. With his division reunited, David Gregg moved north in the direction the Rebels had taken, via Jewsburg and New Windsor. Before long, however, he found the road clogged by elements of the VI Corps, moving toward Meade's new headquarters at Middleburg, Maryland.[35]

Gregg was partially compensated for his misfortune by absorbing, on the road to Westminister, two units from General Schenck's Middle Department. Having been cut off by Stuart while marching from their old post along the Monocacy River to join Schenck in Baltimore, Captain Robert E. Duvall's Company A of the Purnell (Maryland) Legion and a section of Captain William D. Rank's Company H, 3rd Pennsylvania Heavy Artillery (serving as light artillery), fell in with the 2nd Cavalry Division. Though neither unit was experienced in battle, they helped offset Gregg's loss of the 1st Pennsylvania.[36]

At first, they benefited from the same delights that Gregg's division had experienced. At New Windsor, where the column lay over for a spell late on the twenty-ninth, local residents brought the troopers good things to eat and a bevy of schoolgirls swarmed over them in the manner of Stuart's admirers in Rockville.[37] But then the good times ended—replaced by an all-night march that even the veterans considered the longest and hardest they had ever made. "The men fell asleep in their saddles," wrote Captain William E. Miller of the 3rd Pennsylvania, "and whenever the column halted . . . horses would also fall asleep. . . ." To stay alert, the soldiers resorted to extreme measures, pinching themselves, pricking themselves with needles, and slapping each others' faces. Even this did not suffice. Miller noted that "when within about five miles of Westminster it was discovered that the left of the line was not up. A halt was ordered, and, on sending back, the fact was disclosed that the artillerymen and battery horses were sound asleep, and that whilst the portion of the column in front of them had been moving on, that in the rear was standing still." Shaken into consciousness, the men of Rank's battery, unused to the rigors of field campaigning, "implored to be allowed to rest." They begged in vain.[38]

The hardships of travel affected the ranking officers as well. On the way to Westminster General Gregg and Colonel McIntosh became unwell, apparently from intestinal ailments contracted weeks before and aggravated by the grueling march. Both temporarily relinquished command, leaving Pennock Huey in charge. This was an undesirable situation, as neither of the senior officers had confidence in Huey's leadership. They so feared he might go to pieces under the weight of divisional command that for many hours no one told the colonel of his temporary elevation. Finally, McIntosh's inspector-general broke the news—

only to find Huey so "swelled up with importance" that he drafted a formal order naming his own staff. McIntosh's inspector added that "when I told *Mac* about [it], he began swearing and by daylight was *Well!*"[39]

Given Huey's ludicrous pretentions, it was fitting that he was still in command when the main column reached Westminster at about daybreak on 30 June. Learning that Stuart had arrived some twelve hours earlier and uncertain whether he lingered there, Huey took excessive precautions before entering the town. Then a young, devil-may-care officer, Captain Charles Treichel of the 3rd Pennsylvania, gained his permission to lead an attack on the place. A bystander heard Huey caution the captain to "put scabbards under the leg, fasten tin cups so as to make no noise, and go carefully." But Treichel preferred an old-fashioned charge; when out of Huey's earshot, he told the members of his advance guard: "Don't speak until I cheer, then come after me!"

Before the advance struck, Captain Randol, whose battery was attached to McIntosh's brigade, lobbed a few shells at possible enemy nests south of Westminster. Then Treichel went forward along a dirt road that angled onto the Baltimore Pike at the edge of town. First at the trot, then the gallop, the little band rounded some farm buildings on the outskirts, and swept along the main street. Spying some suspicious-looking mounts tethered to nearby posts, Treichel cried: "There they are!" With a shout he charged toward the horses, anticipating a saber-and-pistol battle.

What followed was both pathetic and anticlimactic, for only a few stragglers remained in Westminster, Stuart having departed hours before. Already rattled by Randol's shelling, the Rebels scrambled from homes and stores they had been looting and threw themselves onto their waiting mounts. Some got off before Treichel's party reached them, but others were less agile or less fortunate. Midway down the street, Treichel saw that his grand attack had turned into a farce. He took out his disappointment on one luckless mule-rider, whom he pistol-whipped till the man fell sprawling.[40]

The aftermath of combat proved more rewarding. Although some residents of Westminster had demonstrated Southern sympathies upon Stuart's arrival, several times as many came out to welcome his pursuers. Reported the chaplain of the 1st New Jersey: "From doorways, windows, balconies, handkerchiefs and scarves were waved in welcome; young girls saluted us with patriotic songs; matrons brought out abundant provision for our refreshment; men opened barns, and granaries, and store-rooms, with one impulse of zeal. . . ."[41]

Their quarry still at large, the Federals remained only long enough to stock up on food and forage and to survey the extent of Stuart's depredations. By late in the morning the troopers were in motion toward Hanover Junction, Pennsylvania, in response to an order from Pleasonton on the twenty-ninth. The division proceeded in two columns to Manchester, Maryland, where it got some much-needed sleep, and was back on the road shortly after break of day on 1 July.[42]

A few hours brought the head of Gregg's reunited division to the Pennsylvania line. There "the spirits of all notwithstanding fatigue and hunger, rose to the highest pitch of enthusiasm." Some marked the crossing in memorable fashion. The 10th New York, many of whose members were native Pennsylvanians, sang a rousing chorus of the "Battle Hymn of the Republic" as they crossed the line. Years later the regiment's historian recalled the "grand swelling of loyal voices in spontaneous accord—a sublime crossing of the threshold into the grand old Commonwealth. . . ."[43]

***

Meade and Pleasonton had agreed that Kilpatrick's new division should operate front and center of the army as it advanced. With Buford striving to locate Longstreet and Hill, and Gregg chasing down Stuart, Kilpatrick was left with the task of locating those portions of Ewell's corps pushing eastward from Chambersburg. Meade had received reports that Early and Jenkins were in and about York. Early on the twenty-ninth, Kilpatrick moved out of Frederick with the main body of his division and started in that direction. Pleasonton ordered him to reach Littlestown, Pennsylvania, twenty-five miles southwest of York, by nightfall.[44]

Kilpatrick's itinerary called for Farnsworth's brigade, with the division trains and Lieutenant Elder's Battery E, 4th U.S. Artillery, to move northeastward via Taneytown, Maryland. Meanwhile, Custer's Wolverines would push from Emmitsburg and vicinity to join Farnsworth in Pennsylvania. Custer himself moved with one of two columns, the 1st and 7th Michigan and Lieutenant Pennington's Battery M, 2nd U.S. The other column, composed of the recently detached 5th and 6th Michigan, rode to Littlestown under overall command of Colonel Russell A. Alger of the 5th.[45]

The horse soldiers under Kilpatrick advanced toward Pennsylvania with mixed feelings and muted spirits. They felt keenly the loss of their divisional identity; they had little acquaintance with their brigade and division officers; and their recent wanderings between the Rappahannock and the Potomac had left them bone-weary and in some cases ill or disabled. Their morale gradually improved, however, especially after Alger's regiments came in to swell the command to its limits. Then, too, the people and places the men saw just above the Pennsylvania line had a therapeutic effect. As many of Buford's and Gregg's people had already learned, the commonwealth seemed like "God's country" to the weary travelers; it meant friendly faces, good things to eat and drink, the comforts of home.[46]

Reaching Littlestown shortly before midnight, Farnsworth's command was mobbed by townspeople who, despite the lateness of the hour, greeted the horsemen like deliverers. A member of Kilpatrick's escort observed "a company of young people . . . on the veranda of the hotel singing patriotic songs, with waving flags and handkerchiefs, while their more thoughtful mothers . . . provided baskets of provisions, which were appreciated by the tired soldiers."

Forcing themselves to stay awake long enough to make a gracious response to the welcome, the troopers passed north of town. In meadows and farm fields, they enjoyed a late supper, groomed and fed their horses, and finally caught a few hours' sleep.[47]

Before sunup on the thirtieth, Kilpatrick led the way to Hanover, the last projected stopover below York. Behind him rode Custer's 1st and 7th Michigan, followed by the divisional artillery, the brigade of Elon Farnsworth, and the supply train. Colonel Alger's 5th and 6th Michigan were left behind at Littlestown. From there Alger sent a company of the 6th toward Westminster on a reconnaissance; the remainder of his force, after scouting south of Littlestown, would rejoin Kilpatrick at Hanover.[48]

Signs that Kilpatrick was riding toward combat popped up as his main body neared Hanover. Off to the east his point riders spied mounted Rebels in the near distance, taking note of the column's size and heading. Without slowing his pace, Kilpatrick detached parties from his rear guard, Lieutenant Colonel William P. Brinton's 18th Pennsylvania, to capture or disperse them. Some of these parties, however, never rejoined the column; their absence made their comrades nervous about what lay ahead.[49]

Some time after 8:00 A.M., the advance guard cleared Littlestown, then passed through the hamlets of Pennville and Buttstown and entered Hanover from the southwest. There, as in many other places they had visited, officers and men were showered with baskets of flowers, cheers and applause, and other expressions of greeting—made all the heartier for the town's recent invasion by Lige White. The recipients of this outpouring of affection glowed with self-satisfaction. After so many hero's welcomes they were beginning to see themselves as heroic indeed.[50]

Judson Kilpatrick entered Hanover at the head of Custer's 1st and 7th Michigan. He set up a command post at a local home, where he received citizens who provided details of White's occupation and relayed rumors of movements by other enemy forces. As Kill-cavalry questioned and listened, Custer's horsemen, followed by Pennington's battery and the vanguard of Farnsworth's command, trooped through the town. In Centre Square the line of riders temporarily halted to partake of gifts, ranging from buttermilk to cigars, handed up by the townspeople. The men ate and drank in the saddle, even as they went out the York Pike toward Abbotstown.[51]

At about nine o'clock, after surveying the country toward York from the belfry of the Lutheran church, Kilpatrick departed town with his staff, riding hard to overtake the head of the column. By this time most of Farnsworth's troops had cleared Hanover. As he moved up the road toward Abbotstown, from which point he planned to cross over to the York Pike, the division leader calculated that he could reach York by late afternoon if able to maintain his current progress. By 10:00 A.M. only the 5th New York remained in the town, much of it bunched around Centre Square and the public common nearby. The 18th Pennsylvania and the division's wagon trains and ambulances were ap-

proaching the outskirts of Hanover via Buttstown. Behind the troops and vehicles, scouts continued to search the countryside and to stare down bands of the
enemy.[52]

One of the rear details consisted of forty men drawn from two companies of
the 18th Pennsylvania, under Lieutenant Henry C. Potter. Traveling about a
mile behind their regiment, Potter and his men noted signs of damage done to
roadside homes and farms (the work of White and Gordon). But they saw no
large body of Confederates until they suddenly found perhaps sixty gray-
jacketed horsemen marching east of them, along the road from Westminster.
Though this hinted that larger forces were in the vicinity, the Federals refused
to panic—even when the roads converged at Buttstown and the enemy took a
position across their path.

Potter's troops maintained their marching pace until nearly upon the Rebels.
When the enemy leader called for them to surrender, the lieutenant gave a
prearranged signal and his men burst through the roadblock, blasting away with
their revolvers. Their opposition scattered in surprise, then recovered and put
spurs to their mounts. Keening the Rebel yell, they pursued at top speed
toward Hanover, determined to celebrate in rousing fashion the centennial of
the town's founding.

The sounds of the chase carried far afield. When the Confederates rounded a
bend within sight of Hanover they found Lieutenant Colonel Brinton's rear
echelon dismounted to meet them, many of his troopers positioned behind
roadside fences. The Pennsylvanians opened fire to cover Potter's escape, and
the Confederates backed off. Soon however, other bands of Rebel horsemen
crested the rise south of town. When they pressed forward, the battle began in
earnest.[53]

***

Elon Farnsworth was near New Baltimore, a crossroads about a mile above
Hanover, when the shooting started. At once he turned the head of his column
southward. As the brigade countermarched, he raced ahead to the scene of
action. Though his superior, Kilpatrick, had five minutes before received word
of Stuart's presence in the area, Farnsworth had no idea of the cause of the
fighting.[54] He knew only that an unknown force had struck the shank of his
column; whatever the size and identity of that force, he had to retaliate. Despite
the crisis, the young general was clear-headed and in lofty spirits, intrigued that
his maiden battle in brigade command should come on Northern soil.

Reaching the center of town, he found mass confusion. Parts of his rear
regiments and the wagon train clogged the streets and Centre Square, making
progress difficult in any direction. When regimental leaders reported to him,
Farnsworth learned that Rebel cavalry—presumably Stuart's—had shoved the
rear of the 18th Pennsylvania into town. The regiment's withdrawal had been
complicated by its entanglement with runaway ambulances under the control of

panic-stricken drivers.[55] Still, Farnsworth could not have been pleased by the hastiness of that withdrawal: the road to town lay strewn with the Pennsylvanians' horse equipments, sabers, pistols, and brand-new Burnside carbines.

Major John Hammond's 5th New York had responded to the crisis by charging the attackers, temporarily halting their drive. Now Farnsworth placed himself at the head of the New York outfit and led it down the road to Buttstown, backed by units of Lieutenant Colonel Addison W. Preston's 1st Vermont and Colonel Nathaniel P. Richmond's 1st West Virginia. Cowed by the display of force and determination, the Confederates retreated. The advantage had swung to the Federals—but how long they could maintain it, no one knew.[56]

***

Stuart, of course, had not wanted a battle. But by the time he discovered Kilpatrick's proximity, his advance guard had already made contact. There seemed nothing for the Confederate leader to do but smash through the town as quickly as possible and once on the far side hasten on to York.

Advance guards of Chambliss's brigade, the first in Stuart's main column, had initiated the combat. To Chambliss's rear marched Hampton's men, escorting the division train and most of the artillery. About a mile farther west rode Fitz Lee, seeking to protect his comrades from those Yankees observed near Littlestown. Making his way to the head of the longer line, about two miles below Hanover, Stuart could see only the long, thin column of the 18th Pennsylvania. If no sizable force lay immediately beyond, perhaps Chambliss alone could clear a path through the village. Hampton and Lee might then bypass the place, keeping the march going and protecting the wagons and prisoners.

Stuart had Chambliss's forward regiment, the 13th Virginia of Lieutenant Colonel Jefferson C. Phillips, deploy on both sides of the road to town. He then planted two guns on farmland along Plum Creek, on the left of the brigade.[57] After the cannon had paved their way, some of Phillips's men rushed north and piled into the Federals, creating havoc in their ranks. Their opposition fell back so rapidly that the attackers sensed they were facing raw troops, whose inexperience they could exploit.

While the Federals were reeling, Chambliss sent in William Payne's 2nd North Carolina. A dashing Virginian who had officered the famed "Black Horse Cavalry" in the war's early months, Lieutenant Colonel Payne led a detachment against the very end of the 18th Pennsylvania's line near Buttstown. The larger part of his regiment struck the Yankees in flank closer to Hanover. The two-punch offensive achieved desired results: in minutes the Pennsylvanians gave up all efforts to resist and fled headlong into town.

Carried along by the momentum of the charge, Payne's men ran into the counterattacking 5th New York, Farnsworth at its head. Fighting swirled through the lower end of Hanover, spilling north of Centre Square. As reformed elements of the 18th Pennsylvania threw their weight into the contest, the North Carolinians gave ground. Their retreat was accelerated when they lost their commander. A New York trooper shot away Payne's horse, causing him to fall headfirst into an uncovered vat of dye in the yard of a tannery. When his assailant helped Payne climb out, he found him "a most laughable sight," his uniform, face, and hair a deep, dark brown.[58]

With the pullback of the 2nd North Carolina, Stuart's entire position was in peril. He had no quick means of reinforcing the head of Chambliss's brigade. The rear of the command was prevented from rushing to the front by the artillery and supply wagons that lay between it and Hanover. Hampton, farther to the rear, was at an even greater disadvantage. Meanwhile, Fitz Lee's attention had been distracted by the two Union regiments near Littlestown.

Most of Lee's opposition was provided by Colonel George Gray of the 6th Michigan. Though lacking battle experience and temperate habits (only two weeks ago he had been arrested for drunkenness on duty),[59] Gray fought well against heavy odds, preventing Lee from aiding Chambliss. The colonel finally slipped away to Hanover across roadside fields, joining Colonel Alger's 5th Michigan, which had gone on ahead. In Gray's rear, a single squadron, under Major Peter A. Weber—augmented by gun-toting farmers from the vicinity—made the disengagement possible. Despite losing heavily, especially in prisoners, Weber's men repulsed three assaults and withstood a withering cannonade. Forced to hold his ground till darkness fell, the young major would not rejoin Gray until the next morning.[60]

Hard-pressed to provide Chambliss's vanguard with support, Stuart fed in small units as they became available. As Farnsworth's men braced to meet them, new pockets of combat broke out across fields and ridges below the town. Some of the bitterest fighting raged over the Samuel Forney farm, between the Littlestown Pike and the Westminster road. That encounter expanded until it involved Stuart's own headquarters. Among those who fell was a member of the division staff, who lay unconscious from a saber blow for six hours.[61] Stuart himself narrowly evaded capture when "Virginia" carried him to safety over a fifteen-foot-wide gully that stymied pursuers.[62]

When Chambliss's rear regiments—Colonel Beale's 9th and Colonel Davis's 10th Virginia—made themselves felt, Farnsworth gathered up his strung-out line and withdrew to the town. He placed most of the 1st Vermont and 1st West Virginia on the southern and eastern fringes of Hanover, while leaving the 5th New York in the heart of the town, supported by undemoralized members of the 18th Pennsylvania. The latter two regiments fashioned breastworks from hay bales, packing crates, bar iron, fence rails, and overturned wagons.[63]

The new dispositions brought a long lull to the fighting, during which both sides received reinforcements. Judson Kilpatrick, having raced his horse across fields from Abbotstown at a killing pace, arrived to supervise the defense of the town. He delegated primary authority, however, to Farnsworth, then took up residence at the Central Hotel, where he communicated with Pleasonton's chief of staff, Lieutenant Colonel Alexander, recently arrived at Littlestown. Kilpatrick also spent much time interrogating prisoners, including the discolored William Payne, who tried to convince him that Stuart had twelve thousand sabers poised to sweep his foe into oblivion. In consequence, Kilpatrick buffeted Alexander with pleas for supports.[64]

During the stalemate, Custer's Woverines arrived in force and were placed on the northwestern side of town. Atop an eminence known as Bunker Hill, Pennington's and Elder's batteries went into action, with Colonel Charles H. Town's 1st Michigan and part of the 1st Vermont in support. The cannon soon engaged two guns along Fitz Lee's front. Under this barrage, the rest of the Michigan Brigade—Alger's and Gray's regiments, plus the 7th Michigan of Colonel William D. Mann—gradually took up a post much closer to Lee's position, between the Gettysburg and Littlestown roads. By now Custer held the Union right, Farnsworth the center (in the town) and the left.[65]

The lull also gave Stuart time to absorb Colonel Payne's fugitives and to deploy the bulk of Chambliss's brigade directly below Hanover, connecting with Lee's right. About 2:00 P.M., Wade Hampton at last reached the scene from the rear. Leaving the 125-wagon train behind Fitz Lee, he formed on Chambliss's right, stretching in a line from below Mount Olivet Cemetery, southeast of town, across the Baltimore Turnpike toward the York Pike. He unlimbered four guns astride the Baltimore Pike, protected by the Cobb Legion under Pierce Young. When Hampton's guns opened fire against those Yankees in and east of the town (forcing citizens to huddle for safety in their cellars), they foiled any intentions Farnsworth might have entertained about slipping around Stuart's right.[66]

The stalemate was finally broken late in the afternoon, when George Custer—like Farnsworth eager for his first action in brigade command—moved toward Lee's front west of Hanover. He dismounted about six hundred of Colonel Gray's troopers and directed them against Lee's cannon, which were playing effectively on the other Michigan regiments. This operation marked the first time the 6th Michigan had seen Custer at close range. Though unfamiliar with his military background, including his exploits at Aldie (some thought his name "Custerd"), the Wolverines soon were as impressed by his fighting style as they were amused by his attire.[67]

Gray's six hundred snaked through underbrush toward the Littlestown Pike, their left flank touching Buttstown. Much of the distance they covered on hands and knees, edging up a steep ridge to within three hundred yards of the enemy guns. The Wolverines then let loose with Colt pistols and Spencer rifles. Shocked by the massed fire, the artillery's mounted supports wavered and then broke. Rushing to the rear, they uncovered the cannon and left behind several wounded, fifteen of whom became prisoners.[68]

Concerned for the stability of his brigade front, Lee hustled up enough reinforcements to force Gray back to his original line. There Custer rallied Gray's men and moved then a second time toward the guns on the ridge. Again they failed to seize the position, but most took up vantage points that caused Lee and Stuart to fear for the safety of that flank. In their first fight, Custer and the 6th Michigan had proved themselves a powerful combination.

For the balance of the day, J. E. B. Stuart cast anxious glances not only at his flanks but toward the south, where, he had heard, parts of the Union XII Corps were moving toward his rear. As the hours passed, Custer and Farnsworth shifted parts of their lines, jockeying for advantage, but they could not break through at any point. For his part, Stuart refused to commit himself to an attack in force, now that Hanover was so well covered on all sides. He waited for darkness to facilitate a pullout toward York.

As soon as the sun lowered, Stuart transferred custody of the wagon train to Fitz Lee. While Chambliss and Hampton kept the enemy at bay, the wagons were put in motion toward the Confederate right, in the direction of Jefferson. And when full darkness descended, the rest of the division disengaged, carefully and slowly, to follow the train. After a long engagement under the hot sun, the Confederates faced an all-night march by a roundabout route to an uncertain destination. Stuart, his timetable more warped now than ever, could not afford another long halt short of Early's headquarters.[69]

Kilpatrick appeared content to let them flee. Though he had suffered over two hundred casualties, including thirteen officers, perhaps fifty more than he had inflicted,[70] he knew that his new command had turned in a creditable performance after recovering from its initial disorder. His young subordinates had displayed talent in command—Farnsworth in thrusting Stuart out of Hanover and keeping him out, and Custer by rocking the Confederate left flank. Stuart's latest retreat seemed to indicate another Union victory after a fight involving equal odds.

Unfortunately, Kilpatrick forefited some of the credit due him by failing to mount a pursuit worthy of the name—or even to maintain contact with the enemy. After dark, instead of following Stuart, he placed his command in bivouac along the Abbotstown Pike and permitted it a long sleep. The few patrols he sent north and east toward York, Dover, and East Berlin failed to earn their keep. They merely turned up further indications that Gordon's infantry and White's horsemen had recently visited those locations. Misinterpreting the signs, Kilpatrick, through Lieutenant Colonel Alexander, informed Pleasonton that a large contingent of Robert E. Lee's army lay near East Berlin, ten miles above Hanover. The Knight of Romance not only accepted this absurd deduction but relayed it to Meade along with his praise of Kilpatrick's skill at reconnaissance.[71]

By supposing that he would find the enemy at East Berlin, Kilpatrick ensured that he would waste the day of 1 July. Moving directly north with his main body, he passed far to the west of Stuart's route. All things considered, the division leader's efforts failed to meet the demand that General Meade had made of his cavalry on the thirtieth: that its "most important and sacred" duty was to gather accurate information on the enemy's movements.[72]

Not until the morning of the second—after twenty-four hours spent in fruitless wandering between Hanover and East Berlin—did Kilpatrick act in a manner that made military sense. And he did so only in response to orders to move toward Gettysburg. By slightly divergent routes, Farnsworth's and Custer's brigades marched southwest from East Berlin, passing down the York Pike through New Oxford and turning northward after striking Guldens Station on the Northern Central Railroad. The two columns converged in the direction of Hunterstown, five miles northeast of Gettysburg.[73]

Kilpatrick could have taken a more direct path to the main battlefield, saving considerable time. He had just cause for speed. As early as the afternoon of the first, his men had heard the sounds of battle sweeping east from Gettysburg, indicating that the crisis stage of the Pennsylvania campaign had begun.[74]

[10]
Gettysburg, 1 July

ABOUT 11:00 A.M. on the last day of June, John Buford's main column—a band of skirmishers from the 3rd Indiana, followed by the rest of Gamble's brigade, then Devin's men and Calef's battery—entered Gettysburg under a misty rain. The troopers displayed beards powdered with dust, faces glistening with sweat, and uniforms caked with mud and dirt. Their horses appeared worn down from hard marching. The long column made its way up Washington Street to the Diamond, Gettysburg's oak-shaded center square. From there its riders curved westward and trotted out Chambersburg Street, in the direction from which Lee's army was reported moving.[1]

As always, citizens thronged the streets in welcome. As they had for General Copeland two days before, girls tossed flowers and sang patriotic songs, boys cheered and tried to set off the fireworks they had been saving for the Fourth of July, and their parents bustled about to provide refreshments for the famished-looking soldiers. Though some troopers seemed too tired to notice the greeting, most accepted it with gratification, and amusement. One noted the "state of terror and excitement" into which Jubal Early's invaders had thrown the people. As a new force of Rebels had drawn near the day before, "no wonder that the people should manifest such extreme gladness and joy at our coming."[2]

The people could not shout their welcome loudly enough. "It was to me a novel and grand sight," a teenaged girl recalled. "I had never seen so many soldiers at one time. They were Union soldiers and that was enough for me, for I then knew we had protection, and I felt they were our dearest friends." She and some schoolmates put their greeting into song, making up in enthusiasm what they lacked in voice. Members of Devin's 9th New York responded warmly to their rendition of "Rally Round the Flag, Boys" ("this was the first time most of the 'boys' had heard this song," one commented, "and it was wonderfully inspiring"). Their comrades in the 6th New York cheered "The

Red, White, and Blue," which the girls sang "most loyally and charmingly." A few troopers ventured the minor criticism that the singers seemed to know only a single verse of either song, which they repeated over and over as if determined to get it perfect.[3]

To this tuneful accompaniment, Buford moved his 2,900 men out the Chambersburg Pike, sending scouts far in advance of his vanguard as well as to the north and east. Soon they returned word that A. P. Hill's Confederates had drawn to within nine miles of Gettysburg, with patrols ranging almost to the town itself. In fact, Confederate units were either observed or rumored to be in position both northwest and southwest of the place. Later other scouts told Buford that Ewell had left Carlisle and York, apparently to link with Longstreet and Hill at or near Gettysburg. The day before, Buford had received messengers from Kilpatrick near Frederick, warning of just such a concentration. These reports, added to townspeople's accounts of Rebel activity to the west, told Buford that a pitched battle might lay a few hundred yards off.[4]

Already Buford had seen action in Pennsylvania. The day before, shortly after detaching Merritt and the divisional train, he had stumbled upon a two-regiment, two-gun unit of Major General Henry Heth's division outside the village of Fairfield. Buford met the enemy inadvertently because local residents—apparently fearing Rebel retaliation on their homes and property—failed to warn the Union troopers of Heth's proximity. Though surprised, Buford recovered quickly enough and had men enough to give the Confederates a drubbing. But, aware that his primary task was to reach Gettysburg without delay, he avoided the sort of combat that had bedeviled Stuart on his way north. Fearing that "the cannonading from that quarter might disarrange the plans of the general commanding," he detoured toward Emmitsburg, headquarters of John Reynolds's wing, following a limited skirmish by Gamble's brigade.[5]

At Emmitsburg late that afternoon, Buford doubtless reported the affair to his superior, giving him an assessment of the enemy's position and probable intentions. Reynolds passed such information to Meade and Pleasonton at Frederick, while the first Cavalry Division resumed its movement to Gettysburg. (Although Reynolds was properly appreciative of Buford's reconnaissance, Alfred Pleasonton was not. When, later in the day, Buford sent him detailed and comprehensive reports of Rebel activity north and west of Gettysburg, Pleasonton relayed them to Meade without commendation—even as he praised Kilpatrick for his cockeyed assessment of affairs near East Berlin.)[6]

Once at Gettysburg, Buford surveyed the area for its military-geographical potential. From the first, he liked what he saw. One mile long, a few miles wide, with a population of perhaps 2,400, the town itself appeared no different from other whitewashed villages that dotted the countryside of south-central Pennsylvania, save for two distinctions. It was a center of learning, the home of Pennsylvania College, built thirty-one years ago on the village's northwestern outskirts, and the Lutheran Theological Seminary, founded in 1843 just off the Chambersburg Pike, west of town. Of more significance to men in blue, Gettysburg was the terminus of the Western Maryland Railroad (the road's planned extension northwest of town was as yet an empty cut) as well as the focal point of a dozen thoroughfares radiating in all directions. Each was a strategic byway of advance and withdrawal, and four were hard-surface turnpikes that could accommodate large bodies of troops. Imagining the town to be the face of a clock, Buford found the Centre Mills road running almost directly north between twelve and one o'clock, the Heidlersburg road (also known as the Harrisburg road) at one o'clock, the Hunterstown road between one and two, the York Pike (Oxford road) at two, the Hanover (or Bonaughtown) road between three and four o'clock, the Baltimore Pike (Littlestown road) at about five o'clock, the Taneytown road at six, the Emmitsburg road at seven, the Hagerstown Pike (or Fairfield road) between eight and nine, the Chambersburg Pike (Cashtown road) between nine and ten, the Mummasburg road between ten and eleven, and the Carlisle (or Middletown) road between eleven and twelve o'clock.[7]

These highways not only ran through the heart of lower Pennsylvania but gave access to the industrial centers of the East, as well as Maryland and Washington, D.C. They made Gettysburg a magnet that would draw together forces from distant quarters. For this reason, John Buford considered holding the town not only as a forward outpost but as a grouping-point for Meade's scattered army.[8]

***

It took perhaps three hours for Gamble, Devin, and Calef to reach the ridgeline atop which sat the Lutheran Seminary. Buford bivouacked them on both slopes of Seminary Ridge, from which the men had an almost unobstructed view of the mountains eight miles to the west.[9]

Immediately scouts trotted out the pike toward Cashtown to learn the composition of the Rebel force discovered in that direction. A short distance from their bivouac the scouts exchanged shots with dozens of Confederate infantrymen in line of battle. Having proclaimed their defiance, the enemy retired slowly toward South Mountain, posting four or five pickets several miles from Gettysburg—too far off to pose a threat to the new inhabitants. The skirmish had produced no casualties other than a few captured Rebels.[10]

Though the people of Gettysburg hailed the Rebels' leave-taking as proof of their deliverance, Buford was more realistic. His scouts informed him that the enemy had had enough troops to cause the cavalry a great deal of trouble had they wished to. Perhaps they had resisted the opportunity—as Buford had at Fairfield—because they were bound elsewhere and could not tarry. Buford suspected they would return at a convenient time and in greater force.

After sending a galloper to bring John Reynolds the latest news, the cavalry leader scrutinized the local geography, sizing it up as a battlefield. He rode in all directions, taking sightings from field glasses and comparing notes with his staff, including his signal officer, Lieutenant Aaron B. Jerome. By day's end he was confident that, when the enemy returned, he could successfully oppose them from Seminary Ridge or from several elevations, some wider and higher, farther west. Furthermore, should his men be forced back, they could continue to resist from atop a steep ridgeline parallel to and nearly a mile east of the high ground that held the seminary. This was Cemetery Ridge, which took its name from Evergreen Cemetery on the lower edge of the village. From the graveyard high ground ran south for over two miles, where it was anchored by two knolls: Round Top and Little Round Top, the first heavily wooded. Ordinarily, only infantry could have been expected to utilize fully the defensive potential of these positions. But John Buford knew his people could exploit terrain as skillfully as any foot soldiers alive.

He chose to post only Gamble's brigade on the high ground directly west of the seminary. While keeping a reserve on Seminary Ridge, he placed Gamble's main force on a second elevation about 400 yards beyond: McPherson's Ridge, a stretch of high ground crowned by a patch of woods, with a swale in rear and a meandering stream known as Willoughby Run in front. Gamble stationed advanced pickets on and beyond a third ridgeline, some 1,300 yards west of McPherson's, known as Herr Ridge; the most advanced picket post was about four miles from Gettysburg. When the dispositions were complete, the main line of the 1st Brigade extended for a mile between the Fairfield road and the Chambersburg Pike. From south to north were positioned Lieutenant Colonel Markell's 8th New York, Major John L. Beveridge's 8th Illinois, and the combined companies of the 12th Illinois and 3rd Indiana, under George Chapman.

Buford placed Devin's brigade farther north, stretching from the railroad grading to the Mummasburg road. In that sector it could oppose any force that came in against Buford's right flank and rear. Devin stationed advance pickets on every road north and northeast, as well as northwest, of town: his line of vedettes stretched as far east as York Pike. Running north, the main line of his command consisted of Captain Seymour B. Conger's squadron of the 3rd West Virginia, Lieutenant Colonel William H. Crocker's 6th New York, Colonel Sackett's 9th New York, and the 17th Pennsylvania of Josiah Kellogg. On the far right of the line, almost astride the Carlisle Pike, John Calef had unlimbered his six-gun battery.[11]

By early evening, many of these men lay wrapped in sleep—soundly or otherwise. In the darkness campfires blazed as thousands of insects sawed and chirped away. Other men remained awake, and not only those on the picket lines. Outside Devin's headquarters tent along the Mummasburg road, Buford stood about the fire with his senior subordinates, rehashing dispositions and contingency plans. In the course of the conversation, the brigade leaders expressed faith in their ability to hold their positions the next morning.

Their leader was not so sanguine. A few hours before, Buford had left his headquarters at Tate's Blue Eagle Hotel, one block west of the Diamond. There he had perused reports sent in from the picket lines, from far-ranging scouts, and from citizens who had (or thought they had) information on Rebel movements.[12] He had learned from his vedettes along the Chambersburg Pike that Rebel outposts about a mile beyond Herr Ridge had been reinforced. Other scouts had captured Confederates farther north, along the Mummasburg road. Such signs pointed to a heavy concentration to the northwest. The reports Buford had gathered early in the day indicated that other forces might advance from due north of the town.[13]

From his contacts with Reynolds, Buford was confident that come morning infantry would be within supporting range of him. Still, there was no way of ensuring that the foot troops would arrive in time or in force sufficient to keep the cavalry from being overwhelmed. Had Buford known the strategy that General Meade was mulling over, he would have had further cause for alarm. Though Meade suspected that the army was concentrating at Gettysburg, he did not plan to fight there. The army commander favored taking up a defensive stance in northern Maryland on the banks of Little Pipe Creek, about sixteen miles below Buford's position.[14] When Reynolds came to the aid of the cavalry, would the rest of the army be close behind, or would it remain far off even as Lee massed in Buford's and Reynolds's front?

For these and other reasons, Buford was not impressed by Tom Devin's pronouncement that he could hold his position against any number of Confederates. "No, you won't," he told the colonel. "They will attack you in the morning and they will come *booming*—skirmishers three deep. You will have to fight like the devil to hold your own until supports arrive."[15]

There was no anxiety in his voice; it conveyed resignation to an inexorable fact. Buford had decided to hold his ground, and hold it he would. But he was under no illusion that it was going to be easy.

***

Dawn proved him a seer. At about 5:00 A.M., 1 July, just after sunrise, three lines of Confederate skirmishers came shuffling along the Chambersburg Pike toward Gamble's outposts on McPherson's Ridge. They came on slowly, implacably, with a confidence bred of unbroken success and bolstered by the belief that only Federal militia barred their path.

These were Heth's men of Hill's corps, many of whom had confronted Gamble's scouts from afar the previous afternoon. Yesterday it had been the brigade of Brigadier General James J. Pettigrew that had moved on Gettysburg, involved in foraging and held in check by orders that prohibited an engagement. Today it was Heth's division in its entirety—Brigadier General James J. Archer's Tennessee and Alabama brigade in the lead—looking for supplies thought to be in government warehouses near Gettysburg. And Archer, unlike Pettigrew, was bound by no constraints.[16]

Following his 30 June reconnaissance, Pettigrew had attempted to convince both Heth and Hill that veteran Yankee cavalry held the town and its environs. Neither of his superiors could believe their enemy had moved so swiftly out of

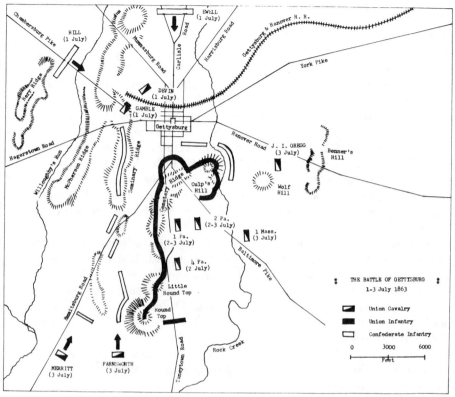

The Battle of Gettysburg, 1–3 July 1863. (Map drawn by Lawrence T. Longacre.)

Maryland, nor that horsemen alone would hold such an exposed post. Another who doubted the accuracy of Pettigrew's report was Robert E. Lee. If a large force of the enemy were truly in Gettysburg, J. E. B. Stuart would have found a way to let him know. Rather than meet him in front, Lee expected General Meade to strike his rear, specifically his communication lines beyond South Mountain. Possibly mounted militia had returned to Gettysburg, or perhaps some of Milroy's stragglers had wandered there—but not the Army of the Potomac! Therefore he gave A. P. Hill permission to retrace his steps of 30 June.[17]

Even as Heth's men started southeastward from Cashtown, Hill massed his other divisions to follow, should his advance discover spoils overlooked by Gordon and Jenkins on the twenty-sixth. And since Hill was moving toward the crossroads, Lee decided to order Ewell, now marching southwest from Carlisle, to swing down to Gettysburg as well. Wishing to group his far-flung units before being forced to accept battle in Pennsylvania or Maryland, Lee—

like Buford and Reynolds—viewed the Adams County seat as his immediate objective.[18]

* * *

Despite yesterday's portents—and although the morning seemed clammy with tension as well as humidity—a mob of youngsters and adults came out before daylight to visit Buford's camps. Young Leander Warren was one of the few privileged to lead the horses of Gamble's main body to drink from nearby streams. But the boy had barely started on his errand when, about 5:30, the fearful staccato of carbine fire drifted down the Chambersburg Pike, spooking the horses in his charge. In a moment, Gamble's bivouac was in tumult and Leander and his friends sensed they had overstayed their time: "The bugles began to blow and the men got their horses ready. We thought we had better start for home. . . ."[19]

Other youngsters were standing in front of Colonel Devin's tent, speaking to his aides, when the shooting started. They saw the brigade leader burst through the flap while buckling on scabbard and holster, an anxious look on his face. He stared westward for a long moment but—though the volume of the firing increased—appeared unable to pinpoint its source. The uncertainty was relieved when a courier galloped up with word from the front: one of the seven outposts Gamble had stationed near the Chambersburg Pike had seen foot soldiers, perhaps two miles out, approaching in triple skirmish lines, and had traded shots with them. But the Rebels appeared determined to keep coming until a larger force stopped them.

Later, several Union troopers would claim to have fired the first shots at Gettysburg. By all indications, the honor belonged to Lieutenant Marcellus E. Jones, of Gamble's 8th Illinois. The commander of a several-man picket post on the east bank of Marsh Creek, a stream that crossed the Chambersburg Pike about half a mile west of Herr Ridge, Jones had spied Archer's skirmishers coming out of the mist that shrouded the pike. Resting a borrowed carbine in the fork of a rail fence, the lieutenant loosed a few rounds at the Rebels. He then fell back and sent messengers to inform General Buford of the incident.[20]

Having foreseen the event, Buford was prepared to respond. From his reserve he strengthened the picket lines, until several hundred of Gamble's and Devin's men held Herr Ridge. Three out of every four scattered through trees and underbrush, taking positions at intervals of perhaps thirty feet. Each fourth man stood to the rear, holding the reins of his and his comrades' mounts. To support this advanced line, Buford transferred Calef's battery from above Gettysburg onto the Chambersburg Pike, one section on its right, the other two on the left.[21]

Thanks to Calef and the troopers in his rear, Buford did a masterful job of delaying the enemy. Amazed by the rapidity of their rifle fire—and seeing no horses nearby—Archer's Confederates decided they were facing veteran foot soldiers. As Buford had hoped, they halted to realign their front. They spread out in long lines of battle above and below the turnpike, and sent skirmishers forward to draw the Yankees' fire. North of the pike, on Devin's front, the first casualties on both sides occurred.[22] Eventually the Rebels learned that cavalry alone confronted them. Even then, they believed that each of Buford's men, rather than a handful, was armed with a repeating rifle.

General Heth required over two hours to align properly his mile-and-a-half-long line. By 8:00 A.M. his rear regiments had closed up, his artillery was in position off the flanks, and his front line again surged forward. The foot soldiers proceeded slowly over plowed ground and through fields of wheat. Then, when almost to Herr Ridge, they charged the front and flanks of Buford's line, threatening to lap around both ends of it simultaneously.

Buford held his men in place till the last minute, then ordered a pullback. Under covering fire from the rear, the dismounted men scrambled east to McPherson's Ridge. Though the new position was less elevated than the old, its proximity to Buford's main force and to Calef's guns made it easier to defend. There the Federals formed a new skirmish line, slightly longer than that they had held on Herr Ridge; as the enemy came on, the troopers attempted to slow them by increasing their rate of fire.

The new position held for another hour and a half. Gamble's carbineers continued to blast away as quickly as they could reload, Calef's shells thundering over their heads to burst in the fields beyond. Close to ten o'clock, however, Heth's men secured advantageous positions on both sides of the pike and brought up enough cannon—two four-gun batteries—to neutralize Calef.[23] Realizing that in minutes he would have to abandon the line, and perhaps the entire field, Buford dispatched couriers to locate Reynolds and hasten him along.

The previous day, Reynolds had moved his I Corps from Emmitsburg to Marsh Creek, only five miles south of Gettysburg. After a brief sleep, the wing commander marched toward the scene of action about 8:00 A.M. on the first. When about three miles from his destination, he met a messenger from Buford, with news of Heth's advance. A mile farther on, a citizen of Gettysburg excitedly told him about the cavalry-infantry contest just up the road. These reports led Reynolds to speed the marching pace of his men and that of Major General O. O. Howard's XI Corps, some miles farther to the south. Then, putting spurs to his charger, Reynolds led his staff and escort far to the front of his vanguard.[24]

A half-hour's gallop up the Emmitsburg road brought his small party into Gettysburg, which was reverberating with sounds of battle. In the center of town, Reynolds learned that Buford had transferred his headquarters to the seminary. With cavalry officers as his guides, he continued through the streets and out the Chambersburg Pike.

Shortly after ten o'clock the major general reached Seminary Ridge. Peering westward through the haze of battle-smoke, he saw Buford's men kneeling and lying on the firing line, striving desperately to hold on. Learning that the cavalry commander had taken up an observation post in the cupola of the seminary building, Reynolds dismounted on the run and leapt up the ladder to the belfry. Halfway to the top, he met Buford descending.

"What's the matter, John?" Reynolds cried.

Relieved to see him, Buford nevertheless replied: "The devil's to pay!"

While outgunned and almost outflanked, however, Buford had not surrendered to pessimism. When Reynolds asked if he could hold his ground till the I Corps could get up, the cavalryman replied with quiet confidence: "I reckon I can."[25]

After Buford familiarized his visitor with the day's events and the local topography, Reynolds returned briefly to the Emmitsburg road to help his escort tear down fences that would block his corps's path to Seminary Ridge. He also dispatched a rider to prod the XI Corps to quicken its pace, while a third courier galloped to Meade's new headquarters at Taneytown, some twenty miles to the south. The latter carried word of Reynolds's decision to fight on the ground that Buford had chosen: "The enemy is advancing in strong force, and I fear he will get to the heights beyond the town before I can. I will fight him inch by inch, and if driven into the town I will barricade the streets, and hold him back as long as possible."[26]

As Reynolds dictated his message, the moment of crisis drew near. By 10:15, the northernmost Federals had been driven from McPherson's Ridge, Calef's gunners were preparing to retire before the gray wave engulfed them, and the rest of the line was being outflanked to the south. By now the cavalry's losses approached one hundred killed or wounded, plus seventy horses dead. Even before leaving the seminary building, Reynolds had met Colonel Gamble, rushing up from the firing line and crying: "Hurry up, General, hurry up! They are breaking our line! They are breaking our line!"[27]

***

To the north of town, the situation was even more precarious, as fighting began to develop on two fronts simultaneously. There Devin's main body stubbornly held the line. Much of the credit for its tenacity was due to Colonel Sackett, who, as commander of the brigade's pickets, had ably deployed his men and had made good use of Calef's upper section. By ten o'clock, the left of that line was finally caving in under pressure from the brigade of Brigadier General Joseph R. Davis, which had come up on the left of Archer's. Part of the problem was that after three hours of heavy skirmishing, Buford's 2nd Brigade was running short of ammunition. Soon Devin's men began to drift rearward and the infanty to press ahead in strength. At about the same time, the skirmishing that had been going on for some hours north of town developed into a full-scale encounter as the lead elements of Rodes's division, Ewell's corps, swept down the Carlisle road. Their attention thus distracted, Devin's people could no longer stop Heth from circumventing Gamble's upper flank.[28]

The Rebels' twin drives, however, came too late. Just as Davis's brigade poised to crush Gamble, the 1st Division, I Corps, Army of the Potomac, double-quicked across the fields to Seminary Ridge. Shouting, swearing, gesticulating, John Reynolds whipped it into line in rear of the cavalry. As the infantry deployed, it opened ranks to allow Buford's troopers to pass through to safety.

Their uniforms torn and bloody, their faces tight from strain and grimy with powder-stains, the men of Gamble's brigade retired with cheers for the foot soldiers and shouts of defiance at the enemy. Some told the I Corps that a brief show of force would send the Rebels scrabbling westward in defeat. "We have got them now," they shouted. "Go in and give them hell!" But the foot soldiers did not reply, aware that victory was far from assured. At the same time, impressed by the troopers' tenacity, they ventured no gibes about a scarcity of dead cavalrymen.[29]

Once the horsemen cleared the front, the I Corps realigned ranks, then began firing volleys. But it had formed so hastily, so few of its men were on the field, and the enemy had gained so much momentum, that part of the new line began to waver. In an effort to steady his embattled right flank, John Reynolds assumed personal command of the "Iron Brigade," which was ensconced in McPherson's Woods astride the latter's namesake ridge. Sitting his dark charger, shouting the brigade forward, the wing commander was knocked from his saddle, a minié ball in his neck. Enraged by his death, his soldiers fought furiously until the right flank regained stability.[30]

Though relieved from the front line, Buford's men were not through for the day. To guard the infantry's lower flank, Gamble massed his brigade and led it to the Hagerstown Pike. There it saw more limited fighting than earlier; still, it calmed the fear of Reynolds's successor, Major General Abner Doubleday, that he would be overwhelmed on the south.[31]

Meanwhile, Devin's brigade became more heavily involved as the fighting stoked up to full fury. By about 10:30, the command had moved into position along a line that stretched from the Carlisle road to the Rock Creek crossing of the road from Harrisburg. Some men took up picket posts on the York Pike as well. For a brief interval, Devin was able to rest his men and replenish their ammunition, while Doubleday's infantry—constantly increased by newly arrived regiments—held A. P. Hill in check. Some time after eleven o'clock, however, Ewell's soldiers appeared in Devin's front in strength at least as great as that Hill had brought to bear against Gamble. Soon both the Carlisle and Heidlersburg roads were flooded with gray infantry (Early's division on the latter) and Devin's position was almost untenable.[32]

The lack of a commanding position such as Herr and McPherson's Ridges ensured that Devin's people would be rapidly driven in. Still, Buford's Hard-

Hitter maintained poise and clear thinking. As the historian of his 9th New York recalled, "Devin retired gradually . . . by successive formations in line by regiment." Employing the fall-back-and-fight tactics that had served both Union and Confederate horsemen so well over the past several weeks, the colonel made his retrograde movement consume two hours.[33]

Devin's tenacity had the desired effect. By 1:00 P.M., when he massed along Rock Creek, leading units of Howard's XI Corps had come up through Gettysburg to form line of battle across the arc of Ewell's advance. When relieved by the infantry and artillery, Devin's brigade fell in on Howard's right along the York Pike, protecting that vulnerable point until the majority of the corps could reach the battlefield.

Devin's men had not only helped frustrate Hill's efforts to crumple Gamble's flank; they had also prevented Ewell from gaining the rear of the I Corps at a crucial time. For their efforts, they got shelled by their own comrades—an XI Corps battery on the outskirts of Gettysburg had mistaken them for Rebels. The cannonade made casualties of several horses but none of their riders.[34]

***

Even with the infantry on the field, it was inevitable that the Union line would collapse. The combined forces of Heth, Rodes, and Early outweighed Doubleday's and Howard's men handily, and Federal reinforcements were hours away. John Buford had foreseen this possibility when considering the use of the lower portions of Seminary and Cemetery Ridges as regrouping points. Therefore, the cavalry leader was not surprised when, about 2:30 P.M., the XI Corps, overwhelmed on the right despite Devin's best efforts, gave way. Within minutes, foot troops and remounted troopers were retreating through Gettysburg toward the higher terrain below.

Pockets of resistance dotted the withdrawal. A squadron of the 9th New York, hard-pressed by pursuers, suddenly turned about and repulsed a much heavier force of Rebels. And dozens of troopers in the 17th Pennsylvania made a stand along the York Pike, delaying the Confederates with massed carbine fire and answering the Rebel yell with "a ringing loyal cheer." Even so, the fallback was mostly a study in chaos, especially when infantry and horsemen collided with citizens in a mad rush through village streets. Many of the latter had been driven into town from outlying farms, herds of cattle and sheep with them. Of course the livestock blocked escape routes, adding to the pandemonium. As one regimental historian recalled, "the bawling and bleating of the animals in straggling herds was in strong contrast to the sharp rattle of musketry and the thunder of cannon."[35]

Scores of Union soldiers were captured or shot down in the streets and alleys of Gettysburg. Most, however, were propelled by survival instincts to the crest of Cemetery Ridge, where they found a phalanx of XI Corps batteries and foot troops posted to aid their escape. Much of the credit for this formidable rear guard was due to Winfield Scott Hancock, commander of the II Corps. He had been sent up to succeed the fallen Reynolds, largely as a result of a dispatch from Buford to Meade decrying the lack of a "directing person" on the field.[36]

While the XI Corps and Devin's brigade fled south, Doubleday and Gamble held Seminary Ridge to the last. Throughout the afternoon, the 1st Cavalry Brigade, plus Calef's guns, continued to support the left flank of the I Corps. The troopers did so by skirmishing with the lower portion of Heth's division and then against infantry coming up on Heth's right. From the McMillan Woods, below the Hagerstown Pike, they poured a shattering volley into Brigadier General James H. Lane's brigade of Major General William D. Pender's division, inflicting many casualties. Gamble suffered several losses of his own in the encounter, including the mortal wounding of Major Charles Lemmon of the 3rd Indiana.[37]

Pender's appearance would have doomed Doubleday and Gamble if the dissolution of the XI Corps had not already done so. Shortly past four o'clock, Rodes's and Early's divisions curved around the right flank of the line on Seminary Ridge. The contest hung in the balance for several minutes as the Confederate pincers closed; then came a Union rout. Doubleday and Gamble emulated Howard and Devin by hustling through Gettysburg, not halting till atop Cemetery Ridge. Most of the troops regrouped on a knoll just south of town, Cemetery Hill.[38]

To prevent a close pursuit, General Hancock asked Buford to make a feint—a show of strength—against the nearest Confederate foot troops. At Buford's order, Colonel Gamble led his tired, bloodied command forward from the west side of Cemetery Hill, the 8th Illinois in the lead. Gamble moved out as a heavy Rebel force emerged in echelon from a belt of woods just beyond the hill and formed for an offensive.[39]

Under a hail of rifle fire, the troopers forged ahead, drawing from observers expressions of acclaim. One of Hancock's staff saw Gamble come on "as steady as if on parade," while Hancock himself thought the troopers' advance "among the most inspiring sights" of his career. For many years he would recall "the splendid spectacle of that gallant cavalry, as it stood there unshaken and undaunted, in the face of the advancing Confederate infantry."[40]

Lane's brigade was just as impressed. Its lead regiment halted, changed front to face the horsemen, and unleashed a volley at close range. When even this failed to halt Gamble's main body—fortified as it was by a covering fire from part of its brigade, holding a stone fence in the rear—Lane's men formed huge, hollow squares, a formation that tactics books prescribed as a defense against a mounted charge.[41]

But an attack proved unnecessary. By huddling together for defense, the Confederates made choice targets. Wrote one of the troopers behind the stone fence: "We went to popping at them. . . . They fell like rain. The ground soon got covered with them. The front collumn [*sic*] broke and started to run but their rear collumn pressed them on with their bayonetts [*sic*]. . . ."[42]

During the melee, Gamble's men kept moving toward the infantry, pistols and carbines flaming. Just short of the human squares, they wheeled about and returned to Cemetery Hill. Their job was done: they had given Hancock time to assimilate Doubleday's and Howard's brigades into his line and to wheel more batteries onto the heights. Intimidated by the men and guns as well as by coming darkness, Dick Ewell—who held overall Confederate command—elected not to storm the high ground, despite discretionary power from Lee to do so. His corps and Hill's drew off toward Seminary Ridge, planning a supreme effort to dislodge the Yankees come dawn.[43]

Ewell's decision—materially influenced by the fortitude of Gamble's brigade—kept the Army of the Potomac from destruction before reinforcements could arrive. Before nightfall elements of Major General Daniel E. Sickles's III and Major General Henry W. Slocum's XII Corps would be on the battlefield, with Meade and the rest of his army not far away.[44]

These units would be sufficient to permit the battle to proceed to its logical conclusion. Thanks to the efforts of the 1st Cavalry Division, which had lost almost 130 men on this day, the horsemen of Gregg and Kilpatrick (as well as those under J. E. B. Stuart) would have the opportunity to test their combat potential to the fullest at Gettysburg.

[11]

Stuart's Expedition—Hanover to Gettysburg

STUART'S decision to head for Jefferson, veering still farther east of his intended route, added ten miles to his march.[1] To worsen his plight, the wounded men and prisoners he had absorbed at Hanover hindered his already slow progress. Notwithstanding, he determined to make the final leg of his journey in record time. From Jefferson he pushed north throughout the night, covering twenty-three miles from Hanover by the morning of 1 July. One result was that his played-out horses went lame by the dozen even as their riders dozed in the saddle. Some of the men fell to the ground when their mounts stumbled or halted abruptly. A few troopers were so exhausted that even after striking the ground they went back to sleep.[2]

En route to Jefferson, Stuart had confiscated local newspapers. Articles they carried confirmed his belief that friendly infantry occupied the York vicinity. But at sunup, when his advance guard reached the York Pike only seven miles west of the city, it saw no sign of Early's presence. Frustrated and concerned, Stuart ordered the march continued to Dover—never realizing that in the darkness his column had crossed the path of Early's march from York to Heidlersburg, a trail only twelve hours old.[3]

Early on the first the Confederate riders crawled into Dover. There, for the first time since breaking contact with Kilpatrick, Stuart permitted them the layover they so desperately needed. Leaving their horses saddled, the troopers dropped off at about the time that the encounter between Heth's infantry and Buford's pickets heated up at Gettysburg.

Not all of Stuart's people were allowed to sleep. Bands of scouts ranged toward York and several other points in a futile attempt to discover Early's whereabouts. Many of the people who lined their march were German immigrants, unable to provide intelligible information. Other locals, with a maddening air of sincerity, disclaimed any knowledge of Rebel infantry movements during the past few days. At Dover, Stuart managed to secure newspapers of more recent date than those procured on the road from Hanover, but they merely repeated old rumors that Lee's ultimate objective was Shippensburg, forty miles west of York, and that Early was probably heading there. To provide more information, Stuart sent from Dover Major A. R. Venable of his staff, to locate Early's route of march. Soon afterward Fitz Lee dispatched a member of his own staff toward Gettysburg to comb the left flank for any indications of Lee's presence.[4]

About midmorning, his men's strength somewhat recruited by four hours' sleep, the Beau Sabreur retook the road north. Just outside Dover, however, he angled westward, in the direction of Carlisle and Shippensburg. His faith in the new route was strengthened when Fitz Lee's outriders reported hearing that Early had left York the day before, heading west. The new route would bring the raiders within range of comrades at some point. If the report about Shippensburg proved false, Stuart knew that other elements of Ewell's corps had recently been in Carlisle. Even if they had departed by this time, perhaps they (unlike Early) had left a rear guard to guide Stuart to the main army.[5] At any rate Stuart's march would bring him into a region in which he could procure provisions, including enough animals to remount his troopers, many of whom were riding two to a horse. In particular, his thoughts fixed on the cavalry depot at Carlisle Barracks, where so many of his prewar cohorts had served years (and, it seemed, another world) ago.

***

The ill luck that had accompanied Stuart out of Virginia refused to desert him. On the morning of the thirtieth Dick Ewell had evacuated Carlisle lock, stock, and rear guard, after appropriating the fresh horses that Stuart hoped to find there. Later in the day Jenkins's brigade passed through the town in an effort to overtake the infantry, and by early evening not one Rebel lingered in the Hamilton County seat. Ewell had left no rear guard to aid Stuart for the simple reason that General Lee had not instructed him to watch for the cavalry leader. For all Ewell and his subordinates knew, Stuart was riding with the main army as it closed up on Gettysburg from the west.[6]

Ewell's and Jenkins's leave-taking cheered the local residents. They were made even happier the next morning by the unexpected arrival of militia under William F. Smith. After exchanging rifle- and cannon-fire with Jenkins along the Susquehanna on the thirtieth, Smith had led 2,000 infantry, plus small units of cavalry and artillery, in an arm's-length pursuit. Smith's tentative march from the Harrisburg defenses indicated his lack of confidence in his troops, but the townspeople readily forgave their deliverers for their inexperience. It was enough to see blue uniforms about town once again.[7]

When he reached Carlisle, Smith exceeded the norms of prudence by occupying the place in force. The risk was real, for Ewell might return just as swiftly as he had left, and without warning. But Smith was committed to making a show of recovering territory lost to the Rebels and to following their withdrawal as closely as possible without actually fighting them. Formerly one of the most respected division leaders in the Army of the Potomac, he had been shelved for quarreling with his associates and undermining the authority of superiors he deemed incompetent. Such conduct had also prompted Congress to reject his nomination as a major general of volunteers. Now Smith was determined to comport himself ably, regardless of the rawness of his troops, to regain prestige, influence, and his old command.[8]

The welcome that the citizen-soldiers received in Carlisle included an elaborate feast which the townspeople served on tables set up along Main Street, near Market Square. While the men gorged themselves on meat, cheeses, lager, and ale, young residents brought forage for the horses of an attached artillery battery. The dinner continued into the early evening, by which time three full brigades of militia had trooped into town via the road from Harrisburg. An officer in an early-arriving unit found the street "crowded with ladies, soldiers, and citizens; the citizens congratulating themselves on being delivered from the Rebels and the soldiers rejoicing in meeting such a reception. . . ."[9]

Then, most abruptly, the festivities ceased. At about seven o'clock, with darkness settling over the town, a cannonball screamed in from the east. Soon came other shells, and with them fires broke out near the cavalry barracks. Pandemonium seized soldiers and civilians alike, "the soldiers running hither and thither to find their regiments; men, women, and children running about, each trying to find a place of safety. Tables loaded with crockery and food were upset, and piles of baggage were knocked over and strewn about. To add to all this, two or three staff officers . . . ordered troops and guns into fifty different positions and at the same time. The guns were drawn up on both sides of the street, the horses were feeding, and the cannoneers [were] without equipment, and drivers were scattered through the crowd."[10]

A shocked General Smith rushed out of his headquarters on South Hanover Street. As still more cannon fire came out of the dusk, he must have wondered if his career had already reached an end here in central Pennsylvania.

***

Stuart's generosity in providing his men with sleep at Dover counted for little. The next leg of their trip proved even more taxing than the night march from Hanover. En route to Carlisle, via Rossville and Dillsburg, the troopers had to march up, across, and down the northernmost spur of South Mountain. Crossing the steep, jagged precipice was almost the death of blown horses and exhausted riders. By the time their next destination came into view, the column had come almost forty miles since morning, and the ordeal had left many riders numb. One of Stuart's subalterns wrote his parents that "from our great exertion, constant mental excitement, want of sleep and food, the men were overcome and so tired and stupid as almost to be ignorant of what was taking place around them." He and fellow officers dozed so soundly in their saddles that Stuart's aides had to slap them awake in order to transmit orders.[11]

One of the few who remained alert to his surroundings was Colonel Beale of the 9th Virginia. Some twenty years before, he had been an undergraduate at Dickinson College, just outside Carlisle, an institution with a large Southern-born student body. Looking about in the fading light, the colonel found that "the whole face of the country, once familiar . . . seemed now changed. Its great natural features, however, remained, and the recollections of boyhood were vividly recalled as, when a student . . . [I] had hunted over these grounds . . . crossed the Yellow Breeches creek in a cider-trough and eaten lunch at a little spring up on the mountainside."[12]

For most of the others in the column, Carlisle seemed to dash their hopes of finding a safe harbor at journey's end. When Fitz Lee's brigade, leading the column, pulled up east of town near the junction of the York and Trindle Spring roads, he found no comrades to greet him. Evidence indicated that Ewell had departed toward the southwest several hours before.

Because Stuart was committed to stopping over, he did not consider bypassing the Union troops he found to have taken Ewell's place. When he heard the garrison was of moderate size and was composed at least partially of militia, the cavalry commander ordered Fitz Lee to press on toward town, while the rest of the column remained farther south, near Dillsburg.

The barracks was the logical objective. Robert E. Lee's nephew marched there directly, passing around the left rear of a mounted picket that Smith had set up east of town. Just beyond the grounds of the cavalry depot, Lee emplaced six cannon, took careful sightings, and launched a few warning shots toward the town.[13]

Despite his preparations, the shelling was inaccurate. Much of it was deflected off course by treetops; other shells failed to carry into downtown Carlisle, due to the small caliber of the guns. Still, chaos erupted in many quarters of the town. Through field glasses, Lee and his subordinates saw residents fleeing to open fields to the north, others scurrying through the streets "with outcries and terrified countenances."[14]

About dusk the brigadier ceased firing and sent a staff officer to Smith's headquarters, under a flag of truce, to demand the town's surrender. Only by acquiescing, said the officer, could Carlisle escape bloodshed and mass destruction.

Though aware he was facing Stuart's cavaliers and suspecting he was outnumbered, Baldy Smith returned a curt refusal. He reasoned that horse artillery could not do extensive damage at such range and that Lee would require an inordinate amount of time to fight his way in closer. With elements of Meade's army not far off, the Rebels could afford no such delay. Of course, too, an aggressive showing in the face of great odds would not hurt Smith's military reputation.[15]

Smith did agree, however, to one of Lee's demands, promising to evacuate the city of women and children. By Smith's account, this condition was then withdrawn; a half hour later, Lee sent a second surrender demand, promising to burn the town if Smith refused. Smith did refuse, expressing his willingness to meet J. E. B. Stuart in hell before he gave up the place.

Annoyed by such recalcitrance, Lee ordered his cannoneers to resume firing. Again their shells flew too high, until return fire from one of the militia batteries permitted them to fix the proper range.[16] Then the rounds landed with more effect, striking midtown edifices including the county courthouse and some government warehouses already plundered by Ewell. A few rounds arched high enough to reach the campus of Colonel Beale's alma mater, just inside the borough limits. Whatever their target, the shells did some damage, for they had been preheated for maximum effect. "We threw hot shot a mile or so," wrote a member of the 2nd Virginia, "and wherever those balls would strike, they would set fire." Later this man stood appalled by the damage his comrades wrought, fearing retaliation by enraged Northerners should the conflict return to Virginia. But not every spectator was horrified by the conflagration. John Esten Cooke felt that "the light fell magnificently upon the spires of the city, presenting an exquisite spectacle."[17]

Magnificent or not, Lee finally tired of it. Shortly before midnight he ceased firing and sent in another demand that Smith capitulate. By now Smith knew that messengers he had sent to bring reinforcements from Harrisburg had been captured. Still he returned the same reply he had made twice before.[18]

This drained the last of Lee's patience. Not only did he resume shelling the place, but he sent his men to torch Carlisle Barracks. Up in flames went the billet area as well as the commandant's headquarters, most recently occupied by Captain David Hastings of the 1st United States Cavalry. The Confederates also set fire to the town's gas works and a nearby lumber yard, sparks from which reportedly destroyed several barns and at least one private home.[19]

The third shelling lasted only an hour. By 1:00 A.M. on 2 July Stuart had decided to ride on, for he had gained the information he had sought since before entering Pennsylvania. It came in the form of sealed orders carried by a courier sent by Robert E. Lee in response to the errand run by Major Venable. Lee's dispatch gave his cavalry chieftain the vital facts. The Army of Northern Virginia was at Gettysburg. It had been fighting the advance of the Army of the Potomac since morning. To support it, Stuart's division was to hasten to the crossroads village by way of Heidlersburg and Hunterstown.[20]

Stuart was immensely relieved to learn the way home. He quickly went about waking the men of Lee's brigade, many of whom had dropped off to sleep, oblivious to the pyrotechnics around them. So tired were they that some of the artillerymen had slumbered even as their guns shelled the town.[21]

While placing Fitz Lee and Chambliss on the road south, Stuart sent word to Hampton, still in the rear at Dillsburg, to move southwestward with the wagons and prisoners, meeting the main column at Heidlersburg. At about 2:00 A.M., Stuart at last led the way out of Carlisle, via Boiling Springs.[22] His departure—which appeared to be the result of the militia's stubborn resistance—meant rejoicing in the town. The locals' joy was magnified because the

134 shells that the Rebels had thrown into Carlisle had produced only a dozen military (and no civilian) casualties, none of them fatalities.[23]

If stung by his opponents' glee, Stuart gave no sign. He was all business as he led his horsemen south, their movements illuminated by the burning garrison. The march proceeded through the night without a halt. By midmorning, after passing through Boiling Springs, the head of the line turned slightly west at Petersburg, scene of Jenkins's bivouac the previous day. This put the cavalry on a direct track to Heidlersburg and, beyond, Gettysburg.

**

Hunterstown, an ancient cluster of wooden dwellings in a tree-shaded corner of Adams County, had been in Confederate hands since the evening of 29 June. At that time a squadron of the Cobb Legion had entered at the end of a far-flung reconnaissance that had begun at Westminster. During the next two days detachments of Kilpatrick's command visited the area but failed to detect the Georgians' presence. This enabled the latter to firm up their hold on the area, while ransacking barns and stables and scouting in many directions, including south toward Gettysburg. The squadron was still in Hunterstown when, shortly after noon on 2 July, Stuart's main body trooped through from the north. At the invitation of the unit's commander, the residents turned out to gape at the long line of gray riders ("it was a great sight to see them riding by in a column, four abreast," thought one farm lad). Instead of joining the column, the Georgians remained in Hunterstown, having been transformed from Stuart's advance echelon into his rear guard.[24]

By 2:00 P.M. the tag end of the column, Hampton's brigade, had moved almost a mile south of town. The rest of the raiding force had halted near Brinkerhoff's Ridge, which overlooked Ewell's position north of Gettysburg. The line remained stationary as Stuart rode on ahead to report to Lee and to learn his proper position.[25]

While the troopers waited, action flared up outside Hunterstown. Sitting his horse along the road to Gettysburg, chatting with his officers, Wade Hampton became the target of small arms fire from a woodlot south of the village. Galloping perhaps two hundred yards in that direction, the general spied his antagonist: a Yankee cavalryman huddling in a thicket another 125 yards to the north. Hampton and he exchanged several volleys, the Yankee working a Spencer repeater and Hampton his pistol. Finally Hampton sank spurs into his mare and charged the underbrush—only to be stopped by a stake-and-rail fence short of his assailant. Frustrated, the brigadier shouted for the Federal to show himself and fight in the open like a man.

The rifleman—a trooper from Custer's 6th Michigan, scouting well in advance of the Wolverine Brigade—remained partially hidden and squeezed off another shot. It missed, as did Hampton's pistol blast in reply. The combatants fired again, and a bullet grazed Hampton's chest. Shrugging off the wound, he prepared to fire yet again before noticing that his enemy's weapon had fouled. The Yankee raised his hand as if to request a pause in the action. The chivalrous brigadier waited for him to clean the carbine's bore. At last the Federal raised his piece for another shot—but this time Hampton put a ball into the man's wrist, ending the strange duel. Conceding defeat, the trooper disappeared among the foliage.

The gentlemanly nature of the encounter abruptly vanished when another antagonist—Major Charles E. Storrs of the rifleman's regiment—burst out of a woodlot to challenge Hampton to swordplay. No devotee of Sir Walter Scott, the major charged Hampton from his blind side and whacked the edge of his saber against the back of his opponent's skull. Only Hampton's slouch hat and thick hair, which lessened the blow, saved him from quick death. Enraged by pain and the perfidy of his assailant, he whirled about and thrust his revolver inches from Storrs's face. Its percussion cap, however, was faulty, and the pistol failed to discharge. Instead of remaining to fight on, the Federal spurred off, bounding along the fenceline toward the thicket that had swallowed Hampton's earlier opponent. The South Carolinian pursued at a furious pace, snapping his inoperative pistol again and again in a display of rage. By desperate riding, Major Storrs escaped, after which Hampton, muttering and growling, returned to his command. There one of his surgeons dressed his chest wound and the four-inch gash that adorned his head.[26]

Hampton's duels foreshadowed his brigade's return to combat. At about 4:00 P.M., a courier reached Stuart to report that a force of Yankees had evicted the Georgians from Hunterstown. Fearing this the prelude to a thrust against Lee's left flank, the major general ordered Hampton to wheel his regiments about and take them back up the road at top speed.

As he moved to obey, Hampton met the fugitives of Cobb's Legion, who provided details of their rout. Learning that the enemy was in heavy strength, Hampton decided to halt and await their coming. It would take time for the rest of his brigade to countermarch and in the interim he could not afford to meet the Yankees head-on. Thus he posted his lead regiments almost a mile south of Hunterstown. He placed the whole of Cobb's Legion in the road itself, with the Phillips Legion on Pierce Young's right and the 1st South Carolina to his left. When available, the rest of the command would take position in Young's rear.

Within minutes a long line of blue-coated troopers marched down the road from town in columns of four. Dismounted marksmen took positions on higher ground on the flanks, apparently to cover an assault. The sharpshooters soon opened fire, but at such a range that they inflicted little damage.

As Hampton had anticipated, a detachment then advanced, preparatory to charging. Unexpectedly, it embraced less than a squadron, though a high-ranking officer rode at its head. For such a small band to challenge three regiments, most of whose men were behind cover, seemed foolhardy. Moreover, the Yankee commander had chosen to attack on a road so narrow that only four horsemen could ride abreast. Still, the unit continued forward as though with unlimited confidence. About three hundred yards from Hampton's line it broke into a gallop, its men waving sabers and pistols and shouting a facsimile of the Rebel yell.[27]

***

Judson Kilpatrick held the notion that cavalry, properly equipped, officered, and supported, could fight anywhere except at sea. Only he could have engineered the assault now being attempted by Captain Henry E. Thompson's company of the 6th Michigan.[28] And only a free spirit with delusions of invincibility such as George Custer could have chosen to lead it.

This was the second saber charge Kill-Cavalry had ordered today. Arriving at Hunterstown at midafternoon, the division leader had sent his advance guard, under the command of his aide, Lieutenant Lewellyn G. Estes, to sweep in from the southeast, nabbing any unfriendly forces in the town. Estes's movement was impetuous enough to have satisfied even Custer, launched as it was without any attempt to study enemy dispositions. The boy who had marveled at Stuart's entrance a few hours earlier stared in awe as the staff officer began his assault: "The officer called out, 'Draw . . . saBERS!' There was a rattling [of steel], then, 'CHARGE!' Down the street they came, hard as they could go, waving their sabers and yelling."[29] Their opponents, alerted by the commotion, took off down the road to Gettysburg just before the attackers struck.

Estes pursued the Georgians out of town until within sight of Hampton's brigade. He then retired under a spattering of rifle fire, although a few of his men remained to snipe at the Rebels.[30] Riding into Hunterstown near sundown, Kilpatrick met Estes on his way back, conferred with him, and learned that he had reestablished contact with the enemy who had evaded him after Hanover. Suspecting Stuart of planning an attack on the upper Union flank—a flank Pleasonton had recently ordered him to defend—Kilpatrick brought up his main body, planning to flay the Confederates with his horse artillery.[31]

When Hampton's rear units turned about and moved north to confront him, Kilpatrick saw he must purchase time for Elder's and Pennington's batteries to pass to the front. He turned to Custer, just coming up with the 6th Michigan. Custer in turn selected Company A, perhaps forty men, he to accompany them. Companies F and G of the 6th, plus elements of other regiments in the Wolverine Brigade, went into position along the sides of the road as skirmishers. In the fading light Custer and Captain Thompson formed for the charge and the artillery came forward—Pennington taking position on the east side of the road, Elder on the west side.[32] Farther to the rear, Farnsworth's brigade turned off onto the Chambersburg Pike to guard Custer's upper flank. As it did so, Farnsworth sent some of his units south to the Hagerstown Pike in response to a report that enemy wagon trains were parked there. Through some "error" of unknown nature, the wagons escaped capture.[33]

In sizing up the strength of Hampton's position, Custer must have recognized the risk in attacking. Yet—even given the narrowness of the road and the fencelines farther south that sheltered Rebel sharpshooters—he made no protest to Kilpatrick. Thompson's opinion was not solicited.

Under a covering fire from flank and rear, Thompson's men went forward— and met an inevitable repulse. Long before coming within saber's range of Hampton's rear, the squadron was blasted apart by small arms fire delivered from many angles. Some of it came from the attackers' comrades; so poorly had the assault been planned that Thompson's own supports poured a crossfire into his ranks. Horses and men toppled into the road, piling up so quickly that the rear of the squadron slammed to a halt, its forward progress blocked. Thirty-two casualties resulted. Thompson and his second-in-command, Lieutenant S. H. Ballard, fell severely wounded, Ballard being captured as well. A lieutenant of Company D was also severely wounded by the errant fire of his own men.[34]

Even George Custer suffered the consequences of his rashness, hurtling through open air when his horse was shot from under him. Slowly regaining his feet, the brigadier found himself the target of numerous marksmen. He was saved only by the courage and agility of a trooper of the 1st Michigan, who galloped up at a critical moment, shot the nearest assailant from his horse, then allowed Custer to mount behind him as he dashed to safety.[35]

Scattered by Hampton's charge, surviving Michiganders galloped back toward Hunterstown. Upon their retreat, their pursuers—Pierce Young's Georgians—became the focus of massed carbine fire. Under a hail of bullets, plus shells from Kilpatrick's now-unlimbered artillery, Young's men suffered more heavily than Thompson's had. Shredded by the dismounted Federals' crossfire, Cobb's Legion turned to retreat. By then Young had been unhorsed (though not injured) and his lieutenant colonel, William G. Delony, had taken a saber slash in the head. Six other officers of the legion also fell dead or wounded, along with fifty-eight troopers. By committing Young's men sans support, Hampton had been as guilty of faulty tactics as his opponent.[36]

Stalemate followed the Confederates' repulse. His artillery having ridden ahead with Stuart, Hampton borrowed guns from the nearby corps of Dick Ewell—a pair of 10-pounder Parrott rifles of Captain C. A. Green's Louisiana Guard Artillery—to oppose further assaults.[37] But none came. Now that he had measured the Rebels, Kilpatrick was content to observe them from long distance, as Elder and Pennington kept up an intermittent fire. In the meantime, he awaited word from Pleasonton as to his next move.

Obliged to proceed to Gettysburg as soon as Fitz Lee and Chambliss moved on, Hampton launched no new offensive of his own. Considering the brevity of the fighting, casualties had run high on both sides. Each commander probably considered the result worth the cost, imagining he had thwarted an enemy drive against his army's flank and rear.[38]

***

While Hampton tangled with Kilpatrick, Stuart reached army headquarters on the Chambersburg Pike a mile west of Gettysburg. Dismounting and striding to General Lee's tent, he saluted his commander and reported the arrival of his raiding force—over sixty hours late.[39]

The lost time had worn away much of the gloss Stuart's reputation had accumulated during the past two years. In the weeks following his expedition, a chorus of critics would indict him for a number of crimes relating to his long absence. Soldiers and civilians alike—even members of the Confederate hierarchy—would accuse him of leaving General Lee sightless and vulnerable ("like unto the blind Samson feeling for the pillars of the temple of Dagon," in the words of one historian), causing him to stumble into battle on terms favorable to his enemy. Among Stuart's colleagues, criticism of his expedition ranged from "a useless, showy parade," to blame for every subsequent misfortune suffered by the Army of Northern Virginia. One of Lee's staff officers even suggested that Stuart be shot for flagrant disobedience of orders.[40]

Perhaps the most balanced assessment of Stuart's expedition was rendered forty years afterward by a veteran of the 9th Virginia Cavalry. "The man is a fool," he wrote, "that contends that Stuart disobeyed orders in riding around the Federal army. General Lee's orders to him plainly permitted him to do this, but the point is that Stuart ought not to have exercised the discretion conferred upon him. His hard horse sense ought to have told him to stick to Lee. That was the place where he was wanted. But . . . the criticism of Stuart is really not criticism. It is a lamentation that so great and powerful a man as he was was not at Lee's right hand to counsel and advise with him about what was best to be done." In short, Lee missed Stuart's cavalry less than he missed Stuart.[41]

Curiously, the man he had failed so deeply wrote little about Stuart's long absence. In his reports of the campaign, Lee confined his criticism to remarks that "the march toward Gettysburg was conducted more slowly than it would have been had the movements of the Federal Army been known," and that prior to the battle the army's operations were "much embarrassed by the absence of the cavalry."[42]

Lee criticized his subordinates so infrequently that when he did he needed few words to drive home his feelings. This trait was evident during his belated rendezvous with Stuart late on 2 July. At first, the army commander regarded his cavalry leader with silence that was itself a rebuke. Finally he asked a quiet question: "General Stuart, where have you been?"

Flustered, Stuart attempted an explanation too long, too involved, and too vague for his superior's patience. Lee cut him short with a voice that smoldered: "I have not heard a word from you for days, and you the eyes and ears of my army!"

Embarrassed staff officers averted their eyes as Stuart struggled to reply. The cavalry leader looked like a man who had just taken a blow in the face.[43]

[12]
Gettysburg, 2 July

FOR the men of the 2nd Cavalry Division, Army of the Potomac, war had never been more hellish. Wrote Pennsylvania Captain David M. Gilmore about the division's journey to Gettysburg: "Think of three weeks marching over hot, dusty roads without regular rest or rations, under constant mental and physical strain, without a wash or change of clothing, and you can have some idea of the exhausted condition of men and horses." Lieutenant Rawle Brooke of Gilmore's regiment added that "the intense heat at times was almost unbearable, the dust almost impenetrable. Horses by scores fell from exhaustion along the road. . . . Officers and men, begrimed past recognition, tramped along on foot, leading their worn-out horses to save their strength, well knowing how much depended upon it. Dismounted cavalrymen, whose horses had fallen dead or dying, struggled along, some carrying their saddles and bridles in hopes of being able to beg, borrow, or help themselves to fresh mounts, others without anything but their arms."[1]

In this condition the troopers crawled into Hanover Junction at about 2:00 P.M. on the first. Despite their exhaustion, they were able to chase off stragglers from the 35th Virginia Battalion and to survey the damage the Comanches had done to trackage and depot facilities.[2] General Gregg hoped to give his men a respite here, but as though the high command felt they had not suffered enough they encountered a torrent of conflicting orders from Cavalry Corps headquarters. Though merely reflecting the uncertainties of the developing campaign, the dispatches harassed Gregg's troopers almost beyond endurance.[3]

Gregg had recently received two communiqués from Pleasonton, written the night before. The first ordered half of his division to return to Westminister while the rest scouted in the direction of Baltimore, covering the army's rear. The second order, dictated just before midnight, instructed him to push a force toward York (including the brigade recently ordered to Westminster) and from there to get in touch with General Couch at Columbia.[4] Gregg had no time to carry out these instructions before the new series of orders reached him, but he did fulfill one obligation by detaching the 1st Massachusetts and sending it to Manchester to picket the supply base now guarded by the VI Corps. Lieutenant Colonel Curtis's outfit would not rejoin its division until late on the third.[5]

The new orders came in rapid succession. The first, dated just before noon, commanded Gregg to take his entire force, not only one regiment, to Manchester. No sooner had the division leader started toward that point than a second courier-borne dispatch told him to fall back upon Westminster if nearby Confederates pressed him, "disputing every inch of ground" in the process. The nature of the threat was unspecified. Gregg was debating whether to place his men on the road to Westminster when another messenger from headquarters reached him. Now he was to send one brigade, with a battery, to Manchester, to protect the northeastern flank of the Westminster supply depot. The rest of his command should hasten to Hanover proper, there to join Kilpatrick.[6]

His patience now threadbare, Gregg complied with this latest directive. He dispatched Huey's brigade, Fuller's battery attached, to Manchester, turned McIntosh and Irvin Gregg northeastward, and marched toward Hanover, praying that this action would not be countermanded. Through the balance of the day and well into the evening the long line of horsemen, artillery, and wagons plodded onward.

It was after daybreak on 2 July when McIntosh and Gregg reached the town that had furnished Stuart and Kilpatrick with their recent battlefield. The newcomers found intact the barricades Farnsworth's men had erected in the village streets. "It was midnight when we passed down through York Street," David Gregg later recalled. "It was full moon and the moving shadows of our horses could be seen on the streets. We halted . . . in Centre Square in Hanover and on the leading streets."

In the square he quizzed residents about the strength, composition, and departure routes of the 30 June combatants. The pastor of Emmanuel Reformed Church got out of bed to inform him that both sides had ridden off in the direction from which Gregg had just come.

While their commander gathered intelligence, Gregg's troopers napped in their saddles. By 3:00 A.M. their dreams were cut short as the column was again prodded into life. Soon it was rocking and jouncing over country roads leading into Adams County.[7]

***

At Gettysburg, dawn of 2 July meant another day of unremitting heat, another day of bloodshed on an epic scale. Today's fighting would be longer and deadlier than the previous day's because Meade and much of his army had reached the field during the night.

Sunrise found General Buford's men southwest of town, guarding Meade's far left on the east side of the Emmitsburg road, three-quarters of a mile from

Little Round Top.[8] During the night the men under Gamble and Devin had been shifted south from Cemetery Hill to salve their wounds out of range of the Rebels who occupied the town.

As Buford must have anticipated, he could not devote full attention to refurbishing his brigades. Though Gamble's men spent what George H. Chapman called a "comparatively quiet" morning, seeing only "a little work between the skirmishers & an occasional shot from the artillery,"[9] Devin's and Calef's people were actively engaged from before dawn until well past noon. About 5:00 A.M., Devin sent a skirmish line forward to reconnoiter suspected enemy positions beyond the Emmitsburg road. Meeting Rebel infantry pickets, his troops and five guns of Calef's battery were drawn into a long and costly firefight against heavy odds.[10]

Fortunately, they enjoyed infantry support: the lower flank of Sickles's III Corps. About noon, in conjunction with Devin's engagement, Sickles sent a phalanx of sharpshooters to oppose enemy skirmishers moving forward from Seminary Ridge. After a sharp engagement, the Federals were driven back, the enemy pressing their left.[11] In turn, the sharpshooters and the cavalry withdrew except for Captain Tim Hanley's squadron of the 9th New York, which remained in position to guard Sickles's left and to warn the corps commander of a renewed enemy advance.[12]

The morning's fighting, sharp though it was, cost Devin fewer than a half dozen casualties. Given its five percent loss rate of the day before, Buford's division remained in good shape, especially since Merritt's brigade, now moving toward Emmitsburg from Mechanicstown, Maryland, had not been engaged. Still, Buford worried about the strength of his command, which he could not recruit without the wagons traveling with Merritt.[13] Early that morning he had requested of Pleasonton (now encamped about a half mile below Meade's headquarters along the Taneytown road)[14] to be allowed to go to the rear for an extensive refit. The petition was especially curious, since Buford's was the only disposable cavalry on the battlefield.

Just as curiously, Pleasonton assented. About 9:00 A.M. Gamble's troopers turned their backs to the enemy and marched south to Taneytown. Devin's people would follow a few hours later. Only Hanley's squadron was left in position along Sickles's lower flank, where it would remain till nightfall.[15] After spending the night in Taneytown, Buford guided his two brigades toward the railhead supply base at Westminster, the sounds of combat growing ever fainter behind him. Arriving at Westminster early on the third, he settled down to restore his command, while guarding the army's rear, thirty miles from the front line.[16]

Buford's decision to leave Gettysburg was questioned by his own troops. As Lieutenant Calef remarked: "Notwithstanding the severe work of the 1st, every one [in the command] showed himself ready for a continuation on the morning of the 2d."[17] To be sure, the division had suffered heavier casualties on other fields without quitting its station.

Pleasonton deserves as much blame as Buford for the withdrawal. If he believed that other mounted units would take Buford's place, he could not have said where he would find them; he must have known that replacements were not immediately available. With Kilpatrick en route to Hunterstown, Gregg far out on the Hanover road, and Merritt still in Maryland, only Buford could have protected the shank of Meade's line on Cemetery Ridge, where mobile reconnaissance units were critically needed. The fact that George Meade must have sanctioned Buford's withdrawal does not absolve cavalry headquarters from censure. In the midst of a growing battle, Meade faced a mob of concerns, Buford's replacement being only one.[18]

Not even Sickles's anxiety over the safety of his left flank, which he repeatedly conveyed to army headquarters, alerted Meade to the problem. Later Sickles attributed to Buford's withdrawal his midafternoon decision to change his position—a change that had dire implications for the entire army. Bereft of cavalry support, Sickles worried that he would be unable to detect an enemy offensive till too late. This worry intensified his belief that his line along Cemetery Ridge was vulnerable to assault.[19] Early in the afternoon, without securing Meade's permission, he led his two divisions, plus attached artillery, toward higher ground almost a mile closer to Seminary Ridge. By stationing his corps on the more favorable terrain, Sickles opened a gap between his troops and the II Corps, north of him. Furthermore, instead of protecting him from attack the new position left him so isolated that he could not stop an offensive by Longstreet's corps, which began about four o'clock.

The Rebels overran Sickles's salient at both ends and then made for the ground the III Corps had vacated along Cemetery Ridge, hoping to roll up the Army of the Potomac from south to north. Only the last-minute placement of reinforcements on Little Round Top saved Meade's left flank from destruction and the army from disaster. By early evening, when the fighting died out, Sickles's corps had been savaged, its commander had lost a leg to a Rebel cannonball, both sides had suffered thousands of casualties, and the Confederates held the western slopes of the Round Tops.[20]

***

About two hours after Buford began to retire from Cemetery Ridge, Gregg's horsemen closed up on Gettysburg from the southeast.[21] Despite their beaten condition, the riders had made extra speed on the road from Hanover. Shortly after daybreak they had turned off the Littlestown road and at McSherrystown struck the road from Hanover to Gettysburg—a more direct route to the west. In this way Gregg cut many minutes from his estimated travel-time.

The column attained a brisk pace as it rode toward the sound of the guns. About 10:00 A.M. it passed Geiselman's Woods, perhaps five miles from the scene of action. The line halted there among the trees while Gregg rode off to Meade's headquarters for further orders. In his absence his junior colonel, Irvin

Gregg, took command, for John McIntosh had again fallen ill from the effects of the journey. Conveyed to the Geiselman farmhouse, McIntosh was cared for by Dr. Theodore T. Tate, chief surgeon of the 3rd Pennsylvania. A native of the region, Dr. Tate had alerted General Gregg to the shortcut via McSherrystown.[22]

The good doctor's ministrations were successful; after an hour McIntosh returned to the head of the column and led it to a point three and a half miles east of Gettysburg, where the Low Dutch (or Salem Church) road intersected the Hanover road. A message from Pleasonton ordered the troopers to remain in that position, guarding Meade's rear and right flank. Thankful men slipped out of their saddles and turned their mounts out to graze in the fields of clover that surrounded the crossroads. McIntosh's brigade bivouacked north of the Hanover road, Gregg's below it.[23]

While the majority of the men rested, McIntosh sent some of Irvin Gregg's people westward across open fields. About a mile and a half from the crossroads,[24] the dismounted men discovered a two-regiment skirmish line of the XI Corps, which had fanned out from Cemetery Hill that morning. Now that Gregg's men had reached the scene, the foot soldiers departed for points closer to General Howard's main body. As they moved off, about 3:00 P.M., much of the 10th New York replaced them atop lofty Binkerhoff's Ridge. In conjunction with this move, Captain Rank's section of artillery moved up the Hanover road, unlimbering near the home of Abraham Reever, about two thousand feet west of the junction.

Troopers in supporting distance of the section began chatting with the Reever family and with other locals who had come out to "see the soldiers." While attuned to the sounds of fighting to the west, other men fed and groomed their horses, played cards around meadowland campfires, and cleaned carbines in anticipation of combat. They also scanned the fields around them for signs of the same enemy the XI Corps had sought.[25]

While awaiting David Gregg's return, McIntosh received another messenger from the front. In response to the order he carried, the colonel detached the 4th Pennsylvania for a trip to Pleasonton's headquarters near the Hummelbaugh farm.

Lieutenant Colonel Doster immediately marched east, guided by officers on the corps staff. He halted his regiment astride the Cemetery Ridge position recently vacated by the III Corps. There he attempted to take the place of Gamble's and Devin's men on the left of the Union line. He and his men spent the balance of the day supporting batteries above Little Round Top and giving Sickles's troops a covering fire against Rebels overrunning their salient. Though never heavily engaged, the 4th Pennsylvania lent a stabilizing influence to the new line that Meade and his subordinates had scrambled to build in rear of the III Corps. By midevening, with Sickles's damage largely repaired, Doster's troopers rejoined their brigade east of town, only to be returned to the infantry's left flank in the wee hours of 3 July.[26]

***

About midday on 2 July—while Gregg reported to Meade, Buford moved to the rear, and Kilpatrick neared Hunterstown—a fourth Union mounted force was becoming engaged. As this force was involved in a feat of derring-do behind the lines, it was fitting that its leader should be Ulric Dahlgren, the young fire-eater who drew his pay as a member of the army headquarters staff but who preferred to do his fighting with the cavalry.

Following his service with Buford's column at Brandy Station, Dahlgren had seen front-line action at Middleburg and Upperville, capering about within range of enemy guns and sometimes beyond support of his own army. After Hooker's demise, Meade had tabbed the captain for courier and escort duty at his headquarters. The work proved too tame for Dahlgren's restless spirit, so he sought transfer to the line. Before his request could be acted on, however, he worked out an arrangement with Meade's intelligence chief, Colonel Sharpe, by which Dahlgren took charge of a detachment of scouts, many of whom were already operating in disguise within the Rebel ranks.

One of the men in Dahlgren's unit was an especially resourceful operative, Captain Milton W. Cline of Indiana, who by some stratagem had ridden out of Salem with Stuart's raiders on 25 June. After passing into Maryland, Cline had deserted his "comrades" and had ridden long and hard to rejoin the Army of the Potomac at Frederick. In that city he relayed to Dahlgren a conversation he had overheard at Stuart's headquarters about a packet of dispatches en route from Richmond to General Lee. The dispatches, signed by Jefferson Davis, were to be conveyed across the Potomac by a courier, protected by a cavalry escort, at a specified hour on 2 July. They would then be forwarded to A.N.V. headquarters via the Greencastle Turnpike.[27]

Here was the sort of mission that gave Dahlgren's life meaning. He had Cline repeat his story to Pleasonton, who, after some hesitation, provided Dahlgren with ten troopers to ride with him to Greencastle to intercept the Rebel mail.[28]

Early on 30 June, Dahlgren set out, crossing South Mountain at Monterey Pass, Pennsylvania. With Cline and the others he veered northwest through Waynesboro, careful to avoid enemy patrols. In the forenoon of 2 July, his men entered Greencastle, some twelve miles west of the site where Lee and Meade were locked in combat.

Having been overrun by a succession of enemy units during the past two weeks, the people of Greencastle were thrilled to see blue uniforms in their streets. "If a band of angels had come down into the town," one resident remarked, "they could not have been more unexpected or welcome. It required only a few minutes to apprise the people of their presence, when all Greencastle seemed to be in the street. Hats flew into the air and cheer followed cheer. Even the old and staid ministers forgot the proprieties and many wept for joy." Dahlgren drank in this exhibition of emotion with great gulps: he loved the role of savior to his native state. Soon, however, he was forced to curtail the rejoicing and to clear the streets. He hid his men at various points around the town, choosing for himself the belfry of the Dutch Reformed Church. From there he scanned the road to the south.[29]

Almost precisely on schedule, the Rebel mailman and his company-size escort came up the trail. Captain Cline had come through magnificently. But just as Dahlgren prepared to signal his men into action, a Rebel supply train, several wagons long, trundled into Greencastle from the opposite direction, bound for Virginia with a harvest of spoils. Its arrival threw Dahlgren into a quandary, for its infantry guard, if teamed with the courier's escort, might overwhelm his little band.

Dahlgren could not let the opportunity pass: he gave the signal to strike. As the wagons and the messenger converged on the middle of town, his men broke from cover and charged them, shouting and shooting. Cutting through the supply train, they stampeded the lead teams, causing some vehicles to overturn. In minutes, the center of Greencastle was bedlam—under cover of which Dahlgren's men sprayed the courier's escort with pistol and carbine fire. As the Rebel company scattered for its life, Captain Cline wrested the dispatch case from its bearer and raced with it to safety.[30]

The wild abandon of Dahlgren's attack convinced the Confederates they were outnumbered. As many as could escape—including the train guards—fled town, leaving behind three officers and fourteen men. For prisoners the captain had no time; he turned them over to local authorities, then remounted and galloped south, his men behind him. Below Waynesboro, fearing pursuit, the band split up. Riding alone with the mail, Dahlgren recrossed the mountains at Monterey Pass and by way of Emmitsburg reached Meade at Gettysburg about midnight, having ascertained the latter's new position from local residents.[31]

Once the army leader perused the captured dispatches, he acknowledged the value of Dahlgren's daring. One letter revealed the Confederate government's anxiety over the distance Lee had put between his army and Richmond. Another missive conveyed Jefferson Davis's regret that because of a Union movement by Major General John A. Dix up the Virginia peninsula toward the capital, some infantry units left in Virginia by Lee could not be released to him as promised. In this same dispatch Davis disabused the army commander of his notion that a heavy force was being assembled at Culpeper Court House to guard his supply line and operate against Washington. Apparently Lee had heard rumors that such a command was being formed from miscellaneous units now idle in Tennessee and the Carolinas. Unknown to him, the Confederate War Office had deemed these troops indispensable in their present locales.[32]

Like Lee, Meade had heard that a second front might be opened in upper Virginia. Now convinced the rumor was false, he no longer needed to worry about the safety of his rear. He could battle Lee secure in the knowledge that the forces on Seminary Ridge were the only troops he had to contend with. Anxious about his ability to hold on at Gettysburg should Lee receive reinforcements from Culpeper or elsewhere, Meade had drawn up contingency plans under which the army would fall back to Pipe Creek. By some accounts, steps had already been taken to implement such plans, and Meade, now assured that his fears were exaggerated, canceled the withdrawal.[33]

As a reward for his resourcefulness, Captain Cline was given the honor of relaying the captured dispatches to Washington. There he would be showered with praise (and gold) by Secretary Stanton. Dahlgren was compensated by Meade's granting his request to lead a larger force of horsemen on a reconnaissance along the length of Lee's communications. Against the better instincts of their regimental commander, 100 members of the 6th Pennsylvania, then stationed at Emmitsburg with the rest of the Reserve Brigade, were selected for the assignment. Before dawn on the third, Dahlgren was leading these men south on another mission dear to his reckless heart.[34]

***

By the time General Gregg returned to his command from Pleasonton's headquarters late on the afternoon of the second, his cousin's skirmishers on Brinkerhoff's Ridge were exchanging shots with Rebel infantry hidden in a woods perhaps a mile to the northwest. David Gregg had anticipated an engagement of this sort; at cavalry headquarters he had learned that his two brigades constituted the rear of the army. Sooner or later the enemy would seek to hit Meade from that direction, possibly in conjunction with an attack against his front.

By 6:00 P.M., with the light and the heat of the day waning, the Rebels in the woods had been reinforced, as indicated by an increased volume of musketry. Fearing an attack, General Gregg ordered his cousin to send some dismounted companies to clear the front. Colonel Gregg selected fifty members of the 10th New York, who swept through the fields toward the woodlot that appeared to harbor the largest source of gunfire. The rest of the troopers, most of whom were still reclining in the clover fields by the road junction, watched with rapt attention, as did some of the civilians in their midst, including a crippled old farm woman bearing a crutch and cane.[35]

Before the skirmishers got halfway to their objective, two dramatic events occurred in rapid succession. From out of the trees came a line of gray-clad infantry, rifles at the ready. A minute later, a mounted man topped a rise several hundred yards to the west and spurred toward the Union line. Behind him raced a party of Rebel horsemen. The fugitive turned out to be Surgeon Tate of the 3rd Pennsylvania, returning from an unsuccessful attempt to enter Gettysburg and visit his wife and family.[36] His pursuers were probably members of White's 35th Virginia Battalion. Two bands of Comanches—each composed of one officer and six men—had been sent that morning to locate the Federal right. One band had passed into Meade's rear, seeking to capture a wagon train erroneously reported in the vicinity.[37]

The historian of Tate's regiment recalled that "in a second Rank's men were at their guns, and, as luck would have it, put two shells into the midst of the party [chasing Dr. Tate]. More beautiful shots were never seen, though they were the first hostile ones the gunners had ever fired. The Confederates fell back instantly under cover of the ridge. . . . The next thing to attract our attention was the old woman running for dear life across the fields with as much activity as a girl in her teens, without crutch or cane, and shrieking with all her might. The two shells had whizzed about six feet over her head and had temporarily cured her of her infirmities."[38]

Turning from such diversion, Gregg's troopers prepared to meet the Rebels advancing on the 10th New York. They proved to be the 2nd Virginia Infantry, Ewell's Corps, then in the process of forming the left flank of an assault on Culp's Hill, a XII Corps position about a mile and a half southwest of Brink-erhoff's Ridge. The Confederates were moving toward a low stone fence that ran along a rise roughly equidistant from Brinkerhoff's and the Federal bivouac. General Gregg saw at once that if the Virginians seized the high ground they could dose his line with minié balls and probably roundshot as well.[39]

The division leader had his buglers sound "To Horse." Before the echoes of the call faded, most of his force had swung aboard their animals, ready for an advance. Gregg sent McIntosh's men forward, keeping Irvin Gregg's in the rear as a mounted reserve. Up the Hanover road cantered the 1st Brigade, passing Rank's busy cannoneers. Just beyond, Lieutenant Colonel Edward S. Jones's 3rd Pennsylvania turned right and entered a stand of timber known as Cress's Woods. Then two squadrons of Jones's regiment, under Captains Miller and Frank W. Hess, advanced dismounted toward the front. Ordered to occupy the fenceline toward which the enemy was straining, the Pennsylvanians waded Cress's Run and pushed westward, Miller on the right and Hess to the left. McIntosh prolonged their line by deploying just south of the Hanover road two battalions of the 1st New Jersey and the Purnell Troop of Captain Duvall. Farther to the rear he stationed the balance of the Jersey outfit under its senior officer, Major Myron H. Beaumont.

Only when reaching the far side of Cress's Run did Miller and Hess see how close the Virginians were to gaining the stone fence. By double-quicking the remaining distance, the Federals reached the barrier barely twenty paces ahead of their adversaries. Opening with their Sharps carbines, they blasted the infantry into retreat. Falling back, the Confederates regrouped and came on again. Again the Pennsylvanians swept the top of the wall with carbine fire, forcing the gray line backward.

Reinforced, the infantrymen charged the wall several times more—an indication of how badly they wished to neutralize Gregg's opposition to the drive against Culp's Hill. Soon darkness came down, shrouding the several casualties on both sides. The shadows finally enabled the Confederates to skirt the troopers' right and pry them loose from their cover. This time, however, the Federals received reinforcements and came back at their enemy. Their numerical advantage enabled them to regain the ridge, but only after desperate, nearly blind fighting.[40]

This effort convinced the Confederates to slip back into the moon-washed timber, carrying off their wounded. Within minutes the fighting degenerated into intermittent skirmishing at long range. About ten o'clock, David Gregg felt able to leave the front and mass his regiments near the crossroads. He seemed content to maintain his bivouac there, but about midnight he received orders to leave only a picket line on the field and to withdraw to a position along the Baltimore Turnpike, near the park of the Artillery Reserve. He marched there via a diagonal road to the southwest, halting where the turnpike crossed White Run. There, beside guns, caissons, and limbers, the troopers bedded down, satisfied that they had fought as hard as they had ridden this day.[41]

The men had rendered more important service than they realized. By preventing the eastward advance of the 2nd Virginia, McIntosh's brigade had helped stall Ewell's push against the key position on the upper flank of Meade's army. The stubborn opposition of Miller, Hess, and their supports prevented not only one regiment but the entire Stonewall Brigade from taking its place in Ewell's assault column. The brigade's commander, Briadier General James A. Walker, was so flustered by the resistance he encountered that he deferred his movement toward Culp's Hill until too late, fearing to uncover Ewell's left to Union observers. For the same reason, he had refused to reinforce the 2nd Virginia's combatants.

In the absence of the Stonewall Brigade, Ewell's assault on Culp's Hill fell short—barely so. In the minds of many veterans on both sides, had Walker's men added their weight to the attack Ewell might have carried that hill, dislodged the XII Corps, unraveled the Union right, and rolled up Meade's line like a giant blue carpet.[42]

***

Having flirted with disaster on both flanks, Meade by evening was in an agitated mood. After some of the most brutal fighting of the war, his army held its ground, though in some places most precariously. By midnight, the whole of his army was in place along Cemetery Ridge and Culp's Hill, but this gave no assurance that the calamity it had averted on the second would not overtake it on the third.

Shortly after midnight the army leader called his ranking subordinates to his headquarters at the Leister farmhouse for a council of war. After they had discussed the strategic situation from every angle, Meade took a vote on whether the army should remain at Gettysburg for a third day of battle or should return to supposedly stronger positions in Maryland. Most of the generals voted to stay and fight. In the end, their harassed but cautiously optimistic commander agreed.

When the conference broke up, Meade was called aside by Major General John Newton, now in command of the I Corps, one of those who had voted to remain on the field. With an ironic smile, the corps leader suggested that Meade "ought to feel much gratified with to-day's results."

The army commander was incredulous. "In the name of common-sense, Newton, why?"

Newton replied with impeccable logic: "They have hammered us into a solid position they cannot whip us out of!"[43]

Colonel William Gamble.
(Photograph courtesy of the Library of Congress.)

Colonel Thomas C. Devin.
(Photograph courtesy of the Library of Congress.)

General Julius Stahel.
(Photograph courtesy of the Library of Congress.)

214

General Alfred Duffié. (Photograph courtesy of the Library of Congress.)

General Wesley Merritt.
(Photograph courtesy of the Library of Congress.)

Colonel J. Irvin Gregg.
(Photograph courtesy of the Library of Congress.)

Colonel Sir Percy Wyndham.
(Photograph courtesy of the Library of Congress.)

Colonel John B. McIntosh.
(Photograph courtesy of the Library of Congress.)

General Elon J. Farnsworth.
(Photograph courtesy of the Library of Congress.)

Colonel Pennock Huey.
(Photograph courtesy of the Library of Congress.)

Captain Ulric Dahlgren.
(Photograph courtesy of the National Archives.)

Lieutenant Alexander C. M. Pennington.
(Photograph courtesy of the Library of Congress.)

Ninth from right, *Lieutenant William Rawle Brooke and officers and men of Company C, 3rd Pennsylvania Cavalry. (Photograph courtesy of the Library of Congress.)*

Warrenton Junction, Virginia. (Photograph courtesy of the Library of Congress.)

The Battle of Upperville, 21 June 1863. (Drawing courtesy of the Library of Congress.)

Scene of Buford's Battle against Confederate Infantry, 1 July 1863. (Photograph courtesy of the Library of Congress.)

[13]
Gettysburg, 3 July

DAWN began with the rise of a blood-red sun, promising oppressive heat. By 6:00 A.M., however, a chill was in the air as J. E. B. Stuart led four brigades of horsemen northeastward along the York Pike. The clip-clopping of hooves on macadam was audible along a wide stretch of the battlefield. Just coming awake, the armies had only begun to blast each other with cannon and small arms.

Stuart's route would take him into the reported position of David Gregg's troopers along the far Union right. The prospect of combat on a large scale, which drew nearer with every passing yard, did not concern the Beau Sabreur. Though lacking still the numbers he had led in the Loudoun Valley (thanks to the absence of Jones and Robertson, whose brigades were closing up in the army's rear), Stuart commanded more troopers than he had at any time in the past ten days. Leading his 6,000-man column was the brigade of Albert Jenkins, spending its first full day under Stuart's command. The horsemen had been placed under the immediate control, however, of Colonel Ferguson, Jenkins having been incapacitated by a sharpshooter while returning from a 2 July visit to Lee's headquarters.[1] Though uncertain of the brigade's usefulness, Stuart seemed satisfied that it was now in the hands of an officer more capable than its namesake commander.

In Ferguson's rear came Chambliss's brigade, followed by the batteries of Griffin and Jackson, then by Hampton's brigade and the section of Green's Louisiana battery that had been assigned to it at Hunterstown. Fitz Lee brought up the rear of the line, conveying the divisional ambulances. The column moved at a more rapid pace than it had for many days, Stuart having unburdened himself of his captured supply train, now in the grateful hands of his army's commissary officers.

Perhaps Stuart should have moved more warily. In addition to Jones's and Robertson's horsemen, he temporarily lacked the services of five batteries.

Those under Breathed and McGregor had run so low on ammunition and supplies that they had remained at army headquarters for replenishment. Chew's and Moorman's batteries had been left with Lee's main army when Stuart began his expedition from Salem; in turn, the army had left them along the north bank of the Potomac until needed supplies could be ferried to them from Winchester. And Hart's battery of Blakely rifles had been temporarily attached to Longstreet's infantry, southwest of Gettysburg.[2] To weaken further Stuart's command, a depleted ammunition supply would limit Ferguson's participation in combat. Due to an oversight by Jenkins, the ten-rounds-per-man quota of Enfield ammunition to which the brigade had been reduced following its campaigning under Ewell had not been increased.[3]

Despite his handicaps, Stuart was determined to make amends for the anxiety and frustration his ride around the enemy had caused General Lee. This day he vowed to meet his commander's expectations, ensuring a coordinated effort on many fronts against Meade's battered ranks. Lee's strategy included a renewed assault by Ewell on Culp's Hill, then a strike by Longstreet and Hill against Cemetery Ridge. Though he had not ordered it, Lee had suggested that Stuart might advance against the Union rear at midday, to exploit a successful attack on the enemy center. If the two-pronged offensive did not achieve a breakthrough, the cavalry might at least divert attention from the infantry's attack.

To conform to this plan, Stuart had consulted his maps long and hard. Now he had a firm plan of his own: to circumvent the Union right by a march out the York Pike, then across the fields into Meade's rear between the Hanover road and the Baltimore Pike. If his path were not blocked, Stuart anticipated delivering a blow both psychologically and physically destructive, one that would compel Meade to quit the high ground and perhaps retreat to less defensible positions farther south.[4]

His troopers rode through the morning in an unusually quiet mood. There was little talking, singing, joke telling—the numberless expedients men resort to in order to break the monotony of travel. Each rider seemed moody and contemplative, as though aware that a crisis lay just ahead. Although they passed through a countryside that had been spared the ravages of combat, the men realized that if the portents held true they would soon be battling for their lives—and the life of their nation.

At about ten o'clock, the head of the line reached the farthest point of Stuart's eastward advance, two and a half miles from Gettysburg. Here, beside the home of Levi Rinehart, Ferguson's brigade descended a country road that led southeastward. As it continued, its point guards scanned the fields and ridges before them. From these positions Yankee cavalry had threatened Confederate infantry the night before. Yet, for the most part, the troopers' view was blocked by the woods through which their road wound. By the time the vanguard reached cleared ground beside the Daniel Stallsmith farm, about half a mile below the York Pike, the scene of last night's fighting was as placid "as if no war existed."

Southwest of the Stallsmith place stood property owned by two other Pennsylvania Dutchmen, George Trostle and John Rummel. Meandering among the three farms was a long and fairly steep elevation known as Cress's Ridge; it ran southwestward through heavy timber, then cut directly south across meadowlands toward the Hanover road. Since the trees on the upper part of the ridge concealed the road by which he had come, Stuart decided to bivouack there while waiting for Chambliss, Hampton, and Lee to catch up to Ferguson. Additionally, as Major McClellan reflected, "the roads leading from the rear of the Federal line of battle were under his [Stuart's] eye and could be reached by the prolongation of the road by which he approached. Moreover, the open fields . . . admitted movement in any direction."[5]

Stuart was especially impressed by the wide, deep, and virtually unobstructed view afforded by Cress's Ridge. Peering southward, he gazed at acre upon acre of farmland—crosshatched by stone and wood fences and dotted by trees—sloping gradually toward Gettysburg under the cloudless sky. Along low ground to the west he could see the puffs of cannon smoke that staked out the positions of the main armies below the town. But the reports were so muffled by distance that the bucolic quiet was nearly total.

It seemed inconceivable that no Federals lurked between Cress's Ridge and Gettysburg. Stuart's eyes shifted to belts of timber in the near and middle distance, including those that fringed the Hanover–Low Dutch roads junction. There or thereabouts, Gregg's cavalry had been stationed less than twelve hours earlier; doubtless some remained. Stuart aimed to flush them out.

While messengers cantered off to hasten forward the main column, the cavalry commander dismounted about 260 members of Lieutenant Colonel Witcher's 34th Virginia Battalion and sent them south to hold the Rummel barn and a line of fences on its right. The rest of Ferguson's brigade closed up on either side of Witcher's party, while Chambliss's brigade formed in Ferguson's right rear. Chambliss's right flank—Lieutenant Colonel Phillips's 13th Virginia—touched the farm of George Trostle, about six hundred yards northwest of the Rummel place.[6]

As Witcher's men moved cautiously forward, Stuart brought up a Parrott rifle from Griffin's battery. From atop the ridge, at his direction, the cannon fired four salvos—one in each compass direction. Though the major general never explained the meaning of this act, his adjutant presumed that it was a signal to Robert E. Lee and his subordinates on various points of the line that the cavalry was in position near Meade's center-rear. Perhaps it was also calculated to provoke nearby Yankees into showing themselves. If so, it had the desired effect.[7]

***

At about 11:00 P.M. on 2 July, Kilpatrick's division had withdrawn from Hunterstown under terms of an order that earmarked it for David Gregg's support. Kilpatrick's withdrawal was also calculated to assuage Meade's concern over an enemy threat against his left rear from the direction of Littlestown.[8]

With Custer's 2,000 men in the van, the 3rd Cavalry Division moved across the fields south of Hunterstown, Farnsworth's rear guard jabbing at long range with Hampton. Crossing the York Turnpike and Hanover road, the column did not halt till it reached the Baltimore Pike just south of Gregg's evening bivouac. Between 3:00 and 4:00 A.M., Custer hove to at a hostelry named Two Taverns, five miles southeast of Gettysburg. Farnsworth's men camped farther west, astride the pike itself. The tired division was permitted only a few hours' rest. By eight o'clock orders from Pleasonton called for it to move across the Emmitsburg road along the extreme southern flank of Meade's line. There, it appeared, the division would compensate the infantry on the army's left for the loss of Buford.[9]

As Kilpatrick prepared for his move west, David Gregg received orders that would affect the 3rd Division as well as his own. Some time after 6:00 A.M., a courier from cavalry headquarters reached his bivouac with instructions to take up a new position farther north and west, guarding a ridge near the Rock Creek crossing of the Baltimore Pike. This post, on the right of the XII Corps line, would enable Gregg to support foot troops engaged in holding Culp's Hill against renewed Rebel assaults. The cavalry's presence there would also ensure that, should the enemy break the XII Corps line, they could not rush headlong into the center of the Union rear.[10]

Gregg thought the shift of position a bad idea. By now he had sized up the field west of the Low Dutch road as a sector to be held at all costs. Anticipating Ewell's continued presence in the area, he foresaw a resumption of fighting along the same ground his men had vied for the previous day. He told all of this to Pleasonton's messenger, but some time after daylight the man returned with word that Gregg must make the move as ordered. The best Pleasonton would do was to assign a 3rd Division brigade to the position Gregg had vacated the night before; Gregg himself was to convey this message to Kilpatrick.[11]

Only partially mollified, Gregg sent an aide to Two Taverns. Upon arriving, the officer found that Farnsworth's men and some of Custer's had already moved toward the Emmitsburg road, leaving only Custer's main body in position. The boy general immediately turned east instead of west, Gregg's messenger guiding him into position along the Hanover–Low Dutch roads intersection. Apparently, no one relayed the news to Custer's superior. Not till noon did Kilpatrick send back for the Wolverine Brigade, supposing its detaching "some mistake."[12]

At his new position, Custer unlimbered Pennington's battery in the southwestern angle of the road junction, near the position Rank's section had held the night before. Unaware that a threat was developing from Cress's Ridge, Custer faced the guns westward. When, shortly afterward, his attention was drawn to the salvos of Griffin's Parrott rifle, he faced four of Pennington's guns and all but four squadrons of the 6th Michigan toward the north. Soon he discovered dismounted cavalry moving toward him from the ridge, but by then he had sent his own foot skirmishers forward, mainly elements of the 5th and 6th Michigan.[13]

Even with Custer on the scene, David Gregg was unwilling to pack up for Culp's Hill. He was especially reluctant to do so after Irvin Gregg's brigade was called to Meade's headquarters for an assignment that made little sense. Arriving at the Leister house about midmorning, Colonel Gregg learned that someone on the army commander's staff—he never learned who—had directed his brigade to proceed up the Taneytown road to study Rebel dispositions inside Gettysburg. Aware that the village was clogged with artillery and sharpshooters, the colonel protested that this was tantamount to a suicide mission. Fortunately, just before Gregg led his men north, Meade found out about the harebrained scheme, quashed it, and allowed the brigade to return to the army's right.[14]

Once back at his cousin's side, Irvin Gregg moved west with one of his regiments to carry out new orders from Pleasonton. Marching across fields below the Hanover road toward the XII Corps picket line on Wolf's Hill, Gregg's 16th Pennsylvania avoided contact with Stuart's skirmishers but encountered opposition from Ewell's infantry. The colonel was forced to halt and dismount part of his outfit. The enemy proved to be in small numbers: the troopers broke through their line, made contact with the XII Corps, and for several hours protected the latter's southern flank. In doing so they met resistance from other, heavier elements of Ewell's corps, many hidden in woods adjacent to Wolf's Hill. To aid the horsemen, David Gregg sent them a section of Randol's battery, which remained near Wolf's until the security of both Gregg and the XII Corps seemed assured. By early afternoon, the fighting on nearby Culp's Hill dwindled down, Ewell's troops having failed to dislodge its defenders. Randol returned east soon afterward, but for much of the day the 16th Pennsylvania continued to hold an extended line from the Hanover road to Wolf's Hill.[15]

By now David Gregg had decided that he was not going to leave the area he had occupied yesterday. He may have reasoned that he could better appreciate its value as a defensive position than an officer chained to the side of the army commander, three miles away. About 10:00 A.M. he directed McIntosh to haul his men out of bivouac and to move toward their position of 2 July. Gregg's ranking subordinate promptly moved up in Custer's rear, till about midway between the Baltimore Pike and the Hanover road. He remained in camp there for three hours.

Gregg's refusal to abandon the area now watched by both Custer and McIntosh was vindicated shortly after noon. At that hour the division leader received another dispatch from Pleasonton, relaying a message from General Howard. The latter's pickets along Cemetery Hill had observed a long line of Rebel horsemen, with cannon and ambulances, marching out the York Turnpike toward the Union right rear.

Realizing that Gregg's concern over his present position had been well-founded, Pleasonton now told him not only to leave McIntosh there but to recall Irvin Gregg as well. Custer, however, should be returned to Kilpatrick, at the lower end of the army's main line. About 1:00 P.M., therefore, McIntosh moved to relieve Custer with his 1,400 men on hand.[16]

While his men broke camp, the colonel rode ahead to Custer's field headquarters northwest of the crossroads. There he complimented the young general on his "fine body of men," and requested a situation report.

Though his outposts had seen only a few Rebels thus far, Custer gestured toward Cress's Ridge and said with a laugh: "I think you will find the woods out there . . . full of them."[17]

To make room for his relief, Custer remounted those of his men who had been lounging in the clover near the crossroads and started them in the direction Kilpatrick and Farnsworth had taken hours earlier. His forwardmost pickets remained in position much longer, for Major Beaumont, whose 1st New Jersey McIntosh had selected to replace them, was slow to appear. Reportedly, Beaumont had come down with a sudden illness. This had happened on several past occasions when battle loomed. Enraged, McIntosh jabbed a finger toward the Jerseymen's bivouac and shouted to an aide: "Damn them, bring them up at a gallop!" In quick time the regiment came forward under the command of an officer of more fortitude, Major Hugh H. Janeway, who at age nineteen had accumulated almost as many wounds as years on earth.[18]

Under Janeway, the 1st New Jersey moved up the Low Dutch road to the Lott farm, about six hundred yards north of the road junction. Many of its men took up posts inside woods on either flank of the road. From his headquarters at the Lott farmhouse, McIntosh placed the balance of his brigade, in column of squadrons, below the woods. Rank's section he unlimbered south of the Hanover road, where it was supported by Gregg's reserve force, the 10th New York, 1st Maine, and the company of District of Columbia cavalry.[19]

Shortly after he completed his dispositions, McIntosh found his attention and that of virtually everyone else drawn to cannon fire erupting along Seminary Ridge. Despite the distance, the din was so terrific that the guns might have been planted just over the next rise. "The very ground shook and trembled," wrote a Pennsylvania trooper, "and the smoke of the guns rolled out of the valley as tho there were thousands of acres of timber on fire." A comrade recalled the sound years later and hoped that "I shall never again hear such terrible thunder as occurred on the afternoon of July 3d."[20]

***

This barrage, generated by 150 cannon along the main Confederate line outside Gettysburg, could be heard 140 miles away. It formed the prelude to the blow Lee had designated for Meade's midsection, a softening-up of the Union lines prior to an attack by 12,500 infantry from the divisions of Major Generals George E. Pickett, Henry Heth, William D. Pender, and Richard H. Anderson.[21]

Across the mile-wide valley separating the armies, Federals hugged the earth to escape the shower of iron. Some huddled behind improvised breastworks. Others, held in the rear where cover was scarce, ran as fast as they could to get beyond range.

Cavalrymen, as well as members of other arms, were targets of the barrage. Because the Rebel cannoneers were firing a bit too high, most of their shells missed the foot soldiers and cannoneers along Cemetery Ridge and wrought havoc among the army's rear-guard population. These included elements of Meade's headquarters force—the 1st, 2nd, and 6th Pennsylvania Cavalry, the Regulars detached from various regiments in Merritt's brigade, and the orderlies and couriers of the Oneida Cavalry.[22]

A trio of horse artillery units from Captain Robertson's brigade also braved the cannonade. Captain Martin's 6th New York, plus Battery B/L of the 2nd United States under Lieutenant Edward Heaton, came under fire while stationed in reserve near Pleasonton's headquarters. Meanwhile, Jabez Daniels's 9th Michigan Battery absorbed shot and shell along the right-center of Meade's main line, where it supported part of the I Corps. Of the batteries, only Daniels's was able to return fire. Its efforts, feeble as they were in the face of such an enormous barrage, helped uphold the morale of General Newton's infantrymen. Its opposition cost the Michigan unit one man killed, four wounded, and twenty-three horses disabled.[23]

Many of the units in rear of the main line were forced to pull up stakes in a hurry. Generals Meade and Pleasonton, chased from their farmhouse headquarters, relocated in woods far down the Taneytown road. So did the troopers detailed to escort them, but not before suffering heavily in horseflesh. The 6th Pennsylvania squadron serving with Meade lost twenty-one horses killed and almost all the others wounded.[24]

Of the several mounted units posted to army headquarters, only the 4th Pennsylvania escaped unscathed. Just before Lee's guns started in, Doster's men were sent down the Baltimore Pike on a scout. They were joined there by Lieutenant Colonel Curtis's 1st Massachusetts—recently detached from VI Corps headquarters—in responding to an erroneous report that an enemy force was driving toward the Union left rear. About 4:00 P.M., their reconnaissance at a close, both regiments crossed over to the Hanover road, where they rejoined David Gregg in time to oppose Stuart.[25]

***

Soon after the barrage along Seminary Ridge began, fighting resumed between Stuart and Gregg. For the next two hours, events on their front moved in rapid and bloody succession.[26]

Stuart began the series of blows and counterblows about one o'clock. The salvos fired by Griffin's cannon had stirred up a nest of Federals—how many and whether infantry or dismounted cavalry, he could not tell—along the cross-

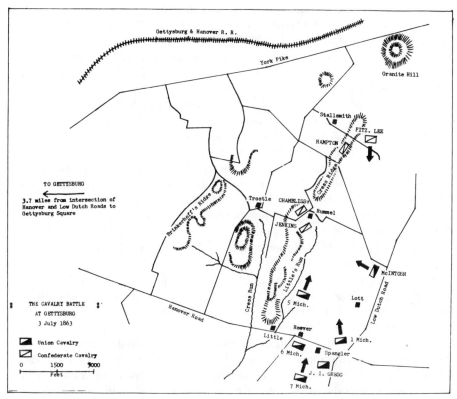

The Cavalry Battle at Gettysburg, 3 July 1863. (Map drawn by Lawrence T. Longacre.)

roads southeast of Rummel's farm. To remove this obstacle to his march toward the Baltimore Pike, he directed Ferguson's dismounted skirmishers to move forward and engage the enemy at long range. At the same time, he had Griffin lash the Yankee position from the middle of Cress's Ridge.

The shelling proved remarkably accurate. Shot and shrapnel dropped into the midst of Custer's main body, inflicting injuries to men and mounts. Quickly Custer moved his men out of range. Because he was about to be relieved, he made no reply to the threat except to bolster his flanks with more members of the 5th and 6th Michigan and to tell Pennington to open fire. The two sections facing north were soon hurling shells at Cress's Ridge. Their accuracy was even greater than their opponent's; within minutes Griffin's guns had been knocked out of action. Soon afterward the Maryland battery had to quit the ridge to refit and replenish ammo chests, leaving Stuart only those cannon under Jackson and Green.[27]

About 2:00 P.M. the Rebel horse artillery fire slackened, and at this point

McIntosh moved to relieve the Wolverines at the front. Two-thirds of his 1st New Jersey—four companies under Major Janeway and four under Captain Robert N. Boyd—moved westward afoot across Little's Run toward the Rummel farm. They took position behind a line of fences within carbine range of Witcher's Confederates. The third battalion of the New Jersey outfit, under Captain James H. Hart, provided cover for Janeway and Boyd from the western flank of Lott's Woods.[28]

Concurrent with McIntosh's advance, Witcher's people seized a fenceline parallel to Janeway's and Boyd's, below the Rummel farm. Since their fence was longer, the Confederates were able to curl around the enemy left. Discovering his comrades imperiled, Custer tried to rescue them by sending forward a heavy skirmish line under Major Noah Ferry of the 5th Michigan. Witcher's men saw the newcomers moving dismounted across open fields toward the run—presenting perfect targets. Having husbanded their remaining Enfield cartridges, the 34th Battalion bobbed up and poured a heavy fire into the Wolverines. Many of Ferry's men fell, others broke and fled. "Rally, boys! Rally for the fence!" shouted their major, seconds before a Rebel bullet drilled him through his red head.[29]

With Janeway and Boyd still trapped, their left collapsing, McIntosh sent up supports of his own, the 3rd Pennsylvania squadrons of Captain Treichel (who had led the 30 June charge into Westminster) and Captain James S. Rogers, plus the Purnell Troop. As these men pressed westward on foot, McIntosh placed the rest of his old regiment—an understrength battalion under Captain Miller and the squadrons of Captains Hess and James Walsh—above the Lott Woods, on the right of Hart's squadron. By moving a few men east of the Low Dutch road, Walsh gained the distinction of holding the farthest point on the Union right flank at Gettysburg.[30]

After splashing across Little's Run, the men of Treichel, Rogers, and Duvall formed on the Jerseymen's embattled flank, securing it. This was no challenge, for Witcher's men, now bereft of ammunition, were withdrawing across the Rummel farm. To replace them, Stuart sent down five companies of the 14th and four of the 16th Virginia. These were the last of Ferguson's available men, the rest of whom were guarding prisoners or picketing in the rear. But all of Chambliss's brigade was now on the field, with Hampton's and Lee's just arriving. Presently, Stuart reinforced Witcher's new skirmish force with part of Chambliss's command and two squadrons of Hampton's 2nd South Carolina.[31]

The Rebels came on with such verve that they pressed not only the troops along Little's Run but also Custer's flanking parties farther north, where part of the 6th Michigan under Major Weber was driven in. Under a barrage of carbine fire the Union line from north to south began to waver.[32]

At this juncture, David Gregg, who had been to the rear, appeared at the Lott house to assume command of the Union forces. He brought with him two sections of Randol's battery. These he placed near his new headquarters to sweep the Rebel position including the Rummel farm, still a nesting-place for snipers. Randol's fire was so heavy and so well directed that Stuart's line began to show signs of weakening.[33]

To keep the Rebels off balance, the troops along Little's Run suddenly pressed forward under cover of the artillery. Converging carbine fire decimated many of Ferguson's men; the heaviest toll occurred in the 14th Virginia, which lost a quarter of its number, including its temporary commander, Major Benjamin F. Eakle, disabled by a fall from his horse.[34] Grudgingly, then rapidly, the Virginians retreated to Cress's Ridge. The Union guns then blasted the Rummel barn and farm buildings, driving out Witcher's sharpshooters. "Never," wrote Gregg, "was there more accurate and effective fire delivered by Artillery than by the guns of Randol and Pennington."[35] Cowed by the barrage, elements of Lee's and Hampton's brigades, which had moved south of the ridge to cover Ferguson, joined the Virginians in their withdrawal.

The Confederates' pullback signaled a lull in the fighting. During the interval Stuart—aware now that he was facing veteran cavalrymen, fighting at the top of their abilities—stabilized his line with the recently arrived cannon of Breathed and McGregor.[36] Soon the resupplied batteries were trading fire with Randol and Pennington. For his part, David Gregg used the breathing spell to importune Custer to remain on the field until the Rebel threat could be neutralized. Though Pennington's guns and most of Custer's troopers remained in position, part of the 6th and 7th Michigan had started southwest in response to orders from Pleasonton and Kilpatrick. Even so, the young brigadier was anxious to stay and fight. He willingly complied with Gregg's request, sending word that his regiments in motion should countermarch. He then reassumed control of his troops still on the firing lines.[37]

The battle lull seemed to end when Fitz Lee began to advance his four regiments. Many of his troops promptly returned to the shelter of the trees on Cress's Ridge—thanks to the fire of Randol's 3-inch rifles, especially that section officered by Lieutenant Ernest Kinney, a converted infantryman. But Lee's people moved forward again nearly a half-hour later, when the ammunition of the troopers along Little's Run began to peter out and the latter tried to disengage. Enemy artillery fire was so fierce, however, that the Federals could not leave their exposed post without courting annihilation.

Custer, nearest their line, attempted to help them out. He managed to place four squadrons of the 6th Michigan on the right of the Purnell Troop, anchoring the lower end of the line along the run. But when he sent the 5th Michigan to relieve Janeway, Boyd, and Duvall, the regiment could get no farther than Treichel's and Rogers's positions. There the Michiganders were forced to take cover behind a post-and-rail fence that ran at right angles to the line along Little's Run, facing northward. In that position they were immediately attacked by Colonel Beale's 9th Virginia, Chambliss's brigade, which swept down from the northwest on foot. Only the combined efforts of McIntosh's troops saved the regiment that Custer had sent to relieve them. Not only did they blast back Beale's men; they also persuaded the 3rd Virginia of Lee's brigade, which had come forward on the 9th's left, to refrain from attacking.

But Fitz Lee would not be stymied. Out of the trees on Cress's Ridge came his storied 1st Virginia. On either flank, other units of the brigade rushed up to provide dismounted support. Soon Colonel Drake's regiment moved toward the Union right center with an unhurried confidence that augured ill for the troops in its front.[38]

With crisis looming, John McIntosh looked about for his final reserve, the 1st Maryland. Unknown to him, General Gregg had moved the regiment from its original position to a line of stone walls southeast of the Lott woods. Still suffering from illness, and overcome by frustration at finding the Marylanders gone, McIntosh "gave way to tears and oaths."[39]

But help was coming up from the south in column of squadrons: Mann's 7th Michigan, the smallest and least experienced member of the Wolverine Brigade. Recruited up to only ten companies, two of which were guarding Custer's supply train,[40] the 7th had seen its first battle only two days ago at Hanover. Still, its men were eager for more and livelier action. Placing himself at the head of the young outfit (its average trooper was eighteen, its commander twenty-four), Custer hollered "Come on, you Wolverines!" and led them in the first full-scale mounted charge of the afternoon.[41]

Breaking into a gallop, the 7th followed Custer with the awkwardness and enthusiasm of rookies. As it thundered diagonally across the battlefield, fugitives from the 1st New Jersey, 3rd Pennsylvania, 5th Michigan, and the Purnell Troop swung wide to let it pass. Rushing by, the 7th closed in on the 1st Virginia—almost oblivious to the dismounted troops that stood between it and its target. It slashed through the scattered ranks of the 9th Virginia as though shredding wastepaper. But a second obstacle in its path, Phillips's 13th Virginia, fired in unison into the head of the regiment, forcing it to make a quarter-turn to the left.

The new heading sent a part of the outfit careening into the post-and-rail fence from which the 5th Michigan had just fled. The barrier transformed the detachment into a "mass of pulp," fusing horses and riders into a giant tangle. Under a brisk fire from many angles, dazed horsemen sorted themselves out and made a stand at the fence, through which they punched holes for their carbines and revolvers. Within minutes they were firing point-blank into the 1st Virginia, many of whose troopers had dismounted along the other side of the barrier. Enjoined by their officers to "kill all you can & do your best each for himself," the Wolverines took a heavy toll of Drake's regiment but lost just as heavily themselves.

That part of the 7th not ambushed by the fence, Custer still at its head, bounded toward the Rummel farm and one of Stuart's batteries just beyond. About two hundred yards short of his prize, however, Custer found Mann's troopers strung out, their momentum gone. He had a bugler sound retreat. But as the troopers wheeled to the south, they were set upon from the rear by two regiments dispatched by Wade Hampton to support the 1st Virginia: Baker's 1st North Carolina and Waring's Jeff Davis Legion. In a desperate fight across the Rummel property, the Rebels took many casualties; their dead included Waring's executive officer, Major W. G. Conner. Even so, they hastened the Federals on their way south, panicking some of the men and stampeding their animals. The Michiganders' retreat was further accelerated when remounted portions of the 9th and 13th Virginia struck their flanks. Then all four Confederate regiments pursued the runaways at top speed.[42]

The 7th Michigan's survivors streamed past Colonel McIntosh, ignoring his plea: "For God's sake, men, if you are ever going to stand, stand now, for you are on your free soil!"[43] Their comrades at the fenceline also remounted and headed south, though many were pounced on by the Virginia and North Carolina regiments and the Davis Legion. Most reached safety after Major Luther S. Trowbridge's battalion of the 5th Michigan dashed into the flanks of the 9th and 13th Virginia, bouncing them back with unexpected force. Trowbridge's band, however, was sliced up and its leader unhorsed when it encountered Baker's and Waring's men, still galloping south in pursuit of the 7th Michigan. In turn, Baker and Waring were struck by Colonel Alger and the rest of Trowbridge's regiment, which had re-formed following its withdrawal from the 1st Virginia's line of advance. A new saber and pistol battle broke out in the middle of the field, the Federals gaining the upper hand.[44]

As the fight intensified, Union observers saw a mounted officer gallop down from Cress's Ridge toward the scene of action. A new line of mounted men left the trees in his rear, following him at a distance. From the length and depth of this line, those watching realized that despite the frenetic succession of charge and countercharge just ended, the day's action was far from over.

***

While the fighting raged outside Gettysburg, all was serene at Westminster, almost thirty miles away. The sound of cannon penetrated to that quarter of Maryland but, as George Chapman noted in his diary, the troopers of Gamble and Devin could get "no reliable word from the battlefield." An enlisted man in Chapman's regiment could hear the guns "plainly. We hear many rumors also but we do not accurately [know] what has been the result of each days work. . . ."

Ten miles to the northeast, at Colonel Huey's depot garrison at Manchester, Union cavalrymen waited and listened in just as much ignorance and anxiety. A member of the 8th Pennsylvania informed his parents that "I haven't heard any news as yet. . . . The firing is getting heavier all the time. I almost wish they would send us there, for I hate to hear a battle going on and not partake of its dangers."[45]

***

Late in the morning, Judson Kilpatrick and Elon Farnsworth approached the lower flank of the main Union line along the Taneytown road. Though lacking Custer's brigade, Kill-cavalry was determined to prevent a resumption of Longstreet's effort to uproot Meade's left. The division leader was in an aggressive mood today and had a preemptive strike in mind. He had been ordered by Pleasonton to "press the enemy, to threaten him at every point, and to strike at the first opportunity." If no such opportunity came about naturally, Kilpatrick planned to create one.[46]

When south of Round Top, he led Farnsworth's men off the road and westward across Plum Run. Before reaching the Emmitsburg road, he turned the column to the north, then angled toward the enemy line along the back slope of Round Top. By 11:00 A.M. Farnsworth's men were within rifleshot of the nearest Rebels, part of the infantry division of Brigadier General Evander M. Law. Law's lowermost force, the Texas and Arkansas brigade of Brigadier General Jerome B. Robertson, held heavily wooded ground at the base of the knoll it had captured the afternoon previous. Under orders from General Longstreet to continue their drive against the Union left, most of Robertson's men were looking eastward instead of toward the cavalry's approach. A thin picket line of the 1st Texas was facing southward as Farnsworth drew near. The only other force guarding Law's southern flank was the 9th Georgia of Brigadier General George T. Anderson's brigade, posted at the Kern house, on the west side of the Emmitsburg road.[47]

When he finally detected Farnsworth's advance, Law took further steps to anchor the lower part of his line. He had a skirmish force from the 1st Texas swing south and west toward the Emmitsburg road, linking with the 9th Georgia while connecting at a right angle with the main line on Round Top. He also turned two of his batteries—under Captain William K. Bachman of South Carolina and Lieutenant James Reilly of North Carolina—to face the south and directed two other Georgia regiments of Anderson's brigade to reinforce the 9th at the Kern house. Not expecting any trouble from beyond the Emmitsburg road, he entrusted that sector to only one hundred medical-train personnel and ambulatory convalescents sent down to him by Longstreet. This force Law placed under Colonel Black of Hampton's 1st South Carolina Cavalry. Having gone home on leave after Brandy Station, Black and a small detachment of his regiment had rejoined the army only a few days before and had not yet located their brigade. Also assigned temporarily to Black were other fugitives from Hampton's brigade: Captain Hart and his battery of three Blakely rifles.[48]

Cautiously approaching Law's new line, Farnsworth's men came under a shelling from the two batteries the Confederate brigadier had trained in their direction. To escape the barrage, the horsemen ducked into woods southwest of Round Top. But they did not remain long under shelter. Seeking ways to make things happen, Kilpatrick ordered up a squadron of Lieutenant Colonel Preston's 1st Vermont, under Captain Henry C. Parsons, and sent it to test the strength of the Rebels. Parsons's men, soon backed by a second Vermont squadron, charged for half a mile up a narrow country lane toward the enemy cannon, pistols drawn. To Kilpatrick's delight, the Vermonters cut through the first troops they met, driving an outpost force back against the main part of the 1st Texas. Although Parsons lost two troopers in the process, Kilpatrick felt this boded well for the future. He rode to Parsons's lodgment at a stone house owned by a family named Bushman, only eight hundred feet to the right of the Emmitsburg road and well within range of Law's batteries. Explaining the importance of the position, he told the squadron leader to hold on for as long as possible, probing the rear of Law's sector. Kilpatrick probably hoped that Parsons's salient would cause Law to extend his flank so far west that Farnsworth would find weak points toward Round Top. The pair of squadrons remained in place till perhaps 4:00 P.M. before returning under fire, but without additional loss, to the main line.[49]

By this time, Kilpatrick had sent other units of Farnsworth's brigade to feel the enemy's position west of Round Top and locate openings for a mounted assault. The report they returned greviously disappointed him. The ground near the timbered knoll was too rugged—its rocky terrain strewn with boulders and sliced up by stone fences—to permit a successful attack.

Kilpatrick's gloom deepened when, close to 5:00 P.M., a messenger from the main line galloped past with news that Lee's infantry attack, launched in the wake of his cannonade, had ended in failure and heavy loss. "We turned the charge," the courier shouted, "nine acres of prisoners!"

The thought that the day's climactic hour was passing with Judson Kilpatrick hardly engaged gnawed at him like the pang of ambition thwarted.[50]

***

For the Confederate brigades of Beverly H. Robertson and Grumble Jones, the road to Gettysburg—which ended late on the morning of the third—was long, rough, and strewn with controversy. The controversy stemmed from the failure of Lee and Stuart to devise a means of certifying that the 3,000 troopers left behind in Virginia would operate to the army's profit.

In his orders of 23 June authorizing Stuart's expedition into Pennsylvania, Lee had stipulated that the horsemen stationed in his rear should follow him north as soon as the Federals departed from their front (but only after leaving pickets to guard the Blue Ridge passes), thence to join him in the Yankee country without delay. On the twenty-fourth, as Stuart prepared to move north, he conveyed these directions to Robertson, who was senior to Jones. Stuart enjoined him to cover the front of Ashby's and Snicker's Gaps as long as Hooker remained east of the mountains. Specifically, he and Jones were "to watch the enemy, deceive him as to our designs, and harrass his rear if you find he is retiring." When Hooker hurried north after Lee's infantry, the troopers were to withdraw to the west side of the Shenandoah, leaving a force near Harpers Ferry, and to push north on Lee's right flank and rear. Stuart directed

Robertson to picket throughout the Shenandoah from Charlestown to the Potomac and to keep in touch with the Confederate infantry via relays of couriers. Both brigades were to avail themselves of every opportunity to refit and recruit as well as to forage in the Valley. Finally, to avoid damage to shod hooves, the horsemen were to avoid macadamized turnpikes on the trip north.[51]

On paper these orders sounded attainable, but they suffered in execution—a fact that produced much criticism of Robertson and Jones.[52] Robertson placed his pickets as ordered, covering the lower (northern end of the) Valley from Winchester to Harpers Ferry and barricading Blue Ridge gaps against incursions. He failed, however, in three duties. He did not maintain contact with Longstreet or even with Jones (the generals placed their brigades several miles apart, apparently by mutual agreement). Even more serious was Robertson's inability to keep in touch with the enemy. Though Hooker left Virginia on the twenty-sixth, the cavalry remained in the mountains until the twenty-ninth. On that day Jones rode from his headquarters at Snickersville to join Robertson at Berryville. The brigadiers compared notes, agreed that no substantial force lingered near the gaps, and decided they had better hustle north. Shortly afterward, they were met by a courier from Lee, en route from Martinsburg, with an order to the same effect.[53]

Not until the thirtieth did the combined force head north, and when it did it moved slowly because of the requirement to avoid the more commodious turnpikes. Early that day it forded the Potomac opposite Williamsport and in Maryland passed long lines of forage wagons bound for Virginia. By late on 1 July the column had reached Greencastle, Pennsylvania. There and thereabouts bands of citizens struck its head and flanks, hoping to preempt attacks on their homes, farms, and stables. Such resistance gave the invaders only bumps and bruises. More demoralizing was their encounter with a vast population of war-age civilians in Pennsylvania. "This," said one of Jones's troopers, "had a rather depressing effect upon us, because it showed us that the North had reserves to draw from, while our men, within the age limit, were all in the army."

But the citizens looked equally depressed. The same Confederate spoke of "the sad faces of the populace as they gathered at their front doors and windows watching us. . . . It resembled a funeral, at which all the people were mourners." A horse artilleryman saw some "beautiful, rosy-cheeked, bonny lassies on the street in Greencastle, but they looked as sour as a crab apple, frowns an inch wide. . . ." He preferred to observe the fields, farms, and foliage of the commonwealth. Everywhere the land seemed under cultivation, "and the barns look like churches."[54]

The column rode throughout 2 July to reach Lee's headquarters at Cashtown. Arriving at Chambersburg early on Friday, the third, they met the cavalry, mounted infantry, and partisan rangers of John Imboden, just up from Virginia via Cumberland, Maryland, and McConnellsburg, Pennsylvania. Leaving Imboden on the western slope of the mountains to guard the army's rear, Robertson and Jones forged ahead in divergent directions. The former moved toward Gettysburg to join Lee, while Jones started for a point eight miles south of

Cashtown. Lee had directed him to Fairfield, just east of South Mountain, to guard supply trains gathered there. Yankee horsemen had been sighted moving toward that same area; they must be headed off.[55]

Today Jones led only three regiments—the 6th, 7th, and 11th Virginia—plus Captain Chew's battery. Lieutenant Colonel Thomas B. Massie's 12th Virginia had been left to observe the Yankees at Harpers Ferry, while White's Comanches, still on detached duty, were stationed on the York Pike northeast of Gettysburg, as part of a reconnaissance in force in conjunction with one of Ewell's foot brigades.[56] Unworried about his missing units, Jones moved south rapidly and confidently, anticipating his first battle since 21 June.

***

At noon on 3 July, Wesley Merritt's brigade left Emmitsburg, Maryland—where it had marched from Mechanicstown the day before—and headed for Gettysburg. Leading his Regulars, Pennsylvanians, and supply trains, Merritt carried orders from Alfred Pleasonton to strike the Rebel left and rear along Seminary Ridge. Aware that the 3rd Division lacked its Michigan brigade, Pleasonton had heeded Kilpatrick's recent suggestion that the Reserve Brigade take Custer's place on that important quarter of the field.[57]

During a rest-stop on the road from Emmitsburg, Merritt took on a second, unofficial assignment. A Unionist citizen rode into his bivouac to report having passed a Confederate forage train about seven miles to the northwest, near Fairfield. Though the wagons were bulging with provisions confiscated in Pennsylvania, their guards seemed few and unprepossessing. Eager to reclaim the plunder for his own brigade, the newly minted brigadier decided to detach part of his largest regiment, the 6th United States, for the mission. He sent Major Starr, with four squadrons, up the road to Millerstown, from which place he was to peel off to the west. The rest of the regiment, under Captain Ira Claflin, remained with Merritt as he resumed his trek north. Forced to travel slowly to match the ponderous pace of his wagons, Merritt soon lost contact with the squadrons ahead.[58]

For about eight miles, the 400-odd troopers under Paddy Starr proceeded unmolested. The major, however, realized he was marching toward Lee's rear—and Lee's rear guard. At the same time, his regiment's poor performance at Upperville rattled in his mind like a sick headache.

At Millerstown, the road to Gettysburg met a trail that cut sharply left toward the mountains. Here Starr divided his force, sending two companies under George Cram and Lieutenant Nicholas Nolan on the westward track. With his remaining squadrons, the major continued north, planning to flank the wagons and their escort.

This tactic would have been effective had the detachments encountered a wagon escort only. After clearing Millerstown, Starr's advance squadron, under Lieutenant Christian Balder, moved to within a half mile of Fairfield, where it spied a few forage wagons—whose drivers had been looting local residents—

leaving town. But just as Balder spurred forward, he discovered on the road above the 7th Virginia Cavalry, the lead unit of Grumble Jones's column. Part of the 7th slammed into him, but another Regular squadron forced the Virginians back, then withdrew along with Balder to apprise Starr of the situation.

To his credit, the major did not lead his main force head-on into a force of unknown strength. He pulled his men off the road, dismounting some within an apple orchard, others behind a post-and-rail fence from which they could not easily be dislodged. From these positions the squadrons opened a fire on the head of the Rebel regiment, inflicting several casualties.[59]

The Virginians appeared paralyzed by the fire; even Lieutenant Colonel Marshall admitted that his outfit "did not at this place and time close up as promptly as it should . . . making our loss greater than it would otherwise have been." The 7th might have made a fight of it even so, had not Cram's and Nolan's companies charged in from the west at a critical moment. With that, the Virginians scattered for safety, every trooper for himself.[60]

Beaten men spurred past Grumble Jones and the next regiment in his column, the 6th Virginia. After vainly calling for the 7th to return, the brigadier turned to Major Flournoy's men and cried: "Shall one damned regiment of Yankees whip my whole brigade?" The troopers answered in unison and in the negative. Shouted one of the men: "Let *us* try them!"[61]

Jones did, he himself at their head. Their charge was so swift that they reached the Regulars before the latter were ready to receive them. Having discovered how badly he was outnumbered, Starr had remounted for a forlorn-hope counterattack. By leaving his cover, however, he offered his force up as a sacrifice. In minutes the Virginians swarmed over it, hacking and slashing in wild abandon. In the melee, Starr was wounded—his right arm mangled by a pistol ball—and captured. Fleeing into the streets of Fairfield, Lieutenant Balder was mortally wounded before he could cut his way to safety. With Balder fell dozens of officers and enlisted men. Before the gyrations of men and animals had ceased, 242 members of the 6th United States were killed, wounded, or taken prisoner. Most became captives; they included Captain Cram, four lieutenants, and two surgeons.[62]

Only two small detachments avoided death or capture. Finding himself cut off from Starr's battalion, Virginians on each side of him, Lieutenant Nolan "commenced retreating, disputing every inch of ground with the enemy." Taking the only exit available, he led the few survivors at high speed toward the Maryland border. Near the old camp at Mechanicstown, beyond range of pursuit, he joined an equally small remnant of Starr's main force, which had been led to safety by the only other officer to avoid capture, Lieutenant Louis H. Carpenter. Assuming command of both parties, Nolan guided them along a circuitous route to Merritt's column, which he joined just south of Gettysburg. There he reported to Captain Claflin the story of Starr's overthrow.[63]

Back on the field of combat, Grumble Jones tended to his forty-four casualties and his gaggle of prisoners, assimilated the wagon train he had been sent to protect, and bivouacked near the South Mountain peak known as Jack Mountain. Though upset that one of his regiments had been routed by a smaller Yankee force, Grumble was proud of having parried a blow against Lee's rear. And by picketing the passes on either side of Jack Mountain—Fairfield Gap on the north and Monterey Pass to the south—he had secured an emergency route for Lee in the event he had to retreat. Ironically, Jones's antagonists felt partially compensated for their losses by reasoning that they had done the same as he, having prevented the enemy from turning their army's southern flank and creating havoc in its rear at a critical time.[64]

***

Shortly after 3:00 P.M., as the 12,500 Confederate infantrymen swept across the valley toward Cemetery Ridge, the cavalry combat east of Gettysburg reached its apogee. While Lee's foot troops gambled everything in a single offensive against Meade's front-center, J. E. B. Stuart readied his main effort against the Union rear. The abrupt silencing of the guns on Seminary Ridge told him that the hour of his advance to the Baltimore Pike had arrived. No time remained in which to outflank the Union horsemen barring his path; he must slash through them as expeditiously as possible.

Without intending to, Wade Hampton had already begun the climactic drive. Seeing his 1st North Carolina and Jeff Davis Legion struck by the 5th Michigan and riddled by the fire of Miller, Hess, Walsh, and Hart, Hampton realized that the two regiments had gone too far, caught up in the momentum of their pursuit of the 7th Michigan. Fearing they might be savaged before supports could reach them, the brigadier rushed alone to their rescue. Spurring his charger, "Butler," down the ridge, he made for the struggling troopers, shouting for them to fall back toward him.

This was the second time Hampton had recalled part of his brigade from an advance. About an hour before, returning from a fruitless errand at division headquarters, he had discovered some of his regiments moving forward without him—supposedly at Stuart's behest. Not wishing to reveal his position, the South Carolinian angrily returned the units to the sheltering trees before harm could be done. On his present mission, however, another errant order thwarted Hampton's effort. Seeing him riding south, his adjutant, Captain T. G. Barker, thought Hampton wished his entire brigade to follow him. Leaving behind only the Cobb Legion (still recovering from its drubbing at Hunterstown), Barker led south the 1st South Carolina, under Lieutenant Colonel John D. Twiggs, Major Lipscomb's 2nd South Carolina, and the Phillips Legion of Lieutenant Colonel W. W. Rich. Minutes later, Stuart sent forward elements of Chambliss's and Lee's brigades to guard Hampton's flanks. After forming ranks, the line began to trot, then to canter.

Whirling about, Hampton was shocked to see so many regiments marching toward him. But he recovered quickly: now that he could not avoid commitment, he prepared to lead an offensive that would sweep the Yankees from the field, once and for all.[65]

As the Rebels came on, their opponents stared open-mouthed at the sight. "A grander spectacle than their advance has rarely been beheld," thought Captain Miller. "They marched with well-aligned fronts and steady reins. Their polished saber-blades dazzled in the sun." To Lieutenant Brooke of Miller's battalion, "the spectacle called forth a murmur of admiration."[66] It also called forth another clearing of the field. McIntosh's staff officers swept their own and Custer's remnants from the area between the Rummel farm and the Lott woods, giving the artillery an unobstructed field of fire.[67]

Minutes later, the guns of Randol and Pennington resumed their cannonade, hurling single and double doses of canister, plus shot and shell, into the gray column. Meanwhile, the sharpshooters on the Union right increased their fire, hoping to stop the attack before well underway. But their commanders soon realized that only a heavy counterthrust could neutralize the threat.[68]

Spurred on by pending disaster, such officers took action. Custer rushed up to the 1st Michigan, his only uncommitted regiment, which had returned to the field during the lull just ended, massing in column of battalions in a field below the Lott house. His most experienced unit, the 1st was exactly the force he would have saved for such a crisis. Its commander, Colonel Town, a sunken-cheeked consumptive who rode strapped into the saddle, was as hard-fighting a subordinate as any brigade leader would have wanted; some said he courted death in battle, preferring it to the wasting away that had long been his lot. Reaching his side, Custer saluted, then announced in a manner ironically polite: "Colonel Town, I shall have to ask you to charge, and I want to go in with you."[69]

In he went, Town and his troopers close behind. Shifting rapidly from one gait to the next, the regiment broke into the gallop almost at the start of its ride. It moved so swiftly that it nearly crossed Pennington's and Randol's lines of fire before the latter ceased their shelling. Careful to avoid the fences that had played hob with Mann's regiment, Custer led it directly at the head of Hampton's force, which had also begun to gallop. The pace increased rather than slackened as the columns converged. Captain Miller described the resulting collision as "like the falling of timber . . . so sudden and violent . . . that many of the horses were turned end over end and crushed their riders beneath them. The clashing of sabers, the firing of pistols, the demands for surrender and cries of the combatants now filled the air."[70]

Having been unhorsed at Brandy Station and again at Hunterstown, George Custer turned the trick a third time, as his charger, "Roanoke," stumbled and fell. He mounted another, riderless horse, aboard which he swiped at one antagonist after another with his long saber. Around him, Town's men chopped and blasted their way through a wall of gray as though determined to win the day's climactic struggle singlehandedly.[71]

They did not have to. Unwilling to let a single regiment take on parts of three brigades, Gregg and McIntosh hurled several other units into the fray. Captain Walter S. Newhall, the latter's acting adjutant general, rallied twenty-one men from the squadrons of Treichel and Rogers and led them against the Rebel right. The band struck with power disproportionate to its size; slicing toward the center of the enemy mass, it made for Hampton's brigade flag. Captain Newhall was within arm's reach of the prize when the flag-bearer lowered his staff like a lance and drove it into his attacker's face. Newhall fell senseless to earth, his jaw ripped apart, before being taken up and carried to the rear, where he recovered from his ghastly wound.

The Confederate right was also the target of Colonel McIntosh himself, who along with Captain Samuel C. Wagner and other members of the brigade staff, joined the melee. To complete the assault on the Confederate right, Colonel Alger led in portions of the scattered 5th and 7th Michigan at a crucial time, making inroads comparable to Newhall's and McIntosh's.[72]

Almost simultaneously, two detachments struck the opposite side of the Rebel line. Emulating his fellow aide Newhall, Captain Hampton S. Thomas placed himself at the head of Hart's New Jersey squadron and led it into the fight. Thomas and Hart penetrated as far as Wade Hampton himself; in a hacking contest with the brigadier, a Jersey trooper inflicted two new gashes on his skull, enough to drive him to the rear for medical aid.[73] Finally, as the saber-and-pistol battle raged in front of him, its outcome in doubt, Captain Miller decided to "go in" on the flank Thomas and Hart had struck, though farther to the rear. Backed by his executive officer, Lieutenant Brooke, Miller left the cover of the Lott Woods, his battalion at his heels. The troopers angled toward the northwest, as though bound for the Rummel farm buildings.

Almost immediately Miller and Brooke found their path blocked by Rebels, but the opposition seemed to melt away as they came on. In one mighty thrust they rode through Chambliss's and then Hampton's men, penetrating about two-thirds of the way toward the Confederate rear. Not till they neared the lane of the Rummel farm, within range of Breathed's battery, were they hemmed in and halted. Trying to break free, Miller was shot through his right arm and saw his saber chopped in two. After several minutes of thrust, parry, and pistol exchanges, the Pennsylvanians turned northward, looping around the enemy rear toward the starting point of their ride, having suffered few casualties.

Their return was made difficult because the Confederates were now streaming north in retreat. Miller's charge (which thirty-four years later would win him the Medal of Honor) had helped curtail the Rebels' offensive by making them fear for the safety of their escape route. Still harassed in front and on both flanks, their commander down and their supports scattered, Hampton's men fell back, slowly and without panic, to Cress's Ridge. Their opponents held back, then withdrew in turn. Surmising that the principal effort against Meade's rear had come and gone, the Federals were content to call it a day.[74]

***

The aftermath of Pickett's charge was a study in contrasting emotions. On Seminary Ridge, Robert E. Lee met his infantry and moaned that "all this has been my fault—it is I that have lost the fight, and you must help me out of it the best way you can." At least one of his subordinates agreed with this assessment of where the blame rested. Years later Evander Law wrote that "General Lee failed . . . because he made his attack precisely where his enemy wanted him to make it and was most fully prepared to receive it." That preparedness had cost him nearly 40 percent of those involved in that final epic charge.[75]

Watching the aftermath of Lee's attack from Cemetery Ridge, George G. Meade knew relief, joy, and pride. He remained impassive, however, even when congratulated on his successful defense by several of his officers. One subordinate came not to congratulate but to badger him. By his own account, Alfred Pleasonton rode up to his superior and announced: "General, I will give you half an hour to show yourself a great general. Order the army to advance, while I will take the cavalry, get in Lee's rear, and we will finish the campaign in a week."[76]

Meade thought Pleasonton's advice presumptuous and his tone offensive. He knew better than anyone that Lee's army had not been destroyed but was regrouping on commanding ground, where it could blow apart such an advance as Pleasonton had in mind. But the cavalry commander did not let up. In subsequent days he called on Meade to make moves he considered bold and enterprising but which the army leader thought foolhardy. The two men had never been fast friends; from this point, relations between them steadily deteriorated. Their falling-out was one factor in Pleasonton's transfer to Missouri the following February. There, far from the big-city newspapers, Pleasonton saw his career slide down the chute to oblivion.[77]

***

Merritt's brigade reached the end of the Confederate right flank at about 3:00 P.M., following a slow march from Emmitsburg. Couriers alerted Kilpatrick, who placed it in position about three hundred yards to the west of Farnsworth's command, just east of the Emmitsburg road. Though Kilpatrick later claimed that he directed Merritt and Farnsworth in unison, the fighting that followed did not suggest close cooperation.[78] Predictably, his opponents— Law's infantry and artillery—were able to defeat each brigade in turn, making a brutal end of the 3 July fighting.

A major reason for the twin Union defeats was Kilpatrick's poor choice of tactics. Although the terrain along the Emmitsburg road was level, wide, and clear, affording the Confederate defenders little cover, the Reserve Brigade made its primary effort on foot. And whereas the ground in Farnsworth's front was steep and broken, the Federals launched mounted attacks there. It was yet another sign that, tactically, the Union cavalry had not yet come of age.[79]

Merritt's advance began at perhaps 4:30 P.M., following ninety minutes of skirmishing. Determined to drive in the enemy, the brigadier moved up the pike with the 6th Pennsylvania, supported in the rear by Captain Graham's battery and on the flanks by the 1st, 2nd, and 5th Regulars, plus what remained of the 6th. At first the movement met success. Graham's shelling drove some of the 9th Georgians from the Kern house and outbuildings, after which Julius Mason's 5th U.S. charged forward on horseback and broke through Colonel Black's patchwork line. In so doing, the Federals inflicted many more than the ten casualties they absorbed.

When the other Georgia regiments in Anderson's brigade, recently placed west of the road, came rushing up to meet the Regulars, they prevented Merritt from gaining a foothold on Law's flank. Watching from the rear, Merritt may have viewed the outcome as a sign that he must dismount his men, for the 6th Pennsylvania then advanced afoot against the Georgians. This was a mistake: not only did the riflemen lace the attackers; so did the cannoneers of Bachman and Reilly, just east of the road. Their combined total of ten cannon staggered the erstwhile lancers as well as the Regulars supporting them.[80]

Merritt tried to hold his advance position, if not to gain further advantage himself then to aid Farnsworth's operations to the east. But this proved impossible. At a crucial moment, General Law came down from Round Top to lead Anderson's 11th and 59th Georgia against Merritt's left. The regiments struck with impressive force, rolling up the Union line from west to east. At first the cavalry gave ground sparingly but then rushed several hundred yards to the south.

As Merritt should have foreseen, it had been foolish to oppose several infantry regiments and two batteries with a few hundred troopers fighting afoot. One of his veterans later observed that "a brigade of infantry backed by an army in position will stop, if it wishes to, a brigade of cavalry outside the lines of its own army, devoid of support. . . ." By five o'clock Merritt's people were in full retreat over fields made muddy by a sudden shower, their enemy pursuing for a short distance. If the Reserve Brigade had intended to rock Law's men on their heels, it had failed decidedly; the Confederates had barely worked up a sweat.[81]

Had Kilpatrick seriously threatened the other end of Law's refused right while Merritt made his push, he might have placed his foe in trouble. As it was, he wasted Merritt's diversion, making an ill-considered assault against the Rebel center and then, when too late and with tragic results, committing a larger force against impregnable positions on Law's left.

By the time the Reserve Brigade began its advance, Kilpatrick had formed Farnsworth's line with the 18th Pennsylvania on the left, connecting with Merritt, and, toward the east, the 1st West Virginia, the 1st Vermont, and the 5th New York, the latter guarding Elder's battery. He directed the artillerymen and carbineers to concentrate their fire against a skirmish line that stretched from near the Emmitsburg road to the rear slope of Round Top. Then he decided to throw the mounted 1st West Virginia against the 1st Texas, which held what he thought was the weak midpoint of the skirmish line.[82]

Kilpatrick guessed wrong; moreover, he botched the attack. Without providing a covering fire by the artillery—a serious omission—he sent Colonel Richmond's West Virginians toward an open valley—only to see them halted by an obstacle that a preliminary reconnaissance would have detected: a rail fence, staked and bound with withes. Watching from the rear, Captain Parsons saw Richmond's men attempting "to throw [down] the rails, tugging at the stakes, cutting with their sabers, and failing in the vain effort." Finding its enemy stymied, the 1st Texas rushed up and blasted the Federals with a volley that cleared the fence. Richmond rallied his men and made a second attempt to pass the barrier but was again repulsed. He returned to the rear after taking heavy losses, making it appear that Kilpatrick was not going to gain his crucial breakthrough after all.[83]

But when Law took personal charge of Merritt's opposition, Kilpatrick took heart anew. As the Confederate commander rushed to the west, the cavalry leader thought he saw his opening. Aiming to strike the rear of Round Top while Law's attention was distracted, he ordered Farnsworth to lead a charge down the wooded, hilly terrain toward the east.[84] The mission smacked of what a Rebel officer later called "wholesale slaughter," and Kilpatrick's subordinate protested it to some degree. Just how much, is difficult to determine, given conflicting testimony—though probably not as loudly or as heatedly as Captain Parsons later recalled in a widely disseminated article. Even so, Farnsworth was upset enough to tell the commander of his 5th New York: "My God, Hammond, Kil is going to have a cavalry charge. It is too awful to think of. . . ."[85]

Nevertheless, he led it. At about 5:30 the brigadier took one battalion of Colonel Preston's 1st Vermont toward the Rebel skirmishers; with him rode Lieutenant Estes, Kilpatrick's fire-eating aide, and perhaps 150 troopers under Major William Wells. A second battalion, under Captain Parsons, simultaneously rushed the skirmish line farther to the east. To the left of both units, the 18th Pennsylvania staged a limited attack to support them, while the rest of Preston's regiment and Elder's cannon provided a covering fire for as long as they could do so without endangering the attackers.

Farnsworth's effort began as badly as it would end. The charge by the 18th Pennsylvania barely got underway before Bachman's and Reilly's guns and their infantry supports shot away its momentum. The Pennsylvanians came rushing back to their line, blasted tree branches tumbling about their heads.[86] Their withdrawal allowed the Confederates to give undivided attention to the 1st Vermont.

Parsons's battalion started out by splitting a seam in the skirmish line and riding north toward Law's guns. But because it passed so close to them, the cannon fired over it, inflicting no losses. Still, Parsons angled eastward down a lane that led past the Slyder home. Thus far opposition had been light, but in changing direction the battalion came abreast of the 4th Alabama of Law's old brigade, which had moved down from Round Top to contest the horsemen's advance. The Alabamians' first fusillade—also pitched too high—did little damage, but a second, ragged volley took a heavy toll and forced the troopers to veer south, jumping a stone wall and seeking shelter in a fenced-in grove. When the Rebel infantry appeared on high ground nearby, the battalion resumed its ride, charging north up a hill, then looping south and topping another wall into an open field.

From that position Parsons saw Farnsworth's force heading northward about two hundred paces closer to Round Top, beyond yet another farm-field wall. Leaping this barrier as well, Parsons's men tried to join the general but found it impossible. Instead they continued south down an incline and broke the same picket line they had ridden through at the outset. Having lost several men but gained almost as many prisoners, the battalion finally reached Kilpatrick and safety.[87]

Parsons's retreat left Elon Farnsworth on his own. Having burst through the Rebel skirmishers in concert with Parsons, the young general soon turned east, crossing his comrades' track, as though planning to strike the rear of Law's line behind Round Top. On the way his force smashed through Colonel William C. Oates's 15th Alabama, another regiment Law had sent down from the wooded knoll but which had lacked the time to form to meet the horsemen. Farnsworth then led Estes, Wells, and the others north along the length of Law's rear. As they passed, infantry facing east turned about to rake the horsemen's flank. Above the Slyder house, Farnsworth curved to the west and then to the south. Suddenly he found himself hurtling directly at the cannon of Bachman and Reilly and the rifles of the 9th Georgia, the latter having rushed east after helping repulse Merritt. Under an artillery-infantry barrage, Farnsworth's horse fell dead just above the Slyder house lane, but the general struggled to his feet.[88]

While most of the battalion ran the gauntlet of artillery fire and rejoined Kilpatrick in three parties, Farnsworth mounted a trooper's horse and rode back in the direction from which he had come. This was madness, for by now the 15th Alabama was lying in wait for him, backed by other units come down from Round Top. Later General Law speculated that the brigade leader had simply lost his bearings. He may have been dazed by his fall. Or perhaps he could not bear to run past the Rebel artillery a second time. Whatever the reason, having lived with death on his shoulders since his college days, Farnsworth now stared death in the eye. At the head of about ten followers, he swerved east and then south, passing foot troops on all sides. A chorus of voices called on him to surrender, but he continued his ride until Colonel Oates's sharpshooters blew him out of the saddle. Wounded in several places, including the pelvis, Farnsworth cried out a refusal to surrender, then fell dead. Rebel observers later claimed he had shot himself to end his agony.[89]

Farnsworth's death capped a charge that had taken sixty-seven lives and a heavy toll in wounded and captured. It also marked the downturn of the career of the man who had ordered the attack. For utter recklessness, for self-indulgent folly, the doomed and senseless assault outshone the many other stains on Judson Kilpatrick's record.[90]

***

As the sun left the battlefield east of Gettysburg, J. E. B. Stuart withdrew his battered brigades from Cress's Ridge to the York Pike, leaving behind a picket line that stretched to the Rummel farm. By departing he appeared to concede the field to his opponents—a claim the latter would advance time and again in after years. Darkness soon halted an artillery duel that had begun following the final Confederate repulse, cloaking the ground where 254 Federals and almost 200 Confederates had gone down dead or wounded. Such statistics would furnish Rebel veterans a basis for victory claims of their own. Though the arguments of both sides had some validity, in the strategic sense the Federals had won the day. Stuart had made a do-or-die effort to break through to the Baltimore Pike, and Gregg, McIntosh, and Custer had thrust him back decisively.[91]

As the cavalries broke contact, medical attendants combed the cluttered plain for bodies that showed signs of life. Kept just as busy were burial teams, groping by lantern-light among corpses, the carcasses of horses, and the splintered remains of battery vehicles. Some of the sights these men encountered illustrated the desperate character of the fighting. Searchers stumbled over two troopers, one in blue and the other in butternut, "who had cut each other down with their sabers, and were lying with their feet together, their heads in opposite directions, and the blood-stained saber of each still tightly in his grip." Not far away were two other combatants, their skulls and torsos riddled with slashes and their fingers so deeply embedded in each other's flesh that no amount of force could pry them apart. On still another part of the field, one of David Gregg's aides found a Rebel sergeant with his head split open by a sword, "so you could put your hand in the gash."

The battlefield yielded up other grisly sights, the work of the living. In the darkness, litter-bearers were joined by local residents, "utterly indifferent to the war and anything pertaining to it," who ransacked the dead for valuables of any kind. And by moonlight the officers of Randol's battery picnicked among windrows of dead horses and the wreckage of limbers and caissons. Despite death all around them, the officers spread a blanket over the littered ground and wolfed down a late supper.

As though in retribution to this sacrilege, a Rebel battery beyond the Rummel farm hurled a final shell toward Randol's position. It burst directly above the officers, scattering them and smashing their crockery to fragments.[92]

[14]

Retreat to Virginia, Pursuit to Maryland

ABOUT midnight, 3–4 July, Lee summoned John Imboden from Cashtown to Gettysburg. As he moved east along the Chambersburg Pike, Imboden found his progress slowed by long lines of ambulances—wagons and carts carrying hundreds of wounded men toward a park in the army's rear. Behind them came supply vehicles, caissons and limbers, and masses of stragglers, the flotsam of a beaten army. Even before reaching army headquarters, Imboden realized that a full-scale retreat was imminent.

Thus far the brigadier had done his utmost to make Lee's campaign in the North a success. Though he had played an auxiliary role in the army's operations, remaining on the western fringes of the vanguard, he had struck heavy blows at communications that might otherwise have fed Union reinforcements into the path of the invasion force.

On 7 June Lee had ordered Imboden's 2,100 cavalry, mounted infantry, partisan rangers, and horse artillerymen to forage off the army's left, to wreck Union railroads and supply bases, and to demonstrate in the vicinity of Romney, West Virginia, in aid of Ewell's offensive against Winchester. Only three days later, Imboden hit Romney and the Baltimore & Ohio garrisons at New Creek and Cacapon Bridge, wrecking resources as well as keeping the troops from interfering with Ewell's operations. A week later the Virginian's command wrecked other railroad property—for the most part track and trestles—near Cumberland, Maryland, while also destroying portions of the Chesapeake & Ohio Canal. Of material benefit to Lee, Imboden mangled every railroad span of importance between Cumberland and Martinsburg, Virginia.[1] Added to Lige White's raid against Point of Rocks, these efforts disrupted the flow of military traffic between Pennsylvania and points west for many days. Afterward, Imboden continued north via Hancock, Maryland, and McConnellsburg, Pennsylvania, confiscating whatever supplies he could find in that picked-over region. On

1 July, Lee called him to Chambersburg, where Imboden assumed the role of the army's rear guard, freeing Pickett's division for its fateful rendezvous at Gettysburg.[2]

Reaching Lee's headquarters in the small hours of the fourth, Imboden learned that his campaign participation would continue to be in a support capacity. Instead of marching south with the main army, his men would escort to Virginia the seemingly endless line of ambulances he had seen going into park beyond Gettysburg. Of perhaps greater importance, Imboden would guard the army's principal supply train, including the forage wagons whose contents gave meaning to Lee's invasion.

Lee told him that his assigned route to Virginia—via the passes beyond Cashtown and the crossing sites near Williamsport, Maryland—would be dangerous, especially given the probability of Yankee cavalry pursuit. Imboden would be reinforced by as many artillery units as available, plus two brigades of Stuart's cavalry, as well as other, miscellaneous units. Lee hoped these would prove sufficient to ward off enemy attacks, but if not, Imboden would have to make do with the only other source of manpower available to him—those convalescents who could still fire a rifle.[3]

Imboden was less concerned with the uncertainties of travel than with the impact of retreat on the army's morale. But Lee saw no help for it; his troops had lost their offensive punch under the weight of thousands of casualties. As he told his visitor in a voice full of emotion: "It has been a sad, sad day to us!"

Due to the complexities of massing the brigade, its additions, and the hundreds of ambulances and supply conveyances, Imboden's column was not ready to march until late that afternoon. By then rain was falling in great, blinding sheets. "The very windows of heaven seemed to have opened," Imboden later recalled. "As the afternoon wore on there was no abatement in the storm. Canvas was no protection against its fury, and the wounded men lying upon the naked boards of the wagon-bodies were drenched. Horses and mules were blinded and maddened by the wind and water, and became almost unmanageable. The deafening roar of the mingled sounds of heaven and earth all around us made it almost impossible to communicate orders, and equally difficult to execute them."

By 4:00 P.M., when the seventeen-mile-long column was in motion at last, Imboden realized his ordeal had just begun. His men and their reinforcements—two infantry regiments, twenty-three guns, and the three thousand troopers under Fitz Lee and Laurence Baker—were assailed by more than thunder and rain. They were forced to listen to a litany of anguish from shattered men whose suffering increased with every bounce taken by the springless wagons. Not even the fury of the storm blotted out their screams, oaths, and pleas for mercy. Imboden would hear them the rest of his life:

"O God! Why can't I die?"

"My God! will no one have mercy and kill me?"

"Stop! Oh! for God's sake, stop, just for one minute; take me out and leave me to die on the roadside!"[4]

***

With his main army Lee planned to retreat to the same point Imboden was marching toward—the Williamsport vicinity—but by a more direct route. Instead of crossing the mountains at Cashtown, his infantry, most of his artillery, and much of his cavalry would move southwest through Fairfield Gap in Jack Mountain, which Grumble Jones had secured on the third. This route should put Lee's army on the Potomac after Imboden got there but long before Meade's infantry arrived. Lee planned to cross only part of his command at Williamsport; the rest would trek over a pontoon bridge recently laid five miles downriver at Falling Waters. The main army's route would not only enable it to reach the river in brief time but would draw Yankees away from Imboden's train, which, if blocked, would clog the crossing sites.

The cavalry would be busy throughout the retreat. While Lee and Baker helped Imboden escort the army's main supply column, those under Robertson and Jones, near Fairfield, would help guard another, smaller train as it passed through Jack and South Mountains. And the brigades of Chambliss and Ferguson would move toward the Potomac via Emmitsburg, guarding Lee's left rear. As the latter was the most strategic of all posts—that nearest the enemy—Stuart would accompany Chambliss and Ferguson.

Throughout 4 July most of Lee's army remained in position west and south of Gettysburg, hoping that Meade would yield to Pleasonton's advice and attack Seminary Ridge. By early evening that hope had guttered out; soon afterward Lee started his command on the first leg of its journey to Virginia. Now the only prospect of salvaging tactical success lay in Meade's attacking him on commanding terrain along the Potomac.

Just after sundown, Hill's corps left its position on Seminary Ridge, followed by Longstreet, then Ewell. Literally in the dark about these movements and uncertain as to his enemy's intentions, Meade made no countermoves for several hours. Having spent the past five days reacting to the tactics of his opponent, the Union commander refused to commit himself until morning, when he could reconnoiter Lee's position.[5]

Meade's indecision led him to issue conflicting orders. Early on Independence Day, believing Lee about to retreat, he told General French, commanding the Harpers Ferry garrison, now removed to Frederick, to return a part of his command to its old post and with the rest block South Mountain passes that Lee might use to escape. Later in the day Meade decided that the Confederates were not ready to withdraw and he countermanded French's instructions. By then, however, the latter had sent detachments of the 13th and 14th Pennsylvania Cavalry, under Major Shadrack Foley, to Falling Waters. Chasing off a band of the 12th Virginia, which Grumble Jones had left there to guard the bridgehead, Foley's tropers broke up the pontoon bridge upon which Lee planned to cross into Virginia.[6] Two days later another mounted element of French's command—the Maryland battalion of Major Cole—would wreck other bridges at Harpers Ferry, which the Rebels might have utilized.[7]

While Meade remained in position at Gettysburg, other Union forces took steps to complicate the Confederate withdrawal. Under orders from General Couch, Baldy Smith's militia marched from Carlisle toward Cashtown early on the fourth. Though slowed by supply problems and the inefficiency of his men, Smith approached the mountains in Lee's rear late in the day. There he might distract the Confederates' attention from the Army of the Potomac. Meade, however, was doubtful that the militia could accomplish much on its own. Later he temporarily added Smith to his own army.[8]

Meanwhile, another of Couch's forces—the infantry and cavalry at Bloody Run under Colonel Pierce—started off for Lee's rear on the fourth. Still other forces were in motion toward Lee's projected line of retreat from points west and south. They included Ulric Dahlgren and his one hundred Pennsylvania troopers, who were again near Greencastle by 4 July; and the few hundred 1st New York Cavalrymen under William Boyd, en route from Shippensburg to Chambersburg. Finally, Brigadier General Benjamin F. Kelley, the newly appointed commander of the Department of West Virginia, was preparing to concentrate at Hancock, Maryland, in response to a War Department order to move against Williamsport and Falling Waters. At those suspected crossing sites, Kelley had been told to capture or destroy the wagon trains that would surely precede Lee's main army.[9]

To these forces, moving to stop Lee's retreat before it was well under way, Meade added the majority of his cavalry. Early on the fourth he started seven of its eight brigades south and west from Gettysburg to harass Lee's line of communications with the Potomac. His orders encompassed two-thirds of Gregg's division (including Huey's brigade at Manchester), both of Kilpatrick's brigades, and Buford's widely dispersed division, including Gamble's and Devin's men at Taneytown. The latter two brigades had marched to their present position from Westminster the previous evening.

Meade's orders were issued through Pleasonton, who remained at army headquarters instead of retaking the field. They called for Gamble and Devin to move to Frederick, where Merritt's brigade would rejoin them; and for Kilpatrick to march southwestward with the brigades of Custer and Richmond (the latter formerly Farnsworth's), assimilating Huey's brigade at Emmitsburg. Perhaps because of a recurrence of his recent illness, David Gregg would not hold division command at the outset of the pursuit. While Huey's brigade operated under Kilpatrick, McIntosh's would be attached to an infantry division in advance of Meade's main body, and Irvin Gregg would play an independent role in pursuing Imboden's column.[10]

***

As though to make amends for his recent misadventures, Judson Kilpatrick moved rapidly south from Gettysburg early on the fourth. At about 3:00 P.M. he reached Emmitsburg, where, as anticipated, he linked with Huey. From there he led his enlarged force southwestward to Frederick, toward which

Buford was moving from the east and Merritt from the north. At Frederick, however, Kilpatrick received a report that caused him to depart before the 1st Division could arrive. Scouts informed him of the passage toward Fairfield of a Rebel supply train that lacked an infantry escort. This proved to be the wagons and ambulances of Ewell's corps, which had moved southwest out of Gettysburg some hours after Imboden's larger train started for Cashtown.

Believing Ewell's train to be Lee's main supply arm, Kilpatrick led his men at a characteristically grueling pace toward Fairfield, despite the continuing rain. At about 10:00 P.M. the head of his column—Custer's brigade—reached a fork from which roads led northwest to Fairfield Gap and southwest to Monterey Pass. There he learned that the wagons had passed onto the upper road a few hours before. After brushing aside a too-small picket force that Beverly Robertson had stationed near the fork, Kilpatrick moved to head off the train before it cleared Fairfield Gap. He sent a single regiment, the 1st Michigan, to strike the rear of the column. The remainder of his force he led along the road to Monterey Pass, confident he could gain the other side in advance of the enemy.[11]

Inside Fairfield Gap, Colonel Town's regiment encountered part of Jones's brigade, which had left its post east of the mountains to escort Ewell's vehicles. The size of this force ensured that the 1st Michigan would do little harm to the train. In a spirited skirmish, Town suffered several casualties including the loss of his lieutenant colonel, Peter Stagg, severely injured when his horse fell with him.

Kilpatrick met a much smaller enemy force inside Monterey Pass, but experienced heavier opposition. This came from barely twenty members of Harry Gilmor's 1st Maryland Cavalry Battalion, under Captain G. M. Emack. Left by mistake to hold Monterey Pass against all comers, the Marylanders should have been as easy to sweep aside as Robertson's pickets had been. Instead, thanks to the bad weather, the treacherous terrain that lined the defile, and its own plucky determination, the little band brought Kilpatrick's column to a standstill a short distance inside the pass. Under a fusillade of bullets from rocks and trees, the Federals halted and ran for cover across the grounds of Monterey Springs, a once-popular health resort. In front of a bridge over a stream that furnished the spa with its mineral water, George Gray's 6th Michigan took up positions from which it returned Emack's fire. Watching from the immediate rear, Colonel Alger of the 5th Michigan could "only see the bridge by the occasional flashes of the guns of the enemy and the 6th Michigan."[12]

The unexpected resistance stymied Gray's men. Repeatedly Kilpatrick ordered them to advance, but their every attempt disintegrated under a hail of gunfire. Custer was forced to send up Alger's men to spell the lead regiment, a process that took much time. More time was lost to a reconnaissance by Alger, which disclosed that, contrary to expectation, the planking of the bridge remained in place. Finally Alger led a dash over the span, placing the 5th Michigan in Emack's midst and leaving the Marylanders "paralyzed." In Alger's rear, the 7th Michigan and Pennington's battery galloped over the planking. But by the time the battery unlimbered, the Confederates had faded into the shadows.

By then, too, it was about 3:00 A.M.; Emack's twenty men had stalled three Union brigades for over five hours.[13]

During the fighting at Monterey Springs, Emack had sent gallopers to Fairfield Gap, seeking Jones's help. Though the brigadier promised aid (and later claimed to have provided it), Emack would insist that his only support came from a dozen members of Robertson's 4th North Carolina, riding in advance of the wagons on the upper road. Jones further dismayed Emack by ignoring his repeated warning to keep the wagons inside the defile. By his own efforts the captain succeeded in preventing two sections of the supply column from debouching from the pass. Hundreds of other vehicles cleared the gap and trundled down the back slope of the mountain along a road that merged into the trail from Monterey Pass.

Thus, when they cut through Emack's band at last, Kilpatrick's people swarmed over the train, sabering mules and horses, shooting drivers, overturning some wagons, burning others, and taking 1,360 prisoners, mostly the inmates of the ambulances. Before Jones's brigade could chase them off, the Federals destroyed or immobilized a large percentage of Ewell's wagons. Appraisals of the number captured or destroyed varied from 150 (Huey's exaggerated claim) to 40 (Stuart's underestimate). Dozens of other wagons had been lost in advance of Kilpatrick's coming when local citizens ambushed the supply column during rest halts—striking with axes and hatchets and racing to safety before train guards could stop them. Other wagons lost their footing on the dark, rain-lashed trails and were overturned and destroyed.[14]

What with these accidents, the depredations of Yankee soldiers and citizens, and the severe weather, Jones's people had a rough time on the road from Gettysburg. One of them summed it up succinctly: "The night was hideous in the extreme."[15]

***

While Kilpatrick struck Ewell's trains and Buford moved toward Frederick to cut off Lee's infantry, the brigades of David Gregg's division that remained at Gettysburg joined in the pursuit. Late on 4 July Meade dispatched Irvin Gregg—accompanied by his division leader—north to another now-quiet battlefield, Hunterstown. There the troopers pried loose a detachment of Cobb's Legion, which, through a communications mixup, had remained in the village following the withdrawal of its brigade. The next morning, after ensuring that no other Confederates occupied the vicinity, Gregg headed out the Chambersburg Pike to overtake Imboden's supply column.[16]

Even with the guiding hand of David Gregg, his cousin did not begin his pursuit auspiciously. First, he lost about five hours in reconnoitering between Hunterstown and Cashtown. Then, when he got underway in earnest, he marched at a pace that his troopers thought "rather tame," prompting some to grumble that Gregg did not wish to overtake the enemy. Part of the reason for his slowness was the frequent stops he made to tend to the casualties along his route. One trooper remarked that for miles around Rebel corpses lay in piles just off the road; some were wounded men who had drowned, unable to pull themselves from fields turned into lagoons by the rain. The chief surgeon of the 1st Maine happened upon four Confederate officers, each missing a freshly amputated limb, stretched out on the floor of a farmhouse where they had lain for two days without postoperative care. As the surgeon changed their dressings, one commented matter-of-factly: "You'uns tried your best to see how many legs and arms you could shoot off; well, you'uns did the job pretty well."[17]

Gregg's march against Imboden's train continued into the evening of the sixth. The Federals clattered through Cashtown and New Caledonia, passing many corpses dumped from the enemy's ambulances. Then, at Greenwood, the point at which the Confederate caravan had turned south, Gregg's advance came up to Imboden's rear guard. An inconsequential fight was the result, though the Federals claimed they captured one hundred prisoners and "a large quantity" of wagons.

Meanwhile, near Marion, on the road between Chambersburg and Greencastle, another part of Gregg's force tangled with Fitz Lee's escort troops. The Rebels gave battle only long enough to allow the wagons, ambulances, and artillery to get beyond range of seizure. Still reluctant to commit himself fully, Irvin Gregg merely held his own; when the Confederates broke free, he let them go. For the next two days his brigade idled between Chambersburg and Boonsboro, Maryland, moving to the latter village on the eleventh. There it saw little action and contributed virtually nothing to the effort to keep Lee north of the Potomac.[18]

John McIntosh's brigade was more energetic and combative in pursuit. Minus the 1st Massachusetts (temporarily detached once again, this time for provost duty), the command marched south from Gettysburg, at Pleasonton's order, to picket the roads toward Maryland. It remained on that duty through Independence Day. On the fifth it started south toward Emmitsburg, where McIntosh found that a large part of Stuart's division had recently passed through, bound for Frederick. Late in the day McIntosh ranged northwestward toward Waynesboro via the Fairfield road; en route, his advance struck troops who turned out to be the tag end of Early's division, then entering the gap outside Fairfield. The force proved too hefty for a single brigade to handle, so McIntosh withdrew to Emmitsburg to await further instructions. He took with him a captured dispatch showing the location of the infantry under Longstreet and Ewell—a communiqué that would give Meade his first definite information about Lee's retreat.[19]

Early on the sixth, McIntosh received orders from Brigadier General Thomas H. Neill, whose newly arrived VI Corps brigade formed the advance of Meade's infantry pursuit. Backed by the foot soldiers and two batteries, McIntosh returned to Fairfield that evening with orders from Meade to observe Ewell's corps and to report when it had passed through South Mountain.

On the seventh, McIntosh and four guns on loan from Neill followed Ewell through Fairfield Gap toward Waynesboro. Then the cavalry fell back to within a few miles of Hagerstown, Maryland, to engage Ewell's left wing. McIntosh's dismounted skirmishers, aided by the cannon, drove numerous Rebels over Antietam Creek in what Neill called "gallant style." In so doing, McIntosh anchored Meade's forward flank only a few miles northeast of the Rebel crossing-points on the Potomac—a strategic position indeed.[20]

McIntosh marked time at Waynesboro until the tenth, when he probed southward toward Smithsburg and Cavetown but located no Rebels. Late that day he retraced his path north and near Leitersburg tangled with a detachment of Stuart's cavalry. After a brief pursuit, he returned to Neill's camp at Waynesboro.

On 12 July, McIntosh detached himself from the infantry in response to orders to report to Boonsboro, seventeen miles to the south. He was to rejoin David Gregg: the 2nd Cavalry Division was massing for the first time since 2 July. McIntosh may have thought this a prelude to renewed combat, but at Boonsboro he as well as Irvin Gregg sat on the sidelines, refitting and scouting, while Buford and Kilpatrick harassed Lee's retreat.[21]

***

The logistics of moving men and wagons, plus the wretched weather, prevented J. E. B. Stuart from departing Gettysburg for Boonsboro until late on the afternoon of the fourth. In consequence, the brigades of Chambliss and Ferguson did not reach their first port of call, Emmitsburg, until the next dawn, several hours after Kilpatrick had passed through.

With the road west clogged by Yankee horsemen, the Beau Sabreur lay over in Emmitsburg, planning strategy and interrogating the sixty-odd Federals he had captured there. At length he decided not to follow Kilpatrick toward Fairfield: the troopers of Robertson and Jones, plus Lee's rapidly approaching infantry, should be more than a match for him. Instead, Stuart turned toward Hagerstown, realizing that if Buford slipped through the passes west of that place he would be able to smite Imboden's column long before it could cross the Potomac.[22]

Leaving Emmitsburg in midmorning, Stuart pushed south to the hamlet of Cooperstown, where he shifted west at a ninety-degree angle. After a short ride his column reached a fork, both branches of which led toward South Mountain and, beyond, the town of Smithsburg—the lower road by the direct route and the upper one by angling north toward Leitersburg. To hasten his crossing, Stuart led Chambliss's men on the northern road, while Colonel Ferguson took the lower trail.

Soon both columns met unexpected resistance. On nearing the western side of the mountain, Stuart and Chambliss discovered Yankees positioned on top of three hills outside Smithsburg: Huey's brigade, with Fuller's battery, in front;

Custer's brigade and Pennington's guns to the left rear; and, in front of the pass through which Ferguson was moving, the troopers of Richmond and the artillerymen of Elder. Stuart was shocked to find that his detour around Kilpatrick had failed. He had not expected the Yankees to cut through Monterey Pass so quickly or to return westward as if seeking another fight.

When they detected Chambliss's advance, Huey's skirmishers deployed in force along both sides of the mountain road, blocking the pass above Smithsburg. Soon Fuller's guns were pounding the head of the Confederate column. His own horse artillery far to the rear, Stuart was in a tight corner. While doing his best to oppose the strategically placed Yankees with his own dismounted carbineers, he sent word for Ferguson—himself engaged with Richmond and Elder—to come to Chambliss's aid. If at all possible, Ferguson was to clear the gap and then curl into Huey's rear; he should countermarch only if he could not force a passage.[23]

Huey had such an advantage in position and strength that, even with Ferguson's support, Chambliss might have remained trapped in the pass. Fortunately for Stuart, his ranking opponent—either through misperception or loss of nerve—refused to press his advantage. When from his headquarters at Smithsburg Kilpatrick saw Ferguson's brigade turn about and retire eastward, he got the impression that Stuart's entire force was retreating. So, at any rate, Kilpatrick claimed in his after-action report. More likely, he overestimated Stuart's strength and panicked at the thought of both halves combining against him. In his report he spoke of departing Smithsburg for Boonsboro, twenty miles to the south, "to save my prisoners, animals, and wagons." If not an admission of pusillanimity, Kilpatrick's pullout was a major tactical blunder.[24]

Though Ferguson's movement had contributed to the Yankees' retreat, Stuart had no praise for him. Instead he berated the colonel for disobeying orders and making a long, slow return to the east, though supposedly on the verge of bursting through his roadblock. Stuart may have done Ferguson an injustice, given the strength of Richmond's position. Even so, he probably entered another black mark against the name of Jenkins's old brigade.

Determined to overcome his problem-plagued march from Gettysburg, Stuart hustled his two brigades through the mountains by the road Huey and Custer had vacated. On the far side he met the Marylanders of Captain Emack, who provided details of the previous night's battle and guided the column to Leitersburg. There Stuart found Beverly Robertson, with his own and Jones's regiments. Learning that Kilpatrick had gone to Boonsboro, apparently to rest and refit, Stuart decided to keep moving while his enemy lay idle. He turned southward, leading all four brigades toward the Potomac.[25]

En route, the column met Grumble Jones, with a handful of his men, just up from Williamsport. The newcomer reported that Imboden had reached that town—minus some wagons lost to Yankee raiders—only hours before. Imboden was in trouble: thanks to the recent downpours, the Potomac was so high and the current so strong that an immediate fording was out of the question. One

Union prisoner described the water as "madly rushing by, carrying logs and trees at a terrific rate, and of the color of yellow mud." Even worse, Buford's horsemen were thought to be closing in from the east. Against them Imboden could pit only his motley command and some artillery; Fitz Lee's troopers were far to the north, tangling with Irvin Gregg, while Laurence Baker was slow to come up from his flank-guard position to the west.[26]

Without hesitating, Stuart resumed his march south, while dispatching Jones's brigade to guard the right flank near Funkstown. The rest of the cavalry headed toward Hagerstown—Robertson, with his own and Chambliss's men, in the lead, Stuart and Ferguson to the rear.

Perhaps they were too late already. Short of Hagerstown, Stuart learned that Kilpatrick had thrown off his lethargy and was himself galloping toward Hagerstown, presumably to cut the Rebels off from the river. Upon Stuart's ability to make headway against Kilpatrick rested, perhaps, the fate of Lee's main supply column. Its loss would deal the Army of Northern Virginia a devastating, perhaps a fatal, blow.

**

As Imboden had suspected, his journey from Cashtown to Williamsport had been replete with danger and loss. Not only had he been forced to contend with Irvin Gregg's pursuit in rear (timid as it was), but he had encountered trouble from an unexpected direction, the west. Early on the fifth his column had been the target of the roving adventurer, Ulric Dahlgren. Having left Emmitsburg on the third, the young captain reached Waynesboro next day, where he lay in wait for Imboden. When the trains approached that point, turning west onto the Greencastle Road, Dahlgren's Pennsylvanians cut between the wagons and their escort—the 18th Virginia Cavalry, led by the brigade leader's brother, Colonel George W. Imboden. The Federals chopped at the wheels of the vehicles with axes borrowed from local farmers, then shot up the teams. After several minutes the marauders left under the violent prodding of Colonel Imboden and Major Benjamin Eshelman of the Washington Artillery of New Orleans. Imboden then resumed his march, but he had to leave behind a few wagons and ambulances, destined to fall into Gregg's hands.[27]

A larger, more destructive strike on Imboden's train came later in the day, after it had reached Greencastle. Some two hundred troopers of Lewis Pierce's command, under Captain Abram Jones of the 1st New York, caught up with the Rebel column late that afternoon after racing down the road from Chambersburg. Pierce's small but determined force struck so unexpectedly that before the train's escort—under Colonel George H. Smith of Imboden's 62nd Virginia (Mounted) Infantry—could beat them back the Federals had burned, overturned, or hacked up almost one hundred wagons, most of them belonging to Fitz Lee's brigade. The Yankees also made off with an artillery piece and some 650 wounded, inmates of captured ambulances. Pierce finally withdrew but he did not stop his work of destruction. Later in the day he captured eighty-three Confederates near Chambersburg and the next day, at Mercersburg, he snatched up sixty additional men and two dozen forage wagons. Afterwards, he fell in with Irvin Gregg near Fayetteville.[28]

If Imboden thought his ordeal was ended when he pulled up near Williamsport at midday on 5 July, he was soon disabused of the notion. With the river almost at flood stage and Stuart's escort far to the rear, he was easy prey for other roving Yankees—especially now that his caravan was immobile.

Uncertain how long he would have to remain, Imboden dug in. He unloaded the ambulances and transferred their inmates to nearby homes and farms (the owners were obliged to cook for the sick and wounded, "on pain of having their kitchens occupied for that purpose"). He fashioned rafts on which he ferried across to Virginia a few of the supply vehicles. And he spread his troops along a wide perimeter to defend his wagon park, which rested at the base of a hill below the town. With Fitz Lee's cavalry still to the north, engaged with Irvin Gregg, and Baker's on roads to the west guarding the far flank, Imboden had to make do with his own brigade and other, miscellaneous troops.

His main defense force was the artillery. He emplaced most of his guns on the roads leading northeast to Hagerstown and southeast toward Boonsboro, both likely avenues of enemy advance. Along each road he positioned four cannon of Eshelman's battery, with two rifles and two 12-pounder howitzers, recently assigned to Hart's battery, in between. Another battery went into position facing north on the Greencastle road, while the cannon attached to Imboden's own brigade, the Virginia battery of Captain J. H. McClanahan, took post on both flanks along the river. To augment these units, Imboden armed every able-bodied man within his reach, including the teamsters and some of the wounded. About five hundred of these he placed under Colonel Black and the wounded Colonel William R. Aylett, 53rd Virginia Infantry.[29]

He did not have to wait long to see his dispositions tested. About 1:30 P.M. Yankee cavalry came in from the west: Buford's reunited division, spoiling for its first fight in four days. Two-thirds of it had moved the previous day from Taneytown to Frederick, a mile west of which Merritt's men rejoined the command. Then, via Middletown and Turner's Gap (both held by French's pickets) Buford moved to Boonsboro, where on the morning of the sixth he conferred with Kilpatrick. After comparing strategies, the two decided to go their separate ways come morning, Buford's men to strike the trains heading for Williamsport and the 3rd Division to go north to Hagerstown in response to reports of Stuart's movement there. Kilpatrick would thus keep the Rebel cavalry from interfering with Buford's operations.[30]

When Buford approached Imboden's position along the Boonsboro road, the variegated group of defenders opened fire. The Rebels hoped to keep the enemy back with a bold show of force, until their cavalry supports could reach them. Despite their ragtag nature, the three thousand effectives nearly matched Buford's manpower; moreover, they enjoyed well-prepared positions and a great edge in artillery. In the end, those advantages saved the wagons and ambulances from capture.

Though at first Buford's range was too great for the guns on the Boonsboro Road, Hart's battery and the cannon beside it struck the Union right flank hard enough to make Buford pull back. Major Eshelman then advanced his cannon—protected by skirmishers—to get a better fix on the cavalry's position. Buford's own artillery, under Lieutenant Calef, laid an enfilading fire along Eshelman's right, but other guns and the troops protecting them drove out Calef's supports and for a time left his battery vulnerable to capture. Gamble's brigade came up to rescue Calef; in a hot skirmish above the Boonsboro road, dozens fell on both sides, including Major William H. Medill, commander of the 8th Illinois, who was mortally wounded. Meanwhile, other artillery and supports kept at bay the Yankees opposite the Confederate left-center, just below the Hagerstown road. Time and again Buford attempted to reach the circle of wagons, but his only success came when some of Gamble's men captured seven vehicles and their drivers on the far Rebel right, along the Downsville road.[31]

While Buford and Imboden squared off, Kilpatrick and Stuart were tilting in the streets of Hagerstown with fluctuating results. The fight had begun about noon with an impetuous charge through the town by a small band in Kilpatrick's advance—led, fittingly, by Ulric Dahlgren. Following his blow at Imboden's trains, the captain had guided his Pennsylvanians against a second Rebel supply column near Waynesboro, cutting off dozens of forage wagons, most of which he burned. Afterward he rode hard to overtake Kilpatrick's column at Boonsboro, seeking an opportunity to strike Stuart's cavaliers.

When Colonel Richmond's brigade, Kilpatrick's leading element, entered the town from the south, Dahlgren by some authority guided two squadrons of the 18th Pennsylvania up the main street. Observing Chambliss's Confederates riding into town from the northeast, Dahlgren led his new command against them without considering how badly he was outnumbered. Ironically, the charge carried the squadrons to a cemetery, where the little band was decimated by rifle fire. Along with many others, Dahlgren fell, his right leg shattered by a minié ball. Amputation of the limb would for several months curtail his deeds of derring-do.[32]

The destruction of its forward unit led the 18th Pennsylvania to rush southward in panic, much as it had at Hanover. Its flight disarranged the next regiment in Richmond's column, the colonel's own 1st West Virginia. As more Rebels entered Hagerstown, the West Virginians also fled, leaving vulnerable their comrades in the 1st Vermont, 5th New York, and Elder's battery. Those units nevertheless took up positions, dismounted, in the streets, and for two hours they resisted the efforts of Chambliss to seize the town. It proved rough going; the Federals not only fought a uniformed enemy but also townspeople sympathetic to the Confederacy. At least one member of Richmond's brigade was killed by a local sniper.[33]

The Rebels lost heavily as well, especially in captured, one of these being Colonel Davis of the 10th Virginia. After some desperate fighting, many of

Chambliss's troopers retreated to the crest of a hill a mile and a half west of the town. Soon afterward, however, Stuart's main force—Robertson's, Jones's, and Ferguson's brigades—reached the scene, as did the head of Robert E. Lee's infantry column, Brigadier General Alfred Iverson's brigade of Ewell's corps. When Iverson opened above Hagerstown with his artillery—firing, among other things, pieces of railroad iron—the Federals began to fall back.[34]

By now Colonel Richmond was on his own, for the rest of Kilpatrick's division had moved toward Williamsport in answer to Buford's call. About 4:00 P.M., having gained little headway against Imboden, the leader of the 1st Cavalry Division sent to Kilpatrick for support. Already the latter had dispatched Custer's brigade toward the river, but due to several factors including Imboden's artillery might, the Wolverines had been of limited assistance to Buford. Now Kilpatrick agreed to add Huey's brigade to the attack on Williamsport; he led it southwest just before Stuart and Iverson pushed their way into Hagerstown.[35]

Though assigned to hold the town for as long as possible, Richmond was steadily shoved out of it. His retreat quickened when the head of Longstreet's corps joined Stuart and Iverson above the place, early in the evening. The enlarged Rebel force pressed Richmond so closely that at one point the colonel turned about and counterattacked in a fit of rage—only to be routed by two of Stuart's regiments, the 5th North Carolina (led today by James B. Gordon) and the 11th Virginia, under Lunsford Lomax. With that, the Union brigade broke apart like cracked glass, pieces flying in all directions. Though some critics later claimed that Buford was responsible for Kilpatrick losing his grip on a strategic position, it seems clear that Kill-cavalry was simply overwhelmed; his retreat from Hagerstown was a matter of time.[36]

Even so it was true that, as Buford's critics also contended, his call for help came too late. By the time Huey joined Custer near Williamsport, it was approaching sundown. Furthermore, the cavalry under Lee and Baker reached the contested field from north and west minutes after Kilpatrick's arrival. This further cheered Imboden's force, whose morale had already been boosted by its ability to keep Buford at arm's length.

Much credit for Imboden's success was due to the general himself and his veteran officers, many of them wounded, who had organized the teamsters and artillerists into a cohesive command and convinced them that they could stand firm against the hardest-fighting veterans in the Union cavalry. Typical of these leaders was Lieutenant Colonel Delony of Cobb's Legion, who left his ambulance to fight despite the wounds he had received at Hunterstown. "I was feeling very miserably," he wrote his wife, Rosa, "but the booming of their cannon aroused me and I gathered up the stragglers about the wagons & went to the field. . . . I managed very soon to inspire the men with confidence and led them in. They fought well, drove the enemy about ¾ of a mile and about dark had completely flanked one of their batteries & if I had had a little more daylight I believe I should have taken it. . . ."[37]

The loss of daylight, as well as Richmond's defeat and the presence of Stuart and Iverson in the Union rear, concerned Buford. As ranking officer, he called off the attack some time after dark. Under a covering fire from Calef, Pennington, and other artillerymen, the Union troopers retired to their led horses—"sullenly," as John Imboden thought. "The news was sent along our whole line," he added, "and was received with a wild and exultant yell. We knew then that the field was won, and slowly pressed forward."[38]

The combined Yankee force retreated southeastward, Buford and Custer toward Jones's Crossroads and Kilpatrick, with Richmond, farther east to Boonsboro. Because the operation lacked planning, the horsemen got in each other's way and clogged the roads. Had darkness not kept Stuart from pressing them (most of the Confederate horsemen elected to remain in Hagerstown), both Buford and Kilpatrick might have tasted disaster.[39] As it was, it seemed a fitting end to a day of advantages wasted through lack of coordination. Much of Lee's army lay trapped along the Potomac, a rising river at its back, but Meade's advance had not been able to capitalize on its predicament.

**

By 7 July, the entire Army of the Potomac was in motion at last. As Meade transferred his headquarters from Gettysburg to Frederick under a day-long downpour, three of his corps moved south from Emmitsburg and nearby Moritz Crossroads. Three other corps, however, began the day still in Pennsylvania. The pursuit seemed determinedly slow, and no commander moved more slowly than General Sedgwick, head of the VI Corps, who led the army's advance. Not for another three days would every major element of the army be within striking range of the Potomac.[40]

In contrast, by the close of the seventh the rear echelon of the Army of Northern Virginia, John B. Gordon's brigade of Ewell's corps, had closed up on Hagerstown; the rest of Lee's troops had moved closer to the river. There they hoped for an opportunity to salvage something from their retreat. Lee had begun to dig a line of works from Williamsport through Downsville, ten miles to the southeast, as far as the river, enclosing several potential crossing points, including Falling Waters. Despite the still-rising river, Confederate engineers were also hard at work fabricating a pontoon bridge to replace that waylaid by French's raiders. Pioneers and fatigue parties had been ferried across the river to initiate construction from below. Other rafts crossed back and forth, hauling artillery and small-arms ammunition (two loads had come over the day before during Imboden's battle with Buford) as well as sick and wounded Confederates and Union prisoners. On the eighth, the artillery with Imboden began to cross to the Virginia side via rafts and a rope-ferry. Thus, instead of being panicked by the swollen river, Lee made his dispositions and labored at his defenses in an unhurried, businesslike manner. The works soon bristled with heavy guns, rifle-pits, and various obstacles for the benefit of his lead-footed pursuers.[41]

***

Because Lee required some days in which to perfect his position, the Union cavalry should have struck his defense perimeter while time remained. Instead, on the seventh Kilpatrick's men and most of Buford's continued toward Boonsboro, their backs turned to Williamsport. The cavalry made only a limited movement toward Stuart and his infantry supports at Hagerstown—and that move ended quite badly.

As Merritt's brigade marched westward in Buford's vanguard, its commander dispatched what remained of the 6th United States, under Ira Claflin, backed by the 1st United States under Captain Lord, north toward the scene of Richmond's recent fighting. En route, the Regulars encountered familiar opponents. Marching down to Funkstown on a reconnaissance similar to Claflin's came the brigade of Grumble Jones. There followed a reprise of the 3 July combat near Fairfield.

When the advance of each force met below Funkstown late in the day, the Regulars initially had the best of it, pushing the Rebels through the village at a rapid clip. But when Claflin's vanguard came up to the place, he caught a minié ball in the shoulder, courtesy of a sharpshooter in the 7th Virginia, the regiment the 6th had routed during their previous meeting. Lieutenant Nolan immediately succeeded him, becoming the only second lieutenant on either side to take command of a regiment of cavalry during the campaign. Nolan advanced his force beyond the town—whereupon he found himself in much the same situation Major Starr had encountered four days ago. Galloping along the road from Hagerstown came Jones's vanguard, led by the 7th Virginia. Despite a covering attack by Lord's Regulars, Thomas Marshall's men piled into the understrength Federal outfits and forced both to retreat. Though Nolan contended that his regiment carried on a "running fight" covering four miles, his and Lord's people did the running. Looking on with a smile, General Jones later expressed his approval in grandiose terms: "Sabers were freely used, and soon 66 bloody-headed prisoners were marched to the rear, and the road of slumbering wrath was marked here and there by cleft skulls and pierced bodies." Pleased to find that the 7th Virginia had redeemed itself, Jones crowed in his report that "the day at Fairfield is nobly and fully avenged."[42]

While cavalry fought cavalry on the Funkstown-Hagerstown road, part of Buford's division engaged in hit-and-run action with Rebels pressing its withdrawal from near Williamsport to Boonsboro. Early in the day—soon after sunup—Devin's brigade, bringing up the rear of the Federal column, experienced pressure from some of Imboden's men and their mounted supports. Turning about, a squadron of Major William E. Beardsley's 6th New York repulsed the pursuers by a "demonstration" charge. That eased things a bit, and Devin resumed his journey to Boonsboro. But about two and a half miles farther on, the colonel was ordered to stop and hold a position near Downsville, west of Antietam Creek, until the rest of Buford's division could cross the stream to Boonsboro. The halt enabled the Confederates to come up again. This time the attackers encompassed infantry and artillery—the brigade of Brigadier General William T. Wofford, whose Georgia foot soldiers General Lee had attached to Stuart's command. Devin gave the post of greatest danger to Colonel Sackett's 9th New York, which did a masterful job of holding Wofford in check until its comrades crossed Antietam bridge. Once the road was clear, Sackett recalled his skirmishers and marched to the creek in good order, occasionally stopping to lash the Rebels with carbine fire. On reaching the bridge, Sackett's men accepted protection from a couple of squadrons of Kellogg's 17th Pennsylvania. Discovering this added support, the enemy did not venture across the stream, allowing Devin's rear to reach Boonsboro minus the eight men Sackett had lost in transit.[43]

Routed near Funkstown and harassed while withdrawing to Boonsboro, the Federals had had a bad day on 7 July. Their evening was worse. Because Buford and Kilpatrick feared Stuart and his infantry friends would strike them before morning, they kept most of their men awake throughout the rain-sodden night. The bivouacs outside Boonsboro became scenes of utter misery. The chaplain of the 6th Pennsylvania recalled that his regiment spent hours "dismounted in a ploughed field in line of battle, in a heavy storm of rain, without fires and with clothes thoughly saturated . . . standing in mud to our knees, every horse remaining saddled and in position, and every man at his horse's head. . . . This was one of the most wretched nights of all our experience in the cavalry service."[44]

The troopers' vigilance was rewarded when, shortly after daybreak, Stuart moved down the rain-swept Hagerstown Pike with the brigades of Lee, Jones, Chambliss, and Baker. His opponents suspected he was heading for the South Mountain passes just beyond Boonsboro. The previous day Pleasonton had ordered the cavalry to keep the gaps clear: Meade's infantry was moving south along the far side of the mountains; it planned to swing west by way of Fox's and Turner's Gaps, within sight of the cavalry's bivouacs. A move toward the gaps, however, was what Stuart wanted his enemy to think he was making. He was merely feinting that way, in order to keep the Federals on the defensive long enough for Lee's rear to clear Hagerstown and reach the defense line along the river.[45]

The initial Confederate threat was directed at Buford, who had formed his brigades in an arc astride the pike, with Devin on the left extending almost to the Williamsport road, Merritt in the center, and Gamble across and east of Stuart's route. In Buford's rear, Kilpatrick's three brigades formed a reserve, with skirmishers thrown out on both flanks.

About 5:00 A.M. Stuart opened the fight with a cannonade from the battery of William M. McGregor, occupying a lofty crest that commanded the Union right. The guns soon enfiladed Gamble's brigade and forced it, along with Calef's battery, to retire to a new line farther south. Stuart then advanced skirmishers across the fields to dislodge other parts of Buford's position; the troopers came on afoot, for Stuart thought the ground "entirely too soft from recent rains to operate successfully with [mounted] cavalry."[46]

As the Union position quivered, Stuart threw in a flank force: Ferguson's brigade, which he sent down the road from Williamsport against the enemy's left. To meet the threat, the skirmishers of Devin and Kilpatrick advanced toward that road but failed in several attempts to seize it. Against opposition from two directions, the Federals held on, Major Beardsley's 6th New York occupying a particularly exposed position. About 2:00 P.M., when he found his ammunition running perilously low, Devin began to fall back, fighting from successive positions. Despite the soggy earth, the Confederates pressed ahead on horseback as well as on foot, shouting in supposed triumph.

At the critical moment, Kilpatrick filled the breach. Shortly after noon he had relieved Merritt's hard-pressed brigade with that of Custer; now he sent Richmond's troops to spell Devin's. On the right, portions of Kilpatrick's command temporarily relieved Gamble as well, but when they were unable to chase Stuart's men out of a flanking position in the woods Gamble returned to his old line and completed the task.

By five o'clock, the momentum had changed and the Federals began to move forward all along the line, Gamble's men afoot and Custer's and Richmond's on horseback, supported by Elder's and Pennington's cannon. When Stuart resisted, heavy fighting covered both sides of the turnpike. During the set-to, Colonel Alger of the 5th Michigan was severely wounded in the thigh and the 7th Michigan's Colonel Mann was unhorsed when a shell burst over his head. When the Federals continued to surge northward, Stuart suddenly decided that he was running out of ammunition. By now he had protected Lee's withdrawal toward Williamsport for several hours.

Stuart's decision to pull back toward Funkstown only encouraged the Federals. As the troopers of Kilpatrick galloped west of the pike, Gamble's men raced along their right, John Buford with them. A member of the 8th Illinois noted that the division leader shook his "fat sides" in trying to keep up with his men. Later, a winded Buford exclaimed: "These boys beat anything in the world in a foot skirmish."[47]

After crossing Beaver Creek, the Confederates took up a strong line below Funkstown, four miles from the battlefield. From a tall hill, the battery of Captain Chew blasted back the leading pursuers, ending the day's combat. Sensitive to their task of guarding the passes, Buford and Kilpatrick were willing to return south. Their troops did so in an enthusiastic mood. "I guess they [the Confederates] will get sick of this side of the Potomac," exulted a Michigan boy the next night. An Illinoisan wrote of his comrades: "They are all bully boys and they don't fear the Rebbs [sic] a bit. . . . Gen. Buford says . . . the only fault he finds with us is that he can't stop us when we once get the Rebbs to running."

Buford was not so jolly—and not merely from tired feet. Despite his troopers' enthusiasm, he was concerned that their three-day diet of combat was reducing their stamina. That night he informed Alfred Pleasonton that "I have had a very rough day of it." Rougher days lay ahead.[48]

***

In his campaign report Stuart claimed that "the fight of the 8th administered a *quietus* to the enemy on the 9th." It was true that Buford and Kilpatrick remained near Boonsboro this day, aware that the head of Meade's column would poke through the mountains momentarily. It was also true that noncombat business took precedence in the Union camps. Among other events, Othneil De Forest returned from leave to resume command of his old brigade, replacing Colonel Richmond, and Huey's brigade was returned to the authority of David Gregg, who was concentrating his division near Boonsboro.[49]

The calm was broken when part of Buford's division returned to battle late in the day. About 4:00 P.M., the tireless men of Tom Devin ranged toward Beaver Creek to report on the new Rebel dispositions. On the way, they rammed into a detachment that Stuart had placed on high ground in advance of his main force. Muscling his way across the Antietam tributary, Devin rushed the enemy position, aided by Gamble's skirmishers and two guns of Lieutenant Heaton's Battery B/L, 2nd United States, ensconced beyond a bend in the stream. In the fading light, two squadrons of Devin's skirmishers broke up Stuart's advanced units and, as one of Gamble's onlookers remarked, "drove them about 2 miles like fun."

However much entertainment was involved, the operation provided another boost to Devin's career. His achievements had not gone unnoticed. This very day, Pleasonton sought for him the brigadier generalship left vacant upon the death of Elon Farnsworth.[50]

***

Late on the ninth, Meade's infantry debouched from Fox's Gap, bringing his army into the main arena. The foot soldiers were in lofty spirits, due not only to Lee's precipitate retreat but to a report recently confirmed: the Confederate stronghold of Vicksburg, Mississippi, had surrendered on Independence Day.[51]

Like John Buford, Meade did not share his men's mood. He was too much aware that Lee was husbanding his strength behind heavy works and the screen erected by his aggressive, hard-hitting cavalry. Suspecting that he might be placed in the same situation as Lee had been on 3 July—forced to operate against strong defenses on commanding terrain—Meade feared that his organic command would prove unequal to such a task. He realized that numerous other forces were moving to his side—with more or less dispatch—to reinforce him. But he suspected that few would reach him in time to fight Lee and that even fewer would be of much assistance.[52]

His pessimism was well-founded. Supposedly General Couch was hastening south from his new headquarters at Chambersburg with thousands of militia of all arms. In reality, only Baldy Smith's division (which Smith himself characterized as "an incoherent mass . . . quite helpless") would reach Meade in time to see action against Stuart at Hagerstown.[53] Couch himself, with 9,000 infantry and eight guns, would never get far beyond Greencastle.[54] Meanwhile, his mounted troops had already reached the limit of their effectiveness in harassing Lee's retreat. Following his attacks on Imboden and the troops at Mercersburg, 5–6 July, the cavalry under Lewis Pierce sat along the fringes of the campaign. The infantry portion of Pierce's force would make fitful, ineffectual efforts to stop Lee from crossing the Potomac near Clear Spring, Maryland.[55] The rest of Couch's mounted force, under Captain Boyd of the 1st New York and Colonel John E. Wynkoop of the 20th Pennsylvania, had made some contributions to the pursuit by capturing men and wagons in the Greencastle-Chambersburg vicinity (Boyd himself, with his remarkable band, had nabbed seven supply vehicles, fifty-two horses, twenty-nine mules, and 165 prisoners). But now that Lee was concentrating along the Potomac, these small units were beyond their depth. They would learn this fact on the eleventh, when a detachment of their combined force ventured far enough south to seize (briefly) Hagerstown. When the Rebel infantry, whose rear guard the horsemen had evicted, returned to the town, Boyd and Wynkoop were sent spinning down the road to the Union lines, minus several casualties.[56]

Other auxiliary forces would aid the Army of the Potomac little or not at all. General Brooks at Pittsburgh had been ordered to Meade's side with his 1,560 troops, but his Pennsylvania militia and emergency units refused to serve outside their state.[57] Brigadier General Henry M. Naglee, commanding on the reoccupied heights above Harpers Ferry, had been directed to send many of his 7,000 men to Meade at Boonsboro; but he was moving too slowly to do the latter any good.[58] Finally, General Kelley, though massing at Hancock for a strike against Lee's rear, would shy away from a commitment at the last minute, despite repeated urgings from the War Department that he cooperate with Meade below the Potomac.[59]

The only parts of Meade's army that received substantial reinforcements were the I and III Corps, which gained some ten thousand troops of all arms from French's garrison at Frederick.[60] At the same time, the Cavalry Corps was strengthened. On 8 July, in response to War Department orders, Sir Percy Wyndham had sent toward Frederick some fifteen hundred troopers, unhorsed veterans whom he had remounted at Giesboro Point following Stuart's raid. By the tenth these troops, including detachments of the decimated 1st Rhode Island and 1st Massachusetts, had rejoined the command of David Gregg.[61]

With them came a report that an older leader, George Stoneman, was returning to the front, replacing Pleasonton. This seemed logical, for since Dan Butterfield's wounding on 3 July, the cavalry leader had been sharing with Major General Gouverneur K. Warren the duties of Meade's acting chief of staff—a post that removed him farther than ever from operational duties. Washington soon quashed the rumor of Stoneman's return and Pleasonton eventually retook the field. But Meade permitted the cavalry division leaders to exercise tactical command through the remainder of the campaign.[62]

Early on the tenth, as Meade's infantry spread out north and west, the cavalry cleared a path for it. In "splendid fighting," Buford's dismounted brigades waded Beaver Creek and advanced determinedly against Stuart. The Confederates soon found too many dismounted skirmishers "crawling up on us" and retired north to Funkstown. But Buford continued to advance at what an Illinois trooper styled "a rappid walk," driving the gray-clad cavalry toward their infantry comrades' entrenchments above Antietam Creek.[63]

About noon Stuart finally made a stand above the Antietam, bolstered by foot soldiers. His supports comprised the brigade of George Anderson (which had opposed Wesley Merritt on 3 July), today under Colonel W. W. White. The infantry marched south across the creek to the northern environs of Funkstown, Fitz Lee guiding it into position against Buford's advance. Though inadvertently shelled by Stuart's horse batteries, the Georgia regiments succeeded in driving dismounted sharpshooters from a barn on the crest of a hill above Funkstown. White later claimed that he would have swept Buford's entire force from the field had not Lee recalled him. As it was, his effort was enough to make the Federals fall back to Beaver Creek, where waited their own infantry supports—a division of Sedgwick's corps. About 3:00 P.M., portions of this division relieved Buford, whose men bivouacked for the night about four miles below the scene of fighting.[64]

While Buford was opening the way for the VI Corps, Huey's brigade—again detached from Gregg's division—moved out of Boonsboro to do the same on behalf of the XII Corps. Passing through Keedysville, the brigade crossed the Antietam circa 10:00 A.M. and, about the time Stuart gave battle to Buford, struck Rebel infantry at Jones's Crossroads, three miles west of Williamsport. In stout fighting—the sort that many colleagues thought Huey incapable of—the troopers drove their opponents from three separate positions, to a point one mile beyond the crossroads. In so doing, Huey uncovered a bridge on the Antietam that his infantry friends could use en route to Lee's main line of defense.[65]

The accomplishments of Buford and Huey meant that when night fell on the tenth, Meade's army had established itself along a line from Bakersville, about two miles from Lee's right flank at Downsville, north to Funkstown, within rifle range of the Rebel rear at Hagerstown. The next morning, Meade began a movement all along this front, determined to shrink the enemy line to its most compact configuration. As usual, the cavalry—except for the brigades of McIntosh and Irvin Gregg, which guarded Meade's center along Marsh Creek, and the men under Wesley Merritt, detached today for special service—moved in advance of the army. Gamble's and Devin's brigades were transferred from the north flank, via Boonsboro and Sharpsburg, to Bakersville, about a mile and a half from the Potomac. A sharp skirmish in this area resulted in Stuart's recalling Fitz Lee from Downsville to his main body outside Hagerstown. Infantry took Lee's place, ensuring that Buford could not seize Downsville without substantial support of his own.[66]

While Buford changed position, Huey's brigade, still backed by the XII Corps, struck Rebel foot troops on the Williamsport road during a reconnaissance in force. Finding the Rebels strongly posted, Huey sprayed them with Fuller's battery, killing three, capturing five others, and driving the survivors westward. Huey held his position till nightfall, when the infantry allowed his men to pass to the rear.[67]

The main Union effort on the eleventh was made by Kilpatrick. That morning Custer's brigade, followed closely by De Forest's, charged up the road to Funkstown. Chasing the last elements of Confederate cavalry and infantry from the village, the 3rd Division gained a lodgment on the pike about a mile and a half below Hagerstown. The Rebels retreated stubbornly toward the southwest in the direction of Williamsport. By late that evening the town was free of Confederates, whose upper flank had been pulled almost two miles closer to the river. It would be an easy chore for Kilpatrick, closely supported by Sedgwick's corps, to occupy the place come morning.

Within two days of emerging from the South Mountain gaps, the Army of the Potomac had pressed to within rifle range of both Confederate flanks and into position to apply pressure to Lee's works at the river. Meade's strategy of contraction and containment had worked splendidly so far—thanks largely to his horsemen. Still, as Captain Adams of the 1st Massachusetts Cavalry cautioned his family, "as to Lee's being routed, he has lots of fight left, and this war is not over yet. . . ."[68]

***

About 8:00 A.M. on 12 July, Kilpatrick's advance guard charged "screaming and yelling" into Hagerstown, occupying the place they had been striving to capture for six days. Though its entry went unopposed and it snatched up fifty Rebels, the division found itself in a brisk fight on the road to Williamsport when it attempted to pursue the evacuees. During the encounter, Custer's brigade suffered several casualties, one being the severe wounding of Lieutenant Colonel Ebenezer Gould of the 5th Michigan. Soon Kilpatrick was joined in and below the town by elements of the VI and XI Corps. The following day Baldy Smith's militia would also reach him—the only sizable body of Couch's infantry to arrive on the scene of action during Lee's retreat.[69]

While Kilpatrick seized Hagerstown, other mounted units pressed westward. Buford launched a reconnaissance of Lee's position at Downsville, while Huey renewed his skirmishing along the Williamsport road. The latter advanced Fuller's battery to the westernmost point of his line and with it drove Rebel infantry into breastworks beyond Saint James College. After holding a position barely 150 yards from the enemy works, Huey was relieved by the VI Corps and again retired to Jones's Crossroads.[70]

On the other side of the lines, Robert E. Lee was putting final touches to the works that enclosed the fords at Williamsport and the new bridge at Falling Waters. The pontoon span was incomplete but this had not stopped Lee from shifting troops and supplies to the right bank of the river. For several days a ferry system had been in operation, with flatboats crossing by means of a rope-wire. A crossing could be completed in seven minutes, and seventy trips was the daily norm. Not only had materiel reached Virginia by this means; by now most of Imboden's command, including his wagons, ambulances, and prisoners, had returned to the Confederacy. Furthermore, the rains having ceased, the water level was falling rapidly: by the end of the day the river at Williamsport would drop eighteen inches. This enabled some elements of the main army to cross on the twelfth, including the 7th Virginia Cavalry, which Grumble Jones sent to guard Lee's communications with Winchester. Still, Lee kept the greater part of his army on Maryland soil, hoping that Meade would chance an assault.[71]

The Union commander wanted to oblige him. On the afternoon of the twelfth he informed the War Department that, barring unforeseen circumstances, he would attack with his entire force the next morning. Soon, however, the unforeseen circumstances came into play. That night Meade called a war council at his headquarters near Boonsboro. Explaining his plan of attack, he solicited his subordinates' opinions as to its efficacy. Five of the seven infantry corps commanders argued strenuously against it, maintaining that Lee's works were too strong to crack. Joining the two who favored assault were Generals Pleasonton and Warren, who had returned to their duties as head of the cavalry corps and the engineer corps, respectively. Also in favor was Major General Andrew A. Humphreys, who had replaced both officers as Meade's chief of staff. But the consensus of the infantry leaders carried great weight with Meade. Though not pleased by their vote, he abided by it until he could make a personal survey of Lee's lines.[72]

The result was that his army saw little activity on the thirteenth, remaining in its rifle-pits between Hagerstown and Bakersville. While Meade made his reconnaissance—which convinced him to order a movement by the entire army at seven o'clock the next morning—only elements of the cavalry were engaged. On the far left, Buford's division, again including Merritt's brigade, shoved its way to within eight hundred yards of Lee's defenses at Downsville. Buford suffered no or few casualties in the process,[73] but a movement by Kilpatrick on the other flank generated more extensive fighting and much greater loss.

Kilpatrick's operation involved only one mounted regiment; the rest of his division got "pretty well rested" in its camps near Hagerstown. That afternoon he sent the 1st Vermont of De Forest's brigade, under its recently returned commander, Colonel Edward B. Sawyer, to reconnoiter Lee's extreme left. To Sawyer's men Kilpatrick added a regiment of Smith's militia, the 33rd Pennsylvania.[74]

With the militia in advance, the 1st Vermont proceeded south of town. Just in front of the nearest earthworks, the combined force met a large band of pickets—against whom Sawyer advanced a line of skirmishers. As the skirmishers, followed by the main body of the cavalry regiment, pressed on, the Rebels steadily retreated, firing as they went. Nevertheless, Sawyer's progress was not rapid enough for Kilpatrick, who ordered the colonel to send in a squadron, mounted. This was typical Kilpatrick: a charge made without prior reconnaissance or an appreciation of the odds against. The results were all too predictable. The two companies of Vermonters galloped down the fence- and woods-lined road until raked by a murderous fire not only from the retiring pickets but from whole regiments in the entrenchments farther south, backed by artillery. The squadron commander was wounded and taken prisoner; his executive officer also took a severe wound; and twelve troopers went down around them. For its efforts, the squadron captured two Rebels.[75]

That night Meade sent Kilpatrick a note rebuking him for the unnecessary loss. The division leader bristled, damned his superior for faintheartedness, and replied that the attack had been necessary to maintain his hold on his position. Later he remarked to his staff: "I know that is not quite true, but I did not want the cowardly militia to return home without meeting the enemy."[76]

***

When Meade failed to attack on the thirteenth, Lee decided he could tarry no longer. The water was now low enough to permit a crossing at Williamsport and the pontoons were in place at Falling Waters. Believing that his enemy would never muster the gumption to strike, he concluded to return to Virginia and renew the contest on more familiar ground.[77]

At 4:15 that afternoon, he instructed Stuart to relieve the infantry at the crossing sites. When darkness fell, the army began crossing at both places, Longstreet—followed by Hill and the artillery—trooping over the bridge, and Ewell fording at Williamsport.[78] With Longstreet crossed the balance of Grumble Jones's brigade, to join the 7th Virginia on the right bank. There it would also rejoin the 12th Virginia, left in its namesake state when Robertson and Jones joined Lee late in June. Lieutenant Colonel Massie had carried on extensive operations against Harpers Ferry prior to its evacuation on 1 July and after its reoccupation by General Naglee on the seventh. Late on 30 June, an advance detachment of the 12th had captured a twenty-one–man picket post above the town and maintained its foothold until the balance of the regiment could arrive. Thereafter Massie occupied the garrison, carrying off prisoners and supplies by the cartload.[79]

Stuart crossed most of his command at Williamsport, under cover of night, in Ewell's rear. Despite the receding water, the fords were deep and the currents treacherous; some men and several wagons were swept away. Captain Blackford watched mule teams slide deeper and deeper into the river: "Soon nothing would be seen but their ears above the water, until by a violent effort the poor brutes would again spring aloft; and indeed after the waters had closed over them, occasionally one would appear in one last plunge high above the surface."[80] Given the bloodletting the Army of Northern Virginia had experienced since 1 July, this could have served as a metaphor for the Confederacy.

Most of Stuart's cavalry reached the Virginia side before dawn on the fourteenth. By 8:00 A.M. the last two squadrons of Lee's brigade trod the pontoons at Falling Waters in a persistent rain, leaving only two divisions of Hill's infantry, commanded by Henry Heth and Brigadier General James J. Pettigrew, on the north shore.[81]

Long before that hour, the Union cavalry detected Lee's pullout. As early as 3:00 A.M. Kilpatrick noticed that the works below Hagerstown were empty; four hours later Buford went forward and discovered that the infantry had vacated its trenches at Downsville. Both divisions began a pursuit, Kilpatrick's from the north and Buford's from the east. Buford notified his colleague that he intended to slice between Lee's rear guard and the river, cutting off Heth and Pettigrew along with numerous cannon, wagons, and supplies. Apparently he expected Kilpatrick to distract the enemy long enough for him to strike.[82]

Kilpatrick had other ideas. Pursuing south with the 5th Michigan, followed closely by the rest of Custer's brigade (De Forest's men remained at Hagerstown), he aimed to land a decisive blow before Lee could escape. At 6:00 A.M. he reached Williamsport, where he found only stragglers from Ewell's corps; these troops the 5th Michigan, now under Major Crawley P. Dake, shoved into the water. Custer's brigade then hastened toward Falling Waters, hoping to bag a greater catch there.[83]

The 6th Michigan, now in the advance, encountered the Rebel rear guard about two miles from Falling Waters. The Wolverines pushed the foot troops steadily toward the river. At 7:30, the cavalry came up to a crescent-shaped line of works on the left of the road, a mile and a half from the Potomac. These defenses, which protected the pontoon bridge, consisted of a half-dozen artillery epaulements and breastworks along a tall crest; they joined woodland trenches about three-quarters of a mile to the north. Held by Pettigrew's men (Heth's had just completed crossing), they were a formidable obstacle to infantry; they should have been impregnable to cavalry.[84]

But as Kilpatrick had reaffirmed as recently as yesterday, he considered a mounted attack appropriate to any occasion. Believing the infantry inside the works demoralized and weak, he instructed Custer to strike with a couple of companies from the 6th Michigan, until the rest of his brigade could reach the scene. Custer selected 100 men and placed them under Peter Weber, who had fought so stubbornly at Hanover and Gettysburg. At Custer's order, the young major dismounted his men, but Kilpatrick had them remount. This was just fine with Weber, who only days before had told a fellow officer that his ambition was to lead a saber charge. At his signal, the hundred men went galloping down the road to the works.[85]

For a time, the Rebels let them advance without opposition; in fact, they had stacked their arms beside the rifle pits. Having heard that a squadron of Stuart's men would be bringing up their rear, they supposed the oncoming horsemen to be Confederates. Stuart's squadron, however, had crossed the river early by mistake. Not till the charging men passed through the epaulements and began shooting and slashing did Pettigrew's men realize they too had erred.[86]

Looking on from the rear, Captain James H. Kidd of the 6th Michigan described the upshot: "Weber, cutting right and left with his saber, and cheering on his men, pierced the first line, but there could be but one result. Recovering from their surprise, the Confederate infantry rallied, and seizing their arms, made short work of their daring assailants." The infantry—elements of the 13th Alabama and the 1st, 7th, and 14th Tennessee—blasted Weber's men along the length of their line at close range. Weber and his second-in-command, Lieutenant Charles E. Bolza, fell dead, while thirty of their men were killed, wounded, or taken prisoner. To the rear, Captain David G. Royce of the 6th, supporting the charge with his dismounted squadron, was also killed, as were several of his troopers.[87]

Coming up from the east, Buford's men observed the slaughter. Colonel Gamble noted sourly that "any competent cavalry officer of experience" could have foretold the result of the charge: though the Wolverines were decimated, "not a single dead enemy could be found." Here Gamble reported falsely, for General Pettigrew himself fell to Weber's squadron. Knocked to the ground when his horse took a trooper's bullet, the division leader was mortally wounded as he regained his feet.[88]

Upon Weber's repulse, Custer threw in the rest of Colonel Gray's regiment, afoot, but Pettigrew's men sent it flying back upon Kilpatrick's main body. Reinforced by the 1st Michigan, the 6th returned to battle and inflicted some loss on the Confederate infantry. Even so, the Wolverines were kept at arm's reach until the bulk of the Rebel rear guard crossed the pontoons.[89]

While Custer tangled with the infantry, Devin's brigade closed in alongside the river, with Gamble's command farther to the right. They discovered that Weber's charge and the attacks that followed it had sent most of Pettigrew's people scrambling across the bridge before they could be cut off. All told, Buford nabbed over five hundred members of the rear guard (Kilpatrick about two hundred others).[90] Yet, had the divisions coordinated operations, many times that number would have fallen into their hands. As it was, Buford's people reached the river a few minutes too late.

The leader of the 1st Cavalry Division told the story concisely: "As our troops neared the bridge, the enemy cut the Maryland side loose, and the bridge swung to the Virginia side."[91]

Afterword

MANY historians regard the Gettysburg campaign as the turning point in the struggle for supremacy between the Union and Confederate cavalries in the East. The accepted view is that Hooker's and Meade's horsemen won a clear-cut victory, demonstrating superior tactical skill, energy, and tenacity throughout the campaign. A dispassionate look at the evidence, however, suggests that while the Union cavalry stood virtually toe-to-toe with its much-vaunted enemy, it gained the clear tactical advantage on only a few occasions. A major reason is that it had yet to strike the proper balance between mounted and dismounted fighting, recognizing which was proper under given conditions. And as long as it retained in command generals such as Alfred Pleasonton and Judson Kilpatrick, the Union cavalry in the East would never truly come of age.

By many indications, the Federals should have triumphed decisively. They possessed great advantages in weaponry, equipment, and horseflesh. They also fought the most crucial part of the campaign in friendly territory, assuring them of a greater opportunity to remount, resupply, and gather intelligence. Moreover, J. E. B. Stuart's horsemen fought much of the campaign on the strategic defensive, which often prevented them from exploiting their natural tendency to attack and overthrow the enemy. Even so, time and again the Southern riders dominated the battlefield, even if forced to quit it at the close of day, giving their efforts the illusion of defeat. The magnitude of Stuart's triumphs between 9 June and 14 July 1863 was also diminished by the stigma that became attached to his ride around Hooker's army and his strategic setback on 3 July at Gettysburg. Admittedly, these were blots on his record, but other commanders including Robert E. Lee himself must accept partial blame for them.

The bottom line is that Stuart held his own or won the day at Brandy Station, Aldie, Middleburg, Upperville, Hanover, Hunterstown, and many of the engagements during Lee's retreat to Virginia. And even on 3 July, along the far Union right, Stuart achieved a tactical draw, while suffering far fewer losses than Gregg and Custer. Additionally, the magnitude of his strategic defeat—to which Union troopers attributed much importance in after years—is open to dispute. The plan by which Stuart was to exploit Pickett's charge was a murky, indefinite one. Even had he reached the rear of the Union main line, it is doubtful he would have exercised a decisive influence on the battle. Quite the contrary: Stuart's chosen route suggests that he would have encountered well-entrenched infantry—two divisions of the XII Corps at Spangler's Spring to the north, and the VI Corps in rear of the Round Tops on the south. It seems highly unlikely that these troops would have been overthrown or even demoralized by attacking cavalry, mounted or afoot. In fact, the foot soldiers might have ensured Stuart's destruction, especially if they had teamed with Gregg's horsemen to pincer the Southern cavaliers.

Admittedly, the men of the Cavalry Corps, Army of the Potomac, did exhibit during the Gettysburg campaign qualities their opponents had not attributed to them for the first two years of the war: speed, strength, endurance, and imagination. Especially at Brandy Station, Aldie, Hanover, along Buford's front on 1 July, on Gregg's the next day, and at Boonsboro, Funkstown, and elsewhere during Lee's retreat, the Union troopers demonstrated that they could no longer be taken lightly in battle. This was merely a restatement of a fact they had made obvious the previous March at Kelly's Ford. Yet it would not be until late 1863 and early 1864 that Meade's troopers would demonstrate a consistent superiority—and their triumph would be muted by their knowledge that the test had not been a fair one. For even as the Union horsemen reached the pinnacle of success, their opponents suffered crippling declines in horseflesh and supplies, as well as the loss of Stuart, Chambliss, Jones, Gordon, and other stalwarts killed in action.

More than any other arm of the nineteenth-century army, cavalry was an extension of the abilities and the personalities of the generals who led. Thus, a summary of the campaign accomplishments of upper echelon commanders may provide an index to the performance of their forces.

In the Army of Northern Virginia Stuart has borne for over a century the aura of selfish indifference to the needs of his own army, thanks to his 25 June–2 July ride around the Army of the Potomac. But while his expedition may have been an exercise of poor judgment, Stuart had ample authority to conduct it. Moreover, he left with Lee horsemen sufficient to the main army's reconnaissance, outpost, and skirmishing needs; the army's failure to use these horsemen properly has never been blamed convincingly on the cavalry leader. Furthermore, had Lee and his staff taken steps to ensure cooperation between Stuart and Dick Ewell, the expedition would have become the effective campaign-within-a-campaign Stuart envisioned it to be at the outset.

From Brandy Station to Boonsboro, Stuart displayed the consistent good sense and tactical precision that had been elements of his reputation since the war's earliest days. Though surprised and outmaneuvered on 9 June, he recovered well enough to hold his ground against enemy foot troops as well as horsemen, forcing their retreat before the day ended. His exercise of more remote command throughout the balance of the campaign was equally judicious when he was on the defensive—as at Aldie, Middleburg, Upperville, and Hanover—and when on the offensive, as at Gettysburg, Hagerstown, and Boonsboro. One should not allow Stuart's lack of strategic perception (perhaps best symbolized by the 125 wagons he lugged from Rockville to Gettysburg, at tremendous cost) to detract from his tactical achievements—and especially his inspired counterreconnaissance efforts—throughout the campaign.

Despite contemporary and postwar assertions to the contrary, Stuart's conduct during the campaign does not conform to the image of a vainglorious fop seeking to salvage his reputation from disgrace. Indeed, during the fighting at Aldie, Middleburg, Upperville, Hanover, Hunterstown, and to a large degree at Gettysburg on 3 July, he took a rear seat while his generals made the crucial tactical decisions; nor did he attempt to steal glory after the event. To be sure, he exercised a firm, guiding hand, and was ready to step in whenever needed; but he preferred to allow his subordinates—many of them new to command—to win the acclaim or suffer the criticism their actions merited.

In large degree, his faith in his lieutenants was borne out by their efforts in the field. With a few exceptions (notably his ill-advised counterattack at Hunterstown and his reluctant charges at Gettysburg) Wade Hampton solidified his role as Stuart's strong right arm. Fitz Lee continued his string of quietly competent performances, while Chambliss proved himself a worthy successor to Rooney Lee. The performances of the other brigade leaders were of mixed or poor quality. Grumble Jones did well on most fields, including Brandy Station, Upperville, and Fairfield, but he was responsible for the loss of many supply wagons at Monterey Pass and was at least as much to blame as Beverly Robertson for dawdling in the Shenandoah Valley after Hooker marched north in pursuit of Lee. Of Stuart's original brigade leaders, only Robertson and Albert Jenkins failed to meet standards expected of Confederate cavalry generals. Robertson's conduct throughout the campaign exhibited a stunted intellect, a constitutional slowness, and a tendency to lose his head while all about him were keeping theirs. His lapses at Brandy Station, in the Shenandoah, and on the road to Jack Mountain were virtually inexcusable; they eventually led to his return to North Carolina, where he resumed command of that part of his brigade which had not made the trip north in June.

Meanwhile, Jenkins erred time and again through a deadly combination of indiscipline and stupidity, causing Ewell and his infantry commanders far more trouble than any Yankee they met on the trip from Winchester to Gettysburg. Perhaps Jenkins's greatest contribution to the Confederate invasion was his wounding on 2 July, which allowed the able Milton Ferguson to succeed him prior to the fighting east of Gettysburg. Those others who held temporary brigade command, Colonels Munford and Baker, served as quietly and as skillfully as Ferguson, with the exception of Munford's unconscionable slowness in supporting Stuart's upper line at Brandy Station.

Finally, John Imboden, whose command was so maligned before and during the campaign, did a masterful job in a difficult role. Throughout the invasion he aided Lee's army by confiscating the rations, forage, animals, and supplies it badly needed. Long before he led Lee's wagon train back to Virginia (fighting stoutly against heavy odds at Williamsport), Imboden had fulfilled every campaign objective assigned to him. Though he lay a rough hand on undefended Pennsylvania towns—which brought him a bad press forever after—the Virginia brigadier performed a number of thankless but vital chores with more efficiency than he was ever credited with.

On the Federal side of the campaign ledger, the red ink is more profuse. At the top of the page stands Alfred Pleasonton, who found his true calling only after he became Meade's acting chief of staff during the pursuit of Lee's army. Certainly Pleasonton accomplished little of consequence as a field leader. Through faulty reconnaissance, misplaced objectives, and overconcern for his line of retreat, he squandered opportunities to overthrow Stuart at Brandy Station. On the march to Pennsylvania he fairly won his appelation of "Knight of Romance" by supplying Hooker and Meade with wild speculation, unfounded rumor, and garbled intelligence instead of the timely, accurate information they needed to chart enemy positions and tendencies. Throughout, he seemed more interested in securing promotion and political gain, besmirching the reputations of his associates, and furnishing newspaper copy, than in leading his troops. When his men achieved tactical success, as at Gettysburg on 3 July, it was through no fault of his, for he served far from the scene of action. When he took a more active role in operations, he blundered—as by removing Buford from Meade's left on 2 July and by spreading his forces so widely during Lee's retreat that they failed to bring maximum weight to bear upon the enemy at any point. A paper-shuffler rather than a field leader, Pleasonton seemed to confirm Meade's belief that a cavalry corps commander should concentrate on administrative duties.

His division leaders had good days and bad. John Buford was outstanding through most of the campaign, winning deserved acclaim for his resistance to the Confederate infantry on 1 July and for sizing up Gettysburg as an advantageous place to fight. His difficulties at Upperville were not his fault, while his operations in Maryland from 4 to 14 July were in the main energetic and successsful. Had he had his way, much of Lee's rear guard would have been captured before able to retreat from Falling Waters. Nevertheless, Buford was culpable for failing to press the Rebel left at Brandy Station, for withdrawing his far-from-shattered division from the 2 July fighting, and for failing to overwhelm Imboden's ragtag force at Williamsport.

David Gregg attained greater fame than Buford, primarily because of his defense of the Union right and rear on 3 July. On that field he expertly shifted forces to meet wide-ranging threats and managed his resources so well that at day's end he had a brigade in reserve while Stuart had none, one indicator of victory emphasized in Napoleonic military theory. But Gregg too made his mistakes and had his setbacks. Though he demonstrated combativeness at Brandy Station, he committed his command piecemeal instead of in combination, ensuring its eventual repulse. He fought in similar fashion at Aldie, Middleburg, and Upperville. Rightly or not, he received much criticism for his inability to overtake Stuart's raiders on 29 June, when he tried to march over roads jammed with Union infantry. And if his performance at Gettysburg constituted the high point of his career, the operations immediately afterward marked its nadir, as Gregg's division was fragmented, its elements added to infantry commands or to other cavalry divisions. Relegated to accompanying Irvin Gregg's brigade, he failed to make it an effective part of Meade's plan to harass and impede the Army of Northern Virginia.

Judson Kilpatrick's record in brigade command from 9 to 27 June and in division command during the balance of the campaign is a study in accelerating incompetence. After a vigorous if not highly successful showing at Brandy Station, he performed less capably at Aldie and Upperville. There, as on later fields, he displayed vague notions of where and how best to strike the enemy, a disregard of his men's welfare, a penchant for leading troops into situations from which he abruptly and awkwardly removed them, and (especially at Aldie, Hunterstown, Gettysburg, Hagerstown, and Falling Waters) an unswerving determination to attack on horseback regardless of the conditions. Even on those occasions when he gained tactical success, such as at Hanover, Fairfield Gap, Smithsburg, and Boonsboro, his erratic efforts to exploit such gains negated their value. Just as the cavalry of the Army of the Potomac would be hurt by the death from illness of John Buford late in 1863, it would be aided by Kilpatrick's transfer to the armies of William T. Sherman early the following year.

The performances of the other division leaders who participated in the Gettysburg campaign, Aldred Duffié and Julius Stahel, are perhaps less worthy of comment because these men served at the behest of other commanders. Each suffered from serious flaws: Duffié from an inflexible, hidebound approach to tactics and discipline, Stahel from a constitutional slowness that smacked of sloth. Still, neither was the avowed incompetent that Pleasonton and other native-born generals made him out to be. To a certain extent, both were victims of prejudice and military politics, which cut short their careers in the main theater of the war.

Throughout the Gettysburg campaign, the Confederate cavalry maintained the advantages of leadership and tactical prowess it had enjoyed at the outset. Statistics bear this out: from 9 June to 14 July, the troopers in gray suffered fewer than two thousand casualties, exclusive of Jenkins's and Ferguson's losses, which were not tabulated. At the same time, they inflicted on their foe 3,650 killed, wounded, and missing (though many of the last-named rejoined their regiments for further service). This the Confederates accomplished despite an inferiority in the quality and quantity of weapons, ammunition, equipment, and horseflesh.

Even so, the campaign also demonstrated that while the Southern horsemen had reached the apex of their power, their almost equally proficient enemy was still improving. Later months would reveal Stuart's cavaliers in rapid decline while their counterparts in blue continued to assimilate tactical innovations and to streamline their application of military technology. Shortly after the end of the campaign in the North, the hypothetical probationary period for most of the Union horsemen then in service passed. The result was a cavalryman who appreciated not only the nuances of field service but the possibilities inherent in a cavalry corps organization. Though adopted four months earlier, the corps system for cavalry exhibited its utility only intermittently during the Gettysburg campaign, mainly because the command lacked a leader with enough imagination and ability to employ horsemen in mass. Not until mid-1864 would the concept prove its worth. The result would be so impressive that Lee's horsemen would adopt a corps organization as well.

One advantage held by the Union troopers, manifest throughout the campaign, was their ability to fight mounted and afoot with comparable effectiveness. Proficiency in dismounted fighting was especially evident on 1 and 2 July at Gettysburg, when Buford and Gregg contested Confederate infantry so tenaciously that the latter thought they were fighting foot troops. It was also evident at Hanover on Custer's front, and in Irvin Gregg's sector at Middleburg, as well as during the several engagements in Maryland after 3 July. Meanwhile, the Federals launched wave after wave of mounted attacks at Brandy Station and on the third day at Gettysburg, with much success. On only a few occasions did the Union horsemen charge mounted when fighting afoot was preferable and vice versa; almost every instance was the work of Judson Kilpatrick.

The lessons they learned during the campaign of Gettysburg redounded to the great benefit of the Federal troopers. In after months they became increasingly adept at perceiving whether mounted or dismounted fighting would prevail on a given occasion. Stuart's troopers, by contrast, remained committed to fighting on horseback, without such consistent success. Further than this, the Union cavalry merely needed better leadership. By 1864 it had rid itself of such pernicious influences as Pleasonton and Kilpatrick, had allowed talented young commanders such as Merritt and Custer to mature, and had acquired dynamic new leaders like Philip H. Sheridan and James Harrison Wilson—men capable of employing cavalry in a style that anticipated the Panzer battalions of a later era. It was then that the seeds sown during the Gettysburg campaign bore fruit.

Notes

ABBREVIATIONS USED IN NOTES

ACPF * Appointments, Commissions, and Personal Branch Document Files, NA
B&L * *Battles and Leaders of the Civil War.* 4 vols. (New York, 1887–88)
BP * Bachelder Papers, New Hampshire Historical Society
BRC * Brooke Rawle Collection, HSP
CWTI * *Civil War Times Illustrated.* 24 vols. to date (Harrisburg, Pa., 1962–)
DAB * *Dictionary of American Biography.* 20 vols. (New York, 1928–36)
GNMPL * Gettysburg National Military Park Library
HEHL * Henry E. Huntington Library
HSP * Historical Society of Pennsylvania
JCCW * *Joint Committee on the Conduct of the War.* 3 vols. in 8 (Washington, D.C., 1863–68)
JMSIUS * *Journal of the Military Service Institution of the United States.* 61 vols. (Governors Island,
    N.Y., 1880–1917)
JUSCA * *Journal of the United States Cavalry Association* [also known as the *Cavalry Journal*]. 48 vols.
    (Fort Leavenworth, Kan., 1888–1946)
LC * Library of Congress
MOLLUS * Military Order of the Loyal Legion of the United States
MSS * Papers
NA * National Archives
OR * *War of the Rebellion: A Compilation of the Official Records of the Union and Confederate Armies.* 4
    series, 70 vols. in 128 (Washington, D.C., 1880–1901) [unless otherwise specified, all references
    are to Series I, Volume 27, parts 1–3]
PHCW * *Photographic History of the Civil War.* 10 vols. (New York, 1911)
RG-, E- * Record Group, Entry
SHSP * *Southern Historical Society Papers.* 52 vols. (Richmond, 1876–1959)
TS * Typescript
UML * University of Michigan Library
USAMHI * United States Army Military History Institute
WL * War Library, MOLLUS National Commandery

CHAPTER 1. THE "BEAU SABREUR" AND HIS CAVALIERS

1. Jim Dan Hill, *The Minuteman in Peace and War: A History of the National Guard* (Harrisburg,
Pa., 1964), pp. 45–46.

2. John Hope Franklin, *The Militant South, 1800–1861* (Boston, 1964), pp. 21, 34; *Volunteer Cavalry—The Lessons of a Decade, by a Volunteer Cavalryman* (New York, 1871), pp. 22–23; Mary Lee Stubbs, "Cavalry in the Civil War," p. 57, TS in the Office of the Chief of Military History, Dept. of the Army; H. B. McClellan, *The Life and Campaigns of Maj. Gen. J. E. B. Stuart* (Richmond, 1885), pp. 257–58; Edward K. Eckert and Nicholas J. Amato, eds., *Ten Years in the Saddle: The Memoir of William Woods Averell* (San Rafael, Calif., 1978), p. 333.

3. Allen C. Redwood, "Following Stuart's Feather," *JMSIUS* 49 (1911): 113–14.

4. *Army and Navy Journal*, 22 Apr. 1865.

5. *Daily Richmond Examiner*, 13 May 1864.

6. Theodore Garnett, *J. E. B. Stuart . . . An Address* (New York, 1907), p. 19.

7. George Cary Eggleston, *A Rebel's Recollections* (New York, 1887), p. 110; James Dearing to His Uncle, 24 Sept. 1861, HSP; John Esten Cooke, *Wearing of the Gray* (New York, 1867), p. 668; Gilbert E. Govan and James W. Livingood, eds., *The Haskell Memoirs* (New York, 1960), p. 19. Foreign observers also left favorable portraits of Stuart: Arthur James Lyon Fremantle, *Three Months in the Southern States, April–June 1863* (New York, 1864), p. 286; William Stanley Hoole, ed., *Seven Months in the Rebel States during the North American War, 1863,* by Justus Scheibert (Tuscaloosa, Ala., 1958), p. 39.

8. Ezra J. Warner, *Generals in Gray: Lives of the Confederate Commanders* (Baton Rouge, La., 1959), pp. 296–97; Curt Anders, *Fighting Confederates* (New York, 1968), pp. 151–52; *DAB*, 18:170–71; Mark Mayo Boatner III, *The Civil War Dictionary* (New York, 1959), pp. 812–13; McClellan, *Life and Campaigns of Stuart*, pp. 1–31.

9. McClellan, *Life and Campaigns of Stuart*, pp. 32–45; John W. Thomason, Jr., *Jeb Stuart* (New York, 1934), pp. 62–133; Richard Lee Tripp, "Cavalry Reconnaissance in the Army of Northern Virginia: J. E. B. Stuart's Cavalry, 1861–64," pp. 45–47, Duke Univ. Lib.; Anders, *Fighting Confederates*, pp. 155–58.

10. McClellan, *Life and Campaigns of Stuart*, pp. 52–71; Thomason, *Jeb Stuart*, pp. 134–55; Douglas Southall Freeman, *Lee's Lieutenants: A Study in Command*, 3 vols. (New York, 1942–44), 1:275–302; Richard Wormser, *The Yellowlegs: The Story of the United States Cavalry* (Garden City, N.Y., 1966), pp. 154–59.

11. *New York Times*, 21 June 1862.

12. McClellan, *Life and Campaigns of Stuart*, pp. 94–95; Cooke, *Wearing of the Gray*, p. 201; Thomason, *Jeb Stuart*, pp. 231–36; Thomas Weber, *The Northern Railroads in the Civil War, 1861–1865* (New York, 1952), p. 147.

13. McClellan, *Life and Campaigns of Stuart*, pp. 136–66; W. W. Blackford, *War Years with Jeb Stuart* (New York, 1945), pp. 164–81.

14. Edward G. Longacre, "Stuart's Dumfries Raid," *CWTI* 15 (July 1976): 18–26; Burke Davis, *Jeb Stuart, the Last Cavalier* (New York, 1957), pp. 261–63; McClellan, *Life and Campaigns of Stuart*, pp. 196–202.

15. Fremantle, *Three Months in the Southern States*, p. 286.

16. McClellan, *Life and Campaigns of Stuart*, pp. 247–56; John S. Mosby, *Stuart's Cavalry in the Gettysburg Campaign* (New York, 1908), pp. x–xii, xvi–xxiii; *OR*, I, 25, pt. 1, pp. 887–89; pt. 2, pp. 769, 792.

17. Manly Wade Wellman, *Giant in Gray: A Biography of Wade Hampton of South Carolina* (New York, 1949), pp. 39–42; Nash K. Burger and John K. Bettersworth, *South of Appomattox* (New York, 1959), pp. 240–43; *DAB*, 8:213–14; Warner, *Generals in Gray*, pp. 122–23.

18. Wellman, *Giant in Gray*, pp. 83, 102–3; Longacre, "Stuart's Dumfries Raid," 18; Boatner, *Civil War Dictionary*, pp. 370–71.

19. Warner, *Generals in Gray*, p. 178; *DAB*, 11:103–5; T. F. Rodenbough, "Some Cavalry Leaders," *PHCW*, 4:277, 286, 288; Eckert and Amato, *Ten Years in the Saddle*, p. 49; John S. Wise, *The End of an Era* (Boston, 1899), pp. 334–36.

20. *OR*, pt 2, p. 692. In 1884, however, Munford recalled that Lee missed action at the outset of the invasion as result of being incapacitated by a kick from a horse or mule: George N. Bliss, "A Review of Aldie," *Maine Bugle* 1 (1894): 131.

21. Boatner, *Civil War Dictionary*, p. 574; Holmes Conrad, "The Cavalry Corps of the Army of

Northern Virginia," *PHCW*, 4:87. The most comprehensive biography of Munford is Robert N. Thomas, "Brigadier General Thomas T. Munford and the Confederacy," Duke Univ. Lib.

22. Wise, *End of an Era*, pp. 333–34.

23. *DAB*, 11:134; Warner, *Generals in Gray*, p. 184; Boatner, *Civil War Dictionary*, pp. 477–78. Another favorable view of Rooney Lee is in James L. Morrison, Jr., ed., *The Memoirs of Henry Heth* (Westport, Conn., 1974), p. 142.

24. In May 1863 the brigades of Hampton and the two Lees (minus two regiments) totaled in mounted effectives 376 officers and 4,695 troopers: *OR*, I, 25, pt. 2, p. 823n.

25. Warner, *Generals in Gray*, pp. 166–67; Boatner, *Civil War Dictionary*, p. 444; Blackford, *War Years with Jeb Stuart*, pp. 51–52; McClellan, *Life and Campaigns of Stuart*, pp. 319–21. Examples of Grumble's testiness and his ability to alienate superiors are found in Jones to John Letcher, 29 Apr., 11 May, 1861, HSP.

26. *DAB*, 9:460–61; Haviland H. Abbot, "General John D. Imboden," *West Virginia History* 21 (1960): 88–103; Boatner, *Civil War Dictionary*, p. 423; Warner, *Generals in Gray*, p. 147; *OR*, pt. 3, p. 985.

27. *OR*, pt. 3, pp. 865–66, 878, 905–6, 924; Douglas Southall Freeman, *R. E. Lee: A Biography*, 4 vols. (New York, 1934–35), 3:14, 29; Wilbur S. Nye, *Here Come the Rebels* (Baton Rouge, La., 1965), p. 49.

28. Boatner, *Civil War Dictionary*, p. 435; Warner, *Generals in Gray*, p. 154; *DAB*, 10:43–44; Freeman, *R. E. Lee*, 3:14, 29, 33; Nye, *Here Come the Rebels*, pp. 142–43; *OR*, I, 25, pt. 2, p. 804; 27, pt. 3, p. 879; Robert E. Lee to J. E. B. Stuart, 2 June 1863, Stuart MSS, HEHL. Originally (as of 25 May 1863) Jenkins led six regiments and three battalions: *OR*, I, 25, pt. 2, pp. 823n., 826n. During the Gettysburg campaign, three of these units were given to Maj. Gen. Samuel Jones for service in his Department of Western Virginia: *OR*, pt. 2, pp. 812–13; pt. 3, pp. 878, 880.

29. *OR*, pt. 3, p. 1006; Bliss, "A Review of Aldie," 128; Warner, *Generals in Gray*, pp. 259–60; Boatner, *Civil War Dictionary*, p. 702; Blackford, *War Years with Jeb Stuart*, p. 229; Mosby, *Stuart's Cavalry*, pp. 215–16; Robert E. Lee to J. E. B. Stuart, 2 June 1863, Stuart MSS, HEHL. Two of Robertson's remaining three regiments had been left in the Tarheel State, while the third was stationed along the Blackwater River in southern Virginia; the two regiments he brought to Lee's army numbered (as of 25 May 1863) sixty-seven officers and 1,068 men, mounted effectives: *OR*, I, 25, pt. 2, pp. 823 and n., 825n., 826nn.

30. Edwin B. Coddington, *The Gettysburg Campaign: A Study in Command* (New York, 1968), p. 16.

31. Boatner, *Civil War Dictionary*, p. 630; Cooke, *Wearing of the Gray*, pp. 116–29; Blackford, *War Years with Jeb Stuart*, pp. 200–202.

32. B. F. Heitman, comp., *Historical Register and Dictionary of the United States Army*, 2 vols. (Washington, D.C., 1903), 1:205; Channing Price to Virginia E. Price, 8, 24 Apr. 1863, Price MSS, Virginia Hist. Soc.; McClellan, *Life and Campaigns of Stuart*, p. 41.

33. Burke Davis, ed., *I Rode with Jeb Stuart: The Life and Campaigns of Major General J. E. B. Stuart*, by H. B. McClellan (Bloomington, Ind., 1958), pp. v–viii; *DAB*, 11:585.

34. Blackford, *War Years with Jeb Stuart*, pp. ix–xiii, 3–8; Davis, *Jeb Stuart, the Last Cavalier*, pp. 54, 59.

35. Philip Van Doren Stern, ed., *Wearing of the Gray*, by John Esten Cooke (Bloomington, Ind., 1959), pp. xi–xviii; Boatner, *Civil War Dictionary*, p. 173; Davis, *Jeb Stuart, the Last Cavalier*, pp. 16, 37; *DAB*, 4:385–86.

36. Boatner, *Civil War Dictionary*, pp. 880–81; Ella Lonn, *Foreigners in the Confederacy* (Chapel Hill, N.C., 1940), pp. 171–74; Thomason, *Jeb Stuart*, pp. 141–42; Blackford, *War Years with Jeb Stuart*, pp. 90–91.

37. Grady McWhiney and Perry D. Jamieson, *Attack and Die: Civil War Military Tactics and the Southern Heritage* (University, Ala., 1982), pp. 126–39; John K. Mahon, "Civil War Infantry Assault Tactics," *Military Affairs* 25 (1961): 67–68.

38. Richard B. Harwell, ed., *Cities and Camps of the Confederate States*, by Fitzgerald Ross (Urbana, Ill., 1958), p. 33; R. A. Preston, ed., "A Letter from a British Military Observer of the American Civil War," *Military Affairs* 16 (1952–53): 52.

39. *Volunteer Cavalry—The Lessons of a Decade*, p. 6; Harwell, *Cities and Camps*, p. 33.

40. *Pennsylvania at Gettysburg*, 2 vols. (Harrisburg, Pa., 1893), 2:779.

41. Mahon, "Civil War Infantry Assault Tactics," 67–68.

42. Redwood, "Following Stuart's Feather," 117; Hoole, *Seven Months in the Rebel States*, p. 37; Blackford, *War Years with Jeb Stuart*, p. 221.

43. James Parker, "Mounted and Dismounted Action of Cavalry," *JMSIUS* 39 (1906): 382, 386–87.

44. Jay Luvaas, "Cavalry Lessons of the Civil War," *CWTI* 6 (Jan. 1968): 25.

45. Redwood, "Following Stuart's Feather," 116–17.

46. Abner Doubleday, *Chancellorsville and Gettysburg* (New York, 1886), p. 83.

47. For a compilation of the factors that governed Lee's campaign planning, see Coddington, *Gettysburg Campaign*, pp. 3–11, and Nye, *Here Come the Rebels*, pp. 3–7.

48. McClellan, *Life and Campaigns of Stuart*, pp. 257–60; Coddington, *Gettysburg Campaign*, pp. 16–17.

49. *OR*, I, 25, pt. 2, p. 793; pt. 3, p. 873.

50. Freeman, *R. E. Lee*, 3:33.

51. Mosby, *Stuart's Cavalry*, p. 5.

52. George M. Neese, *Three Years in the Confederate Horse Artillery* (New York, 1911), p. 166; Ephraim Bowman to His Father, 6 June 1863, Bowman MSS, Univ. of Virginia Lib.

53. McClellan, *Life and Campaigns of Stuart*, p. 261. Jones's brigade reached Culpeper between 4 and 7 June, part of it in time for Stuart's review on the fifth: Jasper Hawse Diary, 7 June 1863, Univ. of Virginia Lib.

54. Freeman, *Lee's Lieutenants*, 3:2.

55. Neese, *Confederate Horse Artillery*, pp. 166–68; Heros von Borcke, *Memoirs of the Confederate War for Independence*, 2 vols. (New York, 1938), 2:265; Festus P. Summers, ed., *A Borderland Confederate* (Westport, Conn., 1973), p. 71.

56. Neese, *Confederate Horse Artillery*, p. 168; Glenn Tucker, "Jeb Stuart Learned on Fleetwood Hill Federals Could Fight on Horseback Too," *Civil War Times* 2 (Dec. 1960): 6; Blackford, *War Years with Jeb Stuart*, p. 212.

57. von Borcke, *Memoirs*, 2:267; Clifford Dowdey and Louis H. Manarin, eds., *The Wartime Papers of R. E. Lee* (Boston, 1961), p. 507; Leiper M. Robinson Memoirs, p. 2, Virginia Hist. Soc.; Cooke, *Wearing of the Gray*, pp. 226–27; Summers, *Borderland Confederate*, p. 71.

58. Daniel A. Grimsley, *Battles in Culpeper County, Virginia* (Culpeper, Va., 1900), p. 8; John N. Opie, *A Rebel Cavalryman with Lee, Stuart, and Jackson* (Chicago, 1899), p. 145.

59. Grimsley, *Battles in Culpeper County*, p. 8; Leiper M. Robinson Memoirs, p. 2; U. R. Brooks, *Butler and His Cavalry in the War of Secession, 1861–1865* (Columbia, S.C., 1909), pp. 150–51; Freeman, *R. E. Lee*, 3:30; Freeman, *Lee's Lieutenants*, 3:4.

60. McClellan, *Life and Campaigns of Stuart*, p. 262; William H. Price, *The Battle of Brandy Station* (Vienna, Va., 1963), p. 2; William V. Kennedy, "The Cavalry Battle at Brandy Station," *Armor* 65 (1956): 28–29; Fairfax Downey, *Clash of Cavalry: The Battle of Brandy Station, June 9, 1863* (New York, 1959), pp. 84–86; *OR*, pt. 2, pp. 680, 727.

CHAPTER 2. THE "KNIGHT OF ROMANCE" AND HIS DRAGOONS

1. Roy P. Stonesifer, Jr., "The Long Hard Road: Union Cavalry in the Gettysburg Campaign," p. 3, Pennsylvania State Univ. Lib.; James M. Merrill, *Spurs to Glory: The Story of the United States Cavalry* (Chicago, 1966), p. 123.

2. Charles D. Rhodes, "The Federal Cavalry: Its Organization and Equipment," *PHCW*, 4:46–50; *The Reminiscences of Carl Schurz*, 3 vols. (New York, 1907–8), 2:230–31; Augustus P. Green Memoirs, p. 65, New-York Hist. Soc.; Walter Kempster, "The Eary Days of Our Cavalry, in the Army of the Potomac," *War Papers: Wisconsin MOLLUS*, 3 (1903): 65; *Thirty-sixth Anniversary and Reunion of the Tenth New York Cavalry Veterans* (Homer, N.Y., 1897), pp. 43–47. For a defense of

Winfield Scott's policy on recruiting volunteer cavalry, see Francis Colburn Adams, *The Story of a Trooper* (New York, 1865), pp. 27–28.

3. *Statutes, 1859–1863* (Washington, D.C., 1863), 12:279–80; William H. Carter, "The Sixth Regiment of [United States] Cavalry," *Maine Bugle* 3 (1896): 232; Mary Lee Stubbs, "Cavalry in the Civil War," pp. 58–59, TS in the Office of the Chief of Military History, Dept. of the Army.

4. Thomas F. Thiele, "The Evolution of Cavalry in the American Civil War, 1861–1863," p. 32, UML; Merrill, *Spurs to Glory*, p. 123.

5. George T. Denison, *A History of Cavalry from the Earliest Times* (London, 1913), p. 359; D. M. Gilmore, "Cavalry: Its Use and Value as Illustrated by Reference to the Engagements of Kelly's Ford and Gettysburg," *Glimpses of the Nation's Struggle: Minnesota MOLLUS*, 2 (1890): 39.

6. *Volunteer Cavalry—The Lessons of a Decade, by a Volunteer Cavalryman* (New York, 1871), p. 24.

7. *JCCW*, 1868, pt. 2, p. 4; James Harrison Wilson, *Under the Old Flag: Recollections of Military Operations*, 2 vols. (New York, 1912), 2:9; Hampton S. Thomas, *Some Personal Reminiscences of Service in the Cavalry of the Army of the Potomac* (Philadelphia, 1889), p. 2; Moses Harris, "The Union Cavalry," *War Papers: Wisconsin MOLLUS*, 1 (1891): 350–51.

8. Silas D. Wesson Diary, 1–2 July 1862, USAMHI; Reuben T. Prentice to "Dear Friend," 16 July 1862, Prentice MSS, Illinois State Hist. Lib.; James B. Turner to His Wife, 18 Aug. 1862, Turner MSS, Illinois State Hist. Lib.; William E. Miller, *War History: Operations of the Union Cavalry on the Peninsula* (Carlisle, Pa., 1908), pp. 9–12.

9. *JCCW*, 1868, pt. 2, p. 6; Charles D. Rhodes, *History of the Cavalry of the Army of the Potomac* (Kansas City, Mo., 1900), p. 24; "Letters of a Civil War Surgeon," *Indiana Magazine of History* 27 (1931): 149; David H. Morgan to His Mother, 18 Sept. 1862, Morgan MSS, Irwin L. Park; John B. McIntosh to His Wife, 19 Sept. 1862, McIntosh MSS, Brown Univ. Lib.; S. L. Gracey, *Annals of the Sixth Pennsylvania Cavalry* (Philadelphia, 1868), p. 100; Charles D. Rhodes, "Cavalry Battles and Charges," *PHCW*, 4:231.

10. Ezra J. Warner, *Generals in Blue: Lives of the Union Commanders* (Baton Rouge, La., 1964), p. 481; Edward J. Stackpole, *Chancellorsville: Lee's Greatest Battle* (Harrisburg, Pa., 1958), p. 26; George A. Custer, "War Memoirs," *Galaxy* 21 (1876): 817; Mark Mayo Boatner III, *The Civil War Dictionary* (New York, 1959), p. 801.

11. Frederic Denison, *Sabres and Spurs: The First Regiment Rhode Island Cavalry in the Civil War, 1861–1865* (Central Falls, R.I., 1876), pp. 208–13; Frank W. Hess, "The First Cavalry Battle at Kelly's Ford, Va.," *Maine Bugle* 3 (July 1893): 3–16; 3 (Oct. 1893): 8–22; Benjamin W. Crowninshield and D. H. L. Gleason, *A History of the First Regiment of Massachusetts Cavalry Volunteers* (Boston, 1891), pp. 115–18; Stackpole, *Chancellorsville*, pp. 48–53.

12. *OR*, I, 25, pt. 1, pp. 804, 1047, 1057–65; "Stoneman's Raid in the Chancellorsville Campaign," *B&L*, 3:152–53; The Comte de Paris, *History of the Civil War in America*, 4 vols. (Philadelphia, 1875–88), 3:115–21.

13. *OR*, I, 25, pt. 1, pp. 1046–48; H. B. McClellan, *The Life and Campaigns of Maj. Gen. J. E. B. Stuart* (Richmond, 1885), p. 233; Douglas Southall Freeman, *Lee's Lieutenants: A Study in Command*, 3 vols. (New York, 1942–44), 2:539–40.

14. Augustus C. Hamlin, *The Battle of Chancellorsville* (Bangor, Me., 1896), pp. 90–103; *JCCW*, 1868, pt. 2, pp. 7–8; Alfred Pleasonton, "The Successes and Failures of Chancellorsville," *B&L*, 3:177–80, 180n., 181.

15. *OR*, pt. 3, p. 11 and n. For unintentionally humorous reading on Stoneman's physical condition (specifically, on his efforts to increase his pension by having his piles declared a war wound), see G. L. Pancoast to HQ, Army of the Potomac, 20 May 1863, Stoneman's General's Papers, RG-94, E-159, NA. See also his Certificate of Disability, 8 June 1863, Stoneman's ACPF, RG-94, NA.

16. *OR*, I, 19, pt. 2, pp. 39–40; Edward G. Longacre, "Alfred Pleasonton: 'The Knight of Romance,'" *CWTI* 13 (Dec. 1974): 15–17.

17. *New York Tribune*, 24 June 1863; Longacre, "Alfred Pleasonton," 11–13.

18. Boatner, *Civil War Dictionary*, p. 275; Warner, *Generals in Blue*, p. 373; *DAB*, 15:8.

19. Paul Fatout, ed., *Letters of a Civil War Surgeon* (Lafayette, Ind., 1961), p. 152; Worthington Chauncey Ford, ed., *A Cycle of Adams Letters, 1861–1865*, 2 vols. (Boston, 1920), 2:8.

20. Edward W. Emerson, *Life and Letters of Charles Russell Lowell* (Boston, 1907), p. 279; Frank Aretas Haskell, *The Battle of Gettysburg* (Boston, 1908), p. 134; A. V. Kautz to Seth Williams, 12 Sept. 1862, Pleasonton's General's Papers, RG-94, E-159, NA.

21. Jennings C. Wise, *The Long Arm of Lee: The History of the Artillery of the Army of Northern Virginia*, 2 vols. (Lynchburg, Va., 1915), 2:594; Ford, *Cycle of Adams Letters*, 2:8; A. R. Hancock, *Reminiscences of Winfield Scott Hancock* (New York, 1887), pp. 182–83.

22. From 22 May to 11 June, 1863, Buford temporarily commanded Pleasonton's division and (for part of that period) Gregg's division as well. During this time, however, his sole permanent command was the Reserve Brigade: *OR*, I, 25, pt. 2, p. 584n.; 27, pt. 3, p. 64.

23. Warner, *Generals in Blue*, pp. 52–53; Fletcher Pratt, *Eleven Generals: Studies in American Command* (New York, 1949), pp. 101–2; Russell F. Weigley, "John Buford—A Personality Profile," *CWTI* 5 (June 1966): 15–19; Kenneth P. Williams, *Lincoln Finds a General: A Military Study of the Civil War*, 5 vols. (New York, 1949–59), 1:325–26; T. F. Rodenbough, "Some Cavalry Leaders," *PHCW*, 4:267, 270, 272, 274. The most comprehensive biography of Buford is Frank B. Borries, Jr., "General John Buford, Civil War Union Cavalryman," Univ. of Kentucky Lib.

24. *DAB*, 3:243; Allan Nevins, ed., *A Diary of Battle: The Personal Journals of Colonel Charles S. Wainwright, 1861–1865* (New York, 1962), pp. 309, 465; James A. Bell to Gusta Ann Hallock, 11 July 1863, Bell MSS, HEHL; George R. Agassiz, ed., *Meade's Headquarters, 1863–1865: Letters of Colonel Theodore Lyman from the Wilderness to Appomattox* (Boston, 1922), p. 21.

25. Russell F. Weigley, "David McMurtrie Gregg: A Personality Profile," *CWTI* 1 (Nov. 1962): 11–12; *New York Tribune*, 24 June 1863; Warner, *Generals in Blue*, pp. 187–88; *DAB*, 7:596; Elmer W. Gray, "Major General David McMurtrie Gregg: Unsung Hero of Gettysburg," *Historical Review of Berks County* 27 (1962): 69; Henry C. Meyer, *Civil War Experiences under Bayard, Gregg, Kilpatrick, Custer, Raulston, and Newberry, 1862, 1863, 1864* (New York, 1911), p. 97.

26. Alphonso D. Rockwell, *Rambling Recollections: An Autobiography* (New York, 1920), p. 164. The most comprehensive biography of Gregg is David McMurtrie Gregg, Jr., "Brevet Major General David McMurtrie Gregg," TS in Gregg MSS, LC.

27. Denison, *Sabres and Spurs*, p. 102; Warner, *Generals in Blue*, pp. 131–32; Rhodes, "Cavalry Battles and Charges," 233; Boatner, *Civil War Dictionary*, p. 250; George N. Bliss, *Duffié and the Monument to His Memory* (Providence, R.I., 1890), pp. 5–7; Ella Lonn, *Foreigners in the Union Army and Navy* (Baton Rouge, La., 1951), pp. 207–8; Ford, *Cycle of Adams Letters*, 2:22.

28. Alfred Pleasonton to John F. Farnsworth, 23 June 1863, Pleasonton MSS, LC.

29. Bruce Catton, *Glory Road: The Bloody Route from Fredericksburg to Gettysburg* (Garden City, N.Y., 1952), p. 158; "Letters of a Civil War Surgeon," 154; E. R. Hagemann, ed., *Fighting Rebels and Redskins: Experiences in Army Life of Colonel George B. Sanford, 1861–1892* (Norman, Okla., 1969), pp. 147–48; David S. Sparks, ed., *Inside Lincoln's Army: The Diary of Marsena Rudolph Patrick, Provost Marshal General, Army of the Potomac* (New York, 1964), p. 256; Henry Norton, *A Sketch of the 8th N.Y. Cavalry: Unwritten History of the Rebellion* (Norwich, N.Y., 1888), p. 26.

30. Warner, *Generals in Blue*, pp. 123–24; *DAB*, 5:263; *New York Times*, 7 Apr. 1878; Hillman Hall to President Abraham Lincoln, n.d. [1862], Devin's ACPF, RG-94, NA; Samuel H. Bradley, *Recollections of Army Life* (n.p., 1913), p. 14. A battalion of Devin's 6th New York was on detached duty at Fort Monroe, Virginia, under Major General John A. Dix, at this time: *OR*, pt. 3, p. 451; Hillman A. Hall, W. B. Besley, and Gilbert G. Wood, comps., *History of the Sixth New York Cavalry* (Worcester, Mass., 1908), pp. 143–44.

31. George F. Price, comp., *Across the Continent with the Fifth Cavalry* (New York, 1883), pp. 331–34; *Official Army Register for 1863* (Washington, D.C., 1863), pp. 17–18, 21–22.

32. Samuel P. Bates, *History of Pennsylvania Volunteers, 1861–5*, 5 vols. (Harrisburg, Pa., 1869–71), 2:741; Frank H. Taylor, *Philadelphia in the Civil War* (Philadelphia, 1913), p. 162 and n.

33. B. F. Heitman, comp., *Historical Register and Dictionary of the United States Army*, 2 vols. (Washington, D.C., 1903), 1:1029; Rhodes, "Cavalry Battles and Charges," 225; Don E. Alberts,

"General Wesley Merritt, Nineteenth Century Cavalryman," pp. 42, 59, 72, Univ. of New Mexico Lib. Whiting was restored to the rank of major in the 3rd U.S. Cavalry after the war: Price, *Across the Continent*, p. 334.

34. *DAB*, 3:583–84; Lonn, *Foreigners in the Union*, p. 242; *New York Times*, 22 Nov. 1904; Crowninshield and Gleason, *First Massachusetts Cavalry*, pp. 307–8.

35. James Grant Wilson and John Fiske, eds., *Appleton's Cyclopaedia of American Biography*, 7 vols. (New York, 1887–1900), 2:759; John Howard Brown, ed., *The Cyclopaedia of American Biography*, 7 vols. (Boston, 1897–1903), 3:408; *The National Cyclopaedia of American Biography*, 63 vols. to date. (New York and Clifton, N.J., 1892–   ), 10:497; *Pennsylvania at Gettysburg*, 2 vols. (Harrisburg, Pa., 1893), 2:845.

36. Edward G. Longacre, "Judson Kilpatrick," *CWTI* 10 (Apr. 1971): 25–29; G. Wayne King, "General Judson Kilpatrick," *New Jersey History* 91 (1973): 35–52; Warner, *Generals in Blue*, 266; *DAB*, 9:374–75.

37. Frank A. Flower, *Edwin McMasters Stanton: The Autocrat of Rebellion, Emancipation, and Reconstruction* (Akron, 1905), p. 133; *House Report 2* (37th Cong., 2nd Sess., 17 Dec. 1861), Testimony, pp. 171–88, 460–61; Theophilus Gaines to Edwin M. Stanton, 13 Jan. 1863, Kilpatrick's ACPF, RG-94, NA; William E. Doster, *Lincoln and Episodes of the Civil War* (New York, 1915), p. 85.

38. Longacre, "Judson Kilpatrick," 33; Nevins, *Diary of Battle*, p. 265; James H. Kidd, *Personal Recollections of a Cavalryman with Custer's Michigan Cavalry Brigade* (Ionia, Mich., 1908), pp. 164–65; Sparks, *Inside Lincoln's Army*, p. 347; Agassiz, *Meade's Headquarters*, p. 79; Ford, *Cycle of Adams Letters*, 2:44–45. The most comprehensive biography of Kilpatrick is G. Wayne King, "The Civil War Career of Hugh Judson Kilpatrick," Univ. of South Carolina Lib.

39. Edward G. Longacre, "Sir Percy Wyndham," *CWTI* 7 (Dec. 1968): 12–17; Lonn, *Foreigners in the Union*, pp. 293–94; Samuel Toombs, *New Jersey Troops in the Gettysburg Campaign* (Orange, N.J., 1888), pp. 402–3; Henry R. Pyne, *The History of the First New Jersey Cavalry* (Trenton, N.J., 1871), p. 24.

40. Earl Schenck Miers, ed., *Ride to War: The History of the First New Jersey Cavalry* (New Brunswick, N.J., 1961), pp. xiii–xvii; Walter S. Newhall to "My Dear George," 2 Oct. 1863, Newhall MSS, HSP; Lillian Rea, ed., *War Record and Personal Reminiscences of Walter Raleigh Robbins* (Chicago, 1923), pp. 12–13.

41. *OR*, I, 25, pt. 2, pp. 584–85; I, 27, pt. 3, pp. 11–12; Boatner, *Civil War Dictionary*, pp. 634, 703; O. E. Hunt, "Federal Artillery and Artillerymen," *PHCW*, 5:37.

42. *OR*, I, 25, pt. 2, p. 585; Boatner, *Civil War Dictionary*, p. 839; *DAB*, 17:529–30.

43. "The Opposing Forces at Gettysburg, Pa.," *B&L*, 3:437; *OR*, pt. 3, pp. 373, 376; James C. Hazlett, "The 3-Inch Ordnance Rifle," *CWTI* 7 (Dec. 1968): 33–35; Warren Ripley, *Artillery and Ammunition of the Civil War* (New York, 1970), pp. 161–64; Fairfax Downey, *The Guns at Gettysburg* (New York, 1958), pp. 10, 14, 262n.–63n.

44. Warner, *Generals in Blue*, pp. 108–9; *DAB*, 5:7–9; Agassiz, *Meade's Headquarters*, p. 17; Catherine S. Crary, ed., *Dear Belle: Letters from a Cadet & Officer to His Sweetheart, 1858–1865* (Middletown, Conn., 1965), pp. 42, 107, 214–15; Marguerite Merington, ed., *The Custer Story: The Life and Intimate Letters of General George A. Custer and His Wife Elizabeth* (New York, 1950), pp. 4–42.

45. Abner Hard, *History of the Eighth Cavalry Regiment, Illinois Volunteers, during the Great Rebellion* (Aurora, Ill., 1868), pp. 56, 73–76; Heitman, *Historical Register and Dictionary*, 1:413; Faculty Minutes, University of Michigan, 3 May 1858, TS in "Elon J. Farnsworth" file, GNMPL; Boatner, *Civil War Dictionary*, p. 275; Warner, *Generals in Blue*, pp. 148–49; *DAB*, 6:284.

46. Thomas Hinds, *Tales of War Times* (Watertown, N.Y., 1904), p. 18; Boatner, *Civil War Dictionary*, pp. 544–45; *DAB*, 11:572–74; Warner, *Generals in Blue*, p. 321; Rodenbough, "Some Cavalry Leaders," 271, 276, 278.

47. "Letters of a Civil War Surgeon," 162; James Albert Clark, *The Making of a Volunteer Cavalryman: MOLLUS Commandery of the District of Columbia War Paper 70* (Washington, D.C., 1907), p. 27; Kidd, *Personal Recollections*, pp. 237–38. The most comprehensive biography of Merritt is Don E. Alberts, *Brandy Station to Manila Bay: A Biography of General Wesley Merritt* (Austin, Tex., 1980).

48. Boatner, *Civil War Dictionary*, p. 218; William Harding Carter, *From Yorktown to Santiago with the Sixth U.S. Cavalry* (Baltimore, 1900), pp. 82–83.

49. T. F. Rodenbough, "Cavalry of the Civil War: Its Evolution and Influence," *PHCW*, 4:20, 22; Weigley, "John Buford," 15.

50. Stephen Z. Starr, "Cold Steel: The Saber and the Union Cavalry," *Civil War History* 11 (1965): 142; Rhodes, *Cavalry of the Army of the Potomac*, p. 7; Rhodes, "The Federal Cavalry: Its Organization and Equipment," 60, 62; Merrill, *Spurs to Glory*, p. 123.

51. Edward P. Tobie, *History of the First Maine Cavalry, 1861–1865* (Boston, 1887), p. 17; Charles H. Greenleaf to His Parents, 7 Dec. 1861, 24 Feb. 1862, Greenleaf MSS, Connecticut Hist. Soc.

52. Charles E. Lewis, *With the First [New York] Dragoons in Virginia* (New York, n.d.), pp. 63–64; Pyne, *First New Jersey Cavalry*, p. 55.

53. Fitz John Porter, "Hanover Court House and Gaines's Mill," *B&L*, 2:340–41; Philip St. George Cooke, "The Charge of Cooke's Cavalry at Gaines's Mill," *B&L*, 2:344–46; Joseph P. Cullen, *The Peninsula Campaign, 1862: McClellan & Lee Struggle for Richmond* (Harrisburg, Pa., 1973), pp. 118–19; Alberts, "General Wesley Merritt," 39–43; Rhodes, "Cavalry Battles and Charges," 220–25; Miller, *War History*, pp. 7–8.

54. Catton, *Glory Road*, pp. 245–46; Francis A. Lord, "Union Cavalry Equipment," *CWTI* 1 (Feb. 1963): 37; Crowninshield and Gleason, *First Massachusetts Cavalry*, p. 129; *Army and Navy Journal*, 14 Nov. 1863.

55. Alfred E. Bates and Edward J. McClernand, "The Second Regiment of Cavalry," *The Army of the United States: Historical Sketches of Staff and Line* (New York, 1896), p. 178; Ford, *Cycle of Adams Letters*, 2:6–7.

56. Rhodes, "Federal Cavalry: Its Organization and Equipment," 58, 62, 64; *History of the Eleventh Pennsylvania Volunteer Cavalry* (Philadelphia, 1902), pp. 22–23; Lord, "Union Cavalry Equipment," 37.

57. Rhodes, *Cavalry of the Army of the Potomac*, pp. 74, 80; Russell F. Weigley, *Quartermaster General of the Union Army: A Biography of M. C. Meigs* (New York, 1959), pp. 256–57; *OR*, I, 25, pt. 2, pp. 533–34; 27, pt. 3, p. 93.

58. Lord, "Union Cavalry Equipment," 37; *Volunteer Cavalry—The Lessons of a Decade*, p. 7; Rhodes, "Federal Cavalry: Its Organization and Equipment," 56; Jack Coggins, *Arms and Equipment of the Civil War* (Garden City, N.Y., 1962), pp. 54–59.

59. Boatner, *Civil War Dictionary*, pp. 766–68; Edwin B. Coddington, *The Gettysburg Campaign: A Study in Command* (New York, 1968), pp. 258–59, 680n.; Fred A. Shannon, *The Organization and Administration of the Union Army, 1861–1865*, 2 vols. (Cleveland, 1928), 1:130–33; *Volunteer Cavalry—The Lessons of a Decade*, pp. 15–16; Carl L. Davis, *Arming the Union: Small Arms in the Civil War* (Port Washington, N.Y., 1973), pp. 77–86, 120–25, 154–57; William B. Edwards, *Civil War Guns* (Harrisburg, Pa., 1962), pp. 110–32, 179–89, 197–203, 273–335.

60. Edwards, *Civil War Guns*, pp. 144–57, 212–16, 305–17; Rhodes, *Cavalry of the Army of the Potomac*, p. 7; Shannon, *Organization and Administration of the Union Army*, 1:141; Davis, *Arming the Union*, pp. 89–94; Robert V. Bruce, *Lincoln and the Tools of War* (Indianapolis, 1956), pp. 113–16; Ralph E. Arnold, "Christopher Spencer's Civil War Repeater," *The Gun Report* 18 (Apr. 1973): 18; William G. Adams, Jr., "Spencers at Gettysburg: Fact or Fiction?" *Military Affairs* 29 (1965): 41–42, 56. The most comprehensive source on the Spencer repeater is J. O. Buckeridge, *Lincoln's Choice* (Harrisburg, Pa., 1956).

61. *OR*, I, 25, pt. 2, pp. 528, 531; Coddington, *Gettysburg Campaign*, p. 623n.

62. Wilbur S. Nye, *Here Come the Rebels* (Baton Rouge, La., 1965), pp. 30–32; *OR*, I, 25, pt. 2, pp. 480, 536, 593.

63. Nye, *Here Come the Rebels*, pp. 32–33; *OR*, I, 25, pt. 2, pp. 566–67, 570–71.

64. Nye, *Here Come the Rebels*, pp. 33–36; *OR*, pt. 3, pp. 5–8, 12–14; *New York Times*, 10 June 1863.

65. Nye, *Here Come the Rebels*, pp. 45–48; Coddington, *Gettysburg Campaign*, pp. 54, 618n.;

John S. Mosby, *Stuart's Cavalry in the Gettysburg Campaign* (New York, 1908), pp. 9–16; E. D. Anderson, "Cavalry Operations in the Gettysburg Campaign," p. 23, Army War College Study, TS in USAMHI; *OR*, pt. 3, pp. 27–28, 30, 34–35, 45; George W. Barbour Diary, 8 June 1863, UML; George Harrington Diary, 7–9 June 1863, Western Michigan Univ. Lib.

66. *OR*, pt. 1, p. 170; pt. 3, pp. 15–17, 27–30; I, 51, pt. 1, p. 1047.

67. Coddington, *Gettysburg Campaign*, pp. 54–56, 615n.; Mosby, *Stuart's Cavalry*, pp. 27–28, 28n., 139; Anderson, "Cavalry Operations in the Gettysburg Campaign," p. 23; Guy S. Norvell, "The Equipment and Tactics of Our Cavalry, 1861–65, Compared with the Present," *JMSIUS* 49 (1911): 368.

68. Ford, *Cycle of Adams Letters*, 2:31; Henry C. Whelan to His Sister, 11 June 1863, HSP; Albert Huntington, *8th New York Cavalry: Historical Paper* (Palmyra, N.Y., 1902), p. 4; Charles Gardner Memoirs, p. 37, USAMHI.

69. William Rawle Brooke to His Mother, 12 June 1863, Brooke MSS, WL; Henry C. Whelan to His Sister, 11 June 1863, HSP; Coddington, *Gettysburg Campaign*, p. 57.

70. Charles W. Ford, "Charge of the First Maine Cavalry at Brandy Station," *War Papers: Maine MOLLUS*, 2 (1902): 273–74.

CHAPTER 3. BRANDY STATION

1. Luther W. Hopkins, *From Bull Run to Appomattox: A Boy's View* (Baltimore, 1908), pp. 90–91.

2. *OR*, pt. 2, pp. 748–49, 754, 757; John N. Opie, *A Rebel Cavalryman with Lee, Stuart, and Jackson* (Chicago, 1899), p. 147; Ephraim Bowman to His Father, 11 June 1863, Bowman MSS, Univ. of Virginia Lib.

3. George M. Neese, *Three Years in the Confederate Horse Artillery* (New York, 1911), p. 171.

4. G. W. Beale, *A Lieutenant of Cavalry in Lee's Army* (Boston, 1918), p. 84; *OR*, pt. 1, p. 1047; James A. Bell to Gusta Ann Hallock, 10 June 1863, Bell MSS, HEHL.

5. Albert Huntington, *8th New York Cavalry: Historical Paper* (Palmyra, N.Y., 1902), p. 9. The time of Buford's crossing is taken from the Ulric Dahlgren Diary, 9 June 1863, LC.

6. Alfred Pleasonton, "The Campaign of Gettysburg," *Annals of the War, Written by Leading Participants, North and South* (Philadelphia, 1879), 448–49.

7. Huntington, *8th New York Cavalry*, p. 10.

8. James W. Milgram, ed., "The Libby Prison Correspondence of Tattnall Paulding," *American Philatelist* 89 (1975): 1116; Huntington, *8th New York Cavalry*, p. 9.

9. Fairfax Downey, *Clash of Cavalry: The Battle of Brandy Station, June 9, 1863* (New York, 1959), p. 94.

10. *OR*, pt. 2, pp. 754–55.

11. Abner Hard, *History of the Eighth Cavalry Regiment, Illinois Volunteers, during the Great Rebellion* (Aurora, Ill., 1868), p. 65; Bushrod C. Washington, ed., *A History of the Laurel Brigade*, by William N. McDonald (Baltimore, 1907), p. 135; *New York Times*, 11 June 1863.

12. *OR*, pt. 1, pp. 1047–48; W. N. Pickerill, *History of the Third Indiana Cavalry* (Indianapolis, 1906), pp. 73–74; Hard, *Eighth Illinois Cavalry*, p. 243.

13. *OR*, pt. 1, p. 1047; Opie, *A Rebel Cavalryman*, p. 152.

14. *OR*, pt. 2, pp. 749, 762–63, 765, 768; Heros von Borcke and Justus Scheibert, *Die Grosse Reiterschlacht bei Brandy Station, 9. Juni 1863* (Berlin, 1893), pp. 86–87.

15. Hopkins, *From Bull Run to Appomattox*, p. 91.

16. Neese, *Confederate Horse Artillery*, p. 172.

17. *OR*, pt. 2, p. 768; George Baylor, *Bull Run to Bull Run: or, Four Years in the Army of Northern Virginia* (Richmond, 1900), p. 142.

18. Marguerite Merington, ed., *The Custer Story: The Life and Intimate Letters of General George A. Custer and His Wife Elizabeth* (New York, 1950), pp. 58–59.

19. Beale, *A Lieutenant of Cavalry*, p. 85; Downey, *Clash of Cavalry*, p. 98.

20. *OR*, pt. 2, pp. 680, 721, 727, 729, 733; H. B. McClellan, *The Life and Campaigns of Maj. Gen. J. E. B. Stuart* (Richmond, 1885), pp. 268–69.

21. *OR*, pt. 2, pp. 743–44; Woodford B. Hackley, *The Little Fork Rangers: A Sketch of Company "D," Fourth Virginia Cavalry* (Richmond, 1927), p. 47.

22. *OR*, pt. 2, p. 737; McClellan, *Life and Campaigns of Stuart*, p. 283.

23. *OR*, pt. 2, pp. 721, 727.

24. McClellan, *Life and Campaigns of Stuart*, pp. 266–67.

25. Beale, *A Lieutenant of Cavalry*, p. 86.

26. McClellan, *Life and Campaigns of Stuart*, pp. 266–67; Opie, *A Rebel Cavalryman*, p. 152.

27. *OR*, pt. 1, p. 1045.

28. *OR*, pt. 1, pp. 1043–44; Edwin E. Bryant, *History of the Third Regiment of Wisconsin Veteran Volunteer Infantry, 1861–1865* (Madison, Wis., 1891), p. 168.

29. Neese, *Confederate Horse Artillery*, pp. 172–74.

30. *OR*, pt. 2, p. 721; McClellan, *Life and Campaigns of Stuart*, p. 267.

31. Milgram, "The Libby Prison Correspondence of Tattnall Paulding," 1116; Daniel Oakey, *History of the Second Massachusetts Regiment of Infantry: Beverly Ford* (Boston, 1884), p. 14.

32. T. F. Rodenbough, comp., *From Everglade to Cañon with the Second Dragoons* (New York, 1875), pp. 288–89; W. H. Carter, *From Yorktown to Santiago with the Sixth U.S. Cavalry* (Baltimore, 1900), pp. 84–85.

33. Daniel Butterfield, "Reminiscences of the Cavalry in the Army of [the] Potomac," pp. 5–6, Wesley Merritt's ACPF, RG-94, NA.

34. *Pennsylvania at Gettysburg*, 2 vols. (Harrisburg, Pa., 1893), 2:823–24; S. L. Gracey, *Annals of the Sixth Pennsylvania Cavalry* (Philadelphia, 1868), p. 164; David H. Morgan to His Mother, 10 June 1863, Morgan MSS, Irwin L. Park; Charles B. Coxe to John Cadwalader, Jr., 12 June 1863, Coxe MSS, HSP.

35. Thomas W. Smith to His Brother, 15 June 1863, Smith MSS, HSP; Baylor, *Bull Run to Bull Run*, p. 143.

36. Milgram, "The Libby Prison Correspondence of Tattnall Paulding," 1117; Gracey, *Sixth Pennsylvania Cavalry*, pp. 160–63; Henry C. Whelan to His Sister, 11 June 1863, HSP.

37. *Pennsylvania at Gettysburg*, 2:823.

38. R. L. T. Beale, *History of the Ninth Virginia Cavalry, in the War between the States* (Richmond, 1899), p. 69.

39. *OR*, pt. 2, pp. 680, 734, 749.

40. Frank M. Myers, *The Comanches: A History of White's Battalion, Virginia Cavalry* (Baltimore, 1871), p. 183.

41. Charles F. Adams, Jr., Diary, 9 June 1863, Massachusetts Hist. Soc.; William Rawle Brooke to His Mother, 12 June 1863, Brooke MSS, WL. Both of these sources dispute the time of crossing as set down by General Gregg in *OR*, pt. 1, p. 950.

42. *OR*, pt. 1, p. 961; Worthington Chauncey Ford, ed., *A Cycle of Adams Letters, 1861–1865*, 2 vols. (Boston, 1920), 2:31.

43. *OR*, pt. 1, p. 1054.

44. *OR*, pt. 1, p. 950; David McMurtrie Gregg to H. B. McClellan, 21 Jan. 1878, McClellan MSS, Virginia Hist. Soc.

45. *OR*, pt. 3, p. 42. Gregg planned that 500 of Russell's troops would guard his rear as well as Duffié's.

46. *OR*, pt. 2, pp. 734–36; W. W. Blackford, *War Years with Jeb Stuart* (New York, 1945), pp. 214–15; Downey, *Clash of Cavalry*, pp. 106–7.

47. Walter S. Newhall to His Father, 12 June 1863, Newhall MSS, HSP.

48. *Philadelphia Weekly Times*, 10 Nov. 1877.

49. *OR*, pt. 1, pp. 965, 1024, 1053; Henry C. Meyer, *Civil War Experiences under Bayard, Gregg, Kilpatrick, Custer, Raulston, and Newberry, 1862, 1863, 1864* (New York, 1911), p. 27; William P. Lloyd, comp., *History of the First Reg't Pennsylvania Reserve Cavalry* (Philadelphia, 1864), p. 53.

50. *OR*, pt. 2, pp. 729, 772; McClellan, *Life and Campaigns of Stuart*, pp. 269–70.

51. *Philadelphia Weekly Times*, 26 June 1880; Douglas Southall Freeman, *Lee's Lieutenants: A Study in Command*, 3 vols. (New York, 1942–44), 3:9.

52. John Esten Cooke, *Wearing of the Gray* (New York, 1867), p. 18.

53. *OR*, pt. 2, pp. 681–82, 721–22, 726–28, 732–33, 755, 768–69.

54. *OR*, pt. 1, pp. 950, 965.

55. Meyer, *Civil War Experiences*, p. 28.

56. Opie, *A Rebel Cavalryman*, p. 153.

57. *OR*, pt. 1, pp. 950–51, 965–66, 1053; pt. 2, pp. 681, 684.

58. *OR*, pt. 1, pp. 965–66; pt. 2, pp. 755, 769; Downey, *Clash of Cavalry*, pp. 118–19.

59. Lloyd, *First Pennsylvania Cavalry*, pp. 54–56; Opie, *A Rebel Cavalryman*, p. 154.

60. Heros von Borcke, *Memoirs of the Confederate War for Independence*, 2 vols. (New York, 1938), 2:273–74.

61. Daniel A. Grimsley, *Battles in Culpeper County, Virginia* (Culpeper, Va., 1900), p. 11.

62. Blackford, *War Years with Jeb Stuart*, p. 216.

63. John Y. Foster, *New Jersey and the Rebellion* (Newark, N.J., 1868), p. 442; Samuel Toombs, *New Jersey Troops in the Gettysburg Campaign* (Orange, N.J., 1888), pp. 56–57.

64. Downey, *Clash of Cavalry*, p. 124.

65. Myers, *The Comanches*, pp. 184–85; *OR*, pt. 1, pp. 1024–25; pt. 2, p. 769.

66. Hampton S. Thomas, *Some Personal Reminiscences of Service in the Cavalry of the Army of the Potomac* (Philadelphia, 1889), p. 11.

67. *OR*, pt. 1, p. 1027; pt. 2, p. 755.

68. *OR*, pt. 1, p. 985; Willard Glazier, *Three Years in the Federal Cavalry* (New York, 1873), p. 218.

69. *OR*, pt. 1, pp. 996–97; N. D. Preston, *History of the Tenth Regiment of Cavalry, New York State Volunteers* (New York, 1892), p. 85.

70. James Moore, *Kilpatrick and Our Cavalry* (New York, 1865), p. 59.

71. Glazier, *Three Years in the Federal Cavalry*, p. 219.

72. Samuel H. Merrill, *The Campaigns of the First Maine and First District of Columbia Cavalry* (Portland, Me., 1866), p. 109; *First Maine Cavalry Association: Record of Proceedings at the First Annual Re-Union* (Augusta, Me., 1872), p. 16; John P. Sheahan to His Father, 10 June 1863, Sheahan MSS, Maine Hist. Soc.

73. Charles W. Ford, "Charge of the First Maine Cavalry at Brandy Station," *War Papers: Maine MOLLUS*, 2 (1902): 278–84.

74. von Borcke, *Memoirs*, 2:276.

75. *OR*, pt. 1, pp. 985–86; Downey, *Clash of Cavalry*, pp. 134–35, 140.

76. *OR*, pt. 2, pp. 722, 732; Lynwood M. Holland, *Pierce M. B. Young, the Warwick of the South* (Athens, Ga., 1964), p. 72.

77. *OR*, pt. 2, p. 763; Beale, *A Lieutenant of Cavalry*, p. 94.

78. *OR*, pt. 1, p. 951.

79. *OR*, pt. 2, p. 722.

80. *OR*, pt. 1, pp. 951, 962.

81. Ford, *Cycle of Adams Letters*, 2:32.

82. *OR*, pt. 1, p. 961; pt. 2, p. 729; Beale, *A Lieutenant of Cavalry*, p. 89; Benjamin W. Crowninshield and D. H. L. Gleason, *A History of the First Regiment of Massachusetts Cavalry Volunteers* (Boston, 1891), p. 129.

83. *OR*, pt. 2, pp. 729–30, 744; U. R. Brooks, *Butler and His Cavalry in the War of Secession, 1861–1865* (Columbia, S.C., 1909), pp. 152, 165–66.

84. *OR*, pt. 1, pp. 961, 975; Crowninshield and Gleason, *First Massachusetts Cavalry*, pp. 129–30. Irvin Gregg's 16th Pennsylvania was detached on 9 June and was serving dismounted on the other side of the Rappahannock: *History of the 16th Regiment Pennsylvania Cavalry, for the Year Ending October 31st, 1863* (Philadelphia, 1864), p. 37.

85. *OR*, pt. 1, p. 961; pt. 2, pp. 729–30; Brooks, *Butler and His Cavalry*, pp. 153, 167–68; Manly Wade Wellman, *Giant in Gray: A Biography of Wade Hampton of South Carolina* (New York, 1949), pp. 108–9.

86. William Rawle Brooke to His Mother, 12 June 1863, Brooke MSS, WL.

87. *OR*, pt. 2, pp. 683, 744; Brooks, *Butler and His Cavalry*, pp. 153, 166–67; McClellan, *Life and Campaigns of Stuart*, pp. 289–90.

88. *OR*, pt. 2, pp. 730–31; McClellan, *Life and Campaigns of Stuart*, pp. 291–92.

89. *OR*, pt. 1, pp. 950, 962; Crowninshield and Gleason, *First Massachusetts Cavalry*, p. 131; Guy S. Norvell, "The Equipment and Tactics of Our Cavalry, 1861–1865, Compared with the Present," *JMSIUS* 49 (1911): 368.

90. Frederic Denison, *Sabres and Spurs: The First Regiment Rhode Island Cavalry in the Civil War, 1861–1865* (Central Falls, R.I., 1876), p. 230; William E. Doster, *Lincoln and Episodes of the Civil War* (New York, 1915), p. 208.

91. *OR*, pt. 1, pp. 170, 1044; Oakey, *Second Massachusetts Infantry*, pp. 7, 10–12; Julian W. Hinkley, *A Narrative of Service with the Third Wisconsin Infantry* (Madison, Wis., 1912), pp. 79–80. The losses suffered by Ames's infantry amounted to seven killed, fifty-seven wounded, and two missing.

92. Henry C. Whelan to His Sister, 11 June 1863, HSP; James McClure Scott Memoirs, p. 10, Virginia Hist. Soc.

93. Rodenbough, *From Everglade to Cañon*, pp. 288–89.

94. T. F. Rodenbough to the War Department, 2 May 1900; Butterfield, "Reminiscences of the Cavalry," pp. 5–6; both, Wesley Merritt's ACPF, RG-94, NA.

95. Grimsley, *Battles in Culpeper County*, p. 12; Beale, *A Lieutenant of Cavalry*, pp. 95–96; *OR*, pt. 2, pp. 682–83, 771, 794, 796.

96. *OR*, pt. 3, pp. 39–40.

97. *OR*, pt. 1, pp. 903–4, 1045; McClellan, *Life and Campaigns of Stuart*, pp. 266, 294–95; Edwin B. Coddington, *The Gettysburg Campaign: A Study in Command* (New York, 1968), pp. 61–63; *Daily Richmond Examiner*, 12 June 1863. Though historians have dismissed Pleasonton's contention that he found on the battlefield papers discussing Stuart's upcoming raid, a member of the 8th Illinois reported finding enemy soldiers' letters stating that on 10 June the Confederates "were to start for Maryland": James A. Bell to Gusta Ann Hallock, 10 June 1863, Bell MSS, HEHL.

98. *OR*, pt. 1, pp. 903, 1045; pt. 2, p. 564; pt. 3, pp. 49, 876; Blackford, *War Years with Jeb Stuart*, p. 216; John S. Mosby, *Stuart's Cavalry in the Gettysburg Campaign* (New York, 1908), pp. 35, 38–39, 46–48, 52; Coddington, *Gettysburg Campaign*, pp. 58, 615n.–16n.

99. Hillman A. Hall, W. B. Besley, and Gilbert G. Wood, comps., *History of the Sixth New York Cavalry* (Worcester, Mass., 1908), p. 128; Daniel Pulis to His Parents, 11 June 1863, Pulis MSS, Rochester Pub. Lib.; William Rawle Brooke Diary, 9 June 1863, Brooke MSS, WL; *OR*, pt. 1, pp. 609, 951, 962, 1045.

CHAPTER 4. ADVANCE TO PENNSYLVANIA

1. *OR*, pt. 1, pp. 168–70, 904; pt. 2, pp. 718–20; H. B. McClellan, *The Life and Campaigns of Maj. Gen. J. E. B. Stuart* (Richmond, 1885), pp. 292–93; Edwin B. Coddington, *The Gettysburg Campaign: A Study in Command* (New York, 1968), pp. 54, 66.

2. *OR*, pt. 1, pp. 903–4; Coddington, *Gettysburg Campaign*, p. 61; Wilbur S. Nye, *Here Come the Rebels* (Baton Rouge, La., 1965), pp. 57–58.

3. R. E. Lee to J. E. B. Stuart, June 16, 1863, Stuart MSS, HEHL.

4. Howard Swiggett, ed., *A Rebel War Clerk's Diary at the Confederate States Capital*, by John B. Jones, 2 vols. (New York, 1935), 1:345.

5. Douglas Southall Freeman, *Lee's Lieutenants: A Study in Command*, 3 vols. (New York, 1942–44), 3:19, 51–52. Some critics believed that such censure, plus the urging of pro-Stuart organs including the *Whig*, prompted him to strive too hard to recover lost prestige—leading to his controversial ride around the Army of the Potomac in late June and early July. Apparently, however, Stuart did not become aware of the extent of the criticism until well after that expedition was underway: Freeman, *Lee's Lieutenants*, 3:52; Nye, *Here Come the Rebels*, pp. 311–12.

6. *OR*, pt. 2, pp. 719–20.

7. Charles M. Blackford III, ed., *Letters from Lee's Army* (New York, 1947), p. 175.

8. George Baylor, *Bull Run to Bull Run: or, Four Years in the Army of Northern Virginia* (Richmond, 1900), p. 146; McClellan, *Life and Campaigns of Stuart*, p. 294.

9. Daniel Pulis to His Parents, 15 June 1863, Pulis MSS, Rochester Pub. Lib.; Walter S. Newhall to His Mother, 25 June 1863, Newhall MSS, HSP; John P. Sheahan to His Father, 10 June 1863, Sheahan MSS, Maine Hist. Soc.; Ulric Dahlgren Diary, 9 June 1863, LC.

10. Allan Nevins, ed., *A Diary of Battle: The Personal Journals of Colonel Charles S. Wainwright, 1861–1865* (New York, 1962), p. 221; Paul Fatout, ed., *Letters of a Civil War Surgeon* (Lafayette, Ind., 1961), p. 69; George G. Meade to His Wife, 11 June 1863, Meade MSS, HSP.

11. *New York Tribune*, 13 June 1863; *Daily Richmond Examiner*, 12 June 1863.

12. Worthington Chauncey Ford, ed., *A Cycle of Adams Letters, 1861–1865*, 2 vols. (Boston, 1920), 2:32; Charles B. Coxe to John Cadwalader, Jr., 12 June 1863, Coxe MSS, HSP; Marsena R. Patrick Diary, 10 June 1863, LC.

13. *OR*, pt. 3, pp. 45–46; Coddington, *Gettysburg Campaign*, p. 66.

14. *OR*, pt. 1, pp. 34–35; Walter H. Hebert, *Fighting Joe Hooker* (Indianapolis, 1944), pp. 235–37.

15. *OR*, pt. 3, pp. 57, 70.

16. *OR*, pt. 3, p. 59.

17. *OR*, pt. 3, pp. 71–72, 83, 89; Nye, *Here Come the Rebels*, p. 166.

18. *OR*, pt. 3, pp. 64–65, 75, 80.

19. *OR*, pt. 1, pp. 1044–46; pt. 3, pp. 57, 64.

20. George H. Chapman Diary, 11 June 1863, Indiana State Hist. Soc.

21. Ezra J. Warner, *Generals in Blue: Lives of the Union Commanders* (Baton Rouge, La., 1964), p. 165; James Grant Wilson and John Fiske, eds., *Appleton's Cyclopaedia of American Biography*, 7 vols. (New York, 1887–1900), 7:110; William Gamble Memorandum,—Oct. 1864, Gamble's ACPF, RG-94, NA; Abner Hard, *History of the Eighth Cavalry Regiment, Illinois Volunteers, during the Great Rebellion* (Aurora, Ill., 1868), p. 35.

22. William Rawle Brooke to His Mother, 22 May, 12 June 1863, Brooke MSS, WL; Warner, *Generals in Blue*, p. 300; *DAB*, 12:69; *History of the Eighteenth Regiment of Cavalry, Pennsylvania Volunteers, 1862–1865* (New York, 1909), p. 49; George F. Price, comp., *Across the Continent with the Fifth Cavalry* (New York, 1883), p. 383; John B. McIntosh to His Wife, 16 May 1863, McIntosh MSS, Brown Univ. Lib.

23. James W. Milgram, ed., "The Libby Prison Correspondence of Tattnall Paulding," *American Philatelist* 89 (1975): 1114; "Colonel Samuel H. Starr," pp. 1–2, TS in Starr MSS, Missouri Hist. Soc.

24. *OR*, pt. 3, p. 64; William Brooke Rawle, ed., *History of the Third Pennsylvania Cavalry* (Philadelphia, 1905), pp. 250, 253, 255. The 8th Pennsylvania was also assigned to Buford's division at this time but was retained for service at army headquarters. It was not returned to the Cavalry Corps until the last week in June, when assigned to Gregg's division: *OR*, pt. 3, pp. 56, 88, 224, 229, 322.

25. *OR*, pt. 3, pp. 57, 90, 177, 373, 376.

26. *OR*, pt. 3, pp. 49–50, 57, 72, 93.

27. *OR*, pt. 2, pp. 313, 340; Freeman, *Lee's Lieutenants*, 3:20.

28. Mosby, *Stuart's Cavalry*, p. 59; Nye, *Here Come the Rebels*, p. 165; John W. Thomason, Jr., *Jeb Stuart* (New York, 1934), p. 412.

29. Mark Mayo Boatner III, *The Civil War Dictionary* (New York, 1959), p. 136; Ezra J. Warner, *Generals in Gray: Lives of the Confederate Commanders* (Baton Rouge, La., 1959), pp. 46–47.

30. *OR*, pt. 2, p. 752; Frank M. Myers, *The Comanches: A History of White's Battalion, Virginia Cavalry* (Baltimore, 1871), pp. 103–4, 188.

31. *OR*, pt. 2, p. 440; W. W. Goldsborough, *The Maryland Line in the Confederate States Army* (Baltimore, 1869), p. 214. Jenkins's force was variously estimated at between 1,500 and 3,800 horsemen; 2,000 effectives seems a prudent calculation: McClellan, *Life and Campaigns of Stuart*, p. 319 and n.

32. Nye, *Here Come the Rebels*, p. 73.

33. *OR*, pt. 2, pp. 70–71; Nye, *Here Come the Rebels*, pp. 74–77; Goldsborough, *Maryland Line*, pp. 215–17.

34. *OR*, pt. 2, pp. 69–70; Nye, *Here Come the Rebels*, p. 77.

35. *OR*, pt. 2, pp. 41–81, 440–42, 459–64, 499–503; Coddington, *Gettysburg Campaign*, pp. 88–89, 624n.–25n.; Nye, *Here Come the Rebels*, pp. 79–123.

36. *OR*, pt. 2, pp. 88–201; pt. 3, pp. 126, 154–55, 157, 183, 190, 198–99, 202–3, 235–37, 277.

37. *OR*, pt. 2, pp. 82–84, 103, 109, 162, 165, 239, 548; Nye, *Here Come the Rebels*, pp. 86–89; Jacob Hoke, *The Great Invasion of 1863* (Dayton, Ohio, 1887), pp. 86–87. For a fuller account of Captain Boyd's exploits, see William H. Beach, *The First New York (Lincoln) Cavalry* (New York, 1902), pp. 247–53.

38. *OR*, pt. 2, pp. 17, 65, 67, 111, 548; Nye, *Here Come the Rebels*, pp. 127–29.

39. *OR*, pt. 2, pp. 16–18, 33–41, 548–49, 564, 592, 599; Nye, *Here Come the Rebels*, pp. 130–36; Manly Wade Wellman, *Harpers Ferry, Prize of War* (Charlotte, N.C., 1960), pp. 107–8.

40. Philip Schaff, "The Gettysburg Week," *Scribner's Magazine* 16 (1894): 22; Hermann Schuricht, "Jenkins' Brigade in the Gettysburg Campaign," *SHSP* 24 (1896): 340.

41. Hoke, *Great Invasion*, pp. 99–104; *Philadelphia Daily Evening Bulletin*, 23 June 1863; *Daily Richmond Examiner*, 2 July 1863.

42. Edwin B. Coddington, "Prelude to Gettysburg: The Confederates Plunder Pennsylvania," *Pennsylvania History* 30 (1963): 133; Samuel P. Bates, *The Battle of Gettysburg* (Philadelphia, 1875), p. 23.

43. Frank Moore, ed., *The Rebellion Record: A Diary of American Events*, 11 vols. (New York, 1861–68), 7:196–97; Hoke, *Great Invasion*, p. 104; Nye, *Here Come the Rebels*, p. 142; *Philadelphia Daily Evening Bulletin*, 23 June 1863.

44. *Philadelphia Press*, 25 June 1863; Hoke, *Great Invasion*, pp. 110–11; Schuricht, "Jenkins' Brigade in the Gettysburg Campaign," 340.

45. Moore, *Rebellion Record*, 7:198; Nye, *Here Come the Rebels*, p. 146.

46. Schaff, "Gettysburg Week," 22–23.

47. *OR*, pt. 3, pp. 186, 201; Nye, *Here Come the Rebels*, p. 146.

48. *OR*, pt. 3, pp. 80–84.

49. *OR*, pt. 3, pp. 81–82, 87–89; Benjamin W. Crowninshield Diary, 13 June 1863, Essex Inst.; Hebert, *Fighting Joe Hooker*, p. 237; Edward J. Nichols, *Toward Gettysburg: A Biography of General John F. Reynolds* (University Park, Pa., 1958), pp. 184–85.

50. *OR*, pt. 3, pp. 106, 116–17; I, 51, pt. 1, pp. 1054–55; Charles F. Adams, Jr., Diary, 15 June 1863, Massachusetts Hist. Soc.; Norman Ball Diary, 13–14 June 1863, Connecticut Hist. Soc.; S. L. Gracey, *Annals of the Sixth Pennsylvania Cavalry* (Philadelphia, 1868), p. 176; Rawle, *Third Pennsylvania Cavalry*, p. 253.

51. Gracey, *Sixth Pennsylvania Cavalry*, p. 176; David H. Morgan to His Mother, 23 June 1863, Morgan MSS, Irwin L. Park; William Rawle Brooke Diary, 17 June 1863, Brooke MSS, WL; John P. Sheahan to His Father, 23 June 1863, Sheahan MSS, Maine Hist. Soc.

52. *OR*, pt. 1, pp. 141–42; pt. 3, pp. 116–17; Nichols, *Toward Gettysburg*, p. 186; Edward J. Stackpole, *They Met at Gettysburg* (Harrisburg, Pa., 1959), pp. 121–22; *Pennsylvania at Gettysburg*, 2 vols. (Harrisburg, Pa., 1893), 2:860.

53. Hebert, *Fighting Joe Hooker*, pp. 238–39.

54. *OR*, pt. 3, pp. 71–72.

55. *OR*, pt. 2, pp. 306, 315, 357, 366, 613, 652, 673–77; pt. 3, pp. 887–88.

56. *OR*, pt. 2, pp. 687–88, 873; I, 51, pt. 2, p. 723; John Swann to "Dear Bettie," 20 June 1863, Swann MSS, Georgia Dept. of Archives and History.

CHAPTER 5. ALDIE AND MIDDLEBURG

1. Heros von Borcke, *Memoirs of the Confederate War for Independence*, 2 vols. (New York, 1938), 2:285.

2. H. B. McClellan, *The Life and Campaigns of Maj. Gen. J. E. B. Stuart* (Richmond, 1885), p. 314.

3. *OR*, pt. 2, p. 688.

4. *OR*, pt. 2, pp. 739, 747.

5. *OR*, pt. 3, pp. 172–73.

6. *OR*, pt. 1, p. 962; pt. 3, p. 105; George N. Bliss, "A Review of Aldie," *Maine Bugle* 1 (1894): 123; William Brooke Rawle, ed., *History of the Third Pennsylvania Cavalry* (Philadelphia, 1905), p. 250.

7. Roy P. Stonesifer, Jr., "The Union Cavalry Comes of Age," *Civil War History* 11 (1965): 280.

8. *OR*, pt. 1, pp. 952–53; pt. 3, p. 171; James Moore, *Kilpatrick and Our Cavalry* (New York, 1865), p. 66.

9. Generals' Reports of Service, War of the Rebellion, 3:120, RG-94, E-160, NA.

10. *OR*, pt. 1, pp. 906, 953; Wilbur S. Nye, *Here Come the Rebels* (Baton Rouge, La., 1965), pp. 171, 173.

11. *OR*, pt. 2, pp. 739, 747; Nye, *Here Come the Rebels*, pp. 173–77; William L. Haskin, comp., *The History of the First Regiment of Artillery from Its Organization in 1821, to January 1st, 1876* (Portland, Me., 1879), p. 520.

12. Benjamin W. Crowninshield and D. H. L. Gleason, *A History of the First Regiment of Massachusetts Cavalry Volunteers* (Boston, 1891), p. 144; Nye, *Here Come the Rebels*, pp. 174–75.

13. *Charles F. Adams, 1835–1915: An Autobiography* (Boston, 1916), p. 131.

14. Crowninshield and Gleason, *First Massachusetts Cavalry*, p. 144; *OR*, pt. 1, p. 1052; pt. 2, p. 745.

15. John Koster, "Count von Zeppelin Visits the Front," *CWTI* 17 (Jan. 1979), 15.

16. Worthington Chauncey Ford, ed., *A Cycle of Adams Letters, 1861–1865*, 2 vols. (Boston, 1920), 2:36–37; *OR*, pt. 1, p. 1052; Bliss Perry, *Life and Letters of Henry Lee Higginson* (Boston, 1921), pp. 194–95.

17. Moore, *Kilpatrick and Our Cavalry*, pp. 66–67.

18. Nye, *Here Come the Rebels*, pp. 177–78.

19. *OR*, pt. 1, pp. 171, 972–73; B. J. Haden, *Reminiscences of J. E. B. Stuart's Cavalry* (Charlottesville, Va., c. 1890), p. 23.

20. Crowninshield and Gleason, *First Massachusetts Cavalry*, pp. 148–49.

21. *OR*, pt. 2, pp. 740, 742; McClellan, *Life and Campaigns of Stuart*, pp. 299–300.

22. Crowninshield and Gleason, *First Massachusetts Cavalry*, p. 149; *OR*, pt. 1, pp. 171, 1052; Charles F. Adams, Jr., Diary, 17 June 1863, Massachusetts Hist. Soc.

23. McClellan, *Life and Campaigns of Stuart*, p. 299.

24. Nye, *Here Come the Rebels*, pp. 180–81.

25. Crowninshield and Gleason, *First Massachusetts Cavalry*, p. 148; Moore, *Kilpatrick and Our Cavalry*, p. 67; *New York Times*, 22 June 1863.

26. *OR*, pt. 1, p. 1052; Ford, *Cycle of Adams Letters*, 2:37; Luigi P. di Cesnola, *Ten Months in Libby Prison* (New York, 1865), p. 1.

27. *OR*, pt. 1, pp. 979–80; pt. 2, pp. 741–43; McClellan, *Life and Campaigns of Stuart*, pp. 300–301.

28. Marguerite Merington, ed., *The Custer Story: The Life and Intimate Letters of General George A. Custer and His Wife Elizabeth* (New York, 1950), pp. 55–56; Jay Monaghan, *Custer: The Life of General George Armstrong Custer* (Boston, 1959), p. 130.

29. *OR*, pt. 1, pp. 979–80; pt. 2, pp. 741, 746.

30. *OR*, pt. 1, pp. 171, 907, 953, 1052; pt. 2, p. 741; Moore, *Kilpatrick and Our Cavalry*, p. 71.

31. *OR*, pt. 2, p. 741.

32. Alfred Pleasonton to John F. Farnsworth, 18 June 1863, Pleasonton MSS, LC.

33. *OR*, pt. 1, p. 907; pt. 2, pp. 357, 366; pt. 3, p. 173.

34. *OR*, pt. 1, pp. 962–63; Albert Porter Tasker, "A Yankee Cavalryman Gets 'Gobbled Up': A First Person Account," *CWTI* 6 (Jan. 1968): 42.

35. *OR*, pt. 1, p. 1055; Frederic Denison, *Sabres and Spurs: The First Regiment Rhode Island Cavalry in the Civil War, 1861–1865* (Central Falls, R.I., 1876), p. 233; Bliss, "A Review of Aldie," 124; Stonesifer, "The Union Cavalry Comes of Age," 279.

36. *OR*, pt. 1, pp. 963, 1055; Nye, *Here Come the Rebels*, p. 183.

37. Bliss, "A Review of Aldie," 126.

38. *OR*, pt. 1, p. 963; von Borcke, *Memoirs*, 2:285–86; Burke Davis, *Jeb Stuart, the Last Cavalier* (New York, 1957), p. 316; McClellan, *Life and Campaigns of Stuart*, pp. 303–4.

39. Tasker, "A Yankee Cavalryman Gets 'Gobbled Up,'" 42.

40. Bliss, "A Review of Aldie," 129; John S. Mosby, *Stuart's Cavalry in the Gettysburg Campaign* (New York, 1908), p. 71; George N. Bliss, *The First Rhode Island Cavalry at Middleburg, Va., June 17 and 18, 1863* (Providence, R.I., 1889), pp. 14–15.

41. *OR*, pt. 1, pp. 963–65; Edwin B. Coddington, *The Gettysburg Campaign: A Study in Command* (New York, 1968), pp. 77–78; Charles O. Green, *An Incident in the Battle of Middleburg, Va., June 17, 1863* (Providence, R.I., 1911), p. 22.

42. *OR*, pt. 1, pp. 963, 1056; Bliss, *First Rhode Island Cavalry at Middleburg*, pp. 11–13; Bliss, "A Review of Aldie," 130.

43. *OR*, pt. 2, p. 688; von Borcke, *Memoirs*, 2:287–88.

44. Tasker, "A Yankee Cavalryman Gets 'Gobbled Up,'" 43; Denison, *Sabres and Spurs*, pp. 234–35; *New York Times*, 22 June 1863.

45. R. L. T. Beale, *History of the Ninth Virginia Cavalry, in the War between the States* (Richmond, 1899), p. 71; Bliss, "A Review of Aldie," 130; *OR*, pt. 1, pp. 963–64, 1056; Denison, *Sabres and Spurs*, pp. 235–36.

46. von Borcke, *Memoirs*, 2:288–90; John W. Thomason, Jr., *Jeb Stuart* (New York, 1934), p. 416.

47. Ulric Dahlgren Diary, 19 June 1863, LC; Denison, *Sabres and Spurs*, pp. 271–72.

48. Benjamin W. Crowninshield Diary, 21 June 1863, Essex Inst.; Denison, *Sabres and Spurs*, p. 271; *OR*, pt. 3, pp. 210–11, 804; F. C. Newhall, *How Lee Lost the Use of His Cavalry before the Battle of Gettysburg* (Philadelphia, 1878), p. 14; Bliss, "A Review of Aldie," 130.

49. Benjamin W. Crowninshield Diary, June 26, 1863, Essex Inst.; *OR*, pt. 3, p. 288; Bliss, *First Rhode Island Cavalry at Middleburg*, p. 27.

50. "Report of Operations of Cavalry Corps [Army of the Potomac] of Battles of Aldie, Middleburg & Upperville," HEHL; Alfred Pleasonton to Adj. Gen., Army of the Potomac, 29 June 1863, Cav. Corps Headquarters, Letters Sent, Feb. 1863–Apr. 1865, RG-393, E-1439, NA; Alfred N. Duffié to Edwin M. Stanton, 4 July 1863, HSP; *OR*, pt. 3, pp. 193, 210–11, 482.

CHAPTER 6. MIDDLEBURG AGAIN AND UPPERVILLE

1. Willard Glazier, *Three Years in the Federal Cavalry* (New York, 1873), p. 230; William Rawle Brooke Diary, 18 June 1863, Brooke MSS, WL.

2. *OR*, pt. 2, pp. 689–90, 758–59.

3. William P. Lloyd, comp., *History of the First Reg't Pennsylvania Reserve Cavalry* (Philadelphia, 1864), p. 57; William Brooke Rawle, ed., *History of the Third Pennsylvania Cavalry* (Philadelphia, 1905), p. 254; *OR*, pt. 1, p. 969.

4. Hillman A. Hall, W. B. Besley, and Gilbert G. Wood, comps., *History of the Sixth New York Cavalry* (Worcester, Mass., 1908), pp. 129–30; *OR*, pt. 3, p. 227; Wilbur S. Nye, *Here Come the Rebels* (Baton Rouge, La., 1965), p. 188.

5. "Report of Operations of Cavalry Corps [Army of the Potomac] of Battles of Aldie, Middleburg & Upperville," HEHL; *OR*, pt. 1, p. 975; Norman Ball Diary, 18 June 1863, Connecticut Hist. Soc.; John D. Follmer Diary, 18 June 1863, UML.

6. *OR*, pt. 1, pp. 908–9, 1029; pt. 3, p. 193.

7. *OR*, pt. 2, p. 689; pt. 3, pp. 117, 175–77, 191, 195; Luther S. Trowbridge, *The Operations of the Cavalry in the Gettysburg Campaign* (Detroit, 1888), pp. 7–8.

8. *OR*, pt. 1, pp. 32, 575; I, 25, pt. 1, p. 1105.

9. *OR*, pt. 1, p. 910; pt. 3, p. 208; Trowbridge, *Operations of the Cavalry*, p. 8; William Wells to His Mother, 21 June 1863, Wells MSS, Univ. of Vermont Lib.

10. John S. Mosby, *Stuart's Cavalry in the Gettysburg Campaign* (New York, 1908), pp. 65–66; H. B. McClellan, *The Life and Campaigns of Maj. Gen. J. E. B. Stuart* (Richmond, 1885), p. 306; *OR*, pt. 1, p. 910; pt. 3, p. 192.

11. *OR*, pt. 1, p. 142; pt. 2, p. 689.

12. *OR*, pt. 3, p. 195; Alfred Pleasonton to David McMurtrie Gregg, 18 June 1863, Gregg MSS, LC.

13. *OR*, pt. 1, pp. 909, 953, 975; pt. 2, p. 690.

14. *OR*, pt. 1, p. 953; Roy P. Stonesifer, Jr., "The Union Cavalry Comes of Age," *Civil War History* 11 (1965): 280–81; Nye, *Here Come the Rebels*, pp. 190–91; Henry C. Meyer, *Civil War Experiences under Bayard, Gregg, Kilpatrick, Custer, Raulston, and Newberry, 1862, 1863, 1864* (New York, 1911), p. 36.

15. *OR*, pt. 1, pp. 953, 972; Nye, *Here Come the Rebels*, pp. 190–91.

16. Meyer, *Civil War Experiences*, p. 38; Nye, *Here Come the Rebels*, pp. 191–92.

17. *OR*, pt. 1, pp. 975–76, 1034; John P. Sheahan to His Father, 20, 23 June 1863, Sheahan MSS, Maine Hist. Soc.; Norman Ball Diary, 19 June 1863, Connecticut Hist. Soc.; Edward P. Tobie, *History of the First Maine Cavalry, 1861–1865* (Boston, 1887), pp. 165–68.

18. *OR*, pt. 1, p. 976; Nye, *Here Come the Rebels*, pp. 193–94; R. L. T. Beale, *History of the Ninth Virginia Cavalry, in the War between the States* (Richmond, 1899), p. 72; *Pennsylvania at Gettysburg*, 3 vols. (Harrisburg, Pa., 1893), 2:846.

19. Heros von Borcke, *Memoirs of the Confederate War for Independence*, 2 vols. (New York, 1938), 2:291.

20. Beale, *Ninth Virginia Cavalry*, p. 73; Nye, *Here Come the Rebels*, p. 194.

21. *OR*, pt. 2, pp. 689–90; McClellan, *Life and Campaigns of Stuart*, pp. 306–7.

22. von Borcke, *Memoirs*, 2:293; W. W. Blackford, *War Years with Jeb Stuart* (New York, 1945), pp. 218–20.

23. *OR*, pt. 1, pp. 193, 911; pt. 2, pp. 712–13; Nye, *Here Come the Rebels*, p. 194.

24. *OR*, pt. 2, pp. 689–90, 759.

25. *OR*, pt. 2, p. 759; Nye, *Here Come the Rebels*, pp. 195–96. This action is misdated in the latter work as occurring on 20 June.

26. George M. Neese, *Three Years in the Confederate Horse Artillery* (New York, 1911), pp. 181–82; Charles F. Adams, Jr., Diary, 20 June 1863, Massachusetts Hist. Soc.

27. E. D. Anderson, "Cavalry Operations in the Gettysburg Campaign," pp. 42–43, Army War College Study, TS in USAMHI; *OR*, pt. 1, p. 911; pt. 3, pp. 227–30.

28. *OR*, pt. 3, p. 213.

29. *OR*, pt. 1, pp. 911–13; Nye, *Here Come the Rebels*, pp. 197, 201; A. M. Judson, *History of the Eighty-third Regiment Pennsylvania Volunteers* (Erie, Pa., n.d.), pp. 63–64.

30. *OR*, pt. 2, p. 690.

31. *OR*, pt. 1, p. 614; John J. Pullen, *The Twentieth Maine: A Volunteer Regiment in the Civil War* (Philadelphia, 1957), pp. 86–87.

32. Nye, *Here Come the Rebels*, p. 198.

33. *OR*, pt. 1, p. 1035; U. R. Brooks, *Butler and His Cavalry in the War of Secession, 1861–1865* (Columbia, S.C., 1909), p. 177.

34. *OR*, pt. 2, p. 690.

35. Nye, *Here Come the Rebels*, pp. 198–200; Eugene A. Nash, *A History of the Forty-fourth Regiment New York Volunteer Infantry in the Civil War, 1861–1865* (Chicago, 1911), pp. 136–37; *OR*, pt. 1, pp. 614, 616; pt. 2, pp. 690–91.

36. *OR*, pt. 1, pp. 954, 972–73; pt. 2, p. 691; Nye, *Here Come the Rebels*, p. 205.

37. George Baylor, *Bull Run to Bull Run; or, Four Years in the Army of Northern Virginia* (Richmond, 1900), p. 149.

38. Brooks, *Butler and His Cavalry*, pp. 180–82; Wade Hampton to H. B. McClellan, 14 Jan. 1878, McClellan MSS, Virginia Hist. Soc.; McClellan, *Life and Campaigns of Stuart*, pp. 311–12; *OR*, pt. 1, p. 954.

39. David McMurtrie Gregg, Jr., "Brevet Major General David McMurtrie Gregg," p. 196, TS in Gregg MSS, LC; Meyer, *Civil War Experiences*, pp. 39–40.

40. In his report of Upperville (*OR*, pt. 1, p. 921), Buford implied that he sent the Reserve Brigade to Gregg's aid of his own volition; years later a sergeant in the 2nd U.S. Cavalry recounted carrying an order from Pleasonton to Buford, detaching the brigade: Benjamin Engle to Samuel H. Starr, 7 Aug. 1891, Starr MSS, Missouri Hist. Soc.

41. James W. Milgram, ed., "The Libby Prison Correspondence of Tattnall Paulding," *American Philatelist* 89 (1975), 1113–14; *OR*, pt. 1, pp. 947–48.

42. *OR*, pt. 1, pp. 945–47, 954. In defense of the Regulars, it should be pointed out that at Upperville their ranks were threadbare; only 825 men remained in the Reserve Brigade, including the 6th Pennsylvania. The rest lacked able-bodied mounts or were on reconnaissance at the mouth of the Monocacy River, not far from Harpers Ferry: *OR*, pt. 3, pp. 258–59, 267, 273, 279.

43. Brooks, *Butler and His Cavalry*, p. 178; Nye, *Here Come the Rebels*, p. 207; McClellan, *Life and Campaigns of Stuart*, pp. 311–12.

44. *Philadelphia Inquirer*, 24 June 1863; Nye, *Here Come the Rebels*, pp. 208–9.

45. *OR*, pt. 1, pp. 984–85; William E. Doster, *Lincoln and Episodes of the Civil War* (New York, 1915), p. 212.

46. *Philadelphia Inquirer*, 24 June 1863.

47. *OR*, pt. 1, pp. 172, 955; pt. 2, p. 712; Nye, *Here Come the Rebels*, p. 210.

48. David McMurtrie Gregg, *The Second Cavalry Division of the Army of the Potomac in the Gettysburg Campaign* (Philadelphia, 1907), p. 9.

49. *OR*, pt. 1, p. 920.

50. *OR*, pt. 1, pp. 920–21; pt. 2, pp. 750–51, 766.

51. *OR*, pt. 1, p. 921.

52. *OR*, pt. 2, pp. 750–51.

53. Ephraim Bowman to His Father, 21 June 1863, Univ. of Virginia Lib.

54. *OR*, pt. 1, pp. 921, 932–33, 1029; Nye, *Here Come the Rebels*, pp. 202–3.

55. William Gamble Memorandum, — Oct. 1864, Gamble's ACPF, RG-94, NA; Abner Hard, *History of the Eighth Cavalry Regiment, Illinois Volunteers, during the Great Rebellion* (Aurora, Ill., 1868), p. 251; *OR*, pt. 1, pp. 921, 933; pt. 2, pp. 751, 756, 759, 766.

56. Daniel Pulis to His Parents, 23 June 1863, Pulis MSS, Rochester Pub. Lib.

57. *OR*, pt. 1, p. 913; pt. 3, p. 255; Edwin B. Coddington, *The Gettysburg Campaign: A Study in Command* (New York, 1968), pp. 121–22.

58. William H. Redman to His Mother, 24 June 1863, Redman MSS, Univ. of Virginia Lib.; Alfred Pleasonton to John F. Farnsworth, 23 June 1863, Pleasonton MSS, LC; Neese, *Confederate Horse Artillery*, p. 183.

59. John P. Sheahan to His Father, 23 June 1863, Sheahan MSS, Maine Hist. Soc.; *OR*, pt. 1, pp. 171–72, 193; pt. 2, pp. 713, 719, 741.

60. Miles A. Cavin to His Sister, 27 June 1863, Cavin MSS, North Carolina State Dept. of Art, Culture and History; John A. Barry to His Sister, 23 June 1863, Barry MSS, Univ. of North Carolina Lib.

61. Charles Brown to His Sister, 23 June 1863, Brown MSS, New York State Lib.; David H. Morgan to His Mother, 23 June 1863, Morgan MSS, Irwin L. Park.

CHAPTER 7. JENKINS'S EXPEDITION—WILLIAMSPORT TO PETERSBURG

1. *OR*, pt. 2, pp. 442–43, 464, 550.

2. *OR*, pt. 2, pp. 442, 550–51; Wilbur S. Nye, *Here Come the Rebels* (Baton Rouge, La., 1965), pp. 146–48.

3. Edwin B. Coddington, *The Gettysburg Campaign: A Study in Command* (New York, 1968), pp. 86–87; *OR*, pt. 3, pp. 443, 810.

4. *OR*, pt. 3, pp. 54–55, 68–69, 145; Samuel P. Bates, *History of Pennsylvania Volunteers, 1861–5*, 5 vols. (Harrisburg, Pa., 1869–71), 5:1222–25; Jacob Hoke, *The Great Invasion of 1863* (Dayton, Ohio, 1887), pp. 93–94; Nye, *Here Come the Rebels*, pp. 60–65, 149–62.

5. *OR*, pt. 3, pp. 138–39, 211–15; Russell F. Weigley, "Emergency Troops in the Gettysburg Campaign," *Pennsylvania History* 25 (1958), 40–41, 51; Nye, *Here Come the Rebels*, pp. 212–21.

6. *OR*, pt. 2, pp. 442–43, 550–51.

7. *OR*, pt. 2, pp. 443, 464, 503.

8. *Philadelphia Press*, 24 June 1863.

9. Hermann Schuricht, "Jenkins' Brigade in the Gettysburg Campaign," *SHSP* 24 (1896): 341–42; Persifor Frazer, "Service of the First Troop Philadelphia City Cavalry during June and July, 1863," *JMSIUS* 43 (1908): 283–84; Nye, *Here Come the Rebels*, pp. 243–44, 267, 271.

10. Samuel P. Bates, *The Battle of Gettysburg* (Philadelphia, 1875), p. 27; Edwin B. Coddington, "Prelude to Gettysburg: The Confederates Plunder Pennsylvania," *Pennsylvania History* 30 (1963): 135; Nye, *Here Come the Rebels*, pp. 244–46, 260.

11. William H. Beach, "Some Reminiscences of the First New York (Lincoln) Cavalry," *War Papers: Wisconsin MOLLUS*, 2 (1896), 284; James H. Stevenson, *"Boots and Saddles": A History of . . . the First New York (Lincoln) Cavalry* (Harrisburg, Pa., 1879), p. 210; Hoke, *Great Invasion*, pp. 124–29; Nye, *Here Come the Rebels*, pp. 236–47.

12. *OR*, pt. 3, pp. 277, 329; Robert Grant Crist, "Highwater 1863: The Confederate Approach to Harrisburg," *Pennsylvania History* 30 (1963): 171; Hoke, *Great Invasion*, pp. 128–35.

13. Richard S. Ewell to His Niece, 24 June 1863, Ewell MSS, LC.

14. *OR*, pt. 2, pp. 565–66; Nye, *Here Come the Rebels*, p. 259; Stevenson, *"Boots and Saddles"*, p. 211.

15. Frank M. Myers, *The Comanches: A History of White's Battalion, Virginia Cavalry* (Baltimore, 1871), pp. 191–92; *OR*, pt. 3, p. 193.

16. *OR*, pt. 2, pp. 203–4; pt. 3, pp. 177, 191.

17. *OR*, pt. 2, pp. 203, 1076n.; pt. 3, pp. 443, 810.

18. *OR*, pt. 2, p. 771; Myers, *The Comanches*, pp. 188–90.

19. *OR*, pt. 2, pp. 203, 771; pt. 3, pp. 191, 193–94, 198, 200–201, 901; Myers, *The Comanches*, p. 191; Bushrod C. Washington, ed., *A History of the Laurel Brigade*, by William N. McDonald (Baltimore, 1907), p. 154; John S. Mosby, *Stuart's Cavalry in the Gettysburg Campaign* (New York, 1908), pp. 70n., 85n., 156n.–58n., 171.

20. *OR*, pt. 2, p. 443.

21. *OR*, pt. 2, pp. 26, 204; pt. 3, pp. 248–49; Harry Gilmor, *Four Years in the Saddle* (New York, 1866), pp. 92–94; C. A. Newcomer, *Cole's Cavalry; or, Three Years in the Saddle in the Shenandoah Valley* (Baltimore, 1895), p. 51.

22. *OR*, pt. 3, pp. 634, 641; Weigley, "Emergency Troops in the Gettysburg Campaign," 42.

23. *OR*, pt. 3, pp. 297, 326; Hoke, *Great Invasion*, pp. 147–52; Edward M. Greene, "The Huntingdon Bible Company," *CWTI* 3 (Apr. 1964): 23–24.

24. *OR*, pt. 2, p. 503; W. W. Goldsborough, *The Maryland Line in the Confederate States Army* (Baltimore, 1869), p. 125; Philip Schaff, "The Gettysburg Week," *Scribner's Magazine* 16 (1894): 23–24.

25. *OR*, pt. 2, pp. 443, 464–65.

26. *OR*, pt. 2, pp. 212, 215; pt. 3, p. 328; Weigley, "Emergency Troops in the Gettysburg Campaign," 45–46.

27. Samuel W. Pennypacker, *The Autobiography of a Pennsylvanian* (Philadelphia, 1918), p. 95.

28. *OR*, pt. 3, p. 344; Hoke, *Great Invasion*, pp. 120–21, 127–30.

29. Nye, *Here Come the Rebels*, pp. 273–74; Myers, *The Comanches*, pp. 192–93; Bates, *Pennsylvania Volunteers*, 5:1225.

30. Frazer, "First Troop Philadelphia City Cavalry," 286–87, 295.

31. *OR*, pt. 3, pp. 344, 363.

32. *OR*, pt. 2, pp. 213, 465; Nye, *Here Come the Rebels*, pp. 276–77; Pennypacker, *Autobiography of a Pennsylvanian*, p. 95.

33. Earl Schenck Miers and Richard A. Brown, eds., *Gettysburg* (New Brunswick, N.J., 1948), pp. 40–41; Edward J. Stackpole, *They Met at Gettysburg* (Harrisburg, Pa., 1956), p. 32.

34. *OR*, pt. 2, p. 465; Nye, *Here Come the Rebels*, p. 275.

35. *OR*, pt. 2, pp. 465–66, 491; *Encounter at Hanover: Prelude to Gettysburg* (Hanover, Pa., 1963), pp. 33–36, 106.

36. *OR*, pt. 2, pp. 212, 278; pt. 3, p. 397; Myers, *The Comanches*, p. 194; *Encounter at Hanover*, p. 35.

37. *Encounter at Hanover*, pp. 35–36.

38. *OR*, pt. 2, pp. 443, 466, 491; pt. 3, pp. 385, 389.

39. *OR*, pt. 2, pp. 466–67; Nye, *Here Come the Rebels*, pp. 285–86.

40. *OR*, pt. 2, pp. 277–79, 443, 466–67, 491–92, 995–96; Nye, *Here Come the Rebels*, pp. 283–92; Weigley, "Emergency Troops in the Gettysburg Campaign," 48, 50.

41. *OR*, pt. 2, pp. 443–44, 467–68, 492; Nye, *Here Come the Rebels*, pp. 296–97; Myers, *The Comanches*, p. 193.

42. *OR*, pt. 2, p. 316.

43. Hoke, *Great Invasion*, p. 173; Schuricht, "Jenkins' Brigade in the Gettysburg Campaign," 342; J. C. Atticks Diary, 24–26 June 1863, USAMHII.

44. Samuel M. Goodyear, *General Robert E. Lee's Invasion of Carlisle, 1863* (Carlisle, Pa., 1942), p. 3.

45. Schuricht, "Jenkins' Brigade in the Gettysburg Campaign," 342; Nye, *Here Come the Rebels*, pp. 307–8, 329–30; "Military History of William Farrar Smith," p. 6, Smith's ACPF, RG-94, NA.

46. Nye, *Here Come the Rebels*, pp. 331–40; Crist, "Highwater 1863," 172–74; Bates, *Pennsylvania Volunteers*, 5:1227.

47. Nye, *Here Come the Rebels*, pp. 340–42; Schuricht, "Jenkins' Brigade in the Gettysburg Campaign," 343–45; Woodruff Jones, "Defending Pennsylvania against Lee," *CWTI* 5 (Oct. 1966): 38; Crist, "Highwater 1863," 177–81.

48. James Longstreet, "Lee's Invasion of Pennsylvania," *B&L*, 3:249–50; Coddington, *Gettysburg Campaign*, pp. 180–83, 188–93.

49. Nye, *Here Come the Rebels*, pp. 347–56; Coddington, *Gettysburg Campaign*, p. 191.

50. Hoke, *Great Invasion*, pp. 229–30.

CHAPTER 8. STUART'S EXPEDITION—SALEM TO HANOVER

1. *OR*, pt. 2, pp. 358, 443, 613.

2. George M. Neese, *Three Years in the Confederate Horse Artillery* (New York, 1911), p. 184; William Brooke Rawle, ed., *History of the Third Pennsylvania Cavalry* (Philadelphia, 1905), p. 255; Charles Brown to His Sister, 23 June 1863, Brown MSS, New York State Lib.

3. Frederick Maurice, ed., *An Aide-de-Camp of Lee*, by Charles Marshall (Boston, 1927), pp. 201–2; Glenn Tucker, *High Tide at Gettysburg: The Campaign in Pennsylvania* (Indianapolis, 1958), p. 32; Douglas Southall Freeman, *Lee's Lieutenants: A Study in Command*, 3 vols. (New York, 1942–44), 3:41 and n.

4. Edwin B. Coddington, *The Gettysburg Campaign: A Study in Command* (New York, 1968), pp. 107–8; Wilbur S. Nye, *Here Come the Rebels* (Baton Rouge, La., 1965), p. 313.

5. *OR*, pt. 3, p. 913.

6. *OR*, pt. 3, p. 923; Maurice, *Aide-de-Camp of Lee*, p. 208; Freeman, *Lee's Lieutenants*, 3:47, 550; Coddington, *Gettysburg Campaign*, p. 108. Later Lee's aide, Charles Marshall, claimed that subsequent orders from Lee to Stuart—copied by Marshall on the 23rd—revoked the 5 P.M. instructions and demanded that Stuart stay close to the right flank of the army. Though afterward lost, Stuart received and later admitted ignoring these orders. So, at any rate, John Mosby quoted Marshall as stating in 1877: John S. Mosby to L. L. Lomax, 19 Feb. 1896, Mosby MSS, USAMHI.

7. *OR*, pt. 3, p. 923; Freeman, *Lee's Lieutenants*, 3:48; Kenneth P. Williams, *Lincoln Finds a*

General: A Military Study of the Civil War, 5 vols. (New York, 1949–59), 2:664; Randolph H. McKim, "The Confederate Cavalry in the Gettysburg Campaign," *JMSIUS* 46 (1910): 418.

8. *OR*, pt. 3, p. 915; Maurice, *Aide-de-Camp of Lee*, pp. 205–6; James Longstreet, *From Manassas to Appomattox: Memoirs of the Civil War in America* (Philadelphia, 1895), pp. 336, 342–43; John S. Mosby to the Editor of the *Philadelphia Weekly Times*, 8 Mar. 1896, Mosby MSS, Missouri Hist. Soc.

9. *OR*, pt. 2, p. 692; H. B. McClellan, *The Life and Campaigns of Maj. Gen. J. E. B. Stuart* (Richmond, 1885), p. 315; John S. Mosby, *Stuart's Cavalry in the Gettysburg Campaign* (New York, 1908), pp. 69–74, 76–81, 85n., 88–92, 194–222; Charles Wells Russell, ed., *The Memoirs of Colonel John S. Mosby* (Boston, 1917), p. 216; Virgil Carrington Jones, *Ranger Mosby* (Chapel Hill, N.C., 1944), pp. 145–46, 149; John S. Mosby, "The Confederate Cavalry in the Gettysburg Campaign," *B&L*, 3:251.

10. *OR*, pt. 2, pp. 692, 696, 708–9; McClellan, *Life and Campaigns of Stuart*, pp. 316–17; Williams, *Lincoln Finds a General*, 2:663.

11. H. B. McClellan, "The Invasion of Pennsylvania in '63," *Philadelphia Weekly Times*, 20 July 1878; Mosby, "Confederate Cavalry in the Gettysburg Campaign," 251–52.

12. Longstreet, *From Manassas to Appomattox*, p. 343; *OR*, pt. 2, p. 915.

13. *OR*, pt. 2, p. 692; McClellan, *Life and Campaigns of Stuart*, p. 321; Burke Davis, *Jeb Stuart, the Last Cavalier* (New York, 1957), p. 324.

14. Miles A. Cavin to His Sister, 27 June 1863, Cavin MSS, North Carolina State Dept. of Art, Culture and History; Jones, *Ranger Mosby*, p. 149; John Scott, *Partisan Life with Col. John S. Mosby* (New York, 1867), p. 107.

15. *OR*, pt. 2, p. 692; McClellan, *Life and Campaigns of Stuart*, p. 321; John Esten Cooke, *Wearing of the Gray* (New York, 1867), p. 230.

16. *OR*, pt. 2, p. 692; McClellan, *Life and Campaigns of Stuart*, pp. 321, 336; W. W. Blackford, *War Years with Jeb Stuart* (New York, 1945), p. 223; Freeman, *Lee's Lieutenants*, 3:61; Jones, *Ranger Mosby*, p. 150; James J. Williamson, *Mosby's Rangers: A Record of the Operations of the Forty-third Battalion Virginia Cavalry* (New York, 1896), pp. 79–80.

17. Theodore Garnett, *J. E. B. Stuart . . . An Address* (New York, 1907), p. 59; McKim, "Confederate Cavalry in the Gettysburg Campaign," 420; Freeman, *Lee's Lieutenants*, 3:550–51; Coddington, *Gettysburg Campaign*, pp. 112–13.

18. *OR*, pt. 2, p. 692; pt. 3, pp. 309–10, 318; McClellan, *Life and Campaigns of Stuart*, p. 321.

19. Cooke, *Wearing of the Gray*, p. 230.

20. *OR*, pt. 2, pp. 692–93.

21. *OR*, pt. 2, p. 693; Coddington, *Gettysburg Campaign*, p. 113; Davis, *Stuart, the Last Cavalier*, p. 325.

22. *OR*, pt. 2, p. 693; Edward G. Longacre, "Stuart's Dumfries Raid," *CWTI* 15 (July 1976): 24–25.

23. Thomas W. Smith, *The Story of a Cavalry Regiment: "Scott's 900," Eleventh New York* (Chicago, 1897), p. 76; Lucien P. Waters to His Parents, 27 June 1863, Waters MSS, New-York Hist. Soc.; Cooke, *Wearing of the Gray*, p. 233.

24. McClellan, *Life and Campaigns of Stuart*, p. 323; *OR*, pt. 2, p. 693; pt. 3, pp. 358, 430; Smith, *Story of a Cavalry Regiment*, pp. 76–100.

25. Howard Swiggett, ed., *A Rebel War Clerk's Diary at the Confederate States Capital*, by John B. Jones, 2 vols. (New York, 1935), 1:366; *OR*, pt. 2, p. 693; R. L. T. Beale, *History of the Ninth Virginia Cavalry, in the War between the States* (Richmond, 1899), p. 78; *Philadelphia Daily Evening Bulletin*, 29 June 1863.

26. Cooke, *Wearing of the Gray*, p. 234.

27. *OR*, pt. 2, p. 693; pt. 3, pp. 376–77; Beale, *Ninth Virginia Cavalry*, p. 78; Blackford, *War Years with Jeb Stuart*, p. 223.

28. Cooke, *Wearing of the Gray*, p. 235.

29. McClellan, *Life and Campaigns of Stuart*, p. 323.

30. *OR*, pt. 2, p. 694; B. J. Haden, *Reminiscences of J. E. B. Stuart's Cavalry* (Charlottesville, Va., c. 1890), p. 23; Nye, *Here Come the Rebels*, p. 317.

31. Ephraim Bowman to His Father, 28 June 1863, Bowman MSS, Univ. of Virginia Lib.

32. Beale, *Ninth Virginia Cavalry*, p. 78; James Harrison Wilson, *Captain Charles Corbit's Charge at Westminster . . . An Episode of the Gettysburg Campaign* (Wilmington, Del., 1913), p. 14.

33. Blackford, *War Years with Jeb Stuart*, p. 225; Cooke, *Wearing of the Gray*, p. 236.

34. Beale, *Ninth Virginia Cavalry*, pp. 79–80; Blackford, *War Years with Jeb Stuart*, p. 224; McClellan, *Life and Campaigns of Stuart*, p. 324; Cooke, *Wearing of the Gray*, p. 238.

35. G. W. Beale, *A Lieutenant of Cavalry in Lee's Army* (Boston, 1918), pp. 112–13; Cooke, *Wearing of the Gray*, p. 238; Blackford, *War Years with Jeb Stuart*, p. 224.

36. *OR*, pt. 2, p. 694; Nye, *Here Come the Rebels*, p. 318.

37. Benjamin F. Cooling, *Symbol, Sword, and Shield: Defending Washington during the Civil War* (Hamden, Conn., 1975), pp. 162–64; Margaret Leech, *Reveille in Washington, 1860–1865* (New York, 1941), p. 256; Cecil D. Eby, Jr., ed., *A Virginia Yankee in the Civil War: The Diaries of David Hunter Strother* (Chapel Hill, N.C., 1961), p. 188.

38. Ezra J. Warner, *Generals in Blue: Lives of the Union Commanders* (Baton Rouge, La., 1964), pp. 284–85; Edward W. Emerson, *Life and Letters of Charles Russell Lowell* (Boston, 1907), pp. 268–70.

39. *OR*, pt. 3, pp. 378, 717; Benjamin W. Crowninshield Diary, 30 June 1863, Essex Inst.

40. *OR*, pt. 2, p. 694.

41. *OR*, pt. 2, p. 694; pt. 3, pp. 396, 403–4; Freeman, *Lee's Lieutenants*, 3:67.

42. McClellan, *Life and Campaigns of Stuart*, p. 326.

43. *OR*, pt. 2, pp. 202, 695; Nye, *Here Come the Rebels*, pp. 319–20; Wilson, *Captain Corbit's Charge at Westminster*, pp. 16–17, 27–28; Frederic Shriver Klein, ed., *Just South of Gettysburg* (Westminster, Md., 1963), pp. 46–47.

44. Wilson, *Captain Corbit's Charge at Westminster*, p. 16.

45. *OR*, pt. 2, p. 695; Everett I. Pearson, "Stuart in Westminster," *Transactions of the Southern Historical Society* 2 (1875): 20; Wilson, *Captain Corbit's Charge at Westminster*, p. 27.

46. *OR*, pt. 2, p. 695; Pearson, "Stuart in Westminster," 22; Cooke, *Wearing of the Gray*, p. 239; Wilson, *Captain Corbit's Charge at Westminster*, pp. 24–25; Klein, *Just South of Gettysburg*, p. 47.

47. *OR*, pt. 2, p. 695; Wilbur S. Nye, "The Affair at Hunterstown," *CWTI* 9 (Feb. 1971): 24; *Encounter at Hanover: Prelude to Gettysburg* (Hanover, Pa., 1963), p. 21.

48. *Encounter at Hanover*, p. 22; William H. Shriver, "My Father Led J. E. B. Stuart to Gettysburg," pp. 3–4, TS in GNMPL; S. C. Shriver to ———, 29 June 1863, Shriver MSS GNMPL.

49. McClellan, *Life and Campaigns of Stuart*, p. 327; *Encounter at Hanover*, pp. 22, 24; Shriver, "My Father Led J. E. B. Stuart to Gettysburg," p. 3.

50. Luther W. Hopkins, *From Bull Run to Appomattox: A Boy's View* (Baltimore, 1908), p. 97.

51. Shriver, "My Father Led J. E. B. Stuart to Gettysburg," p. 5; William Anthony, *History of the Battle of Hanover . . . Tuesday, June 30, 1863* (Hanover, Pa., 1945), p. 1.

52. James L. Morrison, Jr., ed., *The Memoirs of Henry Heth* (Westport, Conn., 1974), p. 174.

CHAPTER 9. PURSUIT TO PENNSYLVANIA

1. Willard Glazier, *Three Years in the Federal Cavalry* (New York, 1873), p. 233.

2. George H. Chapman Diary, 24 June 1863, Indiana State Hist. Soc.

3. Alfred Pleasonton to John F. Farnsworth, 23 June 1863; Elon J. Farnsworth to John F. Farnsworth, 23 June 1863; both, Pleasonton MSS, LC; *OR*, pt. 3, pp. 373, 376.

4. OR, pt. 3, pp. 214–15, 225–26; William Wells to His Mother, 21 June 1863, Wells MSS, Univ. of Vermont Lib.; William H. Rockwell to His Wife, 20 June 1863, Rockwell MSS, Western Michigan Univ. Lib.; Seth Williams to Julius Stahel, 19 June 1863, Generals' Reports of Service, War of the Rebellion, 11:71, RG-94, E-160, NA; John S. Farnill to His Parents, 24 June 1863, Farnill MSS, UML; J. A. Clark to "My Dear Friend," 30 July 1863, Alger MSS, UML.

5. *OR*, pt. 3, pp. 244–45, 254–55, 257–58; Louis N. Boudrye, *Historic Records of the Fifth New York Cavalry* (Albany, N.Y., 1865), p. 62; *Pennsylvania at Gettysburg*, 2 vols. (Harrisburg, Pa., 1893), 2:868; George W. Barbour Diary, 21 June 1863, UML; James H. Kidd to His Father, 28 June 1863,

Kidd MSS, UML; George Harrington Diary, 21 June 1863, Western Michigan Univ. Lib.; Seth Williams to Julius Stahel, 21 June 1863, Generals' Reports of Service, War of the Rebellion, 11:71–75, RG-94, E-160, NA.

6. *OR*, pt. 3, pp. 267, 269–70, 283, 288, 291–92; Walter H. Hebert, *Fighting Joe Hooker* (Indianapolis, 1944), p. 242; Manly Wade Wellman, *Harpers Ferry: Prize of War* (Charlotte, N.C., 1960), pp. 113–14; *Pennsylvania at Gettysburg*, 2:868; Daniel Butterfield to Julius Stahel, 23 June 1863 (and commentary on same), Generals' Reports of Service, War of the Rebellion, 11:75–77, RG-94, E-160, NA.

7. *OR*, pt. 1, p. 143; pt. 3, p. 312; James H. Kidd to His Father, 28 June 1863, Kidd MSS, UML; Hebert, *Fighting Joe Hooker*, pp. 243–44; Edward J. Nichols, *Toward Gettysburg: A Biography of General John F. Reynolds* (University Park, Pa., 1958), p. 187; Edwin B. Coddington, *The Gettysburg Campaign: A Study in Command* (New York, 1968), pp. 121–22, 631n.

8. *OR*, pt. 1, p. 143; pt. 3, pp. 312, 337–38; James H. Kidd, *Personal Recollections of a Cavalryman with Custer's Michigan Cavalry Brigade* (Ionia, Mich., 1908), p. 115; William Wells to His Mother, 28 June 1863, Wells MSS, Univ. of Vermont Lib.; George Harrington Diary, 25–26 June 1863, Western Michigan Univ. Lib.; Coddington, *Gettysburg Campaign*, p. 123.

9. George W. Barbour Diary, 26 June 1863, UML; Frank L. Klement, ed., "Edwin B. Bigelow: A Michigan Sergeant in the Civil War, *Michigan History* 38 (1954): 219; *OR*, pt. 3, pp. 315, 334–36.

10. *OR*, pt. 3, pp. 305–8, 312–13, 322, 334–36, 350; William Wells to His Mother, 28 June 1863, Wells MSS, Univ. of Vermont Lib.; *History of the Eighteenth Regiment of Cavalry, Pennsylvania Volunteers, 1862–1865* (New York, 1909), p. 38; Boudrye, *Fifth New York Cavalry*, p. 63.

11. *OR*, pt. 3, pp. 333–35, 338, 350–52; Nichols, *Toward Gettysburg*, p. 187.

12. *OR*, pt. 3, pp. 349, 353, 370. In the months and years following the campaign, Hooker and Pleasonton both tried to take credit for divining Gettysburg's strategic importance a week in advance of the battle (as witness the 27 June order that sent part of Stahel's division there), and contrary to the thinking of Hooker's less perceptive successor, Meade. Later historians have described their claims as twenty-twenty hindsight: Joseph Hooker to E. D. Townsend, 28 Sept. 1875; Hooker to D. McConaughy, 17 Oct. 1875; both, TSS in Hooker MSS, Gettysburg College Lib.; *JCCW*, 1868, pt. 2, p. 9; Coddington, *Gettysburg Campaign*, pp. 127–29, 633n.

13. *OR*, pt. 3, p. 377; Kidd, *Personal Recollections*, p. 121; Joseph T. Copeland to HQ, Army of the Potomac, 9 July 1863, HSP; Samuel Harris, *The Michigan Brigade of Cavalry at Gettysburg, July 3, 1863* (Chicago, 1894), pp. 5–6; George Harrington Diary, 28 June 1863, Western Michigan Univ. Lib.; Salome Myers Stewart, "Recollections of the Battle of Gettysburg," pp. 2–3; Sarah M. Broadhead, "The Diary of a Lady of Gettysburg, Pennsylvania, from June 15 to July 15, 1863," pp. 4–5; both, TS in Adams County Hist. Soc.

14. "Address of Gen. James H. Kidd at the Dedication of Michigan Monuments upon the Battlefield of Gettysburg, June 12th, 1889," *JUSCA* 4 (1891): 41–46; *OR*, pt. 3, pp. 370, 377; Walter Kempster, "The Cavalry at Gettysburg," *War Papers: Wisconsin MOLLUS*, 4 (1914): 399–400.

15. Jennie S. Croll, "Days of Dread: A Woman's Story of Her Life on a Battlefield," p. 2, TS in Adams County Hist. Soc.; Joseph T. Copeland to HQ, Army of the Potomac, 9 July 1863, HSP; Joseph T. Copeland to Adj. Gen. of the Army, 31 Aug., 30 Nov., 1863, 1 Dec. 1864, Copeland's General's Papers, RG-94, E-159, NA; *OR*, pt. 1, p. 58; pt. 3, pp. 373, 376, 496, 520, 656.

16. *OR*, pt. 1, p. 143; pt. 3, pp. 285–86, 305–6, 314; Coddington, *Gettysburg Campaign*, pp. 122–27.

17. *OR*, pt. 3, pp. 314, 319, 321–22, 333; Charles Gardner Memoirs, p. 38, USAMHI; John L. Beveridge, "The First Gun at Gettysburg," *Military Essays and Recollections: Illinois MOLLUS*, 2 (1894): 87.

18. William E. Miller, "The Cavalry Battle near Gettysburg," *B&L*, 3:397; Henry C. Meyer, *Civil War Experiences under Bayard, Gregg, Kilpatrick, Custer, Raulston, and Newberry, 1862, 1863, 1864* (New York, 1911), p. 42; Glazier, *Three Years in the Federal Cavalry*, p. 237.

19. *OR*, pt. 3, pp. 369, 373–74; Hebert, *Fighting Joe Hooker*, pp. 244–45; Wellman, *Harpers Ferry*, p. 114; Coddington, *Gettysburg Campaign*, pp. 128–33.

20. *OR*, pt. 3, p. 374; George G. Meade to His Wife, 29 June 1863, Meade MSS, HSP.

21. Alfred Pleasonton to John F. Farnsworth, 23 June 1863, Pleasonton MSS, LC; *OR*, pt. 1, p. 154.

22. *OR*, I, 25, pt. 2, p. 588; 27, pt. 1, pp. 166–67; pt. 3, pp. 373, 376, 813; Harris, *Michigan Brigade of Cavalry*, pp. 3–4; Alfred Pleasonton, "The Campaign of Gettysburg," *Annals of the War, Written by Leading Participants, North and South* (Philadelphia, 1879), p. 452.

23. *OR*, pt. 1, pp. 154, 991.

24. John Irvin Gregg, "Private & Confidential Memo," n.d., Gregg MSS, HSP.

25. Samuel Harris, *Major General George A. Custer: Stories Told around the Camp Fire of the Michigan Brigade of Cavalry* (Chicago, 1898), pp. 1–2; Meyer, *Civil War Experiences*, pp. 48–49; Marguerite Merington, ed., *The Custer Story: The Life and Intimate Letters of General George A. Custer and His Wife Elizabeth* (New York, 1950), pp. 60–61; Kidd, *Personal Recollections*, pp. 128–30; George R. Agassiz, ed., *Meade's Headquarters, 1863–1865: Letters of Colonel Theodore Lyman from the Wilderness to Appomattox* (Boston, 1922), p. 17.

26. *OR*, pt. 1, p. 991; Coddington, *Gettysburg Campaign*, p. 246; Samuel L. Gillespie, *A History of Company A, First Ohio Cavalry, 1861–1865* (Washington Court House, Ohio, 1898), pp. 147–48; William H. Rockwell to His Wife, 18 June 1863, Rockwell MSS, Western Michigan Univ. Lib.; William Wells to His Mother, 28 June 1863, Wells MSS, Univ. of Vermont Lib.

27. *OR*, pt. 1, pp. 1020–21; pt. 3, pp. 373, 376.

28. *OR*, pt. 3, p. 211; William Brooke Rawle, ed., *History of the Third Pennsylvania Cavalry* (Philadelphia, 1905), pp. 250, 255; Bliss Perry, *Life and Letters of Henry Lee Higginson* (Boston, 1921), p. 205; William Brooke Rawle, *With Gregg in the Gettysburg Campaign* (Philadelphia, 1884), p. 9.

29. *OR*, pt. 1, pp. 155–67; pt. 3, p. 376; *Pennsylvania at Gettysburg*, 2:781, 789; Frederick Phisterer, comp., *New York in the War of the Rebellion*, 5 vols. (Albany, N.Y., 1912), 2:1187; Charles D. Rhodes, "Outposts, Scouts and Couriers," *PHCW*, 4:195.

30. Isaac R. Pennypacker, *General Meade* (New York, 1901), p. 141; *Personal Memoirs of P. H. Sheridan*, 2 vols. (New York, 1888), 1:356.

31. *OR*, pt. 1, pp. 66–68, 143–44, 488; Newel Cheney, *History of the Ninth Regiment, New York Volunteer Cavalry, War of 1861 to 1865* (Jamestown and Poland Center, N.Y., 1901), pp. 100–101; Flavius J. Bellamy to His Parents, 3 July 1863, Bellamy MSS, Indiana State Lib.; Coddington, *Gettysburg Campaign*, pp. 131–32; D. M. Gilmore, "With General Gregg at Gettysburg," *Glimpses of the Nation's Struggle: Minnesota MOLLUS*, 4 (1898): 97.

32. *OR*, pt. 1, p. 144; George H. Chapman Diary, 29 June 1863, Indiana State Hist. Soc.; Cheney, *Ninth New York Cavalry*, p. 101; Warren W. Hassler, Jr., *Crisis at the Crossroads: The First Day at Gettysburg* (University, Ala., 1970), p. 13.

33. H. P. Moyer, comp., *History of the Seventeenth Regiment Pennsylvania Volunteer Cavalry* (Lebanon, Pa., 1911), p. 58.

34. *OR*, pt. 3, pp. 376–77.

35. *OR*, pt. 3, pp. 397, 469–70; Miller, "Cavalry Battle near Gettysburg," 397–98; Rawle, *Third Pennsylvania Cavalry*, pp. 257, 263; Meyer, *Civil War Experiences*, p. 42; Gilmore, "With General Gregg at Gettysburg," 99; Norman Ball Diary, 29 June 1863, Connecticut Hist. Soc.

36. *OR*, pt. 3, pp. 381, 398; Rawle, *With Gregg in the Gettysburg Campaign*, pp. 4–5; Rawle, *Third Pennsylvania Cavalry*, pp. 262–63.

37. Meyer, *Civil War Experiences*, p. 43.

38. Miller, "Cavalry Battle near Gettysburg," 398; Rawle, *Third Pennsylvania Cavalry*, p. 266; William E. Miller to William Brooke Rawle, 16 Jan. 1886, BRC; William L. Haskin, comp., *The History of the First Regiment of Artillery from Its Organization in 1821, to January 1st, 1876* (Portland, Me., 1879), p. 520.

39. Walter S. Newhall Diary, 29 June 1863, Newhall MSS, HSP; Hampton S. Thomas to William Brooke Rawle, 28 Jan. 1884, BRC.

40. J. C. Hunterson to William Brooke Rawle, 1 Feb. 1884, BRC; Miller, "Cavalry Battle near Gettysburg," 398; Rawle, *Third Pennsylvania Cavalry*, p. 264; Thomas M. Covert to His Wife, 27

July 1863, Covert MSS, William G. Burnett; Walter S. Newhall Diary, 30 June 1863, Newhall MSS, HSP.

41. Henry R. Pyne, *The History of the First New Jersey Cavalry* (Trenton, N.J., 1871), pp. 162–63; Rawle, *Third Pennsylvania Cavalry*, p. 264; John D. Follmer Diary, 30 June 1863, UML.

42. *OR*, pt. 3, p. 399; Miller, "Cavalry Battle near Gettysburg," 399.

43. Rawle, *Third Pennsylvania Cavalry*, p. 265; N. D. Preston, *History of the Tenth Regiment of Cavalry, New York State Volunteers* (New York, 1892), p. 103.

44. *OR*, pt. 1, pp. 144, 991; William Anthony, *History of the Battle of Hanover . . . Tuesday, June 30, 1863* (Hanover, Pa., 1945), p. 1.

45. *OR*, pt. 3, p. 400; Kidd, *Personal Recollections*, pp. 124–25.

46. Anthony, *Battle of Hanover*, p. 60; Frank Moore, ed., *The Rebellion Record: A Diary of American Events*, 11 vols. (New York, 1861–68), 7:184.

47. Gillespie, *Company A, First Ohio Cavalry*, p. 148.

48. *OR*, pt. 1, p. 999; John Robertson, comp., *Michigan in the War* (Lansing, Mich., 1880), pp. 578, 580.

49. *Eighteenth Pennsylvania Cavalry*, p. 39; Anthony, *Battle of Hanover*, p. 2.

50. Charles Blinn Diary, 30 June 1863, GNMPL.

51. Anthony, *Battle of Hanover*, pp. 2, 5, 39; *Encounter at Hanover: Prelude to Gettysburg* (Hanover, Pa., 1963), p. 58.

52. Wilbur S. Nye, *Here Come the Rebels* (Baton Rouge, La., 1965), p. 322; Anthony, *Battle of Hanover*, pp. 2, 9; *Eighteenth Pennsylvania Cavalry*, p. 87.

53. Henry C. Potter Memoirs, p. 2, GNMPL; *Eighteenth Pennsylvania Cavalry*, pp. 87–89.

54. *OR*, pt. 1, p. 986.

55. *OR*, pt. 1, p. 1011.

56. *OR*, pt. 1, pp. 1008–9, 1012, 1018; *Eighteenth Pennsylvania Cavalry*, p. 78; Henry C. Potter Memoirs, p. 2, GNMPL.

57. H. B. McClellan, *The Life and Campaigns of Maj. Gen. J. E. B. Stuart* (Richmond, 1885), p. 328; Anthony, *Battle of Hanover*, p. 2.

58. Anthony, *Battle of Hanover*, pp. 2, 5; *Encounter at Hanover*, pp. 61, 66, 93; W. W. Blackford, *War Years with Jeb Stuart* (New York, 1945), pp. 225–26; Charles Blinn Diary, 30 June 1863, GNMPL; *OR*, pt. 2, pp. 695–96; R. L. T. Beale, *History of the Ninth Virginia Cavalry, in the War between the States* (Richmond, 1899), p. 82.

59. George W. Barbour Diary, 17 June 1863, UML.

60. George W. Barbour Diary, 30 June 1863, UML; Robertson, *Michigan in the War*, p. 580; Kidd, *Personal Recollections*, pp. 127–28.

61. Anthony, *Battle of Hanover*, p. 5.

62. Blackford, *War Years with Jeb Stuart*, pp. 226–27; McClellan, *Life and Campaigns of Stuart*, p. 328.

63. Anthony, *Battle of Hanover*, pp. 6, 9.

64. *OR*, pt. 1, pp. 987–88; Anthony, *Battle of Hanover*, pp. 5–6, 9.

65. *OR*, pt. 1, p. 997; Anthony, *Battle of Hanover*, pp. 6, 9; Kidd, *Personal Recollections*, p. 128.

66. Anthony, *Battle of Hanover*, pp. 6, 60.

67. Anthony, *Battle of Hanover*, p. 9; Edwin R. Havens to "Father, Mother & Nell," 9 July 1863, Havens MSS, Michigan State Univ. Lib.; Kidd, *Personal Recollections*, pp. 128–30.

68. Anthony, *Battle of Hanover*, pp. 9, 14; Robertson, *Michigan in the War*, p. 580; James Moore, *Kilpatrick and Our Cavalry* (New York, 1865), pp. 85–86; John Esten Cooke, *Wearing of the Gray* (New York, 1867), pp. 241–42.

69. *OR*, pt. 2, p. 696; Anthony, *Battle of Hanover*, pp. 9–10; McClellan, *Life and Campaigns of Stuart*, p. 329.

70. *OR*, pt. 1, pp. 193, 992; pt. 2, pp. 713–14; Anthony, *Battle of Hanover*, pp. 14, 30.

71. *OR*, pt. 1, pp. 924, 987–88; Anthony, *Battle of Hanover*, p. 43.

72. *OR*, pt. 1, p. 987; pt. 3, p. 421.

73. *OR*, pt. 1, pp. 145, 992; William Wells to His Father, 7 July 1863, Wells MSS, Univ. of Vermont Lib.; *Encounter at Hanover*, p. 256; *Pennsylvania at Gettysburg*, 2:895.

74. Edwin R. Havens to ———, 6 July 1863, Havens MSS, Michigan State Univ. Lib.

CHAPTER 10. GETTYSBURG, 1 JULY

1. *OR*, pt. 1, p. 923; John L. Beveridge, "The First Gun at Gettysburg," *Military Essays and Recollections: Illinois MOLLUS*, 2 (1894): 89; Glenn Tucker, *High Tide at Gettysburg: The Campaign in Pennsylvania* (Indianapolis, 1958), p. 99.

2. William Gamble to William L. Church, 10 Mar. 1864, Gamble MSS, Chicago Hist. Soc.; Daniel Pulis to His Parents, 6 July 1863, Pulis MSS, Rochester Pub. Lib.; Charles M. Munroe Diary, 30 June 1863, American Antiquarian Soc.; Hillman A. Hall, W. B. Besley, and Gilbert G. Wood, comps., *History of the Sixth New York Cavalry* (Worcester, Mass., 1908), p. 133.

3. Tillie Pierce Alleman, *At Gettysburg; or, What a Girl Saw and Heard of the Battle* (n.p., 1888), pp. 28–29; Salome Myers Stewart, "Recollections of the Battle of Gettysburg," p. 3, TS in Adams County Hist. Soc.; Newel Cheney, *History of the Ninth Regiment, New York Volunteer Cavalry, War of 1861 to 1865* (Jamestown and Poland Center, N.Y., 1901), p. 102; Hall, Besley, and Wood, *Sixth New York Cavalry*, p. 133.

4. *OR*, pt. 1, pp. 922–24; Samuel L. Gillespie, *A History of Company A, First Ohio Cavalry, 1861–1865* (Washington Court House, Ohio, 1898), p. 147.

5. *OR*, pt. 1, pp. 914, 926; George H. Chapman Diary, 30 June 1863, Indiana State Hist. Soc.; Daniel Pulis to His Parents, 6 July 1863, Pulis MSS, Rochester Pub. Lib.; James K. P. Scott, *The Story of the Battle of Gettysburg* (Harrisburg, Pa., 1927), pp. 85–86.

6. *OR*, pt. 1, pp. 923–24; Edwin B. Coddington, *The Gettysburg Campaign: A Study in Command* (New York, 1968), pp. 232–33.

7. Coddington, *Gettysburg Campaign*, pp. 264–65.

8. Walter Kempster, "The Cavalry at Gettysburg," *War Papers: Wisconsin MOLLUS*, 4 (1914): 400; William L. Heermance, "The Cavalry at Gettysburg," *Personal Recollections of the War of the Rebellion: New York MOLLUS*, 3 (1907): 199–200.

9. Charles M. McCurdy, *Gettysburg: A Memoir* (Pittsburgh, Pa., 1929), p. 7.

10. James L. Morrison, Jr., ed., *The Memoirs of Henry Heth* (Westport, Conn., 1974), p. 173; *OR*, pt. 1, pp. 923, 926; pt. 2, p. 637; Coddington, *Gettysburg Campaign*, p. 263; Warren W. Hassler, Jr., *Crisis at the Crossroads: The First Day at Gettysburg* (University, Ala., 1970), p. 16.

11. *OR*, pt. 1, pp. 927, 934, 938; Hassler, *Crisis at the Crossroads*, p. 30; Hall, Besley, and Wood, *Sixth New York Cavalry*, pp. 137–38.

12. *Proceedings of the Buford Memorial Association* (New York, 1895), p. 24; H. E. Jacobs, "How an Eyewitness Watched the Great Battle," *Philadelphia North American*, 29 June 1913.

13. Samuel P. Bates, *The Battle of Gettysburg* (Philadelphia, 1875), p. 55.

14. *OR*, pt. 3, p. 416; Frederic Shriver Klein, "Meade's Pipe Creek Line," *Maryland Historical Magazine* 57 (1962), 133–49.

15. Bates, *Battle of Gettysburg*, p. 55.

16. *OR*, pt. 2, p. 637.

17. Morrison, *Memoirs of Henry Heth*, p. 173; Coddington, *Gettysburg Campaign*, pp. 263–64.

18. *OR*, pt. 2, pp. 307, 444.

19. Leander H. Warren, "Recollections of the Battle of Gettysburg," p. 4, TS in Adams County Hist. Soc.

20. James L. McLean, Jr., "The First Union Shot at Gettysburg," *Lincoln Herald* 82 (1980): 318–23; Beveridge, "The First Gun at Gettysburg," 91–92; Ezra B. Fuller, "Who Fired the First Shot at the Battle of Gettysburg?" *JUSCA* 24 (1914): 793–94; William Gamble to William L. Church, 10 Mar. 1864, Gamble MSS, Chicago Hist. Soc.

21. John H. Calef, "Gettysburg Notes: The Opening Gun," *JMSIUS* 40 (1907), 48; *OR*, pt. 1,

pp. 1030–31; John B. Bachelder to John P. Nicholson, 25 July 1893, "Captain John H. Calef's Battery Position" file, TS in GNMPL.

22. Henry J. Hunt, "The First Day at Gettysburg," *B&L*, 3:274n.–75n.; Cheney, *Ninth New York Cavalry*, pp. 107–8.

23. *OR*, pt. 1, pp. 927, 934, 939; pt. 2, pp. 637, 642–43, 646, 648–49. At least one historian has asserted that Buford's cavalry held the line against Heth's foot soldiers far less than the two or three hours with which it is generally credited: Russell F. Weigley, "John Buford—A Personality Profile," *CWTI* 5 (June 1966): 22.

24. *OR*, pt. 1, pp. 265, 696, 701; pt. 3, p. 457; Charles H. Veil Memoirs, pp. 36–37, WL.

25. Bates, *Battle of Gettysburg*, pp. 59–60; Edward J. Nichols, *Toward Gettysburg: A Biography of General John F. Reynolds* (University Park, Pa., 1958), p. 202. Coddington, *Gettysburg Campaign*, p. 682n., holds that this long accepted account of the Reynolds-Buford meeting may be apocryphal. One resident of Gettysburg claimed to have seen the two generals at Buford's midtown headquarters earlier that same morning: Jacobs, "How an Eyewitness Watched the Great Battle."

26. George Meade, *The Life and Letters of George Gordon Meade*, 2 vols. (New York, 1913), 2:35–36; Charles H. Veil to D. McConaughy, 7 Apr. 1864, Veil MSS, Gettysburg College Lib.

27. William Gamble to William L. Church, 10 Mar. 1864, Gamble MSS, Chicago Hist. Soc.; Albert Huntington, *8th New York Cavalry: Historical Paper* (Palmyra, N.Y., 1902), p. 14.

28. *OR*, pt. 1, p. 939; pt. 2, p. 649; H. P. Moyer, comp., *History of the Seventeenth Regiment Pennsylvania Volunteer Cavalry* (Lebanon, Pa., 1911), pp. 61–63; Cheney, *Ninth New York Cavalry*, p. 109; Hall, Besley, and Wood, *Sixth New York Cavalry*, p. 140.

29. Flavius J. Bellamy to His Parents, 3 July 1863, Bellamy MSS, Indiana State Lib.; Hassler, *Crisis at the Crossroads*, p. 40; Beveridge, "The First Gun at Gettysburg," 93–94.

30. Nichols, *Toward Gettysburg*, pp. 204–5, 253n.–54n.; Charles H. Veil to D. McConaughy, 7 Apr. 1864, Veil MSS, Gettysburg College Lib.; Charles H. Veil Memoirs, pp. 38–39, WL.

31. James A. Bell to Gusta Ann Hallock, 2 July 1863, Bell MSS, HEHL; Abner Doubleday, *Chancellorsville and Gettysburg* (New York, 1886), p. 128.

32. Cheney, *Ninth New York Cavalry*, pp. 109–10; Moyer, *Seventeenth Pennsylvania Cavalry*, p. 63; Augustus P. Clarke, "The Sixth New York Cavalry: Its Movements and Service at the Battle of Gettysburg," *United Service* 16 (1896): 413.

33. Cheney, *Ninth New York Cavalry*, p. 109; *OR*, pt. 1, p. 939.

34. *OR*, pt. 1, p. 939; Hall, Besley, and Wood, *Sixth New York Cavalry*, p. 140; Cheney, *Ninth New York Cavalry*, p. 111; Moyer, *Seventeenth Pennsylvania Cavalry*, p. 63.

35. *OR*, pt. 1, p. 939; Cheney, *Ninth New York Cavalry*, p. 112; Moyer, *Seventeenth Pennsylvania Cavalry*, pp. 63–65.

36. *OR*, pt. 1, p. 925; Freeman Cleaves, *Meade of Gettysburg* (Norman, Okla., 1960), p. 137; Coddington, *Gettysburg Campaign*, pp. 297–98.

37. *OR*, pt. 1, p. 934; pt. 2, pp. 656–57, 662, 665; Calef, "Gettysburg Notes: The Opening Gun," 49–52; George H. Chapman Diary, 1 July 1863, Indiana State Hist. Soc.

38. Coddington, *Gettysburg Campaign*, pp. 294–97.

39. Beveridge, "The First Gun at Gettysburg," 96–97; Charles H. Howard, "First Day at Gettysburg," *Military Essays and Recollections: Illinois MOLLUS*, 4 (1907): 261.

40. Francis A. Walker, *History of the Second Army Corps in the Army of the Potomac* (New York, 1886), p. 266 and n.

41. Charles D. Rhodes, "Cavalry Battles and Charges," *PHCW*, 4:235. One member of Gamble's brigade saw Confederate infantry form "cressent shapes" rather than squares: James A. Bell to Gusta Ann Hallock, 2 July 1863, Bell MSS, HEHL.

42. Daniel Pulis to His Parents, 6 July 1863, Pulis MSS, Rochester Pub. Lib.

43. *OR*, pt. 2, pp. 318, 445.

44. *OR*, pt. 1, pp. 185, 482, 530–31, 758–59.

CHAPTER 11. STUART'S EXPEDITION—HANOVER TO GETTYSBURG

1. James K. P. Scott, *The Story of the Battle of Gettysburg* (Harrisburg, Pa., 1927), p. 121.
2. *OR*, pt. 2, p. 696.
3. *OR*, pt. 2, pp. 467–68, 696; Glenn Tucker, *High Tide at Gettysburg: The Campaign in Pennsylvania* (Indianapolis, 1958), p. 87; Douglas Southall Freeman, *Lee's Lieutenants: A Study in Command*, 3 vols. (New York, 1942–44), 3:71.
4. John S. Mosby, *Stuart's Cavalry in the Gettysburg Campaign* (New York, 1908), pp. 183 and n., 184n.; Freeman, *Lee's Lieutenants*, 3:136; H. B. McClellan, *The Life and Campaigns of Maj. Gen. J. E. B. Stuart* (Richmond, 1885), p. 330.
5. *OR*, pt. 2, p. 696; Mosby, *Stuart's Cavalry*, pp. 182–83.
6. *OR*, pt. 2, p. 444; Wilbur S. Nye, *Here Come the Rebels* (Baton Rouge, La., 1965), pp. 347–49; Edwin B. Coddington, *The Gettysburg Campaign: A Study in Command* (New York, 1968), pp. 206, 660n.–61n.
7. *OR*, pt. 2, p. 220 (the original of Smith's campaign report is in Smith MSS, Vermont Hist. Soc.); pt. 3, p. 493; Russell F. Weigley, "Emergency Troops in the Gettysburg Campaign," *Pennsylvania History* 25 (1985): 53.
8. Edward G. Longacre, "'A Perfect Ishmaelite': General 'Baldy' Smith," *CWTI* 16 (Dec. 1976): 10–14.
9. R. K. Hitner to Mrs. David Hastings, 6 July 1863, Maryland Hist. Soc.; Woodruff Jones, "Defending Pennsylvania against Lee," *CWTI* 5 (Oct. 1966): 40.
10. James W. Sullivan, *Boyhood Memories of the Civil War, 1861–'65: Invasion of Carlisle* (Carlisle, Pa., 1933), p. 27; Jones, "Defending Pennsylvania against Lee," 41.
11. G. W. Beale, *A Lieutenant of Cavalry in Lee's Army* (Boston, 1918), p. 114.
12. Theodore M. Riley, "A Garrison Town in Pennsylvania Fifty Years Ago," *JMSIUS* 40 (1907): 98; R. L. T. Beale, *History of the Ninth Virginia Cavalry, in the War between the States* (Richmond, 1899), p. 84.
13. *New York Times*, 3 July 1863.
14. Jones, "Defending Pennsylvania Against Lee," 43; Nye, *Here Come the Rebels*, p. 325; Burke Davis, *Jeb Stuart, the Last Cavalier* (New York, 1957), p. 331.
15. Samuel M. Goodyear, *General Robert E. Lee's Invasion of Carlisle, 1863* (Carlisle, Pa., 1942), pp. 6–7; Jones, "Defending Pennsylvania against Lee," 42.
16. Although Smith and his subordinate, Brigadier General John Ewen, reported (*OR*, pt. 2, pp. 221, 237) that none of their guns returned Lee's fire, one of their battery officers claimed that militia cannon not only fired back but disabled a Confederate gun crew: Jones, "Defending Pennsylvania against Lee," 42–43.
17. *OR*, pt. 2, p. 221; *New York Times*, 3 July 1863; R. H. Peck, *Reminiscences of a Confederate Soldier of Co. C, 2nd Va. Cavalry* (Fincastle, Va., 1913), p. 32; John Esten Cooke, *Wearing of the Gray* (New York, 1867), p. 245.
18. *OR*, pt. 2, p. 221.
19. *OR*, pt. 2, p. 224; *New York Times*, 3 July 1863; Goodyear, *Lee's Invasion of Carlisle*, p. 7.
20. *OR*, pt. 2, p. 697.
21. Cooke, *Wearing of the Gray*, p. 245.
22. *OR*, pt. 2, p. 697; McClellan, *Life and Campaigns of Stuart*, pp. 330–31.
23. *OR*, pt. 2, pp. 221, 224.
24. *Encounter at Hanover: Prelude to Gettysburg* (Hanover, Pa., 1963), p. 240; T. W. Herbert, "In Occupied Pennsylvania," *Georgia Review* 4 (1950): 109.
25. Wilbur S. Nye, "The Affair at Hunterstown," *CWTI* 9 (Feb. 1971): 29.
26. T. J. Mackey, "Duel of General Wade Hampton on the Battle-Field at Gettysburg with a Federal Soldier," *SHSP* 22 (1894): 125–26; Manly Wade Wellman, *Giant in Gray: A Biography of Wade Hampton of South Carolina* (New York, 1949), pp. 115–16.
27. Nye, "Affair at Hunterstown," 30–31, 33; McClellan, *Life and Campaigns of Stuart*, p. 331.

28. H. C. Parsons, "Farnsworth's Charge and Death," *B&L*, 3:394.

29. Herbert, "In Occupied Pennsylvania," 109.

30. W. C. Storrick, "The Hunterstown Fight," pp. 3–4, TS in GNMPL; C. E. Goldsborough, "Battle of Hunterstown," *Philadelphia Record*, 15 Sept. 1901.

31. *OR*, pt. 1, pp. 992, 999; Storrick, "Hunterstown Fight," pp. 3–4.

32. *OR*, pt. 1, p. 999; Nye, "Affair at Hunterstown," 33; George W. Barbour Diary, 2 July 1863, UML.

33. Frank Moore, ed., *The Rebellion Record: A Diary of American Events*, 11 vols. (New York, 1861–68), 7:194.

34. John Robertson, comp., *Michigan in the War* (Lansing, Mich., 1880), pp. 580, 586–87; James H. Kidd, *Personal Recollections of a Cavalryman with Custer's Michigan Cavalry Brigade* (Ionia, Mich., 1908), p. 134; James H. Kidd to His Parents, 9 July 1863, Kidd MSS, UML; George W. Barbour Diary, 2 July 1863, UML; J. A. Clark to "My Dear Friend," 30 July 1863, Alger MSS, UML; Edwin R. Havens to ———, 6 July 1863, Havens MSS, Michigan State Univ. Lib.

35. *New York Times*, 21 July 1863. This issue contains a long and comprehensive article by E. A. Paul, a correspondent who traveled with Kilpatrick's command, regarding the operations of the 3rd Cavalry Division from Hanover to Falling Waters, 30 June–14 July 1863. Although studded with errors of fact and interpretation, it is an indispensable source on this part of the Gettysburg campaign.

36. *OR*, pt. 2, p. 724; William G. Delony to His Wife, 4, 7 July, 1863, Delony MSS, Univ. of Georgia Lib.; Kidd, *Personal Recollections*, pp. 134–35; Lynwood M. Holland, *Pierce M. B. Young, the Warwick of the South* (Athens, Ga., 1964), p. 73.

37. *OR*, pt. 2, p. 497.

38. Nye, "Affair at Hunterstown," 23.

39. Coddington, *Gettysburg Campaign*, p. 207.

40. R. K. Beecham, *Gettysburg: The Pivotal Battle of the Civil War* (Chicago, 1911), p. 210; Bell I. Wiley, ed., *Recollections of a Confederate Staff Officer*, by G. Moxley Sorrel (Jackson, Tenn., 1958), p. 154; Glenn Tucker, *Lee and Longstreet at Gettysburg* (Indianapolis, 1968), p. 8.

41. William L. Royall, *Some Reminiscences* (New York, 1909), p. 25.

42. *OR*, pt. 2, pp. 307, 321.

43. Davis, *Jeb Stuart, the Last Cavalier*, p. 334; E. Porter Alexander, *Military Memoirs of a Confederate: A Critical Narrative* (New York, 1907), p. 377.

CHAPTER 12. GETTYSBURG, 2 JULY

1. D. M. Gilmore, "With General Gregg at Gettysburg," *Glimpses of the Nation's Struggle: Minnesota MOLLUS*, 4 (1898): 101; William Brooke Rawle, ed., *History of the Third Pennsylvania Cavalry* (Philadelphia, 1905), p. 266; William Brooke Rawle to William E. Miller, 30 Jan. 1886, BRC.

2. John D. Follmer Diary, 1 July 1863, UML; Jonah Yoder Diary, 1 July 1863, USAMHI; Rawle, *Third Pennsylvania Cavalry*, pp. 257, 283; Willard Glazier, *Three Years in the Federal Cavalry* (New York, 1873), p. 242.

3. Gilmore, "With General Gregg at Gettysburg," 101; Walter Kempster, "The Cavalry at Gettysburg," *War Papers: Wisconsin MOLLUS*, 4 (1914): 422; William E. Miller, "The Cavalry Battle near Gettysburg," *B&L*, 3:399.

4. *OR*, pt. 3, pp. 400, 425.

5. Charles F. Adams, Jr., Diary, 30 June, 1–3 July, 1863, Massachusetts Hist. Soc.

6. *OR*, pt. 3, pp. 470–72.

7. *OR*, pt. 1, p. 790; *Pennsylvania at Gettysburg*, 2 vols. (Harrisburg, Pa., 1893), 2:836; David M. Gregg, Jr., "Brevet Major General David McMurtrie Gregg," pp. 201–2, TS in Gregg MSS, LC; Thomas M. Covert to His Wife, 2 July 1863, Covert MSS, William G. Burnett; Norman Ball Diary, 1 July 1863, Connecticut Hist. Soc.; Henry C. Meyer, *Civil War Experiences under Bayard,*

Gregg, Kilpatrick, Custer, Raulston, and Newberry, 1862, 1863, 1864 (New York, 1911), p. 45; Miller, "Cavalry Battle near Gettysburg," 399.

8. Newel Cheney, *History of the Ninth Regiment, New York Volunteer Cavalry, War of 1861 to 1865* (Jamestown and Poland Center, N.Y., 1901), p. 114; Hillman A. Hall, W. B. Besley, and Gilbert G. Wood, comps., *History of the Sixth New York Cavalry* (Worcester, Mass., 1908), p. 142; James A. Bell to Gusta Ann Hallock, 8 July 1863, Bell MSS, HEHL.

9. George H. Chapman Diary, 2 July 1863, Indiana State Hist. Soc.

10. *OR*, pt. 1, pp. 928, 939, 1032; Cheney, *Ninth New York Cavalry*, pp. 114–15; Hall, Besley, and Wood, *Sixth New York Cavalry*, p. 142.

11. *OR*, pt. 1, p. 482; Edwin B. Coddington, *The Gettysburg Campaign: A Study in Command* (New York, 1968), pp. 351–53. Although the time of Buford's withdrawal from the Federal left is usually given as prior to the advance of Sickles's sharpshooters, it would appear that there was a considerable overlap. Most of Devin's brigade remained on the field long enough to support the III Corps during its initial skirmishing: *OR*, pt. 1, pp. 939, 1032.

12. Cheney, *Ninth New York Cavalry*, p. 115.

13. George H. Chapman Diary, 2 July 1863, Indiana State Hist. Soc.

14. *OR*, pt. 1, p. 915. Pleasonton later moved his headquarters a mile farther down the road to Taneytown: *Pennsylvania at Gettysburg*, 2:826.

15. Cheney, *Ninth New York Cavalry*, p. 115.

16. *OR*, pt. 3, p. 490; George H. Chapman Diary, 2 July 1863, Indiana State Hist. Soc.; William H. Redman to His Sisters, 3 July 1863, Redman MSS, Univ. of Virginia Lib.; Flavius J. Bellamy Diary, 2–3 July 1863, Bellamy MSS, Indiana State Lib.; James A. Bell to Gusta Ann Hallock, 8 July 1863, Bell MSS, HEHL; Charles M. Munroe Diary, 2 July 1863, American Antiquarian Soc.; Cheney, *Ninth New York Cavalry*, p. 115; Hall, Besley, and Wood, *Sixth New York Cavalry*, pp. 142–43.

17. *OR*, pt. 1, p. 1032.

18. Edward J. Stackpole, *They Met at Gettysburg* (Harrisburg, Pa., 1956), p. 197; Kempster, "The Cavalry at Gettysburg," 423–25; Coddington, *Gettysburg Campaign*, pp. 351–52. Some hours after Buford had begun his withdrawal, Pleasonton told Gregg to replace both Gamble's and Devin's brigades with a single regiment from the 2nd Division: *OR*, pt. 3, p. 490.

19. "The Meade-Sickles Controversy," *B&L*, 3:415–16.

20. Coddington, *Gettysburg Campaign*, pp. 343–441; Henry J. Hunt, "The Second Day at Gettysburg," *B&L*, 3:301–4. Along with his infantry, Meade shored up Sickles's crumbling line with four regiments from the Cavalry Corps, the 1st Massachusetts and the 1st, 2nd, and 4th Pennsylvania: Worthington Chauncey Ford, ed., *A Cycle of Adams Letters, 1861–1865*, 2 vols. (Boston, 1920), 2:56; *Pennsylvania at Gettysburg*, 2:781, 789–90; *JCCW*, 1868, pt. 2, p. 10; *OR*, pt. 1, pp. 1058–59; William E. Doster, *Lincoln and Episodes of the Civil War* (New York, 1915), pp. 217–19.

21. *OR*, pt. 1, p. 956; Norman Ball Diary, 2 July 1863, Connecticut Hist. Soc.

22. Meyer, *Civil War Experiences*, p. 47; Miller, "Cavalry Battle near Gettysburg," 399–400.

23. Miller, "Cavalry Battle near Gettysburg," 400; Rawle, *Third Pennsylvania Cavalry*, p. 266; *OR*, pt. 3, p. 489.

24. All distances on the cavalry battlefield have been computed by comparing maps of the 1860s and 1880s with a modern U.S. Geological Survey map ("SW/4 Gettysburg 15' Quadrangle," based on a 1951 survey of the field).

25. *OR*, pt. 1, p. 956; Miller, "Cavalry Battle near Gettysburg," 400–401; N. D. Preston, *History of the Tenth Regiment of Cavalry, New York State Volunteers* (New York, 1892), pp. 106–7; William Brooke Rawle, *With Gregg in the Gettysburg Campaign* (Philadelphia, 1884), p. 14.

26. *Pennsylvania at Gettysburg*, 2:817; Doster, *Lincoln and Episodes of the Civil War*, pp. 217–18.

27. Louis Fortescue Memoirs, p. 93; WL; *OR*, pt. 3, p. 266.

28. John A. Dahlgren, *Memoir of Ulric Dahlgren* (Philadelphia, 1872), p. 160; Frank Moore, ed., *The Rebellion Record: A Diary of American Events*, 11 vols. (New York, 1861–68), 7:193.

29. Glenn Tucker, *High Tide at Gettysburg: The Campaign in Pennsylvania* (Indianapolis, 1958), pp. 312–13; Jacob Hoke, *The Great Invasion of 1863* (Dayton, Ohio, 1887), pp. 180–82.

30. Louis Fortescue Memoirs, pp. 93–94, WL; *New York Times*, 8 July 1863; Dahlgren, *Memoir of Ulric Dahlgren*, p. 161; Tucker, *High Tide at Gettysburg*, p. 313.

31. James W. Milgram, ed., "The Libby Prison Correspondence of Tattnall Paulding," *American Philatelist* 89 (1975): 1114; Dahlgren, *Memoir of Ulric Dahlgren*, p. 161; Tucker, *High Tide at Gettysburg*, pp. 313–14.

32. *OR*, pt. 1, pp. 75–77; pt. 3, pp. 931–32.

33. Tucker, *High Tide at Gettysburg*, p. 314; W. J. Seymour, "Some of the Secret History of Gettysburg," *SHSP* 8 (1883): 521–28; Kempster, "The Cavalry at Gettysburg," 428. For an argument against the theory that the captured documents persuaded Meade to cancel his planned withdrawal, see Coddington, *Gettysburg Campaign*, pp. 773n.–74n.

34. Louis Fortescue Memoirs, p. 94, WL; Moore, *Rebellion Record*, 7 : 193; S. L. Gracey, *Annals of the Sixth Pennsylvania Cavalry* (Philadelphia, 1868), p. 189; Dahlgren, *Memoir of Ulric Dahlgren*, p. 163; *Pennsylvania at Gettysburg*, 2 : 827–28; *OR*, pt. 3, pp. 498, 526.

35. *OR*, pt. 1, p. 956; Miller, "Cavalry Battle near Gettysburg," 400–401; Rawle, *Third Pennsylvania Cavalry*, p. 267; Preston, *Tenth New York Cavalry*, p. 110.

36. Rawle, *Third Pennsylvania Cavalry*, p. 267.

37. Frank M. Myers, *The Comanches: A History of White's Battalion, Virginia Cavalry* (Baltimore, 1871), pp. 196, 199. Having marched to Gettysburg the previous day, White's troopers fought Buford's command as part of Ewell's advance. Conceivably, some of the Comanches had ranged toward the Chambersburg Pike, forming a bridge between Ewell and the left flank of Hill's corps. If so, this would explain the cryptic reference in Lieutenant Calef's report to firing on Rebel horsemen advancing along the pike on 1 July: *OR*, pt. 1, p. 1031.

38. Rawle, *Third Pennsylvania Cavalry*, p. 267; Rawle, *With Gregg in the Gettysburg Campaign*, p. 15.

39. *OR*, pt. 2, pp. 504, 518, 521; Kempster, "The Cavalry at Gettysburg," 414.

40. Miller, "Cavalry Battle near Gettysburg," 401; Rawle, *Third Pennsylvania Cavalry*, pp. 267–68.

41. Kempster, "The Cavalry at Gettysburg," 415; Rawle, *With Gregg in the Gettysburg Campaign*, p. 17; William Rawle Brooke Diary, 2 July 1863, Brooke MSS, WL; David McMurtrie Gregg to William Brooke Rawle, 25 May 1878, BRC.

42. Coddington, *Gettysburg Campaign*, pp. 430, 432–33; *OR*, pt. 2, pp. 504, 518–19; *Pennsylvania at Gettysburg*, 2 : 798; Kempster, "The Cavalry at Gettysburg," 415–16.

43. Coddington, *Gettysburg Campaign*, pp. 449–51; Daniel Butterfield, "Further Recollections of Gettysburg," *North American Review* 152 (1891): 283.

CHAPTER 13. GETTYSBURG, 3 JULY

1. E. E. Bouldin to John B. Bachelder, 19 July 1886, BP.

2. H. B. McClellan, *The Life and Campaigns of Maj. Gen. J. E. B. Stuart* (Richmond, 1885), p. 337; Jennings C. Wise, *The Long Arm of Lee: The History of the Artillery of the Army of Northern Virginia*, 2 vols. (Lynchburg, Va., 1915), 2 : 691; Fairfax Downey, *The Guns at Gettysburg* (New York, 1958), pp. 161–62.

3. *OR*, pt. 2, p. 697.

4. *OR*, pt. 2, pp. 697, 699; Edwin B. Coddington, *The Gettysburg Campaign: A Study in Command* (New York, 1968), p. 520; J. G. Harbord, "The History of the Cavalry of the Army of Northern Virginia," *JUSCA* 14 (1904): 456–57; John B. Arnold, Supervisor, Interpretive Services, GNMP, to W. H. Greenleaf, 15 May 1974, TS in GNMPL; Author's Interview with Dr. Frederick Tilberg, Chief Historian Emeritus, GNMP, 10 May 1972.

5. *OR*, pt. 2, p. 697; William Brooke Rawle, ed., *History of the Third Pennsylvania Cavalry* (Philadelphia, 1905), p. 271; McClellan, *Life and Campaigns of Stuart*, p. 338.

6. McClellan, *Life and Campaigns of Stuart*, p. 339; E. E. Bouldin to John B. Bachelder, 29 July

1886; V. A. Witcher to Secretary of War, 27 Mar. 1887; both, BP; V. A. Witcher to L. L. Lomax, 20 Aug. 1908, BRC.

7. McClellan, *Life and Campaigns of Stuart*, pp. 338–39.

8. *OR*, pt. 1, pp. 992, 1059; William E. Doster, *Lincoln and Episodes of the Civil War* (New York, 1915), p. 219.

9. *OR*, pt. 1, pp. 992, 998; James H. Kidd, *Personal Recollections of a Cavalryman with Custer's Michigan Cavalry Brigade* (Ionia, Mich., 1908), p. 135; *History of the Eighteenth Regiment of Cavalry, Pennsylvania Volunteers, 1862–1865* (New York, 1909), pp. 40–41; Henry C. Potter Memoirs, p. 3, GNMPL; *New York Times*, 21 July 1863.

10. *OR*, pt. 3, p. 502; Walter Kempster, "The Cavalry at Gettysburg," *War Papers: Wisconsin MOLLUS*, 4 (1914): 425–26.

11. David McMurtrie Gregg, *The Second Cavalry Division of the Army of the Potomac in the Gettysburg Campaign* (Philadelphia, 1907), p. 10; David M. Gregg, Jr., "Brevet Major General David McMurtrie Gregg," p. 207, TS in Gregg MSS, LC.

12. John Robertson, comp., *Michigan in the War* (Lansing, Mich., 1880), pp. 582–83; Samuel Harris, *Major General George A. Custer: Stories Told around the Camp Fire of the Michigan Brigade of Cavalry* (Chicago, 1898), p. 5; *OR*, pt. 1, pp. 992–93.

13. Robertson, *Michigan in the War*, pp. 582–83; Kidd, *Personal Recollections*, pp. 139–40; J. H. Kidd to His Parents, 9 July 1863, Kidd MSS, UML; Harris, *Major General George A. Custer*, appendix, p. 4.

14. *Pennsylvania at Gettysburg*, 2 vols. (Harrisburg, Pa., 1893), 2:847, 855; *Proceedings at the Dedication of the Monumental Shaft . . . Erected upon the Field of the Cavalry Engagement . . . during the Battle of Gettysburg* (Philadelphia, 1885), p. 39.

15. *OR*, pt. 1, p. 977; *Dedication of the Monumental Shaft*, pp. 39–40; Rawle, *Third Pennsylvania Cavalry*, pp. 269–70; *Pennsylvania at Gettysburg*, 2:870–71; William L. Haskin, comp., *The History of the First Regiment of Artillery from its Organization in 1821, to January 1st, 1876* (Portland, Me., 1879), p. 521; John D. Follmer Diary, 3 July 1863, UML; Norman Ball Diary, 3 July 1863, Connecticut Hist. Soc.

16. *OR*, pt. 1, pp. 956, 1050; Kempster, "The Cavalry at Gettysburg," 426; Rawle, *Third Pennsylvania Cavalry*, p. 270; William E. Miller, "The Cavalry Battle near Gettysburg," *B&L*, 3:401.

17. John B. McIntosh to William Brooke Rawle, 21 June 1878; Hampton S. Thomas, "Notes as to the Cavalry Fight on the Right Flank at Gettysburg," n.d.; both, BRC. The latter work, a memoir by one of McIntosh's staff officers written in the 1870s, is a major source for much of the following account of the 3 July fighting.

18. Thomas, "Notes as to the Cavalry Fight," BRC; Kidd, *Personal Recollections*, pp. 140–41; Samuel Toombs, *New Jersey Troops in the Gettysburg Campaign* (Orange, N.J., 1888), p. 400.

19. *OR*, pt. 1, p. 1050; Rawle, *Third Pennsylvania Cavalry*, p. 273; Miller, "Cavalry Battle near Gettysburg," 400.

20. Charles Gardner Memoirs, p. 39, USAMHI; John D. Follmer Diary, 4 July 1863, UML.

21. *Pennsylvania at Gettysburg*, 2:791–92; Coddington, *Gettysburg Campaign*, pp. 493–502.

22. *Pennsylvania at Gettysburg*, 2:781–82, 785, 790, 815–17.

23. *OR*, pt. 1, pp. 522, 1021–23; Downey, *Guns at Gettysburg*, p. 164.

24. Thomas W. Smith to His Sister, 11 July 1863, Smith MSS, HSP.

25. *Pennsylvania at Gettysburg*, 2:818 and n.; Doster, *Lincoln and Episodes of the Civil War*, p. 219; *OR*, pt. 1, p. 1059.

26. The following account of the 3 July cavalry fighting along the far Union right is derived from dozens of sources and many months of matching them against each other. The discrepancies and inconsistencies in these sources make even compiling a chronology of events extremely difficult. In every case, reliance has been placed on sources written as close to the time of the events depicted as possible, by participants or observers in a position to describe those events knowingly—even when these documents do not agree with long-accepted printed versions of the fighting.

27. *OR*, pt. 2, pp. 697–98; McClellan, *Life and Campaigns of Stuart*, p. 339; Kidd, *Personal Recollections*, pp. 143–44; H. B. McClellan to John B. Bachelder, 12 Apr. 1886, BP; A. C. M. Pennington to Carle A. Woodruff, 5 Dec. 1884, BRC.

28. Miller, "Cavalry Battle near Gettysburg," 402; Rawle, *Third Pennsylvania Cavalry*, p. 274.

29. McClellan, *Life and Campaigns of Stuart*, pp. 339–40; V. A. Witcher to Secretary of War, 27 Mar. 1887, BP; Thomas, "Notes as to the Cavalry Fight," BRC; David M. Cooper, *Obituary Discourse on [the] Occasion of the Death of Noah Henry Ferry* (New York, 1863), pp. 20–22. Many sources—including Kidd, *Personal Recollections*, p. 147; Miller, "Cavalry Battle near Gettysburg," 403; and Rawle, *Third Pennsylvania Cavalry*, p. 276—place Ferry's death much later in the battle, thus skewing the order of events on that field. Three eyewitnesses, including one who tried to recover Ferry's body, agree that the major was killed during or soon after Witcher's initial advance against the 1st New Jersey: Russell A. Alger in Robertson, *Michigan in the War*, p. 578; V. A. Witcher to Russell A. Alger, 2 Aug. 1898, Alger MSS, UML; and Thomas, "Notes as to the Cavalry Fight," BRC.

30. *OR*, pt. 1, p. 1051; Miller, "Cavalry Battle near Gettysburg," 400, 402; Rawle, *Third Pennsylvania Cavalry*, p. 274.

31. E. E. Bouldin to John B. Bachelder, 29 July 1886; V. A. Witcher to Secretary of War, 27 Mar. 1887; both, BP; McClellan, *Life and Campaigns of Stuart*, pp. 339–40.

32. Robertson, *Michigan in the War*, p. 583; Kidd, *Personal Recollections*, p. 146.

33. Haskin, *First Regiment of Artillery*, p. 521; A. M. Randol to John B. Bachelder, 24 Mar. 1886, BP; James Chester to William Brooke Rawle, 3 Dec. 1884, BRC; *OR*, pt. 2, p. 698.

34. E. E. Bouldin to John B. Bachelder, 29 July 1886, BP.

35. Kidd, *Personal Recollections*, pp. 145–46; David McMurtrie Gregg to E. D. Townsend, 12 Mar. 1878, BRC; Miller, "Cavalry Battle near Gettysburg," 402.

36. H. B. McClellan to John B. Bachelder, 28 Dec. 1885, 12 Apr. 1886, BP; *OR*, pt. 2, p. 698.

37. *OR*, pt. 1, p. 956; Robertson, *Michigan in the War*, p. 583; Kidd, *Personal Recollections*, p. 141; Gregg, *Second Cavalry Division*, p. 11; J. B. McIntosh to William Brooke Rawle, 21 June 1878, BRC.

38. William Brooke Rawle to J. W. Kirkley, 21 Dec. 1883, BRC; H. B. McClellan to John B. Bachelder, 14 Apr. 1886, BP; Rawle, *Third Pennsylvania Cavalry*, pp. 275–76; John Y. Foster, *New Jersey and the Rebellion* (Newark, N.J., 1868), pp. 446–49.

39. John B. McIntosh to William Brooke Rawle, 21 June 1878; James M. Deems to William Brooke Rawle, 11 Dec. 1884; Thomas, "Notes as to the Cavalry Fight"; all, BRC; H. S. Thomas to John B. Bachelder, 1 July 1886, BP; *OR*, pt. 1, p. 957; Rawle, *Third Pennsylvania Cavalry*, p. 276.

40. Luther S. Trowbridge to "My Most Precious Julia," 7 July 1863, Trowbridge MSS, UML.

41. Rawle, *Third Pennsylvania Cavalry*, p. 276; Miller, "Cavalry Battle near Gettysburg," 403; Robertson, *Michigan in the War*, pp. 578, 583; Henry C. Meyer, *Civil War Experiences under Bayard, Gregg, Kilpatrick, Custer, Raulston, and Newberry, 1862, 1863, 1864* (New York, 1911), p. 50.

42. Edwin R. Havens to ———, 6 July 1863, Havens MSS, Michigan State Univ. Lib.; J. A. Clark to "My Dear Friend," 30 July 1863, Alger MSS, UML; Asa B. Isham, *An Historical Sketch of the Seventh Regiment Michigan Volunteer Cavalry* (New York, 1893), pp. 22–29; William O. Lee, comp., *Personal and Historical Sketches . . . of the Seventh Regiment Michigan Volunteer Cavalry, 1862–1865* (Detroit, 1904), pp. 56–58, 155–56; Kidd, *Personal Recollections*, pp. 148–52; Rawle, *Third Pennsylvania Cavalry*, pp. 276–77, 277n.; Miller, "Cavalry Battle near Gettysburg," 403–4; *OR*, pt. 2, p. 698.

43. Meyer, *Civil War Experiences*, p. 51.

44. Luther S. Trowbridge to "My Most Precious Julia," 7 July 1863, Trowbridge MSS, UML; R. A. Alger to John B. Bachelder, 4 Jan., 8 Feb., 1886, Alger MSS, UML; Luther S. Trowbridge, *The Operations of the Cavalry in the Gettysburg Campaign* (Detroit, 1888), pp. 12–13; Rawle, *Third Pennsylvania Cavalry*, p. 277; Kidd, *Personal Recollections*, pp. 151–52; Miller, "Cavalry Battle near Gettysburg," 404.

45. George H. Chapman Diary, 3 July 1863, Indiana State Hist. Soc.; Flavius J. Bellamy to His Parents, 3 July 1863, Bellamy MSS, Indiana State Lib.; Daniel H. Woodward, ed., "The Civil War of a Pennsylvania Trooper," *Pennsylvania Magazine of History and Biography* 87 (1963): 53.

46. *OR*, pt. 1, p. 995; H. C. Parsons, "Farnsworth's Charge and Death," *B&L*, 3:393; Henry C. Potter Memoirs, p. 3, GNMPL; *New York Times*, 21 July 1863.

47. Comte de Paris, *History of the Civil War in America*, 4 vols. (Philadelphia, 1875–88) 3:652; E. M. Law, "The Struggle for 'Round Top,'" *B&L*, 3:318–27; *History of the Eighteenth Regiment of Cavalry, Pennsylvania Volunteers, 1862–1865* (New York, 1909), pp. 40–41.

48. E. M. Law to John B. Bachelder, 13 June 1876, 22 Apr. 1886, BP; Law,"Struggle for 'Round Top,'" 327; Eleanor D. McSwain, ed., *Crumbling Defenses, or Memoirs and Reminiscences of John Logan Black, Colonel, C.S.A.* (Macon, Ga., 1960), p. 43; Wise, *Long Arm of Lee*, 2:683–84; Downey, *Guns at Gettysburg*, pp. 165–66.

49. Law, "Struggle for 'Round Top,'" 327; Parsons, "Farnsworth's Charge and Death," 393.

50. *OR*, pt. 1, pp. 993, 1018–19; Parsons, "Farnsworth's Charge and Death," 393; Henry C. Potter Memoirs, pp. 3–4, GNMPL.

51. *OR*, pt. 3, pp. 923, 927–28.

52. See, for example, John S. Mosby, "The Confederate Cavalry in the Gettysburg Campaign," *B&L*, 3:251–52. By 1896, however, even Mosby, one of Robertson's and Jones's sharpest critics, had come to believe that Robert E. Lee was responsible for keeping their brigades in the Valley after Hooker's departure from their front: John S. Mosby to the "Editor of the [*Philadelphia Weekly*] *Times*," 2 Mar. 1896, Mosby MSS, Missouri Hist. Soc.; John S. Mosby, *Stuart's Cavalry in the Gettysburg Campaign* (New York, 1908), pp. 195, 198–201, 215–18.

53. Mosby, "Confederate Cavalry in the Gettysburg Campaign," 251–52; Beverly H. Robertson, "The Confederate Cavalry in the Gettysburg Campaign," *B&L*, 3:253; Jasper Hawse Diary, 3 July 1863, Univ. of Virginia Lib.; John S. Mosby to L. L. Lomax, 19 Feb. 1896, Mosby MSS, USAMHI; George M. Neese, *Three Years in the Confederate Horse Artillery* (New York, 1911), pp. 184–86; Bushrod C. Washington, ed., *A History of the Laurel Brigade*, by William N. McDonald (Baltimore, 1907), p. 153; McClellan, *Life and Campaigns of Stuart*, pp. 336, 347; Coddington, *Gettysburg Campaign*, pp. 184–86.

54. Luther W. Hopkins, *From Bull Run to Appomattox: A Boy's View* (Baltimore, 1908), p. 109; Neese, *Confederate Horse Artillery*, p. 186.

55. *OR*, pt. 2, pp. 752, 756, 760; pt. 3, pp. 947–48; Neese, *Confederate Horse Artillery*, p. 187; Jacob Hoke, *The Great Invasion of 1863* (Dayton, Ohio, 1887), p. 231; William F. Loftin to His Mother, 29 Aug. 1863, Duke Univ. Lib.

56. George Baylor, *Bull Run to Bull Run; or, Four Years in the Army of Northern Virginia* (Richmond, 1900), p. 150; Washington, *Laurel Brigade*, p. 153; Frank M. Myers, *The Comanches: A History of White's Battalion, Virginia Cavalry* (Baltimore, 1871), pp. 201–3.

57. *OR*, pt. 1, p. 943; *New York Times*, 8 July 1863.

58. *OR*, pt. 1, p. 948; James W. Milgram, ed., "The Libby Prison Correspondence of Tattnall Paulding," *American Philatelist* 89 (1975): 1114–15; *Pennsylvania at Gettysburg*, 2:850; W. H. Carter, *From Yorktown to Santiago with the Sixth U.S. Cavalry* (Baltimore, 1900), p. 95; William H. Carter, "The Sixth Regiment of [United States] Cavalry," *Maine Bugle* 3 (1896): 299; S. L. Gracey, *Annals of the Sixth Pennsylvania Cavalry* (Philadelphia, 1868), p. 179; T. F. Rodenbough, "The Regular Cavalry in the Gettysburg Campaign," *JMSIUS* 44 (1909): 29.

59. Milgram, "Libby Prison Correspondence of Tattnall Paulding," 1115; Carter, *From Yorktown to Santiago*, pp. 95–96; *OR*, pt. 2, p. 752.

60. *OR*, pt. 1, p. 948; pt. 2, pp. 752, 760.

61. *OR*, pt. 2, p. 756; Washington, *Laurel Brigade*, p. 155.

62. "Colonel Samuel H. Starr," p. 2, TS in Starr MSS, Missouri Hist. Soc.; Milgram, "Libby Prison Correspondence of Tattnall Paulding," 1115; *OR*, pt. 1, p. 948; McClellan, *Life and Campaigns of Stuart*, p. 384 and n.; Hopkins, *From Bull Run to Appomattox*, p. 113.

63. *OR*, pt. 1, p. 948.

64. Washington, *Laurel Brigade*, p. 156; Coddington, *Gettysburg Campaign*, pp. 537–38; Neese, *Confederate Horse Artillery*, p. 188; Carter, *From Yorktown to Santiago*, p. 98; E. D. Anderson, "Cavalry Operations in the Gettysburg Campaign," pp. 64–65, Army War College Study, TS in USAMHI.

65. *OR*, pt. 2, pp. 724–25; Manly Wade Wellman, *Giant in Gray: A Biography of Wade Hampton of South Carolina* (New York, 1949), pp. 118–19; Rawle, *Third Pennsylvania Cavalry*, p. 277.

66. Miller, "Cavalry Battle near Gettysburg," 404; Rawle, *Third Pennsylvania Cavalry*, p. 277.

67. H. S. Thomas to John B. Bachelder, 1 July 1886, BP.

68. A. M. Randol to John B. Bachelder, 24 Mar. 1886; H. B. McClellan to John B. Bachelder, 12 Apr. 1886; both, BP; James Chester to William Brooke Rawle, 27 Sept. 1879, 3 Dec. 1884; A. C. M. Pennington to Carle A. Woodruff, 5 Dec. 1884; both, BRC; Kidd, *Personal Recollections*, pp. 153–54; Downey, *Guns at Gettysburg*, p. 164.

69. Asa B. Isham, *The Michigan Cavalry Brigade* (Ionia, Mich., 1911), p. 1; Meyer, *Civil War Experiences*, p. 52; Asa B. Isham, "The Cavalry of the Army of the Potomac," *Sketches of War History, 1861–1865: Ohio MOLLUS*, 5 (1903): 309; Harris, *Major General George A. Custer*, p. 6.

70. Miller, "Cavalry Battle near Gettysburg," 404.

71. George Armstrong Custer to His Sister, 26 July 1863, Custer MSS, United States Military Academy Lib.; Robertson, *Michigan in the War*, pp. 576, 583; Kidd, *Personal Recollections*, pp. 154–55; Rawle, *Third Pennsylvania Cavalry*, pp. 277–79; William Brooke Rawle to John B. Bachelder, 22 May 1878, BRC.

72. Rawle, *Third Pennsylvania Cavalry*, p. 279; Miller, "Cavalry Battle near Gettysburg," 404–5; *OR*, pt. 1, p. 1051; John B. McIntosh to His Wife, 17 July 1863, McIntosh MSS, Brown Univ. Lib.; Meyer, *Civil War Experiences*, pp. 51–52; Frederick C. Newhall to His Father, 4 July 1863, Newhall MSS, HSP; Harrison S. Newhall to William Brooke Rawle, 3 Dec. 1877; David McMurtrie Gregg to J. Edward Carpenter, 27 Dec. 1877; both, BRC; Kidd, *Personal Recollections*, pp. 154–55; Sarah Butler Wister, *Walter S. Newhall: A Memoir* (Philadelphia, 1864), pp. 111–13.

73. Miller, "Cavalry Battle near Gettysburg," 405; Rawle, *Third Pennsylvania Cavalry*, p. 280; Wellman, *Giant in Gray*, p. 120; Charles E. Cauthen, ed., *Family Letters of Three Wade Hamptons, 1782–1901* (Columbia, S.C., 1953), p. 94; Rufus Barringer, *The First North Carolina—A Famous Cavalry Regiment* (n.p., c. 1866), p. 5; William G. Delony to His Wife, 4 July 1863, Delony MSS, Univ. of Georgia Lib.; Thomas, "Notes as to the Cavalry Fight," BRC.

74. Miller, "Cavalry Battle near Gettysburg," 404–5; Rawle, *Third Pennsylvania Cavalry*, pp. 279, 307–12; D. M. Gilmore, "With General Gregg at Gettysburg," *Glimpses of the Nation's Struggle: Minnesota MOLLUS*, 4 (1898): 110–11; William E. Miller to William Brooke Rawle, 5 June 1878; William E. Miller to John B. McIntosh, 8 June 1878; William Brooke Rawle to William E. Miller, 12 June 1878; William Brooke Rawle to Cecil Battine, 21 Feb. 1908; all, BRC. For a rebuttal to the claims of effectiveness traditionally made for Captain Miller's attack, see Andrew J. Speese, *Story of Companies H, A and C, Third Pennsylvania Cavalry at Gettysburg, July 3, 1863* (Germantown, Pa., 1906), especially pp. 7–8, 15.

75. Arthur James Lyon Fremantle, *Three Months in the Southern States, April–June 1863* (New York, 1864), pp. 266–70; Bruce Catton, *Never Call Retreat* (Garden City, N.Y., 1965), p. 191; Law, "Struggle for 'Round Top,'" 322.

76. *JCCW*, 1868, pt. 2, p. 10; Alfred Pleasonton, "The Campaign of Gettysburg," *Annals of the War, Written by Leading Participants, North and South* (Philadelphia, 1879), p. 455.

77. Edward G. Longacre, "Alfred Pleasonton, 'The Knight of Romance,'" *CWTI* 13 (Dec. 1974): 18–23.

78. *OR*, pt. 1, pp. 916, 943, 993; *Pennsylvania at Gettysburg*, 2:829; Kempster, "Cavalry at Gettysburg," 421; Cecil Battine, *The Crisis of the Confederacy: A History of Gettysburg and the Wilderness* (New York, 1905), p. 260.

79. William L. Richter, "The Federal Cavalry in the Gettysburg Campaign: The Development of the Mobile Arm of the Army of the Potomac," p. 137, Arizona State Univ. Lib.; Coddington, *Gettysburg Campaign*, pp. 524–25.

80. *OR*, pt. 1, p. 943; Law, "Struggle for 'Round Top,'" 327; E. M. Law to John B. Bachelder, 11, 13 June 1876, BP; Gracey, *Sixth Pennsylvania Cavalry*, pp. 179–81; Comte de Paris, *Civil War in America*, 3:653; T. F. Rodenbough, comp., *From Everglade to Cañon with the Second Dragoons* (New York, 1875), p. 295; Don E. Alberts, "General Wesley Merritt, Nineteenth Century Cavalryman," p. 81, Univ. of New Mexico Lib.

81. *OR*, pt. 2, p. 402; Law, "Struggle for 'Round Top,'" 328; E. M. Law to John B. Bachelder, 13 June 1876, 22 Apr. 1886, BP; *Pennsylvania at Gettysburg*, 2:852–53.

82. Parsons, "Farnsworth's Charge and Death," 393; Henry C. Potter Memoirs, p. 3, GNMPL; *Eighteenth Pennsylvania Cavalry*, pp. 79–80.

83. *OR*, pt. 1, pp. 1018–19; Parsons, "Farnsworth's Charge and Death," 394; Law, "Struggle for 'Round Top,'" 328; Downey, *Guns at Gettysburg*, p. 165.

84. Charles D. Rhodes, "Cavalry Battles and Charges," *PHCW*, 4:230; James Moore, *Kilpatrick and Our Cavalry* (New York, 1865), p. 92; Charles D. Rhodes, *History of the Cavalry of the Army of the Potomac* (Kansas City, Mo., 1900), p. 68.

85. McSwain, *Crumbling Defenses*, p. 43; *John Hammond: Died May 28, 1889* (Chicago, 1890), p. 61; Parsons, "Farnsworth's Charge and Death," 394. An even more fanciful unpublished version of the latter source is in LC. In many respects it is similar to the *B&L* piece, though containing further embellishments such as an assertion that Meade personally ordered Farnsworth's charge and later suppressed his directive to that effect. The facts of the Kilpatrick-Farnsworth exchange preceding the attack are muddled. While Confederate infantrymen supposedly overheard a heated argument (William C. Oates, *The War between the Union and the Confederacy* [New York, 1905], p. 236; *Pennsylvania at Gettysburg*, 2:830; E. M. Law to John B. Bachelder, 13 June 1876, BP), many Union witnesses—including the officer who conveyed the attack order from Kilpatrick to Farnsworth—heatedly denied that an acrimonious confrontation took place: L. G. Estes to the Editors of the *Century*, 7 July 1888, Estes MSS, New York Public Lib.; Henry C. Potter Memoirs, p. 4, GNMPL; *Dedication of the Statue to Brevet Major-General William Wells . . . on the Battlefield of Gettysburg* (Burlington, Vt., 1914), pp. 134–36.

86. *Eighteenth Pennsylvania Cavalry*, pp. 40–41, 80–82; Henry C. Potter Memoirs, p. 4, GNMPL; *OR*, pt. 1, pp. 993, 1011–12; *Pennsylvania at Gettysburg*, 2:852–53, 895–98.

87. Parsons, "Farnsworth's Charge and Death," 394–96.

88. *OR*, pt. 1, pp. 993, 1005, 1009, 1011–14, 1018–19; pt. 2, pp. 391–92, 396–97, 400, 402–3; Parsons, "Farnsworth's Charge and Death," 395–96; Law, "Struggle for 'Round Top,'" 328–29; William Wells to His Parents, 7 July 1863, Wells MSS, Univ. of Vermont Lib.; Charles Blinn Diary, 3 July 1863, GNMPL; Oates, *War between the Union and the Confederacy*, pp. 235–36; *Eighteenth Pennsylvania Cavalry*, p. 81; Francis F. McKinney, "The Death of Farnsworth," *Michigan Alumnus Quarterly Review* 66 (1959): 77–79.

89. Parsons, "Farnsworth's Charge and Death," 396n.; James Barnet, ed., *The Martyrs and Heroes of Illinois in the Great Rebellion: Biographical Sketches* (Chicago, 1865), p. 44; Rhodes, "Cavalry Battles and Charges," 232, 234; Oates, *War between the Union and the Confederacy*, pp. 236–37; William C. Oates, "The Battle [of Gettysburg] on the Right," *SHSP* 6 (1878): 182; McSwain, *Crumbling Defenses*, p. 43; E. M. Law to John B. Bachelder, 13 June 1876, BP. The surgeon of the 1st Vermont and Farnsworth's stepmother, both of whom examined the body, reported that it had been riddled with bullets, many of the wounds being extensive enough to have proved fatal. Thus Farnsworth's comrades asserted that he would not have possessed the strength to commit suicide: P. O. Edson to H. N. Jackson, 3 June 1914, TS in "South Cavalry Field" file, GNMPL; E. A. Carpenter to the Editor of the *Century*, 3 Jan. 1887, Carpenter MSS, New York Public Lib.

90. Fitz Lee, for one, wrote that neither Farnsworth nor Merritt was in a position to accomplish anything of strategic consequence: Fitzhugh Lee, *General Lee* (New York, 1895), p. 276. Some Federals claimed that Farnsworth's charge prevented General Law from aiding Longstreet's renewed effort against the Round Tops. But Law had determined this to be an impossibility—given his position and the constraints placed on him by the surrounding terrain—long before the Union troopers advanced against him: Law, "Struggle for 'Round Top,'" 326–27. On the other hand, had Kilpatrick employed Farnsworth's brigade farther to the west, on Merritt's left, he might have menaced the Confederate rear and, in the words of James Longstreet, "made more trouble than was ever made by a cavalry brigade": James Longstreet, *From Manassas to Appomattox: Memoirs of the Civil War in America* (Philadelphia, 1895), p. 396. Longstreet's chief of artillery agreed: E. Porter Alexander, *Military Memoirs of a Confederate: A Critical Narrative* (New York, 1907), p. 425. Even so, the myopic Pleasonton told Kilpatrick the next day that he was "highly delighted" with the division

leader's operations against the enemy right, though Pleasonton grieved over the death of his former aide: Generals' Reports of Service, War of the Rebellion, 3:695, RG-94, E-160, NA; Alfred Pleasonton to John F. Farnsworth, 15 July 1863, Pleasonton MSS, LC.

91. McClellan, *Life and Campaigns of Stuart*, pp. 341–49; *OR*, pt. 1, pp. 186, 193, 957–58; pt. 2, pp. 699, 714–15. The Federals contended that at battle's end they, not Stuart, held the Rummel farm. This became a hotly contested issue for years afterward: J. H. Rummel to William Brooke Rawle, 17 Nov. 1884, 14 Jan. 1886; H. B. McClellan to William Brooke Rawle, 1 July 1885; both, BRC; H. S. Thomas to John B. Bachelder, 1 July 1886; H. B. McClellan to John B. Bachelder, 28 Dec. 1885, 12 Apr. 1886; all, BP; Miller, "Cavalry Battle near Gettysburg," 406; Rawle, *Third Pennsylvania Cavalry*, pp. 280–82.

92. Miller, "Cavalry Battle near Gettysburg," 405n.; Meyer, *Civil War Experiences*, pp. 54–55; James Chester to William Brooke Rawle, 12 Nov. 1884, BRC.

CHAPTER 14. RETREAT TO VIRGINIA, PURSUIT TO MARYLAND

1. *OR*, pt. 2, pp. 296–97, 305, 307; pt. 3, pp. 183–84, 187, 201, 221–22, 232, 236, 296, 345, 389–90, 508, 595, 610, 865–66, 878, 905–6, 924; Jacob Hoke, *The Great Invasion of 1863* (Dayton, Ohio, 1887), pp. 172–73; Edwin B. Coddington, *The Gettysburg Campaign: A Study in Command* (New York, 1968), pp. 17, 105–7, 173–74, 808n., 810n.; *Philadelphia Daily Evening Bulletin*, 25 June 1863; Philip Schaff, "The Gettysburg Week," *Scribner's Magazine* 16 (1894): 25–26.

2. *OR*, pt. 3, pp. 345, 389, 394, 924, 947–48; Hoke, *Great Invasion*, pp. 172, 200–205; *New York Times*, 1 July 1863.

3. John D. Imboden, "The Confederate Retreat from Gettysburg," *B&L*, 3:420–22; Coddington, *Gettysburg Campaign*, p. 538; *OR*, pt. 3, pp. 966–67.

4. Imboden, "Confederate Retreat from Gettysburg," 421–24; Coddington, *Gettysburg Campaign*, pp. 810n., 814n.–15n.

5. *OR*, pt. 2, pp. 299, 309, 311, 322, 669; pt. 3, p. 531; Coddington, *Gettysburg Campaign*, pp. 535–41.

6. *OR*, pt. 1, p. 489; pt. 3, pp. 517–18, 524, 538, 1069; I, 51, pt. 1, p. 540; Hoke, *Great Invasion*, p. 471; Coddington, *Gettysburg Campaign*, p. 542; *New York Times*, 6 July 1863.

7. *OR*, pt. 1, pp. 81, 489; C. A. Newcomer, *Cole's Cavalry; or, Three Years in the Saddle in the Shenandoah Valley* (Baltimore, 1895), p. 55; Manly Made Wellman, *Harpers Ferry: Prize of War* (Charlotte, N.C., 1960), p. 118.

8. *OR*, pt. 2, pp. 221–22, 238, 246; "Military History of William Farrar Smith," p. 6, Smith's ACPF, RG-94, NA; Coddington, *Gettysburg Campaign*, pp. 542–43.

9. *OR*, pt. 1, p. 85; pt. 3, pp. 506–8, 549–50; S. L. Grace, *Annals of the Sixth Pennsylvania Cavalry* (Philadelphia, 1868), p. 189; *Pennsylvania at Gettysburg*, 2 vols. (Harrisburg, Pa., 1893), 2:827–28, 850; *New York Times*, 21 July 1863.

10. *OR*, pt. 1, pp. 916–17, 928, 939, 943, 958–59, 967, 970, 977, 993–94; Coddington, *Gettysburg Campaign*, pp. 543–44.

11. *OR*, pt. 1, pp. 970, 993–94, 998; pt. 2, p. 326; William Brooke Rawle, ed., *History of the Third Pennsylvania Cavalry* (Philadelphia, 1905), p. 283; *Pennsylvania at Gettysburg*, 2:836; H. B. McClellan, *The Life and Campaigns of Maj. Gen. J. E. B. Stuart* (Richmond, 1885), pp. 352–53; E. D. Anderson, "Cavalry Operations in the Gettysburg Campaign," p. 67, Army War College Study, TS in USAMHI.

12. *OR*, pt. 1, pp. 994, 998; pt. 2, pp. 752–53; John Robertson, comp., *Michigan in the War* (Lansing, Mich., 1880), pp. 576–77, 579; McClellan, *Life and Campaigns of Stuart*, pp. 353–55; Russell A. Alger to S. L. Gillespie, 27 Apr. 1899, Alger MSS, UML.

13. Russell A. Alger to L. G. Estes, 12 Feb. 1897; Russell A. Alger to S. L. Gillespie, 27 Apr. 1899; both, Alger MSS, UML; L. G. Estes to Secretary of War, 11 Feb. 1897, Alger's ACPF, RG-94, NA; McClellan, *Life and Campaigns of Stuart*, pp. 353–55; George Wilson Booth, *Personal Reminiscences of a Maryland Soldier in the War between the States, 1861–65* (Baltimore, 1898), p. 93.

14. *OR*, pt. 1, pp. 970, 994; pt. 2, pp. 700–701, 753; Robert E. Lee to Jefferson Davis, 7 July 1863, Lee MSS, Chicago Hist. Soc.; *New York Times*, 21 July 1863; G. W. Mattoon to His Sisters, 16 July 1863, Mattoon MSS, Michigan State Univ. Lib.; Gilbert W. Chapman to "Friend James," 29 July 1863, Detroit Pub. Lib.; John R. Morey Diary, 4–5 July 1863, Morey MSS, UML; Charles Blinn Diary, 4–5 July 1863, GNMPL; James H. Kidd to His Parents, 9 July 1863, Kidd MSS, UML; Willard Glazier, *Three Years in the Federal Cavalry* (New York, 1873), pp. 267–69; James Moore, *Kilpatrick and Our Cavalry* (New York, 1865), pp. 99–101; James H. Kidd, *Personal Recollections of a Cavalryman with Custer's Michigan Cavalry Brigade* (Ionia, Mich., 1908), pp. 168–71; Samuel L. Gillespie, *A History of Company A, First Ohio Cavalry, 1861–1865* (Washington Court House, Ohio, 1898), pp. 154–59; John N. Opie, *A Rebel Cavalryman with Lee, Stuart, and Jackson* (Chicago, 1899), p. 173; George M. Neese, *Three Years in the Confederate Horse Artillery* (New York, 1911), pp. 190–91; John O. Casler, *Four Years in the Stonewall Brigade* (Guthrie, Okla., 1893), p. 260.

15. Luther W. Hopkins, *From Bull Run to Appomattox: A Boy's View* (Baltimore, 1908), p. 105.

16. *OR*, pt. 1, pp. 959, 977, 981; pt. 3, p. 517; William E. Doster, *Lincoln and Episodes of the Civil War* (New York, 1915), pp. 232–33; Henry C. Meyer, *Civil War Experiences under Bayard, Gregg, Kilpatrick, Custer, Raulston, and Newberry, 1862, 1863, 1864* (New York, 1911), pp. 56–57; Norman Ball Diary, 4–5 July 1863, Connecticut Hist. Soc.; David M. Gregg, Jr., "Brevet Major General David McMurtrie Gregg," p. 217, TS in Gregg MSS, LC; John P. Sheahan to His Father, 5, 6 July, 1863; John P. Sheahan to His Sister, 13 July 1863; all, Sheahan MSS, Maine Hist. Soc.; Glazier, *Three Years in the Federal Cavalry*, p. 266; Rawle, *Third Pennsylvania Cavalry*, p. 285.

17. Meyer, *Civil War Experiences*, pp. 56–57; Charles Gardner Memoirs, pp. 39–40, USAMIHI; Norman Ball Diary, 4–6 July 1863, Connecticut Hist. Soc.; John D. Follmer Diary, 4–5 July 1863, UML; Edward P. Tobie, *History of the First Maine Cavalry, 1861–1865* (Boston, 1887), p. 180.

18. *OR*, pt. 1, pp. 917, 977–78, 1059; pt. 3, pp. 582, 584, 593, 602, 621; Gregg, "Brevet Major General David McMurtrie Gregg," p. 218; Rawle, *Third Pennsylvania Cavalry*, p. 285; Doster, *Lincoln and Episodes of the Civil War*, pp. 233–34; Norman Ball Diary, 7–14 July 1863, Connecticut Hist. Soc.; John D. Follmer Diary, 6–14 July 1863, UML; *Pennsylvania at Gettysburg*, 2:818–19; Coddington, *Gettysburg Campaign*, pp. 813–14.

19. *OR*, pt. 1, pp. 959, 967; pt. 3, pp. 560–61; Benjamin W. Crowninshield Diary, 4 July 1863, Essex Inst.; Rawle, *Third Pennsylvania Cavalry*, pp. 285–86; Generals' Reports of Service, War of the Rebellion, 6:177, RG-94, E-160, NA; John B. McIntosh to His Wife, 6 July 1863, McIntosh MSS, Brown Univ. Lib.

20. *OR*, pt. 1, pp. 80, 967; pt. 3, pp. 559–62, 595–96; I, 51, pt. 1, pp. 196–97; Generals' Reports of Service, War of the Rebellion, 6:275, RG-94, E-160, NA; Coddington, *Gettysburg Campaign*, pp. 550–51.

21. John B. McIntosh to His Wife, 17, 19, 22 July, 1863, McIntosh MSS, Brown Univ. Lib.; Gregg, "Brevet Major General David McMurtrie Gregg," p. 218; *OR*, pt. 3, pp. 653–54.

22. *OR*, pt. 2, pp. 311, 700.

23. *OR*, pt. 1, pp. 971, 994–95, 1006, 1014; pt. 2, p. 700; *New York Times*, 21 July 1863; Louis Fortescue Memoirs, pp. 167–68, WL; Edwin R. Havens to ———, 6 July 1863, Havens MSS, Michigan State Univ. Lib.; John R. Morey Diary, 5 July 1863, Morey MSS, UML; A. B. Throckmorton, "Major-General Kilpatrick," *Northern Monthly* 2 (1868): 596.

24. *OR*, pt. 1, pp. 994–95; William Ball to His Parents, 9 July 1863, Ball MSS, Western Michigan Univ. Lib.; James H. Kidd to His Parents, 9 July 1863, Kidd MSS, UML; Moore, *Kilpatrick and Our Cavalry*, p. 101.

25. *OR*, pt. 2, pp. 700–701.

26. *OR*, pt. 2, pp. 701, 753–54; pt. 3, p. 548; *New York Times*, 6 July 1863; Louis Fortescue Memoirs, p. 177, WL.

27. Imboden, "Confederate Retreat from Gettysburg," 425; John A. Dahlgren, *Memoir of Ulric Dahlgren* (Philadelphia, 1872), p. 166; Gracey, *Sixth Pennsylvania Cavalry*, p. 190; *Pennsylvania at Gettysburg*, 2:827–28, 850; *New York Times*, 21 July 1863; Charles E. Cadwalader to His Mother, 10 July 1863, Cadwalader MSS, HSP.

28. *OR*, pt. 2, pp. 214, 280, 437, 703; pt. 3, pp. 547–49; Coddington, *Gettysburg Campaign*,

pp. 542–43, 552; Samuel P. Bates, *History of Pennsylvania Volunteers, 1861–5*, 5 vols. (Harrisburg, Pa., 1869–71), 3:1145–46; Schaff, "Gettysburg Week," 27.

29. *OR*, pt. 2, pp. 436–38, 498–99, 653, 655; Imboden, "Confederate Retreat from Gettysburg," 425–27; Coddington, *Gettysburg Campaign*, p. 554.

30. *OR*, pt. 1, pp. 916, 928, 943, 995; pt. 3, p. 586; Newel Cheney, *History of the Ninth Regiment, New York Volunteer Cavalry, War of 1861 to 1865* (Jamestown and Poland Center, N.Y., 1901), p. 117; H. P. Moyer, comp., *History of the Seventeenth Regiment Pennsylvania Volunteer Cavalry* (Lebanon, Pa., 1911), p. 66; George B. Davis, "From Gettysburg to Williamsport," *Papers of the Military Historical Society of Massachusetts*, 3 (1903): 457; Flavius J. Bellamy Diary, 4–6 July 1863, Bellamy MSS, Indiana State Lib.; William H. Redman to His Mother, 6 July 1863, Redman MSS, Univ. of Virginia Lib.; James A. Bell to Gusta Ann Hallock, 8–10 July 1863, Bell MSS, HEHL; Charles M. Munroe Diary, 4–6 July 1863, American Antiquarian Soc.

31. *OR*, pt. 1, pp. 928, 935, 939–40, 943; pt. 2, pp. 436–38; Imboden, "Confederate Retreat from Gettysburg," 427–28; Cheney, *Ninth New York Cavalry*, pp. 117–18; Gracey, *Sixth Pennsylvania Cavalry*, p. 189; Hillman A. Hall, W. B. Besley, and Gilbert G. Wood, comps., *History of the Sixth New York Cavalry* (Worcester, Mass., 1908), pp. 145–46; Moyer, *Seventeenth Pennsylvania Cavalry*, pp. 66–67; James Barnet, ed., *The Martyrs and Heroes of Illinois in the Great Rebellion: Biographical Sketches* (Chicago: 1865), pp. 74–76; Charles M. Blackford III, ed., *Letters from Lee's Army* (New York, 1947), p. 189; Joseph T. Durkin, ed., *Confederate Chaplain: A War Journal* (Milwaukee, Wis., 1964), p. 49; E. Porter Alexander, *Military Memoirs of a Confederate: A Critical Narrative* (New York, 1907), p. 438; *New York Times*, 21 July 1863; Coddington, *Gettysburg Campaign*, p. 554; Jasper Hawse Diary, 6 July 1863, Univ. of Virginia Lib.; Bailey Clement to His Wife, 9 July 1863, Clement MSS, North Carolina State Dept. of Art, Culture and History.

32. *OR*, pt. 1, pp. 995, 1006; Gracey, *Sixth Pennsylvania Cavalry*, pp. 190–91; *History of the Eighteenth Regiment of Cavalry, Pennsylvania Volunteers, 1862–1865* (New York, 1909), pp. 17–18, 41, 85, 94–95; Dahlgren, *Memoir of Ulric Dahlgren*, pp. 168–69; *Pennsylvania at Gettysburg*, 2:872; W. W. Goldsborough, *The Maryland Line in the Confederate States Army* (Baltimore, 1869), pp. 218–19; *New York Times*, 21 July 1863; Charles E. Cadwalader to His Mother, 12 July 1863, Cadwalader MSS, HSP.

33. *OR*, pt. 1, pp. 995, 1006, 1009–11, 1014–15; *New York Times*, 21 July 1863; *Eighteenth Pennsylvania Cavalry*, pp. 94–97; William Wells to His Parents, 7 July 1863, Wells MSS, Univ. of Vermont Lib.

34. *OR*, pt. 1, pp. 995, 1006; pt. 2, pp. 322, 581, 701–3; McClellan, *Life and Campaigns of Stuart*, p. 359; *New York Times*, 21 July 1863; Gillespie, *Company A, First Ohio Cavalry*, pp. 161–62; *Eighteenth Pennsylvania Cavalry*, p. 18; Coddington, *Gettysburg Campaign*, p. 553.

35. *OR*, pt. 1, pp. 928, 995, 999–1000; Kidd, *Personal Recollections*, pp. 173–76; James H. Kidd to His Parents, 9 July 1863, Kidd MSS, UML.

36. *OR*, pt. 1, pp. 1006, 1010–11, 1014–15; pt. 2, pp. 361, 370, 702, 764–65; James H. Kidd to His Parents, 9 July 1863, Kidd MSS, UML; Glazier, *Three Years in the Federal Cavalry*, p. 276; *Eighteenth Pennsylvania Cavalry*, p. 98; Moore, *Kilpatrick and Our Cavalry*, pp. 102–3; Comte de Paris, *History of the Civil War in America*, 4 vols. (Philadelphia, 1875–88), 3:712–14; William Wells to His Parents, 7 July 1863, Wells MSS, Univ. of Vermont Lib.; G. Wayne King, "The Civil War Career of Hugh Judson Kilpatrick," pp. 134–35, Univ. of South Carolina Lib.; *New York Times*, 21 July 1863; Neese, *Confederate Horse Artillery*, pp. 193–94.

37. W. G. Delony to His Wife, 7 July 1863, Delony MSS, Univ. of Georgia Lib.

38. Imboden, "Confederate Retreat from Gettysburg," 427–28.

39. *OR*, pt. 2, p. 702; Kidd, *Personal Recollections*, pp. 174–75; King, "Civil War Career of Hugh Judson Kilpatrick," p. 135.

40. *OR*, pt. 1, pp. 81–89, 145–47; Coddington, *Gettysburg Campaign*, pp. 551–52, 555.

41. *OR*, pt. 2, pp. 299–301, 322–23, 438, 493; Jennings C. Wise, *The Long Arm of Lee: The History of the Artillery of the Army of Northern Virginia*, 2 vols. (Lynchburg, Va., 1915), 2:700; Coddington, *Gettysburg Campaign*, pp. 565–66, 818n.

42. *OR*, pt. 1, pp. 928, 944, 948–49, 966; pt. 2, pp. 754, 760–61; *New York Times*, 12, 21 July 1863; W. H. Carter, *From Yorktown to Santiago with the Sixth U.S. Cavalry* (Baltimore, 1900), pp. 99–102; Flavius J. Bellamy Diary, 7 July 1863, Bellamy MSS, Indiana State Lib.

43. *OR*, pt. 1, pp. 928, 940; pt. 2, p. 703; Cheney, *Ninth New York Cavalry*, pp. 188–91; Hall, Besley, and Wood, *Sixth New York Cavalry*, pp. 146–47; Flavius J. Bellamy Diary, 7 July 1863, Bellamy MSS, Indiana State Lib.

44. Gracey, *Sixth Pennsylvania Cavalry*, p. 186.

45. *OR*, pt. 2, p. 703; Gracey, *Sixth Pennsylvania Cavalry*, p. 187.

46. *OR*, pt. 1, pp. 929, 935, 940–41; pt. 2, p. 703.

47. *OR*, pt. 1, pp. 929, 935–36, 940–41, 996, 999, 1007, 1010–11, 1015–16, 1020; pt. 2, pp. 703–4; Cheney, *Ninth New York Cavalry*, p. 120; Hall, Besley, and Wood, *Sixth New York Cavalry*, pp. 147–48; Moore, *Kilpatrick and Our Cavalry*, pp. 103–4; *Eighteenth Pennsylvania Cavalry*, p. 41; Robertson, *Michigan in the War*, pp. 579, 581–82; Kidd, *Personal Recollections*, pp. 178–81; James A. Bell to Gusta Ann Hallock, 9 July 1863, Bell MSS, HEHL; John R. Morey Diary, 8 July 1863, Morey MSS, UML; Charles M. Munroe Diary, 9 July 1863, American Antiquarian Soc.; Flavius J. Bellamy Diary, 8 July 1863, Bellamy MSS, Indiana State Lib.; William H. Rockwell to His Wife, 9 July 1863, Rockwell MSS, Western Michigan Univ. Lib.; John E. Hoffman Diary, 8 July 1863, West Virginia Univ. Lib.; James H. Kidd to His Parents, 9 July 1863, Kidd MSS, UML; Comte de Paris, *Civil War in America*, 3:716; *New York Times*, 10 July 1863; Edwin R. Havens to "Father, Mother & Nell," 9 July 1863, Havens MSS, Michigan State Univ. Lib.; Abner Hard, *History of the Eighth Cavalry Regiment, Illinois Volunteers, during the Great Rebellion* (Aurora, Ill., 1868), pp. 262–63.

48. *OR*, pt. 1, p. 925; William V. Stuart to "Dearest Friend," 9 July 1863, Detroit Pub. Lib.; William H. Redman to His Mother, 10 July 1863, Redman MSS, Univ. of Virginia Lib.

49. *OR*, pt. 1, pp. 958, 1007; pt. 2, p. 704.

50. *OR*, pt. 1, pp. 929, 941; Cheney, *Ninth New York Cavalry*, pp. 120–21; Hall, Besley, and Wood, *Sixth New York Cavalry*, pp. 148–49; Neese, *Confederate Horse Artillery*, p. 197; Daniel Pulis to His Parents, 11 July 1863, Pulis MSS, Rochester Pub. Lib.; Flavius J. Bellamy to His Brother, 11 July 1863, Bellamy MSS, Indiana State Lib.; Charles M. Munroe Diary, 9 July 1863, American Antiquarian Soc.; Alfred Pleasonton to HQ, Army of the Potomac, 9 July 1863, Thomas C. Devin's ACPF, RG-94, NA.

51. *OR*, pt. 1, pp. 83, 146; pt. 3, p. 621.

52. Coddington, *Gettysburg Campaign*, pp. 561–62.

53. *OR*, pt. 1, p. 86; pt. 2, pp. 221–28, 238, 242–43, 246, 261–66; pt. 3, pp. 577–81, 585, 593, 611, 621, 633–34, 640–42; "Military History of William Farrar Smith," pp. 6–7, Smith's ACPF, RG-94, NA; Coddington, *Gettysburg Campaign*, pp. 542–43, 562; John S. Mosby, *Stuart's Cavalry in the Gettysburg Campaign* (New York, 1908), pp. 187–88.

54. *OR*, pt. 3, pp. 611, 613, 634, 651, 677–78, 704.

55. *OR*, pt. 3, pp. 595, 612–13, 634; Bates, *History of Pennsylvania Volunteers*, 2:1145–46; Schaff, "Gettysburg Week," 27–28.

56. *OR*. pt. 3, pp. 391, 446, 448, 496, 563–64, 594–95, 613 and n., 623, 634; Bates, *History of Pennsylvania Volunteers*, 5:32; J. C. Atticks Diary, 2 July 1863, USAMHI; *New York Times*, 15 July 1863.

57. *OR*, pt. 1, pp. 85, 88; pt. 3, p. 643.

58. *OR*, pt. 1, pp. 83–84, 87; pt. 3, pp. 600, 615–16, 628, 668–69, 703; Wellman, *Harpers Ferry*, p. 119.

59. *OR*, pt. 1, p. 88; pt. 2, p. 280; pt. 3, pp. 625, 652, 681, 698; Charles L. Jefferds to "Mrs. Barns," 10 July 1863, USAMHI.

60. *OR*, pt. 3, p. 584; Coddington, *Gettysburg Campaign*, pp. 559–60.

61. *OR*, pt. 3, pp. 546, 568, 717. On or about 14 July the Cavalry Corps got further reinforcements, though not in time to see action before Lee's escape into Virginia. This came about after General Gregg sent Colonel McReynolds of the 1st New York to Couch's headquarters to gather up McReynolds's own regiment as well as Colonel Wynkoop's 20th Pennsylvania: *OR*, pt. 3, p. 694.

62. *Detroit Advertiser & Tribune*, 8 July 1863; Freeman Cleaves, *Meade of Gettysburg* (Norman, Okla., 1960), p. 175; Coddington, *Gettysburg Campaign*, p. 558; *OR*, pt. 1, p. 90.

63. *OR*, pt. 1, pp. 925–26, 929, 936, 941–42, 1033; Hall, Besley, and Wood, *Sixth New York Cavalry*, p. 149; Cheney, *Ninth New York Cavalry*, p. 120; Neese, *Confederate Horse Artillery*, pp. 197–98; James A. Bell to Gusta Ann Hallock, 10 July 1863, Bell MSS, HEHL; Flavius J. Bellamy to His Brother, 11 July 1863, Bellamy MSS, Indiana State Lib.; Charles M. Munroe Diary, 10 July 1863, American Antiquarian Soc.; Daniel Pulis to His Parents, 11 July 1863, Pulis MSS, Rochester Pub. Lib.

64. *OR*, pt. 1, pp. 663–64, 929, 936, 942; pt. 2, pp. 398–99, 704; Hoke, *Great Invasion*, pp. 462–64.

65. *OR*, pt. 1, pp. 971, 1036; pt. 3, p. 627; Glazier, *Three Years in the Federal Cavalry*, p. 283; Rawle, *Third Pennsylvania Cavalry*, p. 284; Thomas M. Covert to His Wife, 27 July 1863, Covert MSS, William G. Burnett.

66. *OR*, pt. 1, p. 929; pt. 2, p. 704; pt. 3, p. 633; Cheney, *Ninth New York*, p. 120; Hall, Besley, and Wood, *Sixth New York Cavalry*, pp. 149–50; Comte de Paris, *Civil War in America*, 3:723; Flavius J. Bellamy Diary, 11 July 1863, Bellamy MSS, Indiana State Lib.; Charles M. Munroe Diary, 11 July 1863, American Antiquarian Soc.; James A. Bell to Gusta Ann Hallock, 12 July 1863, Bell MSS, HEHL.

67. *OR*, pt. 1, pp. 958, 971, 1036.

68. *OR*, pt. 1, pp. 664, 999–1000; pt. 3, pp. 649, 651; *Eighteenth Pennsylvania Cavalry*, p. 41; Comte de Paris, *Civil War in America*, 3:723; Kidd, *Personal Recollections*, pp. 181–83; Worthington Chauncey Ford, ed., *A Cycle of Adams Letters, 1861–1865*, 2 vols. (Boston, 1920), 2:45.

69. *OR*, pt. 1, pp. 988–89, 999; pt. 2, pp. 704–5; pt. 3, pp. 657–58, 664; Robertson, *Michigan in the War*, p. 579; Moore, *Kilpatrick and Our Cavalry*, p. 107; Comte de Paris, *Civil War in America*, 3:726; Gillespie, *Company A, First Ohio Cavalry*, pp. 163–64; *New York Times*, 21 July 1863; Frank L. Klement, ed., "Edwin B. Bigelow: A Michigan Sergeant in the Civil War," *Michigan History* 38 (1954): 223; John R. Morey Diary, 12 July 1863, Morey MSS, UML.

70. *OR*, pt. 1, pp. 929, 971; pt. 3, p. 660; Cheney, *Ninth New York Cavalry*, p. 121; Comte de Paris, *Civil War in America*, 3:726.

71. *OR*, pt. 2, pp. 753, 762; pt. 3, pp. 657–58, 664–65, 669, 987–88; Coddington, *Gettysburg Campaign*, p. 566; Robert E. Lee to J. E. B. Stuart, 12 July 1863, Stuart MSS, HEHL.

72. Coddington, *Gettysburg Campaign*, p. 567.

73. *OR*, pt. 1, pp. 118, 929; pt. 3, p. 675.

74. Klement, "Edwin B. Bigelow," 223; *OR*, pt. 1, p. 1016; pt. 2, pp. 226, 1008; Gillespie, *Company A, First Ohio Cavalry*, pp. 165–66.

75. *OR*, pt. 1, pp. 996, 1016–17; pt. 2, pp. 226, 246; Generals' Reports of Service, War of the Rebellion, 3:697, RG-94, E-160, NA; E. B. Sawyer to William Wells, 23, 24 Aug. 1863, Wells MSS, Univ. of Vermont Lib.; *New York Times*, 21 July 1863.

76. Gillespie, *Company A, First Ohio Cavalry*, p. 166.

77. Imboden, "Confederate Retreat from Gettysburg," 428; William Stanley Hoole, ed., *Seven Months in the Rebel States during the North American War, 1863*, by Justus Scheibert (Tuscaloosa, Ala., 1958), p. 120; Davis, "From Gettysburg to Williamsport," 458; Coddington, *Gettysburg Campaign*, pp. 569–70.

78. *OR*, pt. 2, p. 705; pt. 3, p. 1001; Coddington, *Gettysburg Campaign*, p. 570.

79. *OR*, pt. 2, pp. 705, 765–67; pt. 3, p. 676; George Baylor, *Bull Run to Bull Run; or, Four Years in the Army of Northern Virginia* (Richmond, 1900), p. 150; Bushrod C. Washington, ed., *A History of the Laurel Brigade*, by William N. McDonald (Baltimore, 1907), p. 153; Wellman, *Harpers Ferry*, p. 117; General Orders #1, 29 June 1863; Special Orders #12, 26 June 1863; both, Garrison HQ Records, Harpers Ferry, West Virginia, HSP.

80. *OR*, pt. 2, p. 327; Neese, *Confederate Horse Artillery*, p. 199; W. W. Blackford, *War Years with Jeb Stuart* (New York, 1945), p. 235.

81. *OR*, pt. 2, pp. 639–40, 705; Coddington, *Gettysburg Campaign*, p. 570.

82. *OR*, pt. 1, pp. 929, 990; pt. 3, p. 685.

83. *OR*, pt. 1, pp. 990, 999; *New York Times*, 21 July 1863; John R. Morey Diary, 14 July 1863, Morey MSS, UML.

84. *OR*, pt. 1, p. 990; pt. 2, pp. 640–42; *New York Times*, 21 July 1863.

85. *OR*, pt. 1, pp. 990, 1000; Gillespie, *Company A, First Ohio Cavalry*, pp. 169–70; Kidd, *Personal Recollections*, pp. 147, 184–86; *New York Times*, 21 July 1863.

86. *OR*, pt. 2, pp. 640, 705; James Longstreet, *From Manassas to Appomattox: Memoirs of the Civil War in America* (Philadelphia, 1895), p. 430.

87. *OR*, pt. 1, pp. 990, 1000; pt. 2, p. 648; Robertson, *Michigan in the War*, p. 581; Kidd, *Personal Recollections*, pp. 185–86.

88. *OR*, pt. 1, p. 936; pt. 2, p. 641; James L. Morrison, Jr., ed., *The Memoirs of Henry Heth* (Westport, Conn., 1974), p. 179.

89. *OR*, pt. 1, pp. 990–91, 998; Comte de Paris, *Civil War in America*, 3:732–33; Robertson, *Michigan in the War*, p. 581; Benjamin J. Clark to His Brothers and Sisters, 17 July 1863, Central Michigan Univ. Lib.; James H. Kidd to His Parents, 16 July 1863, Kidd MSS, UML; *New York Times*, 21 July 1863; Bailey Clement to His Wife, 16 July 1863, Clement MSS, North Carolina State Dept. of Art, Culture and History.

90. *OR*, pt. 1, pp. 929, 937, 942, 990; pt. 3, p. 698; Cheney, *Ninth New York Cavalry*, p. 122; Hall, Besley, and Wood, *Sixth New York Cavalry*, p. 150; Glazier, *Three Years in the Federal Cavalry*, p. 294; Kidd, *Personal Recollections*, pp. 187–89; Moyer, *Seventeenth Pennsylvania Cavalry*, pp. 67–68; Coddington, *Gettysburg Campaign*, pp. 571, 820n.

91. Casler, *Four Years in the Stonewall Brigade*, p. 264; *OR*, pt. 1, p. 929.

Bibliography

Note: Space considerations necessitate omitting the nearly six hundred printed sources consulted during the preparation of this book. Most of these have provided material incorporated in the text and are identified in the chapter notes. This bibliography lists only the manuscripts and unpublished records drawn upon in research.

Adams, Charles F., Jr. Diary. Massachusetts Historical Society, Boston.

Alberts, Don E. "General Wesley Merritt, Nineteenth Century Cavalryman." Ph.D. diss., University of New Mexico, Albuquerque, 1975.

Alger, Russell A. Correspondence. University of Michigan Library, Ann Arbor.

Allen, Winthrop S. G. Letter of 30 June 1863. Illinois State Historical Library, Springfield.

Anderson, E. D. "Cavalry Operations in the Gettysburg Campaign." Army War College Study, 1912. U.S. Army Military History Institute, Carlisle Barracks, Pa.

Armstrong, John E. Memoirs. U.S. Army Military History Institute.

Atticks, J. C. Diary. U.S. Army Military History Institute.

Ayer, Osborn. Correspondence. Nebraska State Historical Society, Lincoln.

Ayres, Chauncey. Correspondence. Rutgers University Library, New Brunswick, N.J.

Bachelder, John. Correspondence. New Hampshire Historical Society, Concord.

Ball, Norman. Diary. Connecticut Historical Society, Hartford.

Ball, William. Correspondence. Western Michigan University Library, Kalamazoo.

Barbour, George W. Diary. University of Michigan Library.

Barnett, Joel C. Correspondence. Georgia Department of Archives and History, Atlanta.

Barry, John A. Correspondence. University of North Carolina Library, Chapel Hill.

Beane, Thomas O. "Thomas Lafayette Rosser: Soldier, Railroad Builder, Politician, Businessman (1836–1910)." M.A. thesis, University of Virginia, Charlottesville, 1957.

Bell, James A. Correspondence. Henry E. Huntington Library, San Marino, Calif.

Bellamy, Flavius J. Correspondence and Diary. Indiana State Library, Indianapolis.

Blackford, William W. Diary. University of Virginia Library.

Blinn, Charles. Diary. Gettysburg National Military Park, Gettysburg, Pa.

Bliss, George N. Correspondence. Rhode Island Historical Society, Providence.

Borries, Frank B., Jr. "General John Buford, Civil War Union Cavalryman." M.A. thesis, University of Kentucky, Lexington, 1960.

Bowman, Ephraim. Correspondence. University of Virginia Library.

Broadhead, Sarah M. Diary. Adams County Historical Society, Gettysburg, Pa.

Brooke, William Rawle. Correspondence and Diary. War Library, National Commandery, Military Order of the Loyal Legion of the United States, Philadelphia, Pa.

————. Correspondence. Historical Society of Pennsylvania, Philadelphia.

Brooks, N. John. Correspondence and Diary. University of North Carolina Library.

Brown, Charles. Correspondence. New York State Library, Albany.

Buck, Andrew N. Letter of 9 July 1863. University of Michigan Library.

Butler, M. Calbraith. Correspondence. Historical Society of Pennsylvania.

Cadwalader, Charles E. Correspondence. Historical Society of Pennsylvania.

Cadwalader, J. Iredell. Letter of 9 July 1863. U.S. Army Military History Institute.

"Captain John H. Calef's Battery Position [at Gettysburg, 1 July 1863]." Gettysburg National Military Park.

Carpenter, E. A. Correspondence. New York Public Library, New York, N. Y.

Carpenter, Louis H. Correspondence. Historical Society of Pennsylvania.

Case, Howard. "General Judson Kilpatrick, New Jersey's Forgotten Hero." In Possession of the Author, Sussex, N.J.

Cavin, Miles A. Correspondence. North Carolina State Department of Art, Culture and History, Raleigh.

Chapman, George H. Diary. Indiana State Historical Society, Indianapolis.

Chapman, Gilbert W. Letter of 29 July 1863. Detroit Public Library, Detroit, Mich.

Chew, Robert Preston. Correspondence. Duke University Library, Durham, N.C.

Clark, Benjamin J. Letter of 17 July 1863. Central Michigan University Library, Mount Pleasant.

Clark, J. A. Letter of 30 July 1863. University of Michigan Library.

Clement, Bailey. Correspondence. North Carolina State Department of Art, Culture and History.

Comte, Victor. Letter of 7 July 1863. University of Michigan Library.

Cooke, John Esten. Correspondence. Virginia Historical Society, Richmond.

Copeland, Joseph T. Letter of 9 July 1863. Historical Society of Pennsylvania.

Corselius, Edward. Correspondence. University of Michigan Library.

Covert, Thomas M. Correspondence. In Possession of William G. Burnett, Rocky River, Ohio.

Coxe, Charles B. Correspondence. Historical Society of Pennsylvania.

Croll, Jennie S. Memoirs. Adams County Historical Society, Gettysburg, Pa.

Crowninshield, Benjamin W. Diary. Essex Institute, Salem, Mass.

Custer, George Armstrong. Correspondence. United States Military Academy Library, West Point, N.Y.

Dahlgren, Ulric. Diary. Library of Congress, Washington, D.C.

Dearing, James. Correspondence. Historical Society of Pennsylvania.

Delony, William G. Correspondence. University of Georgia Library, Athens.

Devin, Thomas C. Correspondence. In Possession of M. Catherine Devin, Midland Park, N.J.

Duffié, Alfred N. Letter of 4 July 1863. Historical Society of Pennsylvania.

"Elon J. Farnsworth." Gettysburg National Military Park.

Estes, Lewellyn G. Correspondence. New York Public Library.

Ewell, Richard S. Correspondence. Library of Congress.

Farnill, John S. Correspondence. University of Michigan Library.

Faxon, John H. Diary. University of Michigan Library.

Flack, George W. Diary. Rutgers University Library.

Follmer, John D. Diary. University of Michigan Library.

Fortescue, Louis. Memoirs. War Library, National Commandery, Military Order of the Loyal Legion of the United States.

Gamble, William. Letter of 13 July 1863. Historical Society of Pennsylvania.

———. Correspondence. Chicago Historical Society, Chicago, Ill.

Gardner, Charles. Memoirs. U.S. Army Military History Institute.

Graham, William A., Jr. Correspondence. North Carolina State Department of Art, Culture and History.

Green, Augustus P. Correspondence and Memoirs. New-York Historical Society, New York, N.Y.

Greenleaf, Charles H. Correspondence. Connecticut Historical Society.

Gregg, David McMurtrie. Correspondence. Historical Society of Berks County, Reading, Pa.

———. Correspondence. Library of Congress.

———. Correspondence. Gettysburg National Military Park.

Gregg, J. Irvin. Correspondence. Historical Society of Pennsylvania.

Hampton, Wade. Correspondence. University of North Carolina Library.

———. Correspondence. University of South Carolina Library, Columbia.

Harpers Ferry, West Virginia. Garrison Records, June–July 1863. Historical Society of Pennsylvania.

Harrington, George. Diary. Western Michigan University Library.

Havens, Edwin R. Correspondence. Michigan State University Library, East Lansing.

Hawse, Jasper. Diary. University of Virginia Library.

Headquarters, Cavalry Corps, Army of the Potomac. Letters and Telegrams Sent and Received, General Orders and Circulars Issued, Reports of Officers, etc. Record Group 393, Entries 1439–40, 1442–43, 1449, 1451–53, 1463–64, National Archives, Washington, D.C.

Hitner, Mrs. R. K. Letter of 6 July 1863. U.S. Army Military History Institute.

Hoffman, Elliott Wheelock. "Vermont General: The Military Development of William Wells, 1861–1865." M.A. thesis, University of Vermont, Burlington, 1974.

Hoffman, John E. Diary. West Virginia University Library, Morgantown.

Holley, Turner W. Correspondence. Duke University Library.

Hooker, Joseph. Correspondence. Gettysburg College Library, Gettysburg, Pa.

———. Correspondence. Henry E. Huntington Library.

Imboden, John D. Correspondence. New York Public Library.

———. Correspondence. University of Virginia Library.

———. Correspondence. West Virginia University Library.

Jefferds, Charles L. Letter of 10 July 1863. U.S. Army Military History Institute.

Jones, William E. Correspondence. Historical Society of Pennsylvania.

Kennon, R. B. Correspondence. Virginia State Library, Richmond.

Kidd, James H. Correspondence. University of Michigan Library.

Kilborn, George H. Correspondence. University of Michigan Library.

King, G. Wayne. "The Civil War Career of Hugh Judson Kilpatrick." Ph.D. diss., University of South Carolina, 1969.

Kitzmiller, Anna Garlach. Memoirs. U.S. Army Military History Institute.

Langhorne, George T. "The Cavalry in the Gettysburg Campaign. . . ." Army War College Study, 1913. U.S. Army Military History Institute.

Lee, Fitzhugh. Correspondence. Henry E. Huntington Library.

Lee, Robert E. Correspondence. Chicago Historical Society.

———. Correspondence. Virginia Historical Society.

Loftin, William F. Letter of 29 August 1863. Duke University Library.

McClellan, Henry B. Correspondence. Virginia Historical Society.

McIntosh, John B. Correspondence. Brown University Library, Providence, R.I.

Macomb, A. C. "Cavalry in the Gettysburg Campaign." Army War College Study, 1915. U.S. Army Military History Institute.

Marshall, William C. Correspondence. Virginia Historical Society.

Martin, Harmon. Letter of 25 August 1863. U.S. Army Military History Institute.

Mattoon, G. W. Correspondence. Michigan State University Library.

Meade, George Gordon. Correspondence. Gettysburg College Library.

———. Correspondence. Historical Society of Pennsylvania.

Medill, William H. Correspondence. Library of Congress.

Mobley, B. L. Correspondence. Emory University Library, Atlanta, Ga.

Morey, John R. Correspondence and Diary. University of Michigan Library.

Morgan, David H. Correspondence. In Possession of Irwin L. Park, Philadelphia, Pa.

Mosby, John Singleton. Correspondence. Duke University Library.

———. Correspondence. Library of Congress.

———. Correspondence. Missouri Historical Society, Saint Louis.

———. Correspondence. New York Public Library.

———. Correspondence. U.S. Army Military History Institute.

———. Correspondence. University of Virginia Library.

Munroe, Charles M. Diary. American Antiquarian Society, Worcester, Mass.

Newhall, Walter S. Correspondence and Diary. Historical Society of Pennsylvania.

Nunn, Jesse C. Correspondence. Georgia Department of Archives and History.

Parsons, H. C. Memoir of Farnsworth's Charge at Gettysburg, 3 July 1863. Library of Congress.

Patrick, Marsena R. Diary. Library of Congress.

Payne, William H. F. Correspondence. Virginia State Library.

Pleasonton, Alfred. Correspondence. Chicago Historical Society.

———. Correspondence. Gettysburg College Library.

———. Correspondence. Library of Congress.

———. Correspondence. New-York Historical Society.

———. Correspondence. New York Public Library.

———. "Report of Operations of Cavalry Corps [Army of the Potomac] of Battles of Aldie, Middleburg & Upperville. . . ." Henry E. Huntington Library.

Potter, Henry C. Memoirs. Gettysburg National Military Park.

Prentice, Reuben T. Correspondence. Illinois State Historical Library.

Preston, N. D. Memoirs. New York Public Library.

Price, R. Channing. Correspondence. Virginia Historical Society.

Pulis, Daniel W. Correspondence. Rochester Public Library, Rochester, N.Y.

Readnor, Henry W. "General Fitzhugh Lee, 1835–1915." Ph.D. diss., University of Virginia, 1958.

Redman, William H. Correspondence. University of Virginia Library.

Reynolds, John F. Correspondence. Franklin and Marshall College Library, Lancaster, Pa.

————. Correspondence. Gettysburg College Library.

Rheney, John W. Correspondence. Georgia Department of Archives and History.

Richter, William L. "The Federal Cavalry in the Gettysburg Campaign: The Development of the Mobile Arm of the Army of the Potomac." M.A. thesis, Arizona State University, Tempe, 1965.

Robinson, Leiper M. Memoirs. Virginia Historical Society.

Rockenbach, S. D. "The Gettysburg Campaign: The Cavalry Fight at Rummel's Farm [3 July 1863]." Army War College Study, 1912. U.S. Army Military History Institute.

Rockwell, William H. Correspondence. Western Michigan University Library.

Rosser, Thomas L. Correspondence. University of Virginia Library.

Ryder, Alfred G. Letter of 24 June 1863. University of Michigan Library.

Scott, James McClure. Memoirs. Virginia Historical Society.

Sheahan, John P. Correspondence. Maine Historical Society, Portland.

Shriver, S. C. Correspondence. Gettysburg National Military Park.

Shriver, William H. "My Father Led General J. E. B. Stuart to Gettysburg." Gettysburg National Military Park.

Smith, Thomas W. Correspondence. Historical Society of Pennsylvania.

Smith, William Farrar. Correspondence and Memoirs. Vermont Historical Society, Montpelier.

"South Cavalry Field [at Gettysburg, 2–3 July 1863]." Gettysburg National Military Park.

Starr, Samuel H. Correspondence. Missouri Historical Society.

Stewart, Daniel. Letter of 24 July 1863. Western Michigan University Library.

Stewart, Salome Myers. Memoirs. Adams County Historical Society, Gettysburg, Pa.

Stonesifer, Roy P., Jr. "The Long Hard Road: Union Cavalry in the Gettysburg Campaign." M.A. thesis, Pennsylvania State University, University Park, 1959.

Storrick, W. C. "The Hunterstown Fight [2 July 1863]." Gettysburg National Military Park.

Stuart, James E. B. Correspondence. Henry E. Huntington Library.

————. Correspondence. Virginia Historical Society.

"Stuart's Absence—Gettysburg, July 1863." Gettysburg National Military Park.

Stuart, William V. Letter of 9 July 1863. Detroit Public Library.

Stubbs, Mary Lee. "Cavalry in the Civil War." Office of the Chief of Military History, Department of the Army, Washington, D.C.

Swann, John T. Correspondence. Georgia Department of Archives and History.

Thiele, Thomas F. "The Evolution of Cavalry in the American Civil War, 1861–1863." Ph.D. diss., University of Michigan, 1952.

Thomas, Robert N. "Brigadier General Thomas T. Munford and the Confederacy." M.A. thesis, Duke University, 1958.

Tidball, John C. Correspondence. United States Military Academy Library.

Tripp, Richard Lee. "Cavalry Reconnaissance in the Army of Northern Virginia: J. E. B. Stuart's Cavalry, 1861–64." M.A. thesis, Duke University, 1967.

Trowbridge, Alamin. Correspondence. Georgia Department of Archives and History.

Trowbridge, Luther S. Correspondence. University of Michigan Library.

Turner, James B. Correspondence. Illinois State Historical Library.

Various Cavalry Commanders, Army of the Potomac. Appointments, Commissions, and Personal Branch Document Files. Record Group 94, National Archives.

———. General's Papers. Record Group 94, Entry 159, National Archives.

———. Generals' Reports of Service, War of the Rebellion (13 vols.). Record Group 94, Entry 160, National Archives.

Veil, Charles H. Correspondence. Gettysburg College Library.

———. Memoirs. War Library, National Commandery, Military Order of the Loyal Legion of the United States.

Venable, Andrew R. Correspondence. Virginia Historical Society.

Waring, J. Frederick. Diary. University of North Carolina Library.

Warren, Leander H. Memoirs. Adams County Historical Society, Gettysburg, Pa.

Waters, Lucien P. Correspondence. New-York Historical Society.

Weaver, Augustus C. Memoirs. Indiana State Library.

Wells, William. Correspondence. University of Vermont Library.

Wesson, Silas D. Diary. U.S. Army Military History Institute.

Whelan, Henry C. Letter of 11 June 1863. Historical Society of Pennsylvania.

Wigfall, Halsey. Correspondence. Library of Congress.

Yancy, Benjamin C. Correspondence. University of North Carolina Library.

Yoder, Jonah. Diary. U.S. Army Military History Institute.

Index